Chinese Characters
Learn & Remember 2,178 Characters and Their Meanings

How to Retain the Meanings for More Than 2000 of the Most Common Characters in Mandarin Chinese

Alan Hoenig,]

GW00645490

Use an Innovative Memory Method To Put 'Ease' Into 'Chinese'!

SIMPLIFIED CHARACTER EDITION

EZChinesey.com

PO BOX 2346, HUNTINGTON, LONG ISLAND, NEW YORK 11743

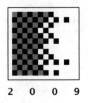

2 0 0 9

About the cover. Cover design by Jim Hannan. Cover photo shows the panda couple Mei Xiang (female, left) and Tian Tian (male, right) and appears courtesy of Ann Batdorf/Smithsonian's National Zoo.

The red Chinese characters are symbols of good luck and fortune. Reading down, here are their meanings and official pinyin phonetic transliteration: beautiful (měi), longevity (shòu), lucky (jí), wealth (cái), good fortune (fú), harmonious (hé), love (ai), virtue (dé), happiness (xǐ), and emolument (lù). The character on the spine is hóng (large, vast), the author's Chinese surname.

The interior body types are drawn from the family of Linux Libertine fonts, designed by Philipp H. Poll. The typesetting was done by means of the XeTEX program of Jonathan Kew, itself an extension of Donald Knuth's TEX typesetting program.

Copyright ©2009 by Alan Hoenig

GBS.080731.V01.Foo.foo

All rights reserved
Printed in the United States of America
First Edition

Library of Congress Cataloging-in-Publication Data

Hoenig, Alan.
   Chinese Characters: Learn & Remember 2,178 Characters and Their Meanings/ Alan Hoenig —1st ed.
      p. cm.
Includes indices.

ISBN 978-0-9822324-0-8
1. Chinese language. 2. Mandarin language. 3. Chinese characters. 4. HanZi characters.

WWW.EZCHINESEY.COM
PO BOX 2346, HUNTINGTON, LONG ISLAND, NY 11743
631–866–6146

www.EZChinesey.com

1 2 3 4 5 6 7 8 9 0

2008912226

Dedicated to the memory of

BLOSSOM HOENIG

1924–2005

loving mother, iconoclast, woman of valor

人去留影

Preface

Chinese characters have been in use for thousands of years, and despite arguments that have probably raged for about the same amount of time, the Chinese people have never bothered to reform these characters in any meaningful way. Oh, sure, in the mid-50s, the People's Republic *did* revamp a couple of thousand of them, thereby providing us with the so-called simplified character set (the subject of this volume), but you *could* argue that this step only made the situation—at least for us poor foreign students—ever more burdensome. For now, it has become necessary to learn not one system, but both systems (traditional and simplified) in order to cope with mainland and overseas documents, as well as with the oceans of legacy documents that remain—older material printed before simplification.

Nevertheless, the very fact that these characters have persevered for such a long time must mean something. It means that in some allegorical and mystical sense they "want" to be learned, and indeed in my strictly empirical and anecdotal research, I've not run into a person brought up in China who complained about all the work it took to learn them. That's cold comfort for us non-native speakers, and the purpose of this book is to advance a method which makes this daunting task much less so for us. Please see the 'Read Me First!' introduction for a fuller, far more expansive discussion of this innovative method.

I will conclude this section with a plethora of acknowledgments. First off, I must point out that many of my ideas in this presentation drew upon the earlier work of James W. Heisig and Michael Rowley dealing with Japanese kanji.

My old college chum Chris Rider possesses critical acuity that I swear is second to none. She graciously proofread the entire text, not only keeping silly errors to a minimum, but also ensuring that my little stories stay on point, remain consistent, and maintain their pedagogical integrity—a far more demanding endeavor. I am grateful beyond words.

Matters artistic were the province of Jim Hannan, who performed yeoman service in the design of the cover. If you don't agree, you can blame me, for I'm the one who transformed it (as best I could) to electronic media.

Thanks to Web-meister (and Meistersinger) Mitch Clarvit for his expertise in setting up www.EZChinesey.com. His bemused patience in the face of my fearsome naivety had to be seen to be believed.

I fear that errors remain in this book, despite the scrupulous care I took (or attempted to take). Most of them are mine and mine alone, but not all. I relied heavily on a small handful of remarkable reference works, but they did not always agree, and not knowing whom to follow in those instances may have led me down the wrong path. The three books in this personal canon are the "Oxford Concise English-Chinese Chinese-English Dictionary" (I used the second edition); Rick Harbaugh's "Chinese Characters: A Genealogy and Dictionary" (1998, published by Zhongwen.com; mine is the fourteenth printing); and the "Chinese-English Comprehensive Dictionary," edited by John DeFrancis (2003, University of Hawai'i Press). These books, especially the last two, should be at hand to every serious student.

Speaking of errors, I hope that I can rely on you, gentle reader, to assist me in ruthlessly rooting them out. If you find any mistakes, or if you have suggestions for improving the stories in any panels, or any suggestions for improvement whatsoever, and if you include permission for me to use this material in any and all subsequent editions and printings, then I will cheerfully list the name of the first person who finds an error, and the names of all readers whose suggestions are incorporated into the volume. Many thanks in advance.

Without my kids Hannah and Sam, this book would have been written in half the time! Thanks, kids. Hey, Max, thank you, too. My wife, Jozefa, has been, as she has so frequently in the past, my bulwark against stupor, discouragement, crankiness, and lassitude, the four horsemen of the authorial apocalypse. More positively, she has supported and encouraged this venture with good cheer, great advice, and unstinting love.

I deeply regret my mother not living to see this volume in print. The example of her endlessly inventive creativity, nurturing care, and maternal love was a remarkable role model for myself and my siblings and, indeed, for anyone who knew her. I therefore dedicate this book to her. This one's for you, Ma.

—Alan Hoenig
Huntington, Long Island, New York
2008 August 8, 8:08AM

Table of Contents

Read Me First!

...Or in other words, should I buy this book?

EZChinesey™: **the method.**

Begin by staring at some Chinese text. No matter how intense your concentration, it's simply not possible to extract any meaning from the characters. After a while, though, you may become sensitive to differences in appearance. For example—and this is key—some characters have a simpler structure than others. Compare, for example, a pair (of admitted extremes) such as 二 and 猿.

Okay, so any one character may be more complex than any other. What's the point?

Here's how we can turn this observation to our advantage: Let's decide to arrange the characters of interest—the 2000 most common—in order of their complexity. That is, we'll arrange this list in order from simple to somewhat less simple, to more complex, to downright frightening.

So how does this help? With luck, the simplest character is so simple you can learn it instantly. Move forward to the next character in the list. If our luck continues to hold, we should be able remember this next character by means of some simple story or memory aid which relates the first character—which we learned easily—to the change we need to get to the second, current character we are focusing on.

Now keep on doing this. That is, we try to express every character as some combination of a previous simpler character plus some small change, a change so small that it's easy to remember the current character as well. By great good fortune, this method works splendidly! (See the technical notes at the end of this introduction for additional details.) Actually, though, we have to be a little more forgiving than this statement implies. We may need to look at more than one of the previous characters, and from time to time we need to introduce into our master list some components which comprise various arrangements of strokes that aren't themselves independent Chinese characters.

EZChinesey™ at work: an example.

Now let's see how this helps us learn the meanings of the eight simplest characters. The three simplest are 一, 二, and 三, which mean 'one', 'two', 'three' respectively, and you'll agree that it's easy to learn them just as they are. It won't always be *quite* this easy, for there aren't any additional legal characters you can build up solely from horizontal strokes.

To move forward, we'll need to introduce a component that provides flexibility in constructing new characters. Here's one that looks like an upright stick: ' | '. Sturdy sticks are useful as primitive but effective tools, and as scepter-like symbols of authority that identify kings, politicians, and other self-important riffraff. This staff combines with bars to form new characters, and we can keep track of them by creating simple stories which combine the meanings of each component and embedded character. We show no mercy in the creation of these stories—outrageous puns, incredible settings, and striking images—in short, anything that makes it easy to remember them—are grist for our mill.

Let's keep going to show this method in action.

The next character on our list is 十, Chinese for '**ten**' and constructed from the single bar meaning '*one*' and this new '*stick*' component. It's easy to remember this meaning, for the crossed strokes look like the 't' which begins the word 'ten'.

Now, what might you make of this character: 士, which features '*ten*' on top of '*one*'? Someone smart enough to count backwards from *ten* to *one* would have regarded themselves as a **scholar**, and that's one meaning for this character.

The *stick* can combine with 二, '*two*', in several ways. First, imagine trying to force the stick between the two bars to keep them far apart, like this: 工. You can do it, but it takes **work**, which is one meaning for this character.

In 土, '*stick*' pierces '*two*'. Perhaps the stick is a hoe, and the bars represent the top and bottom of the layer the hoe passes through. Layer of what? Why, layers of earth, of course—and this character often means **earth** or **soil**.

Sometimes, perhaps in time of drought, the earth is so soft and powdery, that the hoe slips all the way through the earth until only its top is at the surface, like this: 干. This happens when the soil is thirsty and **dry**, and that's what this character often means.

Reviewing our work.
Okay, now don't look back. Here are the eight characters we just discussed.

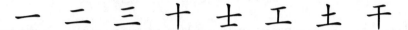

Can you remember their meanings? I bet you did better than you expected.

EZChinesey™: **results.**
In this way, we build up the meanings for the two thousand most frequent characters. With knowledge of these meanings, you will recognize—on average—97% of all the characters in any piece of modern Chinese writing. Not bad. (In other volumes of this series, we'll consider more characters and methods for learning how to read and pronounce characters.)

You may still have many questions, but let's pause for an important message. We need to emphasize what **EZ**Chinesey™ is *not*. It is *not* a calligraphy manual. *Nor* is it an historical survey of the development of character forms from ancient times until now. These and related topics are certainly important and interesting, but you'll need to go elsewhere to learn more. Moreover, some scholars may find that the mnemonic scenarios I use fly in the face of scholarly study—well, too bad! My goal here is a simple one, and that is to present a simple method for *remembering* Chinese characters, period.

One character, one panel.
Pause now to flip through this book to see how it's organized. You'll see a bunch of numbered panels, each of which contains information about a single character or component. Each panel deliberately displays the character or component in two font styles, so you get practice learning to recognize the character. Out in the margin, you also get the pinyin pronunciation for it.

A visual graphic lets you know what components or previous characters we use to construct *this character*. Attached to the several little squares in this display are the names of these components and panel numbers in which *they* are defined, so you can easily flip back if you need to refresh your memory. Moreover, the squares are filled in interesting ways which suggest what portion of the character is occupied by which component. For example, this display

    ■ man r 953   ▫ inch 210

tells you that, roughly speaking, the left half of the character contains the component named '*man r*', presented first in §953, and the character '*inch*' from §210 appears on the right. ('§' is the 'panel' symbol; '§§' means 'panels'.) Chinese scribes build up one character that means '**to pay**' (see §971) from these components.

The components for 'eagle' (§1006) provide another illustration, and

wild goose 1005 (altered)   bird 885

shows how the allocation of space can be a bit more complex. Sometimes, components find themselves altered a bit, and the accompanying label makes that clear.

(Rarely, characters contain miscellaneous strokes that are hard to identify with any other components, and never again appear in any other character. You'll see a descriptive label to help you make sense of its shape, but there won't be any panel reference number to go along with it.)

The narrative scenario.

But the heart and soul of each panel is the central narrative which provides a scenario for learning and remembering its meaning. You can see how some words in this little story merit special typographic treatment. Words that use type that appears *like this* refer to the components—that is, the building blocks—of the current character. Words looking **like this** refer to the meaning of the character. In this way, you can look at the narrative and see how the *parts* contribute to the **whole**. You may have noticed that we have already used these conventions above.

Sometimes, a story line begins with the abbreviation 'BF' which stands for 'bound form'. This means that the character never stands by itself, but with at least one other character that precedes or follows it. Essentially, a bound form character is only part of a Chinese word.

A little extra information appears just for fun. You learn how many pen strokes it takes to draw the character, and the frequency ranking of the character. The particle 的, pronounced 'de', has a frequency ranking of one; it's the most common character in written Chinese.

Of course, components also get their own panels. The abbreviation 'cmp' lets you know this is a component panel, and some other typographic conventions differ slightly. Components do not have pronunciations, but do have names. Sometimes components and characters coincide. For a variety of reasons, it seems a good idea to present the item twice—once as a component, and a second time, immediately thereafter, as a character.

There's one more convention that proves useful from time to time. An asterisk * that follows a definition flags another character with the un-asterisked definition which has appeared previously with a different character. For example, in addition to 哥, 'elder brother', this volume presents characters 兄 and 昆, 'elder brother*' and 'elder brother**'.

Now you're good to go. If you'd like, you're can skip the remainder of this introduction, and start the first unit.

We've prepared some on-line resources to assist you. For example, at our Web-site, WWW.EZChinesey.COM, you'll find:

- ☞ downloadable flash cards,
- ☞ review material for each unit,
- ☞ graded reading practice, and
- ☞ much more—**all free.**

Further discussion of this material appears on our Web site and in this volume's Appendix. The remainder of this introduction contains more about **EZChinesey**™.

Exactly what does it mean to 'learn' a character?

This question has two answers, and both miss the mark by a bit. Should we concentrate learning the character's *pronunciation*, or should its *meaning* be our focus?

I rejected the 'pronunciation' alternative for several reasons. First off, a significant minority of characters has several different pronunciations, depending on context and meaning. More important, though, is the fact that, in general, Chinese pronunciation is so different from English so as to render any memory schemes seriously deficient, for how can an *English* mnemonic refer to a pronunciation with no English counterpart?

We are led to the second candidate—*meaning.* That is, we tie our memory scheme to the meaning of each character. But even here there are difficulties. Most of the time, there is not one single meaning for each character. Other times, the character stands not for a 'word' in our usual sense, but for a portion of word. Sometimes, too, the character represents a special Chinese grammatical construct, for which no English equivalent occurs.

Even so, this seems to me the best method to choose. It was my intention at all times to choose the most prominent meaning for each character, although sometimes that's a matter more of personal preference than actual Chinese usage. I found it a particular challenge to provide a correspondence between untranslatable 'words'—particles and the like—and some reasonable English pseudo-equivalent.

Of course, how *do* you learn the pronunciation of each character? Other titles in the '**EZChinesey**™' series address this important issue, but for the time being, refer to the pinyin pronunciation in the right margin.

Advantages and disadvantages of EZChinesey™.
One finding of this book is that it is possible to deconstruct virtually every character in terms of one hundred or so components. That's certainly a lot more than the 26 letters of the English alphabet, but it's vastly less than the figure of 'thousands' that unthinking instructors use to frighten would-be students of Chinese.

Nevertheless, there *is* one striking disadvantage to this method. The order in which we learn characters the **EZChinesey™** way matches that of no known Chinese language curriculum. How could it? Language courses go from common vocabulary to challenging words (more or less). This book presents words from the *visually* simple to the *visually* complex, and the two orderings will hardly ever line up. Although it may be difficult to use this material in a traditional classroom setting, the author hopes that the ease and rapidity with which novice learners can commit meanings to memory will mitigate this problem.

Who decides what the 2000-most common characters are?
The earliest survey I know of Chinese character frequencies was made in 1928. According to it, 2000 distinct characters account for 96.5% of the text selections in this study, which comprises over 900,000 characters. Most recently, in an analysis of over 87 million characters of non-technical material, Jun Da basically reproduced this result—2000 characters account for 96.5% of the text. [Please refer to *Proceedings of the Fourth International Conference on New Technologies in Teaching and Learning Chinese* (edited by Pu Zhang *et. al.*), pp. 501-11, 2004. (Beijing: Tsinghua University Press) for further details.] Moreover, there were only 8,435 distinct characters in this large sample—a far cry from the "tens of thousands" that the uninformed claim need be learned. This scholar has made his list of character frequencies available for downloading (from lingua.mtsu.edu/chinese-computing), and it is the first 2000 of these characters with which we concern ourselves in these pages. I am grateful to this researcher for allowing me to use his results.

Components versus characters.
I've spoken above of "characters" and "components," but I'd like to spend a few minutes clarifying the distinction between them. Basically, if a glyph can stand by itself in a Chinese document, and be recognized as having its own pronunciation, then it's a *character*. Otherwise, it's a *component*, a building block for other independent characters.

You may already know about *radicals*, which are special types of components used by scribes to categorize all Chinese characters. Many radicals (but not all!) show up in this book as components. Radicals often appear independently as characters. For example, a common radical is 口 (it means "**mouth**"), which is a character in its own right, but appears as a radical in words like 叶, 古, 右, and many, many others.

Sometimes, when a component in the **EZChinesey**™ method coincides in form with one of the more-or-less two hundred recognized radicals, we identify it as such with the suffix 'r'. So while '**man**' is 人, the man radical '*man r*' looks like 亻, and frequently makes an appearance in this volume as a component.

'Words' themselves sometimes play the role of components: 古 '**ancient**' is part of 估; 末 '**end, tip**' appears in 抹 and 沫; and there are numerous other instances.

Although our purpose is to present narratives for the two thousand most common characters, it was sometimes necessary to relax this restriction. It often happens that a well-defined portion of a common character contains a sub-unit which is itself an independent character, but a rare one. For example, the Chinese use 隹 to mean a generic form of **short-tailed bird**. However, while this character is only the 5837th most common character in use, it itself appears often in other, far more frequent characters; 堆 (meaning '**heap up**', rank 1370), 推 ('**push**', 505), 准 ('**criterion**', 379), 惟 ('**-ism**', 1856), 集 ('**gather**', 406), 焦 ('**burnt**', 1554), and 瞧 ('**look at**', 1551) barely scratch the surface. I deemed it closer to the *spirit* of this work to include '隹' among the list of characters for this book. After all, even though it is rare, it still occurs from time to time, it can't hurt to know it, and it helps learn many of its offspring. That's why all told, this book includes narratives for 2178 characters and another hundred or so components (2280 in all).

What's the best way use this book?

Using our method to learn characters is a skill, and skill sets improve and strengthen the more you use them. You may find the ideas of learning character meanings daunting at first—that's why the first few units are much shorter than most of the units in this volume.

You should strive to do some of this work each day. Of course, if you stick to the book while doing this, it's easy to wonder—are you really learning the meaning for each character (and vice versa), or are you learning to regurgitate this material in the order it appears? For that reason, I *strongly* recommend the use of flash cards (which can be shuffled) and other memory aids. Our Web site—forgive us for bragging one more time—contains several kinds of practice material, including flashcards, end of unit review material, and graded reading practice. Fuller discussion appears on-line and in the book's Appendix.

I myself seem to have gravitated to a two-ply system, and I have become addicted to using flashcards for review. It's 'two-ply' for while I am reviewing or learning the words in some current unit, I also review the material in a previous unit. I review a units-worth of entries in two ways. From the definition (that is, I cover the left-hand, 'character' side of the cards), I try to recreate its form in my mind (actually, I tend to 'draw' it on the palm of one hand with the index finger of the other). Then, (after shuffling the pack of cards) while looking at the characters (this time covering the right side), I identify its definition. And I try to do this three times a day for each of the two units I am learning and reviewing.

In conclusion...

Learning Chinese is rewarding and challenging, but the problem of grappling with Chinese characters threatens the success of the whole endeavor. With this book, you will learn a method that takes the sweat out of learning them, a method that, well, puts the 'ease' into 'Chinese'.

Abbreviations Used

BF	bound form
CMP	component
LIT	literary
M	measure word
r	radical
SB	somebody
STH	something
V	variant

Unit 1
New Beginnings

1 ⎯ ⎯ **bar**
CMP What else could this be?

2 ⎯ ⎯ **one** ⬛ bar 1   yī
Chinese tally marks are evidently horizontal rather than vertical. One such *bar* stands for **one**. [1 STROKES RANK 2]

3 ⎯ ⎯ **two** ⬛ one (times 2) 2   èr
One tally twice stands for **two**. Notice that the upper bar is shorter than the bottom one.

     Sometimes this character, especially at a character's bottom, represents two horizontals. [2 STROKES RANK 157]

4 ⎯ ⎯ **three** ⬜ one 2   ⬛ two 3   sān
Three bars generate the number **three**. Since the middle stroke is the shortest, it is natural (and important!) to interpret this symbol as *one* plus *two*.
[3 STROKES RANK 125]

5 | | **scepter**
CMP This is a simple vertical stroke, and it's helpful to assign to such primitive forms a similar shape, such as a **scepter**, which is what we'll do here. The presence of a **scepter** often conveys impressions of authority and leadership, used as this object often is by rulers and leaders.

     The **scepter** is a tool conferring authority, and we might sometimes regard it as a symbol of such. But sometimes, too, we'll just regard it as a stick-like tool.

6 ╈ ╈ **ten**   ▬ one 2   ▐█ scepter 5   shí

  1 The character ╈ looks like the letter 't' which stands for '**ten**'.
  2 The upright *stick* in this character resembles a European '*one*'. The horizontal bar of the Chinese '*one*' closely mimics the horizontal hand motion people use to show there's nothing left. A '*one*' and the 'zero' of 'nothing left' and you've got **1 0**, a perfect **ten**.
  When used as a component, this character will sometimes take on the meaning of 'a good several'.   [2 STROKES   RANK 112]

7 ⼯ ⼯ **labor, work**   ██ two 3   ▐█ scepter 5   gōng

The components of ⼯ are ⸗ and ⎮ . Normally, though, the horizontal strokes of *two* are close together. If we pry these strokes apart, and keep them propped open with our *scepter*, we have done some useful **work**.

                                                            [3 STROKES   RANK 118]

8 ⼠ ⼠ **scholar**   ██ ten 6   ▭ one 2   shì

  1 A **scholar** is someone so smart they can count backwards from *ten* to *one*.
  2 A **scholar** combines many positive attributes—as many as *ten*—within *one* individual.   [3 STROKES   RANK 372]

9 ⼟ ⼟ **earth, soil**   ▬ two 3   ▐█ scepter 5   tǔ

Our scepter has uses other than conveying authority. Now let's use it in farming. Imagine the **earth**, and that the ⸗ component shows *two* layers of the ground in a sideways, cut-away view. The upper stroke shows the surface, and the lower, represents the level to which we dig the hoe. Times are so tough that even the king needs to participate—even he must use his *scepter* for hoeing, and that's what we see here. The scepter pierces the surface of the **soil** for some small distance...   [3 STROKES   RANK 515]

10 ╀ ╀ **dry**   ▬ two 3   ▐█ scepter 5   gān

...but if the soil is exceptionally **dry**, as during a drought or in the desert, the *stick* might well plunge through the *two* layers to its very tip, as we see here.   [3 STROKES   RANK 353]

Unit 2

Onion-Like Layers

11 王　王　**king**　☐ one 2　▬ two 3　▐ scepter 5　wáng

Because the middle horizontal *scepter* is shorter than the other *two*, we can group the horizontals as '*one*' followed by '*two*'. This character's components are therefore '*one*'–'*two*'–'*lead*'; a **king** is chosen by a nation as some *one to* (sounds like '*two*'—get it?) *lead*. A *scepter* is a symbol of authority, and therefore of *leadership*.　[4 STROKES　RANK 299]

12 丰　丰　**plentiful**　▮ king 11 (altered)　fēng

BF In times of abundance, or **plentiful** economics, a *king*'s authority grows and expands. In this character, his scepter overflows the bounds of the horizontal components to emphasize this abundance.　[4 STROKES　RANK 1189]

13 非　非　**not**　▮ three 4　▐ scepter 5　▐ scepter 5　▮ three 4　fēi

The left and right halves of 非 consist of a pair of *three*-toothed combs which are mirror images of each other. Each comb looks alike but they are nevertheless **not** equal.　[8 STROKES　RANK 283]

14 圭　圭　**jade tablet**　▬ earth, soil (times 2) 9　guī

A **jade tablet** was a symbol of great authority in ancient societies and possessed very great value. How do you safeguard such an item? Here's one way—create several piles of *earth* and secrete it in one of them, but only you (the tribal leader) know which one.　[6 STROKES　RANK 3537]

15 且　且　**moreover**　▮ bar (times 4) 1　▐ scepter (times 2) 5　qiě

Do you like this small system of shelves? With it, you can stack **more** stuff **over** each other.　[5 STROKES　RANK 296]

16 直 直 straight, vertical   ⬛ ten 6   ⬛ moreover 15 (altered)   zhí

If we pile *ten* bookshelves from the definition of '*moreover*' on top of each other, they need to be as **straight** and **vertical** as possible so they don't topple over. *Moreover*, we need to add an extra horizontal 'shelf' to each bookcase for additional strength and support. (As if to tempt fate, the vertical shaft of 十 lists a bit to starboard in this character—look closely!)   [8 STROKES   RANK 255]

False identity alert: At first blush, it seems that 且 'moreover' acts as a component in 直 'straight, vertical'. But look very closely—the stovepipe hats have different numbers of bars: 且 versus 直.

17 臣 臣 subject of a ruler   ⬛ king 11 (altered)   □ scepter 5   chér

What do **subjects** do to acknowledge their servile status to the *king*? They kneel. Here's a view from the top of one such servant. His back is to the left (next to the *king*'s *scepter*), and the servant's head is between his kneeling legs. The two short verticals represent his knees, which are all you can see of his legs.   [6 STROKES   RANK 1138]

18 巨 巨 huge   ⬛ subject of a ruler 17   ⬚ vertical struts   jù

(In the schematic, gray indicates removal or subtraction or minor alteration of some elements.) If you've ever gone off a diet, you know the 'overshoot' effect at first hand. Not only do you regain—instantly—all your lost weight, but you overshoot the mark and now weigh more than you did originally. In the same way, when we erase the *vertical* 'knee' *marks* (of §17) to show that the *subject* is standing up, in some magical way, he overshoots his original height to become **huge**.   [4 STROKES   RANK 913]

19 五 五 five   ⬛ labor, work 7   ⊟ one 2   ⬚ unexpected stroke   wǔ

Here's the profile of a royal throne, and we see the supports for the **five** major limbs of the queen—supports for the head, two arms, and two feet.

[4 STROKES   RANK 279]

20 互 互 **mutual**   ■ five 19 (altered)   hù

Look carefully to see the stylized arm reaching down to grab a second arm reaching up to grab it. Imagine they are giving each other **mutual** assistance.

[4 STROKES   RANK 819]

Unit 3

Curiouser and Curiouser

21 山　山　**mountain**　　　■ three ₄ (altered)　▢ one ₂　shān

Three peaks form *one* **mountain**.　[3 STROKES　RANK 259]

22 出　出　**exit**　　　■ mountain (times 2) ₂₁　chū

Although this character looks like it has some connection to 山, it's better to focus on the five vertical strokes, which have the appearance of bony fingers. In fact, when you stare at it, 出 resembles a hand, highly contorted perhaps, like that of the wicked queen in the guise of the hag who beckoned Snow White out of the dwarfs' cottage, persuading her to **exit** from the safety of the room and so to her fate.　[5 STROKES　RANK 28]

23 击　击　**strike**　　　▢ earth, soil ₉　■ mountain ₂₁　jī

BF *Earth* from a *mountain* is a landslide—it **strikes** with great force.

[5 STROKES　RANK 395]

24 亅　亅　**hooked stick**

CMP The long vertical 'scepter' stroke of the preceding panels sometimes appears with a hook. In this context, the vertical can refer to something hook-like, but sometimes the hook acts as an 'abbreviation' sign. That is, the hooked vertical will remind you of a more elaborate shape.

25 丁 丁   **fourth**   ☐ one 2   ▥ hooked stick 24   dīng

(The definition here refers to 'fourth in a series of items or fourth in a list'.) This shape reminds me of the special *hook*-like keys you use to open *one* can of sardines. With the layers of cramped fish finally exposed, they are free to go **forth** (sounds like *fourth*) for your gustatory delight.

    We will sometimes use this shape to refer to a platform or table, because that's what it looks like.   [2 STROKES   RANK 1168]

26 于 于   **in; at; to**   ☐ two 3   ▥ hooked stick 24   yú

Prepositions are the worst part of learning foreign languages—they never translate cleanly, which is why we must append three meanings to 于. How do you even visualize prepositional relationships? Here's our *hook*—we've already compared two horizontals to the surface of dry earth (see §10), but the *hook* helps lock the stick **in** place or **at** our location. Furthermore, the '*two*' strokes which indicate the earth sound like **to**.   [3 STROKES   RANK 40]

27 手 手   **hand**   ☐ three 4   ▥ hooked stick 24   shǒu

The *hooked stick* is shorthand for an entire arm; the hook is the elbow, but only the forearm is explicitly drawn. The *three* horizontal strokes are the stylized fingers of the **hand**, so stylized that no one cares that we show six fingers!   [4 STROKES   RANK 143]

28 拜 拜   **do obeisance, salute**   ▥ hand 27 (altered)   ▥ king 11 (altered)   bài

Is this character evidence for subtle subversion on the part of ancient scribes? Observe a slightly disfigured left *hand* performing a **salute** to a trumped-up *king*—too many chevrons and a scepter threatening to drop out of the frame.   [9 STROKES   RANK 1218]

29 扌 扌   **hand r**

CMP When the character 手 appears as a component in another character, it takes this somewhat abbreviated and distorted form—now there are only four fingers! (Or perhaps there are five—the four ends of the more-or-less horizontal strokes, and the upper protruding end of the central hook.)

30 挂 挂 hang   ▮ hand r 29   ▮ jade tablet 14   guà

If you take your *hand* and **hang** the *jade tablet* which symbolizes our leadership and power, then everyone can inspect it and render proper respect to you.   [9 STROKES   RANK 1232]

Sometimes, when we use a character as a component, it suffers mild distortion. For example,

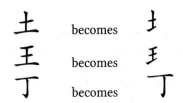

土   becomes   土

王   becomes   王

丁   becomes   丁

Sometimes, though, the distortion is more severe. We will draw your attention to instances of these disfigurations by including the word 'altered' in the label that identifies the component.

Unit 4

Action and Inaction

31 拒 拒　**resist or repel**　　□ hand r 29　□ huge 18　jù
BF The giant's *hand* is *huge*. With it, it's easy for him to **resist** and **repel** his enemies.　　[7 STROKES　RANK 1331]

32 排 排　**put in order**　　□ hand r 29　□ not 13　pái
The straight lines of '*not*' suggest the ordered arrangement of soldiers who are drilling. Here's a young boy using his *hand* to **put** his toy soldiers **in order**. And in fact another meaning for 'pái' is '**platoon**'.　　[11 STROKES　RANK 682]

33 打 打　**hit**　　□ hand r 29　□ fourth 25　dǎ
The *hand* (on the left) is clutching the '*fourth*' component on the right, which we earlier compared to a metal key, as if it were a pair of brass knuckles. We are getting ready to **hit** someone with a vengeance. What's the point of fighting if you're not going to win?　　[5 STROKES　RANK 223]

34 ヨ ヨ　**boar's head**
CMP The design emphasizes the stiff bristles that cover a **boar's head**.

35 扫 扫　**sweep**　　□ hand r 29　□ boar's head 34　sǎo
Officially, the right component represents a *boar's head*, but we'll interpret it as the bottom of a broom, which is what it looks like! After all, we have to put these stiff bristles to good use. We see a *hand* holding a broom getting ready to **sweep**.　　[6 STROKES　RANK 1435]

36 彗 彗 **broom**   ■ plentiful (times 2) 12   ■ boar's head 34   huì

I'm a champion sweeper, and I wear out **brooms** *plenty* fast. The bristles come from a *boar's head*, and I use an *abundance* of them.   [11 STROKES   RANK 3591]

37 丑 丑 **hideous**   ■ boar's head 34 (altered)   Ⅱ scepter 5   chǒu

The underlying '*boar's head*' is a variant of the form shown above in §34. Wild, feral boars are far more **hideous** and frightening than their domestic cousins. This character shows one so ancient and mighty that a giant fang extends upward from his horizontal jaw to the top of his *head*. The fangs are weapons and, like a *scepter*, a symbol of his authority within the pack.

[4 STROKES   RANK 1901]

38 扭 扭 **twist, wrench**   ■ hand r 29   Ⅱ hideous 37   niǔ

Twisting and especially **wrenching** are ugly motions, often accompanied by ugly emotion. It's not surprising that a *hand* accompanied by *ugliness* has this meaning.   [7 STROKES   RANK 1805]

39 聿 聿 **pen, writing instrument**

■ boar's head 34   Ⅱ scepter 5   ■ two 3   yù

BF There are a total of five horizontal strokes in this rare character, representing five fingers holding the vertical **pen**. The first and third fingers are linked, to emphasize that the first three fingers of a hand are the strongest and most dexterous.   [6 STROKES   RANK 3526]

40 囗 囗 **enclosure**

CMP Normally, only 囗 contains additional elements inside it; 囗 never does.

41 口 囗 **mouth**   ■ enclosure 40   kǒu

Almost everyone already knows this is a stylized representation of an actual **mouth**. It's square rather than round because the calligraphy brush made circular curves difficult to execute, but it represents a small *enclosure*. It's often useful to imagine that 口 represents a speaking person, or sometimes just a person. It's only possible to reliably distinguish 囗 from 口 when they're next to each other.   [3 STROKES   RANK 212]

42 回 回 **return**   ■ enclosure 40   ■ mouth 41   huí

Here, a lonely man imprisoned in an *enclosure* uses his *mouth* to signal his distress, his desire to **return** home to friends and family.

[6 STROKES   RANK 172]

43 吕 吕 **bamboo pitch pipes**   ▬ mouth 41   ▬ mouth 41   lǚ

BF **Bamboo pitch pipes** are flute-like things we blow into to get a pure musical tone. Here are two of the holes—mini-*mouths*, so to speak.

[6 STROKES   RANK 1716]

44 品 品 **product**   ■ mouth 41   ■ mouth 41   ■ mouth 41   pǐn

Here is a stylized crowd of merchants, represented by their *mouths*. They are busy hawking the **product**s they have for sale.   [9 STROKES   RANK 308]

45 中 中 **middle**   ▬ enclosure 40   Ⅱ scepter 5   zhōng

An *enclosure*—a small pen—pierced by a *scepter* through the **middle** nicely illustrates this concept.   [4 STROKES   RANK 14]

46 串 串 **strung together**

            ▭ mouth 41   ▬ mouth 41   Ⅱ scepter 5   chuàn

Here's a grisly tale—natives from a cannibal isle take their shrunken heads, symbolized by a pair of *mouths*, and use a small pole or *scepter*, to **string** them **together**.   [7 STROKES   RANK 1832]

47 申 申 **express**   ■ mouth 41   ■ ten 6   shēn

BF A skilled orator can **express** herself on any subject—figuratively speaking, *ten* words emerge effortlessly from her *mouth*.   [5 STROKES   RANK 1110]

48 由 由 **let sb do sth**   ■ mouth 41   ■ ten 6   yóu

You can think of the '田' part as the portcullis on a medieval castle. Someone has just raised the central vertical to **let** you walk through.

[5 STROKES   RANK 136]

Unit 5

Moving and Standing Still

49 抽 抽 **take out**　　　■ hand r 29　□ let sb do sth 48　chōι
The vertical on the right looks for all the world like a thorn embedded in a *hand* or a paw. The fingers of the '*hand*' on the left are about to **take out** this offending object by clamping on it.　[8 STROKES　RANK 1178]

50 甲 甲 **first in a series**　　　□ mouth 41　■ ten 6　jiǎ
A protest rally is getting under way. You are at the head of the line holding a sign which looks just like this character. You hold it by its long handle, so people can read it. It lets them know to stand behind you. You are **first in the series** of *ten* marchers, all of whom are loud*mouths*.　[5 STROKES　RANK 1106]

51 古 古 **ancient**　　　■ ten 6　■ mouth 41　gǔ
This character shows *ten mouths*. Mouths next to each other in time (rather than space) can represent generations. Thus, something like ten generations ago is **ancient**.　[5 STROKES　RANK 509]

52 叶 叶 **leaf**　　　■ mouth 41　■ ten 6　yè
If you rotate 古 (§51) by ninety degrees, you get this character, 叶 'leaf'. The rotation means ten mouths in space, not time, *ten* people ('*mouths*') clamoring for food. Fortunately, there's enough—to the host's **relief** (sound like **leaf**!).　[5 STROKES　RANK 920]

53 固 固 **solid**　　　■ enclosure 40　■ ancient 51　gù
Ancient ruins, surrounded or protected by an *enclosure* must be pretty **solid** to have lasted this long.　[8 STROKES　RANK 893]

54 咕 咕 **cluck**   ▮ mouth ₄₁   ▯ ancient ₅₁   gū

For some *ancient* people, the sounds from their *mouths* often resemble muttering or the **clucks** of chickens.   [8 STROKES   RANK 2418]

55 吐 吐 **spit**   ▯ mouth ₄₁   ▮ earth, soil ₉   tǔ

From your *mouth* to the *earth*—that pretty much sums up the act of **spitting**.   [6 STROKES   RANK 1653]

56 吉 吉 **lucky**   ▱ scholar ₈   ▰ mouth ₄₁   jí

BF The words from a *scholar's mouth* are considered **lucky**. I assume this is a scholar's definition of luck!   [6 STROKES   RANK 856]

57 田 田 **field**   ▮ enclosure ₄₀   ▮ ten ₆   tián

Officially, this pictograph represents a **field** with irrigation ditches. In keeping with our methods, it's better to think of a cultivated **field** as an *enclosure* containing any number of crops, perhaps *ten* or so.   [5 STROKES   RANK 778]

58 呈 呈 **appear**   ▯ mouth ₄₁   ▬ king ₁₁   chéng

In ancient societies, *kings* were often isolated from their subjects. Their **appearance** for ceremonial or ritual purposes would have been a key event in ancient life, so it makes sense to use this event to stand for the verb **appear**. The *mouth* represents the physical features of the *king*.   [7 STROKES   RANK 1563]

59 扣 扣 **to button**   ▮ hand r ₂₉   ▯ mouth ₄₁   kòu

Here, you use your *hand* to **button** the button, which looks like nothing so much as a doll's *mouth*.   [6 STROKES   RANK 1625]

60 可 可 **can; may**   ☐ fourth 25   ■ mouth 41   kě

Children's tales often involve an important character who succeeds in a task only after several trials. A big, bad wolf, for example, may need several attempts to huff and puff to blow a house down. Here, only after the expulsion of a mighty breath from its *mouth* on the *fourth* attempt **can** the wolf succeed in his demolition work.

可 often appears as part of another character. Then, it will often receive the interpretation of 'ability', the noun referred to by *can* and *may*.

[5 STROKES   RANK 30]

61 呵 呵 **breathe out**   ☐ mouth 41   ☐ can; may 60   hē

Breathing out is one of a *mouth's* special *abilities*.   [8 STROKES   RANK 1861]

62 哥 哥 **elder brother**   ☐ can; may 60 (altered)   ■ can; may 60   gē

1   BF If you have an **elder brother**, you know it's not an easy life, especially when you're young. Lots of fights break out, so you really need physical a *double dose* of *ability* to survive.

2   **Elder brothers** are frustrating creatures. Since they're older than you, they have so many more *abilities*.   [10 STROKES   RANK 804]

63 日 日 **day, sun**   ■ enclosure 40   ☐ one 2   rì

BF A stylized pictograph of the **sun**. A **day** *encloses one* major time period.

[4 STROKES   RANK 101]

64 曰 曰 **speak**   ■ mouth 41   ☐ one 2   yuē

1   *One mouth* is used for **speaking**.

2   The horizontal line represents the expulsion of breath when **speaking**.

[4 STROKES   RANK 1656]

65 旦 旦 **dawn**   ■ day, sun 63   ☐ one 2   dàn

How can you help but see the *sun* rising above the horizon *line* at **dawn**?

[5 STROKES   RANK 1300]

66 坦 坦 flat   ■ earth, soil 9   ■ dawn 65   tǎn

BF No matter what the terrain, the *earth* at *dawn* appears **flat**.

[8 STROKES   RANK 1017]

Unit 6

Up and Down

67 担 担 undertake   ◨ hand r 29   ◨ dawn 65   dān

Undertaking the tasks of daily life begins early. At *dawn*, people begin using their *hands* to perform their various chores.   [8 STROKES   RANK 720]

68 旧 旧 old; bygone   ◨ scepter 5   ◨ day, sun 63   jiù

An aged leader, with her *scepter* as symbol of authority, has seen many *days* and reflects on past, **bygone** times.   [5 STROKES   RANK 915]

69 昌 昌 flourishing   ◨ speak 64   ◨ speak 64   chāng

BF Merchants **flourish** when they *speak* a lot. Their sales pitches nail their deals.   [8 STROKES   RANK 1606]

70 早 早 morning   ◨ day, sun 63   ◨ ten 6   zǎo

1 The *sun* is jauntily perched on a *ten*—it's 10:00, a frabjous time to finally begin the **morning**.

2 The horizontal line of the 'ten' component represents ground level. The vertical stroke is a flower stalk, on top of which sits a *sun*-flower bud. In the **morning**, the bud opens and prepares to follow the sun.

         [6 STROKES   RANK 462]

71 里 里 inside   ◨ field 57   ◨ earth, soil 9   lǐ

Inside a *field*'s *soil* are the roots of a goodly number of crops.

         [7 STROKES   RANK 50]

72 埋 埋 **bury**   ⬛ earth, soil 9   ⬛ inside 71   mái

When are you part of the *earth's insides*? When they come to **bury** you!

[10 STROKES   RANK 1640]

73 理 理 **rational**   ⬛ king 11   ⬛ inside 71   lǐ

How does a king get to be in charge, at least in theory? The *king's insides* supposedly endow him with superior logic and **rationality**, so much so that he deserves our fealty.

[11 STROKES   RANK 89]

74 哩 哩 **enumeration**   ⬛ mouth 41   ⬛ inside 71   lī

I've chosen a slightly non-standard use for this glyph. The enumeration I refer to has to do with listing items:

> Yīngwén lī, Déwén lī, Fàwén lī, tā dōu huì shuō.
> *He can speak English, German, and French.*

When speaking, you **enumerate** items by speaking each item (with your *mouth*, naturally) as it bubbles up from within (*inside*) you.

[10 STROKES   RANK 1949]

75 唱 唱 **sing**   ⬛ mouth 41   ⬛ flourishing 69   chàng

It's possible to think of song as enhanced speaking, that is, the expressive powers of the **singing** *mouth* have *flourished* beyond normal.

[11 STROKES   RANK 1252]

76 晶 晶 **crystal**   ⬛ day, sun 63   ⬛ day, sun 63   ⬛ day, sun 63   jīng

BF The light on the facets of a **crystal**, so bright and brilliant, looks just like several *suns*.

[12 STROKES   RANK 1725]

77 量 量 **measure**   ⬛ dawn 65   ⬛ inside 71   liáng

At the break of *dawn*, visibility improves *inside* your room, making it easy to **measure** things by natural light.

[12 STROKES   RANK 241]

78 目 目 eye · enclosure 40 · two 3   mù

BF The *two enclosures* in the upper half of your head are your **eyes**. Also, you can imagine yourself taking an open **eye**, turning it on its end, and simplifying all curves to horizontal and vertical segments, to get 目.

[5 STROKES   RANK 239]

79 冒 冒 brave · helmet · two 3 · eye 78   màc

It's easy for a soldier to be **brave** when he is *helmeted* in such a way to protect his *two eyes*. (We have no component called 'helmet', but to me, this seems an obvious piece of imagery.)   [9 STROKES   RANK 1222]

80 盯 盯 stare · eye 78 · fourth 25   dīn

A **stare** is a fixed gaze, in which *one* person *hooks* you with his *eye*. (Here, we are decomposing the 丁 component of §25 into its components.)

[7 STROKES   RANK 1906]

81 吾 吾 me · five 19 · mouth 41   wú

I don't know about you, but my head, with its *five 'mouths'* or orifices (two ears, two nostrils, mouth) is the essence of **me**, the center of consciousness.

[7 STROKES   RANK 1649]

82 耳 耳 ear · eye 78 (altered)   ěr

Ears and eyes are the main sensory receptors of a person. The **ear** is shown here as a slightly deformed *eye*. The horizontal extensions emphasize the additional external structures that surround our **ears**. The lower vertical stroke on the right is the earlobe of the right **ear**.   [6 STROKES   RANK 887]

83 而 而 express add'l but contrasting info · one 2 · eye 78 (altered)   ér

Think of this diagram as a sketch whereby the little '*dab*' connects two contrasting forms, the smooth *horizontal* surface on the top, and the rough, beard-like form below it. Consequently, we'll use this character to express **contrast**.

Also, an *eye*, subject to rotation and gross alteration, surveys the *horizon*. All kinds of stuff are visible, similar and **contrasting**.   [6 STROKES   RANK 36]

84 面　面　face, aspect

■ express add'l but contrasting info 83 　　　 a few alterations 　　miàn

BF Regard this character as a triptych of mirrors, perhaps on a lady's dressing table. The topmost stroke is a light bar connected to the top of the mirrors. The lady of the house **faces** the mirrors and can inspect any of three **aspects** of her reflection. 　　　　　　　　　　　　　　　　　　　　[9 STROKES　RANK 74]

Unit 7

From Side to Side

85 雨 雨 **rain**

■ express add'l but contrasting info 83 (altered)   ▪▪ drops of rain   **yǔ**

1 What a *contrast* with yesterday! It was bright sun yesterday—today it's pouring **rain**!

2 Look at the driving **rain** outside the dual windows. (It's a double window, with a long decorative sill on top.)   [8 STROKES   RANK 928]

86 雷 雷 **thunder**   ■ rain 85   ■ field 57   **léi**

It's not enough to have *rain* to water the crops in the *fields*. The rainfall must be intense, otherwise you tease the crops but don't let them grow. Typically, intense *rain*storms, sufficiently intense to nourish the *fields*, are accompanied by **thunder**, so this character is fitting for this natural noise.

[13 STROKES   RANK 686]

87 雪 雪 **snow**   ■ rain 85   ■ boar's head 34   **xuě**

1 Here's precipitation lying in white layers on the ground. Can't be *rain*, so it must be **snow**.

2 Here's *precipitation* that needs sweeping away with my *boar's head* broom. It's **snow**!   [11 STROKES   RANK 1003]

88 需 需 **needs, requirements**

■ rain 85   ■ express add'l but contrasting info 83   **xū**

BF *Rain* often marks a *contrast* with previous conditions. Moreover, once it starts raining, you will **need** other stuff—hats, umbrellas, boots, raincoat—to stay comfortable, so this is a good way to indicate **needs** and **requirements**.

[14 STROKES   RANK 408]

89 瑞 瑞 auspicious

◻ king 11   ◼ mountain 21   ◼ express add'l but contrasting info 83   ruì

BF The right pair of components combines soaring *mountains* seemingly connected to a *contrasting* image, roots firmly anchored underground. The Chinese people must have felt that the ideal *king* combines lofty ideals— *mountains*—with down-to-earth practicality, symbolized by the roots. A *king* thus endowed would surely have an **auspicious** reign.

[13 STROKES   RANK 1332]

90 喘 喘 gasp for breath

◻ mouth 41   ◼ mountain 21   ◼ express add'l but contrasting info 83   chuǎn

BF Consider a *mountain* and its *contrast*, the valley down below, and suppose you run like the wind from the *mountain* down to the other. Through your *mouth*, you'll be **gasping for breath**.

Could the gasping be due to asthma? **Asthma** is another meaning for this character. [12 STROKES   RANK 1977]

91 押 押 mortgage, pawn, give as security

◼ hand r 29   ◼ first in a series 50   yā

Before I get a bank loan, I *hand* over the item that's *first* in my affections, as a guarantee they get their money back. This is the essence of **pledging** collateral or **mortgaging** your house. [8 STROKES   RANK 1775]

92 ㄐ ㄐ speak up!

CMP Here's someone cupping their ear with their left hand to better hear what someone is saying.

93 叫 叫 to be called

◻ mouth 41   ◼ speak up! 92   jiào

It looks like someone is standing attentively, cupping their ear with their left hand to *better hear* what the *mouth* is saying. The person with the *mouth* (on the left) is **calling something** to the hearing-challenged friend.

[5 STROKES   RANK 387]

94 艹 ⧺   grass r
CMP

1 Short **grass** plants emerge vertically from the horizontal ground.
2 Here, in the United States, where these words are being written, we think of **grass** as a charming, but bland, garden ornament. In fact, the many species of grasses throughout the world belie this blandness. Many are highly colored and highly ornamental. Some, like some majestic forms of bamboo, are breathtaking. Consequently, it sometimes behooves us to interpret this component as a form of decoration, particularly outdoor decoration.
3 Remind yourself of the hand component of §29. That character looks like our bit of **grass**, but arranged vertically instead of horizontally. Sometimes it's useful to refer to this image as another hand.

95 草 草 grass   ☐ grass r 94   ■ morning 70   cǎo

1 The small 'grass' component on top of this character is the actual **grass**. To get the whole character, think of your gardener arriving to cut the *grass* in the *morning*.
2 **Grass** is even *grassier* in the *morning*. Glowing in the morning light, freshened by its breakfast of dew, a perfect lawn seems even more perfect at this hour.   [9 STROKES RANK 789]

96 苦 苦 bitter   ☐ grass r 94   ■ ancient 51   kǔ

It's famine time. **Bitter** experience soon teaches you that *grass* which is *ancient* tastes the most **bitter**.   [8 STROKES RANK 634]

97 苗 苗 seedling   ■ grass r 94   ■ field 57   miáo

The product of **seedlings** sprouting in the fenced-in *field* is a whole bunch of *grasses*. Later on, we transplant the mature plants.   [8 STROKES RANK 1920]

98 描 描 **to trace**   ▮ hand r 29   ▮ seedling 97   miáo

1 The 'grass' component on the right top of 描 looks sorta kinda like the left-hand 'hand' component rotated by ninety degrees and distorted somewhat. 'Hand' becomes 'grass'—a poor job of **tracing** the original. The 'field' component is your grade for this assignment—only 'ten' marks (out of one hundred) circled by a mouth-like enclosure.

2 Sometimes, when plants sprout, we use our *hand* to manipulate the *seedlings* and their fine, hairlike leaves. Think of plucking these tiny *seedlings*, turning them upside down, and holding them to **trace** a picture—a type of primitive Chinese calligraphy.   [11 STROKES   RANK 1246]

99 菲 菲 **luxuriant**   ▢ grass r 94   ▮ not 13   fēi

BF We've previously (§13) identified the components as *combs* in the hair of a royal princess. She further affixes a costly gold hair clip at the top of her head. The clip, with its clasp mechanism, looks like a tuft of golden *grass* in her hair. How **luxurious!**   [11 STROKES   RANK 1418]

100 廿 廿 **horned animal**

CMP Every so often, we'll come upon a component that appears in a handful or so of characters. We'll call this one a **horned animal**, something like a cow or ox. The verticals represent the horns and the sides of the head. A horizontal stroke shows the top of the head. Sometimes, as we see here, the component includes a short stroke connecting the bottom of the verticals—the base of the head.

101 革 革 **animal hide**   ▮ horned animal 100   ▮ mouth 41   ⊞ ten 6   gé

1 When you skin a *horned animal* to get its **hide**, there are lots of cutouts in the leather representing places where the poor **animal** used to have four hooves, two eyes, one nose, one actual mouth, and two ears. These openings are like *mouths* in the **hide**, and there are *ten* of them .

2 We're looking down at the tanned **hide** of some unfortunate **animal** (sheep, antelope, etc.). That's the head of the *horned animal* at the top, followed by the *mouth* component, which here suggests the animal's body, and finally the strokes of the *ten* which sketch the spine, tail, and limbs.   [9 STROKES   RANK 521]

102 鞋　鞋　shoe　　█ animal hide 101　▙ earth, soil 9　▟ earth, soil 9　　xié

To create **shoes**, the cobbler uses *leather* in which you can comfortably put both feet on the *ground*, which is why the '*soil*' component occurs twice.

[15 STROKES   RANK 1638]

Unit 8

Getting Stroked

103 甘 甘 **sweet**　■ horned animal 100　⊟ one 2　gān

BF Animals respond voraciously to intense flavors that are **sweet**. Here our favorite *horned animal* enjoys sucking on *one* peppermint stick.

[5 STROKES   RANK 1408]

104 曲 曲 **bend**　■ mouth 41　▥ horned animal 100　qū

Some *horned animal* with a huge open *mouth*, perhaps something like a horned hippopotamus, is ready to chomp on your umbrella. For sure, the animal will **bend** it.

[6 STROKES   RANK 1066]

105 曹 曹 **plaintiff and defendant**　▢ one 2　▤ bend 104　▥ speak 64

cáo

In a courtroom setting, *one* of either the **plaintiff or defendant** is *bent* when they *speak*.

[11 STROKES   RANK 1570]

106 世 世 **generation**　■ ten 6　■ horned animal 100　▢ one 2　shì

BF Certain animals don't live as long as people. Metaphorically speaking, it takes *ten* or so *animal* lifespans to equal *one* human **generation**.

[5 STROKES   RANK 181]

107 ⼫ ⼫ **net r**

CMP This radical corresponds to the full character 网, wǎng, '**net**', often used today for '**Internet**'. Interpret this glyph as a snapshot of a small portion of a **net**, focusing on three adjacent gaps in its fabric and the strands framing them.

108 罪 罪 **crime, guilt**   ▢ net r 107   ■ not 13   zuì

Becoming enmeshed in **crime** and covered in **guilt** is a lot like becoming entangled in a *net* that is *not* arranged properly—you're all *knotted up* ('knot' sounds like 'not', get it?).   [13 STROKES   RANK 718]

109 置 置 **to place, put**   ▢ net r 107   ■ straight, vertical 16   zhì

  1 Pictographically, here is a *net* emptying its load (of fish?) which cascades down a chute into the tall, *vertical* storage container. The result—we've **placed** the stuff where it belongs.

  2 At the end of the day, we take our *net*, carefully clean it, and then *straighten it up* and perhaps hang it *vertically* on the wall. We've **put** it where it belongs, ready for tomorrow's use.   [13 STROKES   RANK 677]

110 皿 皿 **vessel, dish**   ■ net r 107   ▢ one 2   mǐn
BF

  1 You can think of this drawing as *one net* stretched to become tense and rigid, attached to a lower boundary. In this tense mode, the strands of the net are like wires, keeping the contents from slipping out. Thus, it becomes like a **vessel** or **dish**.

  2 Imagine the profile of a fancy bowl. The scribes have sketched here its footing and the lines of texture on the walls of the bowl.

                    [5 STROKES   RANK 3763]

111 𠃌 𠃌 **place of refuge**

CMP This land form, like an arm which encircles and protects a loved one, provides a place for people with like interests, skills, or characteristics to congregate safely, or a place where people can come together for mutual assistance and help—a **place of refuge**.

112 司 司 **company**   ▢ place of refuge 111   ▬ one 2   ▣ mouth 41   sī

BF A **company** is a *place of refuge*—so to speak—for people who have come together to work for a common goal—that of the company. And so, metaphorically, they speak with *one mouth*.   [5 STROKES   RANK 278]

113 卫 卫 **guard, protect** ⬛ place of refuge 111 ▯ scepter 5 ▯ one 2   wèi
BF

    1 At the *place of refuge* for the clans, the leader wields his *scepter* of authority to **guard** and **protect** his people from the danger just over the *horizon.*

    2 This character clearly shows the profile of a fist ready to challenge and defend, to **guard** and **protect**.   [3 STROKES   RANK 669]

114 节 节 **festival** ▭ grass r 94 ⬛ guard, protect 113 ▯ one 2   jié
BF The earliest **festivals** were times of celebration following the successful safekeeping and *guarding* of a tribe following attack—enemies over the horizon are a distant bad memory! (The grayed horizon tells you that this component should be removed from consideration.) Fronds of decorative *grass* were hung everywhere to serve as convenient and cheap decorations.

[5 STROKES   RANK 514]

115 韦 韦 **leather** ⬛ plentiful 12 ⬛ place of refuge 111   wéi
BF Note how the horizontal part of '*place of refuge*' coincides with the bottom horizontal of '*plentiful*'.

    Look at the spot we've scouted out. *Plentiful* resources and well-fortified to make a *refuge*. It'll make a good place to **hide** from our enemies, and '**hide**' is a synonym of '**leather**'!   [4 STROKES   RANK 1667]

116 围 围 **surround, enclose** ▢ enclosure 40 ⬛ leather 115   wéi
We *hide* (a synonym for *leather*, remember!) in an *enclosure* for protection against our enemies who **surround** us.   [7 STROKES   RANK 576]

117 韩 韩 **South Korea** ⬛ ten 6 ⬛ morning 70 ⬛ leather 115   hán
Those businessmen from **South Korea** are too canny for me! We've had meetings for the last *ten mornings*, and we still have yet to come to terms about exclusive importing of their *leather* chopsticks! (See those upper two horizontal strokes that are part of the 'leather' component? It's a set of those chopsticks!)   [12 STROKES   RANK 1221]

118 斤 斤　catty　　■ place of refuge 111 (altered)　▐ fourth 25 (altered)　jīn

Although a full-blown character in its own right, this structure is also a very common component of other characters. Incidentally, **catty** is a noun, a Chinese unit of weight. It's about one-half a kilogram, so therefore about 1.1 pounds.

By itself, this structure looks like the left half of a table. To see this, imagine butting its right edge alongside its mirror image. The table is covered by a table cloth, too. The half we see here stands upright, but it's very unstable. If you **pound** on it too hard, down it goes.

When this character itself serves as component, we may assign it the meaning of '**unstable**' or '**unbalanced**'. Other times, we interpret it in a '**pound**' or weight-related sense.　　[4 STROKES RANK 1866]

119 听 听　hear, listen　　▇ mouth 41　▐ catty 118　tīng

That guy is talking really crazy. Are we in any danger? Whenever someone *mouths* off in an *unbalanced* manner, I **listen** very carefully to see if emergency measures are called for.　　[7 STROKES RANK 285]

120 折 折　broken (stick, rope)　　▌ hand r 29　▐ catty 118　shé

Could this be the source of the *broken table* of §118? Some *unbalanced* person's *hand* has **broken** it.　　[7 STROKES RANK 1131]

121 哲 哲　wise, sagacious　　▭ broken (stick, rope) 120　▬ mouth 41　zhé

BF On those long winter nights, tribal elders recounted ancient historical epics. From the elder's *mouth* proceeds a tale of things *broken* during the course of great adventures. The conclusion to the tale contains **wise** and **sagacious** lessons to be learned from the story.　　[10 STROKES RANK 1117]

122 岳 岳　high mountain peak

　　　　　▭ catty 118　▬ one 2　▬ mountain 21　yuè

BF If *mountains* truly had *one*, definable, sharp **peak**, then something placed on a *platform* on top of this hypothetical peak would be *unbalanced*.

In other words, you'll be *unbalanced* at *one high mountain's* **peak**.

[8 STROKES RANK 1844]

123 羽　羽　feather, wing

◼ place of refuge 111　◼ two 3 (altered)　◼ place of refuge 111　◼ two 3 (altered)　yǔ

BF The ancient scribes sketched the *two* **wings** of a bird with economical strokes. The wings themselves can enfold you to provide *places of refuge*. The inner '*two*'s (somewhat misaligned) suggest how the **feathers** themselves become distorted by the air flow during flight.　　[6 STROKES　RANK 1865]

124 丘　丘　mound, little hill　　　　　　　◼ catty 118　◻ one 2　qiū

BF The vagrant is a little *unbalanced*. He looks towards the distant *horizon*, and thinks he sees a **little hill** because it's so far away.

[5 STROKES　RANK 1929]

125 习　习　practice, study　　　　◼ feather, wing 123　◻ feather, wing 123　xí

BF *Half a feather, half of a wing* suggests that we have to **practice** more in order to fully earn our *wings*!　　[3 STROKES　RANK 676]

126 弱　弱　weak, feeble, inferior　　　◼ feather, wing 123 (altered)　ruò

The *wings* and *feathers* of a young fledgling look quite different from those of its parents. The chick is **weak** and **feeble**.　　[10 STROKES　RANK 1038]

127 冂　冂　borders　　　　　　　◻ scepter 5　◼ place of refuge 111

CMP The **borders** of a country mark a region in which a well-defined governmental *authority* provides *refuge* and safety to its citizens.

128 再　再　again　　　　　　　◼ king 11　◼ borders 127　zài

The *king* and his court have an uncontrollable urge, an itch, to extend their reach beyond their *borders*, and to do so **again** and **again**. (The interweaving of the two components is subtle and fascinating.)　　[6 STROKES　RANK 242]

Unit 9

Wordplay and Word Play

129 同　同　**same, similar**　■ borders 127　▬ one 2　■ mouth 41　tón

BF People living within the **same** set of *borders* speak the **same** language—that is, they speak as if with *one mouth* (metaphorically).　[6 STROKES　RANK 69]

130 巾　巾　**towel**　▬ borders 127　▯ scepter 5　jīn

1　**BF** Picture our *scepter* in use as a drying rod; some one's smelly old **towel** is hanging limply on it to dry out—that's what the *borders* represent.

2　See how the neighboring king (symbolized here by his royal *scepter*) invades our *borders*. Could it be time for us to throw in the **towel**?

By extension, since a towel is a cloth with a special purpose, we will feel free to interpret this character as a towel or other special purpose piece of fabric when it appears as a component.　[3 STROKES　RANK 2281]

131 吊　吊　**hang, suspend**　▯ mouth 41　▬ towel 130　dià

1　What *special cloth* **hangs** below a man's *mouth*? A necktie.

2　A freshly-**hung** person must look like this, suspended from the noose, body **hanging** limply down below the head.　[6 STROKES　RANK 2050]

132 帽　帽　**hat**　▮ towel 130　▮ brave 79　mà

Some men need fancy clothes to bolster their self-esteem. In this case, the *special cloth* that makes them *brave* is a **hat**. (It's a helmet-like structure, protecting our two eyes.)　[12 STROKES　RANK 1750]

133 帚 帚 broom*

⬚ boar's head 34   ▭ borders 127 (altered)   ▬ towel 130   zhǒu

BF The *boar's head* bristles on the **broom** have been wrapped with *towels* and other cloths to sweep or mop some large area within the *borders* of four walls.   [8 STROKES   RANK 3630]

134 册 册 book, booklet

▮▮ borders (times 2) 127   ▭ one 2   cè

BF Hold an old **book** upright and look down on the top edge. The book is a collection of folded sheets, sewn together. This character is a schematic of that structure. Here are two of these gatherings, sewn together to form *one* **booklet**.   [5 STROKES   RANK 1525]

135 ㄴ ㄴ mineshaft

CMP If the component in §111 is a place of safety, this component is its opposite, a place of danger! Think of it perhaps as a **mineshaft**. You fall right down the shaft of this tunnel. When you regain consciousness, you can walk horizontally, at least for a short bit.

136 黾 黾 tadpole

▭ mouth 41   ▮ mineshaft 135   ▬ day, sun 63   mǐn

BF Here's a scribe's-eye view of a **tadpole**. A giant *mouth*-head is attached to a wiggling, wriggling *shaft*-shaped body. A round, *sun*-shaped stomach provides nourishment until the cute little creature achieves a measure of self-sufficiency.   [8 STROKES   RANK 5223]

137 七 七 seven

▬ mineshaft 135   ▭ one 2   qī

Go ahead—turn this character over so it's upside-down. You'll see a Roman 'seven', crossed in the European fashion.   [2 STROKES   RANK 530]

138 电 电 electricity　　　■ day, sun 63　　▯ mineshaft 135　　diàr

Look closely at this portion of an **electric** grid. The current enters or exits via the *mineshaft*-shaped wire, and disperses through the other wires in a regular pattern that looks like the *sun*.

For readers with some background in physics, a moving current gives rise to an **electro**magnetic field, nicely symbolized by the '*sun*' component. The *sun* itself has a massive **electro**magnetic field associated with it.

[5 STROKES   RANK 230]

139 扎 扎 pierce, prick　　　▮ hand r 29　　▯ mineshaft 135　　zhā

The *hand* grabs the *wire* (the shape of a *mineshaft* suggests a segment of a live wire) in a careless manner. The sharp end **pierces** his *hand* and it bleeds a bit.　　[4 STROKES   RANK 1411]

140 也 也 also*, too*

　　　■ mineshaft 135　　▯ scepter 5　　■ place of refuge 111 (altered)　　yě

The central *scepter* represents the court of a powerful king. His court can be a *place of refuge* but **also** a *mineshaft* of danger, depending on how well you play politics.

When present as a component, 也 combines contrasts together.

[3 STROKES   RANK 31]

141 地 地 earth, ground　　　▮ earth, soil 9　　▯ also*, too* 140　　dì

This is a more descriptive character for '**earth**' than we saw 'way back in §9. In addition to suggesting the *soil* itself, we are reminded that our planet is both dangerous—watch out for *mineshafts!*—but *also* secure, a place of refuge. It is arid, but *also* fertile, high and *also* low, dry and wet, and so on and so on.　　[6 STROKES   RANK 21]

142 匕 匕 ancient ladle　　　■ seven 137 (altered)　　bǐ

Ancient ladles and spoons were more substantial than their modern-day descendants. That's because their ways of making them were imprecise. As a result, you could serve *seven* guests with a single gargantuan scoop. Remember that the bottom curve represents the part that holds the soup.

[2 STROKES   RANK 3252]

143 旨 旨 **intention, meaning**   ▨ ancient ladle 142   ▪ day, sun 63   zhǐ

BF Here's how the ancients signalled their **intentions** and **meanings** during their meetings. The polished bottoms of *ladles* focused the rays of the *sun* on each item on a poster during a presentation.   [6 STROKES   RANK 1685]

144 指 指 **finger**   ▪ hand r 29   ▨ intention, meaning 143   zhǐ

BF I use the **fingers** of my *hand* to point and so make my *intentions* and *meanings* clear.   [9 STROKES   RANK 261]

145 北 北 **north**   ▪ ancient ladle 142 (altered)   ▪ ancient ladle 142   běi

Although we see *two ladles*, the left being a mirror image of the right, the long parts of each are actually levees on a river channeling water from the **north**, the top part of the picture, and letting the water flow down to the lands of the south. The short horizontal strokes are supports keeping the levees from toppling.   [5 STROKES   RANK 315]

146 比 比 **compared with**

         ▪ ancient ladle 142 (altered)   ▪ ancient ladle 142   bǐ

Here are *two ancient ladles*. **Compared with** the first, the second is more elegant.   [4 STROKES   RANK 199]

147 批 批 **annotate**   ▪ hand r 29   ▨ compared with 146   pī

Annotations by *hand* allow authors (and future scholars) to *compare* their revisions *with* the original versions.   [7 STROKES   RANK 569]

148 毕 毕 **finish, conclude**   ▨ compared with 146   ▪ ten 6   bì

BF **Finishing** a task, *compared with* doing only *ten* percent of it, is better.   [6 STROKES   RANK 1093]

149 昆 昆 **elder brother****   ▨ day, sun 63   ▪ compared with 146   kūn

BF This guy is an **elder brother** because, he saw the *sun* first, at least *compared with* his younger brothers.   [8 STROKES   RANK 1759]

150 屯 屯 **stockpile, store up**   ■ electricity 138 (altered)   tún

Electricity flows when a **stockpile** of electrons—the particles that give a charge to the current—is drawn to a region with an electron deficit.

[4 STROKES   RANK 2864]

151 吨 吨 ton   □ mouth 41   ■ stockpile, store up 150   dūn

There are several pretentious idiots in my class. Here's how to identify them: they open their *mouths,* and the worthless trivia they've *stockpiled* over the years comes pouring out—a **ton** of it.   [7 STROKES   RANK 1700]

152 匚 匚 **basket, box**   □ one 2   ■ mineshaft 135

CMP There are two ways to enclose a mineshaft. One way is to put a *lid* on it, as we do here, to **box** it in completely. Another way…

153 匪 匪 bandit   □ basket, box 152   ■ not 13   fěi

BF Gangs of **bandits** posed a real problem in many pre-modern societies. *Boxes* of valuables were *not* safe.   [10 STROKES   RANK 2201]

154 匠 匠 craftsman   ■ basket, box 152   ■ catty 118   jiàng

BF Give a true **craftsman** raw materials as funky and clunky as an old *box* and *an unbalanced table,* and soon you get a creative work of art.

[6 STROKES   RANK 2110]

Unit 10

In Nature's Realm

155 凵 凵 **receptacle** ◼ mineshaft 135 ☐ one 2

CMP We can stop off the *one* horizontal leg of the *mineshaft*, damming it up with a vertical fence to form some kind of **receptacle**.

156 画 画 **draw** ☐ one 2 ◼ field 57 ◼ receptacle 155 huà

What better symbolizes a landscape that you're busy **drawing** than a *field*. Discerning critics have always said your paintings are larger than life, and look how the drawing explodes out of the frame formed by '*one*' plus '*receptacle*'. Another tour de force! [8 STROKES RANK 883]

157 卩 卩 **single ear**

CMP The ear sticks out a bit from the side of the head, so try not to laugh.

158 印 印 **seal, stamp** ◼ boar's head 34 (altered) ◼ single ear 157 yìn

The point of a **stamp** or **seal** is to make a mark that's uniquely yours. Stick some *one's ear* at the *back of a boar's head* (that's how it has been altered) and use the *single ear* as a handle. Now, simply ink the head and press it to paper for a unique and memorable mark. [5 STROKES RANK 640]

159 丽 丽 **beautiful, elegant**

☐ one 2 ◼ single ear (times 2 and altered) 157 lì

BF Here are two shell-like *ears* each with *one* earring to make up a *single* pair. The jewelry is exquisite and oh-so **elegant**. [7 STROKES RANK 834]

160 卬 卬 **head held high**   ▯ basket, box 152   ▯ single ear 157

CMP The *box* and the *single ear* resemble a prominent pair of ears plainly visible as their owner **holds his head high**.

161 昂 昂 **hold your head high**   ▢ day, sun 63   ▬ head held high 160   áng

When you **hold your head high**, you get as close as you can to the *sun*.

[8 STROKES   RANK 1952]

162 抑 抑 **restrain, restrict**   ▮ hand r 29   ▯ head held high 160   yì

BF Could the *hand* in his face, forcing him to *hold his head high*, suggest some one's trying to bully him? It sure looks like it—his movements are being **restricted**.   [7 STROKES   RANK 1748]

163 畐 畐 **size range**   ▭ one 2   ▬ enclosure 40   ▬ field 57

CMP Let's read this component top down—*one, enclosure*, and *field*. The objects become increasingly two-dimensional and more structured. We imagine this juxtaposition to represent **a range of sizes**, from small to large (or the other way around).

164 幅 幅 **width of cloth**   ▮ towel 130   ▯ size range 163   fú

This word represents the extent of sheet-like items, cloth, pictures, photos, and so on.

The *towel* part reminds us that we're talking about things like **cloth**, with area but little depth. How much of the thing? Well, the possibilities are many—any of a whole *size range*. If the length stays the same, we get this range by varying the **width**.   [12 STROKES   RANK 1444]

165 事 事 **matter, affair**   ▬ size range 163 (altered)   ▯ scepter 5   shì

Human **affairs** come in all *sizes and shapes*. In order to make sense of them, people try to group them together, as if to skewer them with a sharp *stick*. But these **matters** are notoriously prickly, and the '*size range*' component has been altered to emphasize the presence of sharp, prickly points.

[8 STROKES   RANK 58]

166 刂 刂 knife r

CMP Normally, Chinese readers associate this shape with the compressed form of the character '刀', dāo, 'knife'. In my mind, this component shows the blade represented by the straight stroke in the Swiss-army-knife holder, the outer hooked vertical. Almost always, you'll see this component on the right edge of a character.

You use a **knife** to perform a job, so sometimes this component represents **completion of a task**, work activity, or something similar.

167 刊 刊 publish   ■ dry 10   ▢ knife r 166   kān

BF Here at the Surreal Publishing Company, the *dry* books we **publish** all have pages made from *dry* sheets cut by extremely sharp *knives*.

[5 STROKES   RANK 1241]

168 副 副 vice-   ■ size range 163   ▢ knife r 166   fù

Vice-president, **vice**-chairman, and so on sound impressive, but often these job titles serve as screens to get people to perform a *range* of *activities*, often with only a dull *knife* as a tool.   [11 STROKES   RANK 764]

169 ﹨ ﹨ dab

CMP …this little dab of ink that appears all the time, often on or near the top of characters (for example, 主). Sometimes, it takes an elongated form, as on the top stroke of 丢 or 睡 Look closely, for it's barely distinguishable from a true horizontal.

As a component, it's useful to let it mean 'a drop of something' or 'a little bit' of some larger quantity.

170 卜 卜 foretell   ▯ scepter 5   ▭ dab 169   bǔ

BF

1 The act of accurate **foretelling**, of prediction, is an act of high magic; what we see here is a magic wand, a *scepter* endowed with a *dab* of extraordinary power.

2 Historically, this glyph refers to the cracks in a tortoise shell by which the ancient priests **foretold** the future.   [2 STROKES   RANK 1979]

171 扑 扑 **dedicate oneself**   ▮ hand r 29   ▮ foretell 170   pū

1 With *wand* in *hand*, you're ready to **dedicate yourself** to good works.
2 **Dedication** to a cause requires a tremendous amount of self-discipline, so much so that when you use your *hand* in this activity, you need some sorcery from a *magic wand* to keep you on task.   [5 STROKES RANK 1509]

172 占 占 **practice divination**   ▮ foretell 170   ▬ mouth 41   zhā▮

BF When you **practice divination**, you rely on two main tools—your magic wand, with which you *foretell* the future, and your *mouth*, with which you woo credulous followers.   [5 STROKES RANK 737]

173 卓 卓 **stand firm**   ▯ foretell 170   ▮ morning 70   zhuō

Sometimes, a *magic wand* in the *morning* is the only thing that gets me up and out of bed, perky enough to **stand firm** at that time of day.
   [8 STROKES RANK 1942]

174 罩 罩 **bamboo fish trap**   ▯ net r 107   ▮ stand firm 173   zhào

Rope *nets* are notoriously floppy things, but if we make it out of bamboo, the strands of the net *stand firm*, so the resulting **bamboo fish trap** is very effective.   [13 STROKES RANK 1978]

175 上 上 **on**   ▮ foretell 170   ▭ one 2   shàn▮

We use the *magic wand* on *one* single surface to mark the most interesting side, which in this case is the side **on** top.   [3 STROKES RANK 16]

176 下 下 **under**   ▭ one 2   ▮ foretell 170   xià

We use the *magic wand* under *one* single surface to mark the side of interest—in this case, the **under** side.   [3 STROKES RANK 42]

177 斥 斥 **scold, reprimand**   ▮ catty 118   ▬ dab 169   chì

BF You try to reduce the *instability* of this table (see §118) by adding a *dab* of something, but no use—down it goes. The boss **scolds** you, yet again.
   [5 STROKES RANK 1857]

178 卧 卧 lie down, crouch (animals)

subject of a ruler 17   foretell 170   wò

Animals are good at hiding. They **crouch down** out of sight as the loyal *subjects* of the king hunt fresh meat for the royal supper. The hunters have been *foretold* where to locate and subdue the well-concealed animals.

[8 STROKES   RANK 1944]

179 卡 卡 card

on 175   under 176   kǎ

The silvery, stiff stuff of a credit **card** with its strange imprints and designs *on* top and *underneath* is a universal part of modern life.   [5 STROKES   RANK 717]

180 吓 吓 frighten

mouth 41   under 176   xià

Imagine a face with the *mouth* located *under* the chin. How **frightening**!

[6 STROKES   RANK 1466]

Unit 11

More and More

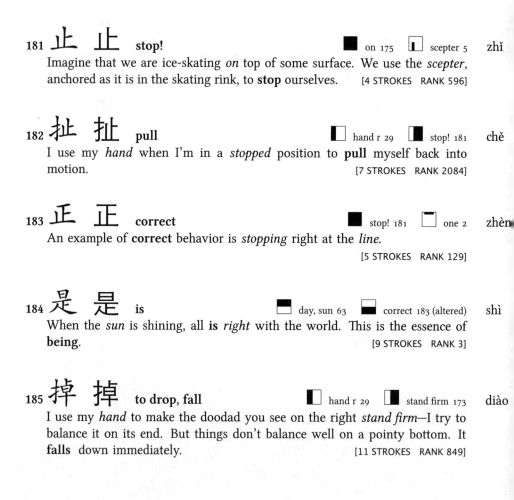

181 止 止 **stop!** ■ on 175 ⊔ scepter 5 zhǐ

Imagine that we are ice-skating *on* top of some surface. We use the *scepter*, anchored as it is in the skating rink, to **stop** ourselves. [4 STROKES RANK 596]

182 扯 扯 **pull** ▯ hand r 29 ▮ stop! 181 chě

I use my *hand* when I'm in a *stopped* position to **pull** myself back into motion. [7 STROKES RANK 2084]

183 正 正 **correct** ■ stop! 181 ▢ one 2 zhèn

An example of **correct** behavior is *stopping* right at the *line*. [5 STROKES RANK 129]

184 是 是 **is** ▬ day, sun 63 ▬ correct 183 (altered) shì

When the *sun* is shining, all **is** *right* with the world. This is the essence of **being**. [9 STROKES RANK 3]

185 掉 掉 **to drop, fall** ▮ hand r 29 ▮ stand firm 173 diào

I use my *hand* to make the doodad you see on the right *stand firm*—I try to balance it on its end. But things don't balance well on a pointy bottom. It **falls** down immediately. [11 STROKES RANK 849]

186 牛 牛 ox   ▯ scepter 5   ▬ two 3   ▫ dab 169   niú

1 This pictograph is a stylized **ox** or **cow**. The central spine is just that, the *two* horizontals are the legs, and the little *dab* of ink shows the left horn of the animal.

2 **Ox** or cow meat can provide some *royal* eating; that's what the scepter means. We get at least *two* good steaks from the animal, and the *drop* of blood still visible is to some people's taste.   [4 STROKES RANK 1018]

187 制 制 make, manufacture

       ▬ ox 186   ▪ towel 130   ▯ knife r 166   zhì

Here are the kinds of things you need to **manufacture** things in a pre-modern society. The *cow* or *ox* provides power. The *cloth* polishes and cleans the finished product, and the *knife* symbolizes the instruments you need for fine detailing.   [8 STROKES RANK 163]

188 午 午 noonish   ▪ dry 10   ▫ dab 169   wǔ

BF (午 can refer to 'noon', but also to the period between around 11AM and 1PM—'noonish'.)

     I start to get a *little bit dry* at **around noon**—it's been a long time since my breakfast coffee.   [4 STROKES RANK 1004]

     The two characters, 牛 and 午 in §§186 and 188, are confusing to beginners! How can you tell them apart? They are the same except that 'cow' has a central protuberance; could it be the second horn of the animal? 'Noonish' is flat up top, so people can lie comfortably on it for their afternoon siesta.

189 告 告 tell   ▪ earth, soil 9   ▫ dab 169   ▪ mouth 41   gào

BF It's a windy day outside. As you **tell** a buddy some crucial news, the wind blows a *little bit* of *earth* into your *mouth*.   [7 STROKES RANK 310]

190 靠 靠 depend upon   ▪ tell 189   ▬ not 13   kào

If I **depend upon** you to take the garbage out, then I do *not* have to *tell* you twice.   [15 STROKES RANK 808]

191 生 生 **give birth to**   ■ three ₄   ▯ scepter ₅   ▪ dab 169   shē
Giving birth creates a family of *three* out of what had been two. The newborn little guy is the guy on top. We know he or she is little, because the little *dab* tells us so. The *scepter* acts as a fastener to bind and bond the new family together.   [5 STROKES   RANK 34]

192 年 年 **year**   ■ give birth to 191 (altered)   ▪ an unexpected stroke   niár
Here's 生, 'to give birth'. It's been altered—subtly—so the central stroke points down instead of up. As the **years** pass, we journey away from *birth* and towards death. The *unexpected little stroke* of ink suggests that the years themselves are full of unexpected strokes of luck.   [6 STROKES   RANK 45]

193 星 星 **star**   ■ give birth to 191   ▢ day, sun 63   xīng
An ancient legend says that sparks given off by the *sun* serve as the seminal material by which it *gave birth* to **stars**.   [9 STROKES   RANK 537]

194 牲 牲 **domestic animal**   ▮ ox 186   ▮ give birth to 191   shēr
BF What's one surprising difference between **domesticated animals** and their wild counterparts? It's easy to get animals like *oxen and cows* to *give birth* in captivity, but not so for their wild cousins.   [9 STROKES   RANK 1582]

195 竹 竹 **bamboo**   ▪ dab (times 2) 169   ■ fourth (times 2) 25   zhú
BF Young **bamboo** shoots are among the fastest growing plants on the planet, sometimes growing an inch or two per hour! Bamboo grows so fast that the ancient Chinese artists could not paint them convincingly in the square grid that calligraphic custom demands. So they split a young plant in two, and we see here two sections of the seedling plant next to each other, with one *dab*-like leaf at the top of each section.   [6 STROKES   RANK 1588]

196 门 门 **door**   ▯ scepter 5   ▢ dab 169   ▮ place of refuge 111   **mén**

1 **Doors** lead to safety and comfort, to cozy houses where everything 'will be all right'. Anyone, be she among the high (symbolized by her *scepter*) or low (a mere *dab* of a person) can enter through here to a *place of refuge*.

2 The dab of ink up top at the left is the hinge around which the door—the right-angle stroke on the right—swings.

When used as a component, 门 can symbolize a 'place of gathering' in addition to 'gate'. People often do mill around entrances and exits.

[3 STROKES   RANK 185]

197 问 问 **ask**   ▮ door 196   ▣ mouth 41   **wèn**

People gather at special places to exchange information and gossip. A person at one such *place of gathering* opens their *mouth* to **ask** a question.

[6 STROKES   RANK 137]

198 间 间 **room**   ▮ door 196   ▣ day, sun 63   **jiān**

BF Here's how to get into your **room**: retreat from the *sun*, go through the *door*, and you're in! Or, from within your **room**, you can look through the *door* and see the *sun* outside.   [7 STROKES   RANK 135]

199 闰 闰 **intercalary month**   ▮ door 196   ▮ king 11   **rùn**

BF In ancient China, the *king* did in fact sit at the *gate* during the **intercalary months** that were added to the lunar calendar.   [7 STROKES   RANK 4183]

200 闻 闻 **hear, smell**   ▮ door 196   ▣ ear 82   **wén**

At the *doorway*, with your *ear* properly placed, you can both **hear and smell** anything going on inside.   [9 STROKES   RANK 825]

201 白 白 **white**   ▢ dab 169   ▮ day, sun 63   **bái**

How poetic to think of the color **white** as a *little bit* of *sun*!

[5 STROKES   RANK 286]

202 自 自 self   ☐ dab 169   ■ eye 78   zì

The *eye* is the gateway for all visual information into our brain. A *small portion* of this material influences our behavior, and becomes part of our core **self**.   [6 STROKES   RANK 43]

203 百 百 hundred   ☐ one 2   ■ white 201   bǎi

We've been trying to sell our old house for months. Finally, we figured out if we applied *one* coat of *white*wash, the place would look a **hundred** percent better.   [6 STROKES   RANK 407]

204 拍 拍 clap   ■ hand r 29   ■ white 201   pāi

Go ahead—**clap** your *hands* especially hard. Your palms will briefly turn *white* as the force of the clap pushes the blood out of your tissues.

[8 STROKES   RANK 1167]

205 帕 帕 handkerchief   ■ towel 130   ■ white 201   pà

BF A *special cloth* which is *white*!? How much clearer can these components be! This is a **handkerchief**.   [8 STROKES   RANK 1519]

206 帛 帛 silk   ■ white 201   ■ towel 130   bó

The symbolism of *white cloth* is clear—such fancy duds could only be **silk**.

[8 STROKES   RANK 3682]

   Both characters 帕 and 帛 (§§205 and 206) use the same components but place them differently. Keep them straight in our mind by remembering that silk is famous for the elegance of the way it handles—it drapes beautifully. In 帛, the white substance seems to hang on a central pole, which will emphasize this elegance.

Unit 12

Coming to Terms

207 皇 皇 **emperor**   ⬜ white 201   ⬛ king 11   **huáng**
BF 'White' often suggests purity and sometimes superiority. The Chinese portray an **emperor** as a *white king*, a king-among-kings.

[9 STROKES RANK 759]

208 咱 咱 **you and me**   ◨ mouth 41   ⬜ self 202   **zán**
BF (This is the 'inclusive we'—that is, it includes the speaker.) The two components here suggest the presence of at least two people. The *mouth* refers to someone else, and the *self* component is the speaker. Altogether, this is **we**, as long as the speaker is included.   [9 STROKES RANK 1265]

209 血 血 **blood**   ⬜ dab 169   ⬛ vessel, dish 110   **xiě**
Blood was always a by-product of the animal sacrifices of ancient societies. Gathered in *vessels* for easy disposal, the only clue to their contents was the rich, dark *drops* at the rim of the container.   [6 STROKES RANK 658]

210 寸 寸 **inch**   ⬛ hand 27 (altered)   ⬜ dab 169   **cùn**
(A 'Chinese inch' is one-third of a decimeter, approximately 1.3 American inches.) Hand? Where do you see a *hand*, or anything remotely like the image in §27? Some artistic license is in order. The fact that the 'hook' of §24 extends above the horizontal 'one' indicates that some other strokes are missing, namely the top two horizontals. The little *dab* of ink marks a special point on the wrist—the point where you can feel your pulse, about an **inch** below the heel of the hand.

    We will sometimes use this component for 'little' or 'small'.

[3 STROKES RANK 1904]

211 时 时 time   ■ day, sun 63   ■ inch 210   shí

As the *sun* journeys from sunrise to sunset, what is the appropriate dimension that's equivalent to linear *inches*? The answer is **time**.   [7 STROKES   RANK 25]

212 封 封 m for correspondence

■ earth, soil 9   ■ earth, soil 9   ■ inch 210   fēng

A **letter** is something *small* traveling from one part of the *earth* to another part of the *earth*.   [9 STROKES   RANK 871]

213 寺 寺 Buddhist temple   ■ earth, soil 9   ■ inch 210   sì

BF In the very old days, **Buddhist temples** were not much grander than any other house. Here's one, made of *earth*, and only a *small bit* taller than anything else and with only a *small* sign out front to identify it.   [6 STROKES   RANK 1892]

214 持 持 grasp, hold   ■ hand r 29   ■ Buddhist temple 213   chí

The insurgents are almost upon you! The huge *Buddhist temple* ahead of you is a literal life-saver, as everybody recognizes it as a place of refuge. When you get there, you are so exhausted, you need your *hand* to be able to **grasp** the walls of the structure for support.   [9 STROKES   RANK 357]

215 特 特 special, unusual   ■ ox 186   ■ Buddhist temple 213   tè

BF Buddhists don't eat meat. The circumstances are **special** indeed when you find *cow* meat in a *Buddhist temple*.   [10 STROKES   RANK 173]

216 耐 耐 bear, endure

■ express add'l but contrasting info 83   ■ inch 210   nài

The 'dab' in the '*inch*' component marks the sensitive spot near the wrist where you can feel your pulse. The bristles from the '*contrasting*' component on the left lightly brush across this spot. It's hard to **bear** this ticklish sensation.   [9 STROKES   RANK 1409]

217 寻 寻　search, seek　　　　　■ boar's head 34　■ inch 210　　xún

With a specialty whisk broom in hand, all of whose bristles come from a *boar's head* and are *one inch* long, you **search** high and low for your missing wallet.　　　　　　　　　　　　　　　　　　[6 STROKES　RANK 962]

218 斗 斗　cup-shaped　　□ dab 169　■ dab 169　■ ten 6　　dǒu

What do you use a **cup-shaped object** for? Why, to hold coffee, of course! Here you see two knuckles of somebody's hand on the rim of the cup, right by the handle.　　　　　　　　　　　　　　　　　[4 STROKES　RANK 580]

219 抖 抖　tremble　　　　　■ hand r 29　□ cup-shaped 218　　dǒu

Wow, that cup from §218 is *way* too heavy for me. My *hand*, from the effort of holding the *cup*, gets weak and starts **trembling**.　　[7 STROKES　RANK 1757]

220 主 主　master　　　　　　　□ dab 169　■ king 11　　zhǔ

BF Just as the master of the country is the king, so too the **master** of a house is a *little bit* of a *king*.　　　　　　　　　　　　[5 STROKES　RANK 87]

221 玉 玉　jade　　　　　　　　■ king 11　□ dab 169　　yù

Some essence of the king resides in his valuable possessions, make them even more valuable than if you or I owned them. Of special significance is **jade**, so permeated with royal essence, that owning a piece of it is like owning a *bit* of the *king*.　　　　　　　　　　　　　　[5 STROKES　RANK 1001]

222 国 国　country　　　　　　　■ enclosure 40　■ jade 221　　guó

Here, *jade* symbolically represents all the king's possessions—the entire country. 国 represents an *enclosure* containing everything belonging to the king, that is, the **country**.　　　　　　　　　　　[8 STROKES　RANK 20]

223 书 书 **book** ▬ place of refuge (times 2) 111   ⬜ dab 169   ▯ scepter 5   shū

There are few experiences like losing yourself in the depths of a really good book. A book is the ultimate *place of refuge*, perhaps why this component appears twice. Moreover, **books** extend their grace to all and sundry, from those with riches and wealth and material trappings (the '*scepter*') to those with *virtually nothing* to their names.   [4 STROKES   RANK 282]

224 千 千 **thousand**   ⬜ dab 169   ▬ ten 6   qiān

Sometimes we will s-t-r-e-t-c-h our little "dab" of ink:

Think of the '*dab*' as a snapshot of a clothes line from which are hanging many freshly-washed items of clothes, each worth an average of *ten* dollars. There's lots of clean clothes hanging, perhaps as many as one hundred, so the whole wash is worth one **thousand** dollars in all.   [3 STROKES   RANK 599]

Reader alert: in certain font styles, this character 千 bears a striking resemblance to 干 'dry' (§10). Learn to pay attention to see whether the top stroke is truly horizontal or a near-horizontal smear.

225 舌 舌 **tongue**   ▬ thousand 224   ▣ mouth 41   shé

BF A human mouth is relatively small, yet capable of great expressive power. Any one of *thousands* of different sentiments come out of your *mouth* by virtue of your **tongue's** versatility.   [6 STROKES   RANK 1958]

226 括 括 **draw together**   ▯ hand r 29   ▯ tongue 225   kuò

The definition refers to the *drawing together* or *contracting* together of things like muscles. The muscles in your *hand* and in your *tongue* are examples of body parts that **contract** quickly under sharp pain.   [9 STROKES   RANK 850]

227 甜 甜 **sweetness**   ▯ tongue 225   ▯ sweet 103   tián

We already considered 'sweet' in §103, although that character 甘 was a bound form. This is a more 'intense' sensation, because it can stand by itself. Anyway, we can imagine a *tongue* licking something *sweet and pleasant* because of its **sweetness**.   [11 STROKES   RANK 2020]

228 重 重 **heavy** ☐ thousand 224 ■ inside 71 zhòng

After Thanksgiving dinner, with what feels like *one thousand* pounds of food *inside* me, I can hardly budge from the table—I feel so **heavy**.

[9 STROKES   RANK 140]

229 董 董 **director** ☐ grass r 94 ■ heavy 228 dǒng

BF Nowadays, **trustees**, **members of Boards of Directors**, and other **bigwigs** wear clothes suitable of their high station in life. In ancient days, they advertised their status by wearing *grassy* laurels on their heads and dragging around a *heavy*, overweight body.   [12 STROKES   RANK 1629]

230 帀 帀 **money, currency** ☐ dab 169 ■ towel 130 bì

BF A little *bit* of *towel*, perhaps a small strip, was a forerunner to what would become **currency**.   [4 STROKES   RANK 1188]

231 毛 毛 **hair** ■ mineshaft 135 ☐ dab 169 ▤ two 3 máo

That's not a *mineshaft* pictured here, but rather the chin of a teenage boy on the verge of shaving. Already he can see a *dab*-like whisk of a whisker surmounting *two* genuine **hairs**. He can't wait to start shaving!

[4 STROKES   RANK 623]

232 乱 乱 **in disorder** ■ tongue 225 ■ mineshaft 135 luàn

Go ahead, wrap your *tongue* around a live *wire*. You'll find your thoughts and sensations temporarily jumbled up and in great **disorder**.

[7 STROKES   RANK 765]

Unit 13

Practice Makes Perfect

233 此 此 **this** ▮ stop! 181 ▮ ancient ladle 142 cǐ

This must *stop*! *Stop* banging the *spoon* on the sidewalk—I can't take the noise. [6 STROKES   RANK 116]

234 些 些 **some** ▬ this 233 ▭ two 3 xiē

When I apply the specifier '*this*' to *a couple* of things, why now I have **some** stuff. [8 STROKES   RANK 86]

235 皆 皆 **each and every** ▭ compared with 146 ▬ white 201 jiē

Scientists tell us that *white* light contains light rays of all other colors. In that respect, some quality that appears in **each and every** item can be *compared with* the color *white*. [9 STROKES   RANK 1419]

236 托 托 **hold in the palm** ▮ hand r 29 ▮ ancient ladle 142 (altered) ▛ dab 169 tuō

If you cup your *hand* to imitate a *ladle*, you'll be able to **hold liquid in your palm**, too—at least for some *small* amount of time. [6 STROKES   RANK 799]

237 监 监   **inspect, supervise**

⬚ lie down, crouch (animals) 178 (altered)   ⬛ blood 209 (altered)   jiān

BF The scribes have taken lots of liberties with the components of this character. The '*crouch*' bit (卧, §178) has suffered the most. The kneeling subject part on its left has been reduced to two parallel verticals, and the stem of the magic wand leans to the right. The drop of blood that identifies '*blood*' has moved from the left to the right side of the vessel (血, §209).

Here's a *crouching* courtier, bent over a bowl of *blood*, **inspecting** it to see that it is ritually okay.   [10 STROKES   RANK 838]

238 提 提   **carry, take, lift**   ⬛ hand r 29   ⬛ is 184   tí

Carrying is the use of your *hands* to change the location of something that *is* in some initial location.   [12 STROKES   RANK 196]

239 临 临   **face, overlook**

⬛ lie down, crouch (animals) 178 (altered)   ⬛ product 44 (altered)   lín

BF The boss in the warehouse was **overlooking** everything. My girlfriend and I, who were behaving like animals just a minute ago, were behind a pile of his *products, crouched down* and quiet.   [9 STROKES   RANK 839]

240 蓝 蓝   **blue**   ⬚ grass r 94   ⬛ inspect, supervise 237   lán

I'm very sad and **blue**. The best job I could get is one *inspecting* the height of Kentucky *bluegrass*.   [13 STROKES   RANK 1190]

241 卸 卸   **unload, take sth off**

⬛ noonish 188   ⬛ stop! 181   ⬛ single ear 157   xiè

What made me take this summer job as airport baggage handler! We all look forward to the *noon* break so we can **unload** the bags for a bit. We all keep a *single ear* cocked for the whistle announcing the time to *stop* work.   [9 STROKES   RANK 2479]

242 址 址   **foundation, site**   ⬛ earth, soil 9   ⬛ stop! 181   zhǐ

BF The purpose of a building's **foundation** is to *stop* it from sliding or moving to the *earth*.   [7 STROKES   RANK 1848]

243 竹 竹
        bamboo r   ⬜ bamboo 195 (altered)

CMP Take a knife and slice off the bottom stems of these bamboo segments. This radical treatment gives rise to the **bamboo radical** that often appears in Chinese characters.

244 等 等 **wait**   ⬜ bamboo r 243   ⬛ Buddhist temple 213   děn₤

I am not a particularly religious person. I can imagine myself attending a service in a *Buddhist temple* out of curiosity, but then I'd stare at the *bamboo* walls, **waiting** with impatience for the service to end.

[12 STROKES   RANK 158]

245 简 简 **simple, simplified**   ⬜ bamboo r 243   ⬛ room 198   jiǎn

BF The elegant **simplicity** of the *room* is stunning. Everything is made from *bamboo*.
[13 STROKES   RANK 716]

246 笔 笔 **pen**   ⬜ bamboo r 243   ⬛ hair 231   bǐ

Ancient **pens** were made from *bamboo*, which provided the part to hold, and *hair*, which served as nib.
[10 STROKES   RANK 956]

247 宀 宀 **roof**

CMP This stylized **roof**, with the little dab up top for the pitch line, tops traditional Chinese houses.

248 定 定 **decide***   ⬜ roof 247   ⬛ correct 183 (altered)   dìng

Because the *roof* was not installed *correctly*, we have leaks whenever it rains. We've **decided** to bite the bullet and rip off the old one, and do it all over again.
[8 STROKES   RANK 77]

249 它 它 **it**   ⬜ roof 247   ⬛ ancient ladle 142   tā

It takes hard work to make a home function. Here is a *roof* covering all the internal tasks that must be done—the *ladle*, prominent in the preparation of food, symbolizes all of them. Remember these internal tasks by their acronym, **it**.
[5 STROKES   RANK 107]

250 害 害 **harm, injure**   ☐ roof 247   ▤ plentiful 12   ▤ mouth 41   hài

The worst **harm** people do to each other is via gossip—*too much talk* under
the supposed protection of someone's *roof*.   [10 STROKES RANK 579]

251 富 富 **rich, wealthy**   ☐ roof 247   ■ size range 163   fù

Rich people own much more than they need. It's common to find similar
items, but in a *range of sizes*, under their *roof*.   [12 STROKES RANK 733]

252 審 審 **examine, go over**   ☐ roof 247   ■ express 47   shěn

When I study for a test, I need to **go over** all the material out loud. I feel
comfortable under my own *roof*, where I can *express myself* out loud with
no one giving me funny looks.   [8 STROKES RANK 746]

253 宣 宣 **declare, proclaim**

☐ roof 247   ▤ two 3 (altered)   ▤ speak 64 (altered)   xuān

BF The '*roof*' is really a decorated handle, attached to the upper of *two* horizontal rods. The rods serve to anchor a scroll, which *speaks* the words of the
emperor's **proclamation**.   [9 STROKES RANK 770]

254 守 守 **guard, defend**   ☐ roof 247   ■ inch 210   shǒu

The leprechauns live in tiny houses—there are their *roofs*, only one *inch* off
the ground. They use their magical powers to **guard** and **defend** us.

[6 STROKES RANK 796]

255 宝 宝 **treasure, precious jewel**   ☐ roof 247   ■ jade 221   bǎo

People hide their **treasures** under their own *roof*. Scribes use the symbol for
'*jade*' to represent these valuables.

Or else, this character shows a *house* made of *jade*. What a **precious
treasure**!   [8 STROKES RANK 811]

256 宫 宫 **palace**   ☐ roof 247   ◼ bamboo pitch pipes 43   gōn

BF The blocks of the *pitch pipes* also suggest rooms, many rooms. What kind of structure consists of a *roof* surmounting many rooms? Why, a royal **palace**, of course.   [9 STROKES   RANK 982]

257 宁 宁 **rather, would rather**   ☐ roof 247   ◼ fourth 25   nìn

BF Help! The *roof* is collapsing for the *fourth* time. I **would rather** that this didn't happen. Next time, I'm making the roof supports out of **wood** (sounds like '**would**').   [5 STROKES   RANK 1019]

258 街 街 **street**   ▮ rather, would rather 257 (altered)   ▮ jade tablet 14   jiē

Compared to crude earthen paths, paved **streets** must have seemed like roads paved with *jade tablets*. Of course, everyone *would rather* travel on these!

[12 STROKES   RANK 1101]

Unit 14

Hit the Ground Running

259 宇　宇　**building, house**　🔲 roof 247　⬛ in; at; to 26　yǔ

BF Here's a *roof* spreading over a place that you go *to*, that you stay *at*, and you're never happier than when *in*. It's your ancestral **house**.

[6 STROKES   RANK 1156]

260 宜　宜　**proper, suitable**　🔲 roof 247　⬛ moreover 15　yí

BF It's **proper** and **suitable** to be *home* in our cozy den, with *bookcases* lining the wall.　[8 STROKES   RANK 1290]

261 宙　宙　**all time, past, present, and future**

🔲 roof 247　⬛ let sb do sth 48　zhòu

BF A man's *home* is his castle—he *can do* whatever he wants in it, for **all time**.　[8 STROKES   RANK 1421]

262 割　割　**cut apart, sever**　⬛ harm, injure 250　🔲 knife r 166　gē

The bad guys in a movie might use their *knife* to *harm* the hero. They try to **sever or cut** some major blood vessel, but (Hollywood being Hollywood) invariably fail.　[12 STROKES   RANK 1665]

263 牢　牢　**pen, prison**　🔲 roof 247　⬛ ox 186　láo

A **pen** is a place which provides a figurative *roof* over the heads of *farm animals*.　[7 STROKES   RANK 1696]

264 宅 宅　**residence, house**　　　⬜ roof 247　⬛ hair 231 (altered)　zhái

BF It looks like I lost some of my *hair*—because I've been living under the same *roof* for so long. That's the comfort of a true **residence**.

[6 STROKES   RANK 1858]

265 冖 冖　**safe house, security**

CMP This is really just a Chinese roof (§247) modified to emphasize how the roof of a house encloses and protects its inhabitants. Therefore, rather than think of it as a 'modified roof', it seems better to imagine it as a symbol of the **security** that such a roof implies.

266 向 向　**to face**　　　⬛ safe house, security 265　⬜ mouth 41　xiàn

It's been a hard journey, and now you're almost home. With joy in your heart, you **face** your home, the source of greatest *security*. The '*mouth*' symbolizes 'you' enveloped by the protective home.　[6 STROKES   RANK 146]

267 响 响　**make a sound**　　　⬛ mouth 41　⬛ to face 266　xiǎn

One way to **make a sound** that's easily heard is to use your *mouth* while *facing* the direction you're talking.　[9 STROKES   RANK 503]

268 亠 亠　**cover**

CMP The image and the title say it all.

269 亡 亡　**perish**　　　⬜ cover 268　⬛ mineshaft 135　wán

BF Here's a scene right out of *Indiana Jones*. The villain takes off the horizontal *cover*. After knocking you unconscious, he throws you down the *mineshaft*, covers it, and leaves you to **perish**.　[3 STROKES   RANK 957]

270 言 言　**speech**　　　⬜ cover 268　⬛ two 3　⬛ mouth 41　yán

BF **Speech** is *two mouths* gossiping. The *cover* is there to (try to) keep a lid on this chatter, to make sure harmful rumors don't spread.

[7 STROKES   RANK 355]

271 誓 誓 **vow, pledge**   ▪ broken (stick, rope) 120   ▪ speech 270   shì

BF *Speech* acts metaphorically to hold up and support a statement that could be *broken*. The support ensures that it will not be broken, that the statement is a proper **vow** or **oath**.   [14 STROKES   RANK 2095]

272 詈 詈 **scold, curse**   ▫ net r 107   ▪ speech 270   lì

BF During the angry *speech*, your mother-in-law shows a lot of teeth—that's what the '*net*' suggests. She is really **cursing** you out!

[12 STROKES   RANK 4626]

273 市 市 **market**   ▫ cover 268   ▪ towel 130   shì

BF Ancient **marketplaces** generated lots of filth, dust, and soot! Surrounding householders would have had to *cover* their white linen and *towels* to protect them from this dirt.   [5 STROKES   RANK 254]

274 闹 闹 **make a noise**   ▪ door 196   ▪ market 273   nào

You live right on the main square of the town. Today is market day. There's **lots of noise**, because the *market* is going on right outside your *door*.

[8 STROKES   RANK 1336]

275 高 高 **high**

▪ cover 268   ▫ mouth 41   ▪ borders 127   ▪ mouth 41   gāo

The essence of **high**-ness is a tower. Here, the '*mouths*' represent building blocks, bricks or stones or whatever, which are piled higher and higher. The '*borders*' here are supports on the lower portion of the tower, to help buttress the bricks from the instability of supporting lots of stuff on top. The *cover* at the top, like a finial, provides a decorative flourish.   [10 STROKES   RANK 134]

276 搞 搞 **do, work, manage, etc**   ▪ hand r 29   ▪ high 275   gǎo

Here's someone **doing work** by using their *hands* to pile things up *high*.

[13 STROKES   RANK 1146]

277 芒 芒   **spike, sharp point**   ☐ grass r 94   ■ perish 269   máŗ
BF Don't be fooled—bamboo and other tough *grasses* make potent weapons.
Unwary travelers have *perished* in traps where lengths of these *grasses* are
used as **sharp spikes**.   [6 STROKES   RANK 2251]

278 罚 罚   **punish, penalize**   ▣ scold, curse 272 (altered)   ☐ knife r 166   fá
In the altered form of '*scold, curse*', the 'speech' part has been simplified to a
common form we'll encounter later.
    Amid all the *cursing* and screaming, if someone pulls out a *knife*, you're
really in for a severe **punishment**.   [9 STROKES   RANK 1215]

279 鬲 鬲   **cauldron for meat or cereal**
        ■ high 275 (altered)   ▣ metal stand   lì
This **cauldron** (often found in archaeological sites) is sufficiently *tall* and well-
balanced on its *stand* that the ancients could easily have stuffed large slabs
of meat in there for stewing.   [10 STROKES   RANK 6856]

280 ⌐ ⌐   **smooth cover**
CMP It's smooth because there's no little handle on top; compare with the
'regular' cover in §268.

281 亭 亭   **pavilion, kiosk**
    ☐ cover 268   ▪ mouth 41   ▤ smooth cover 280   ▣ fourth 25   tínɡ
We've seen in §275 how useful it can be to use our components as architectural
building blocks. A **pavilion** is a decorated, ornate building used for some
special purpose. The bottom components of 高 have been replaced by some
fancier counterparts. That's how we construct a **pavilion**.
                               [9 STROKES   RANK 2002]

282 营 营 **battalion**

☐ grass r 94   ▭ smooth cover 280   ▬ mouth 41   ▭ mouth 41   yíng

A multitude of *mouths*—here there's only two, because that's all there's room for—symbolizes lots of men, the men of a **battalion**. We know this is a battalion because battalions need food—symbolized by vegetable *grass*—and shelter (*cover*).   [11 STROKES   RANK 536]

283 带 带 **bring, band, belt**

☐ towel 130 (altered)   ▭ smooth cover 280   ▬ towel 130   dài

1 (BAND, BELT) The *towel* component—really, fancy cloth—appears twice, once (on top) with extra decoration. Together, they form an ancient ensemble, **belted** in the middle.

2 (BRING) Use the **belt** as a leash to **bring** somebody along with you.

     [9 STROKES   RANK 342]

284 垂 垂 **spider web**

CMP Sometimes opposite concepts are helpful in remembering the meaning of a character. Here, mentally strip away the top 'dab' stroke and the bottom 'one' stroke. We're left with an intriguing grid of horizontals and verticals, three of each. It's easy to interpret as a *bit* of a stylized **spider web**. This portion is mounted on a *horizontal base*, so it looks like our web is pretty close to the ground.

Unit 15

There's Always a Tomorrow

285 垂 垂 droop ■ spider web 284 chuí

A freshly-woven *spider web* is a marvel of intricacy and tight, tense strands. Oops, a bug or twig or some other little something has blundered into the *web*. The spider may prepare to feast, but the struggling bug or some windblown chaff destroys the tension of the web, causing all strands to **droop**.

    A word on the structure of the web. Both horizontals and verticals consist of strokes in the pattern short-long-short, but the horizontals are a bit longer than the verticals. Calligraphic strokes are like people—they spread out a bit more when lying down! [8 STROKES RANK 1592]

286 睡 睡 sleep ▌ eye 78 ▌ droop 285 shuì

When you lie down, and your *eyes* begin to *droop*, then **sleep** can't be far behind. [13 STROKES RANK 964]

287 儿 儿 walking man

CMP Imagine an amateur photographer, a very clumsy amateur photographer, trying to take a candid shot of a walking man. Good shot—too bad it's off-center. All we got were the legs, and that's what we see here.

288 儿 儿 son ■ walking man 287 ér

Here are the *legs of a man*, but the rest of him is missing—there's no head or other limbs! It's an undeveloped man—a **son**. [2 STROKES RANK 192]

289 四 四 **four** ■ enclosure 40 ■ walking man 287 **sì**

The restless prisoner wants to get out of his cell. With no respite, this *walking man* circuits his *enclosure* looking for a way out of the **four** walls.

[5 STROKES   RANK 226]

290 匹 匹 **be a match for** ■ basket, box 152 ■ walking man 287 **pǐ**

Fights on television are staged from start to finish. To build up tension and excitement, they will bring on a challenger in a *box*, open one side, and focus on the 'champion' from the *legs* up. They claim that this guy will **be a match for** anyone. [4 STROKES   RANK 1908]

291 西 西 **west** □ one 2 ■ four 289 (altered) **xī**

The restless prisoner has earned some free time outside his cell, so part of him is outside. The clumsy photographer from §287 did a little better this time—he captured our guy from the waist down, but still wandering around the small courtyard bordered by *four* mighty walls. The *horizontal line* is his belt. His recess ends at sunset, when the sun sets in the **west**. [6 STROKES   RANK 167]

292 牺 牺 **sacrificial animal** ■ ox 186 ■ west 291 **xī**

BF An *ox* facing the setting sun in the *west* makes a picture perfect **sacrificial animal**. [10 STROKES   RANK 1814]

293 元 元 **dollar** ■ two 3 ■ walking man 287 **yuán**

(This character also refers to the unit of currency in the People's Republic of China.) *Two* guys aimlessly *walking around* discussing various get-rich schemes to increase their stock of **dollars**. [4 STROKES   RANK 370]

294 园 园 **garden** ■ enclosure 40 ■ dollar 293 **yuán**

BF **Gardens** and parks demand huge amounts of labor to keep them looking neat and attractive to tourists. Vast infusions of *dollars* are necessary keep the park lands inside the *boundaries* looking tip-top. [7 STROKES   RANK 988]

295 玩 玩   **have fun, amuse oneself**   ▮ king 11   ▮ dollar 293   wán▸

(This is a famously tough verb to translate into English!) Anyway, with some *money* in your pocket, you're all set to have a *royal* **good time**.

[8 STROKES   RANK 1072]

296 完 完   **finish, complete**   ▭ roof 247   ▬ dollar 293   wán▸

The *roof* on top of a *dollar* is the Chinese way of reminding shoppers that when they've *capped* their *spending*, they're **finished**. It's time to call it a day.   [7 STROKES   RANK 301]

297 冠 冠   **hat, cap**

▭ smooth cover 280   ▮ dollar 293 (altered)   ▮ inch 210   guā▸

BF See how the slightly distorted '*dollar*' scoops up the '*inch*'? That refers to the *little* decorative ribbon that you forgot to buy originally for this cute little sailor **hat**. Now your head *cover* is complete.   [9 STROKES   RANK 1713]

298 兄 兄   **elder brother***   ▬ mouth 41   ▬ walking man 287   xiōn▸

BF This character shows a *walking man* whose *mouth* does all the talking. Younger siblings think about their **elder brothers** in this way! (The very different character of §62 also means 'elder brother'.)   [5 STROKES   RANK 1089]

299 克 克   **subdue**   ▬ ancient 51   ▬ walking man 287   kè

BF

1 It's easy to **subdue** an *ancient walker*.

▭ ten 6   ▬ elder brother* 298

2 Here's another way to parse the components. The bottom portion consists of an *elder brother* with a *ten*-shaped spike atop his head. When *ten brothers* get together, they can **subdue** anyone.   [7 STROKES   RANK 262]

300 先 先   **first**   ▭ dab 169   ▬ earth, soil 9   ▬ walking man 287   xiān▸

Because he was **first** in line, a *little bit* of muddy *dirt* splashed onto his pants during the *walk*.   [6 STROKES   RANK 188]

301 见 见 **see** ▣ borders 127 ▣ walking man 287 jiàn

Here's a *guy walking around* who has, for some reason, placed a paper bag over his head. You can see its *borders*. As a result, he can't **see**.

Alternatively, the *borders* represent the shape of his head, so as he *walks around*, he can **see** where he's going.   [4 STROKES   RANK 153]

302 现 现 **now** ▣ king 11 ▣ see 301 xiàn

BF The *king* is the *king*, and he can look at whatever he wants, and he wants to *see* the thing right **now**!   [8 STROKES   RANK 70]

303 酉 酉 **new wine** ▣ west 291 ▬ one 2 yǒu

By itself, this low-frequency character refers to the late afternoon (specifically, the time between 5PM and 7PM). As a component, it occurs often, where it means 'alcohol'. To people from other parts of the world, what's the *one* thing that seems to mean so much to *Western* party-goers? **Alcohol!**

[7 STROKES   RANK 3839]

304 醒 醒 **wake up** ▣ new wine 303 ▣ star 193 xǐng

The parts of this character refer to things that vanish, at least temporarily. When the influence of *alcohol* disappears, and the sun chases the *stars* away, then it's time to **wake up**!   [16 STROKES   RANK 1075]

305 酷 酷 **cruel, 'cool'** ▣ new wine 303 ▣ tell 189 kù

BF Under the influence of *alcohol*, a person is apt to *tell* things to a friend that he wouldn't dream of mentioning while sober. How **cruel** these revelations can be. In vino veritas...

The Chinese have adopted the English word 'cool', meaning great, nifty, way to go!, and use this character and pronunciation for it.

[14 STROKES   RANK 1867]

306 览 览 **look at, display** ▣ inspect, supervise 237 (altered) ▣ see 301 lǎn

BF When the museum painting is properly **displayed**, it makes it easy to *see* what you are *inspecting*.   [9 STROKES   RANK 1886]

307 苋 苋 amaranth   ☐ grass r 94   ■ see 301   xiàn

BF **Amaranth** is an ancient grain recently rediscovered. Its seeds, when roasted, pop like popcorn. The ancient Chinese treated it as a leafy *vegetable* which they used to stir fry. They thought it was good for one's *vision*.   [7 STROKES   RANK 4820]

308 宽 宽 wide, broad, lenient   ☐ roof 247   ■ amaranth 307   kuā

Amaranth kernels are tiny but extremely numerous. (And they are very nutritious. This combination of nutrition plus bounty is what makes this grain so appealing to food scientists.) Anyway, imagine someone making a carpet from the seeds of a single *amaranth* plant. They are so plentiful that the house, and its *roof*, would have to be both **wide and broad** to encompass it.   [10 STROKES   RANK 1155]

309 宪 宪 law, statute, constitution   ☐ roof 247   ■ first 300   xiàn

BF The experience of the United States is salutary in the following respect: a **constitution** is the first responsibility of a country's founders. If done properly, it is as a *roof*, protecting and nurturing the infant nation.

[9 STROKES   RANK 1484]

310 人 人 standing man

CMP The pictograph shows a highly stylized drawing of a standing man. Used as a freestanding character, it's very common, but it also makes frequent appearance as a component.

Unit 16

A Fighting Chance

311 人　人　**man**　■ standing man 310　rén

Sometimes our **man** maintains its shape (for example in the simplified form of the measure word 个; see below), but most of the time 人 gets squished, like this: 亻, as we'll see. [2 STROKES　RANK 7]

312 个　个　**non-specific measure word**　▭ man 311　▯ scepter 5　gè

1 How can we remember that this is the non-specific Chinese measure word, used whenever a noun does not call for a special measure word? We see a *man* distinguished by his *scepter*. Thus, this pictograph identifies a very particular **specimen** of humanity, and by extension to any definite person, and thence to any noun requiring a measure word.

2 A *man* with a *scepter*—someone 'way up there—strolls around the marketplace, taking advantage of his position to sample all kinds of stuff. There's no pattern behind all this sampling, so we use this **non-specific measure word**. [3 STROKES　RANK 12]

313 从　从　**from**　■ man (times 2) 311　cóng

Here's two pictures of the same man. The hindmost component in the rear left shows the same man's original position, while front picture shows him in his present location. The rear picture shows where he came **from**.

We sometimes use 从 for the concept of '**source**', since this character shows the progress made by somebody traveling from this source to his present position. [4 STROKES　RANK 98]

314 众　众　**multitude**　■ man (times 3) 311　zhòng

BF The components say it all—you see here a **multitude** of *men*.

[6 STROKES　RANK 510]

315 丛 丛 cluster   ▪️ from 313 ☐ one 2   cón

BF A **cluster** is a group of *people* or other things bound together by *one* common characteristic.   [5 STROKES RANK 1678]

316 两 两 **both, two**   ☐ one 2 ▪️ borders 127 ▪️ man (times 2) 311   liǎn

Within the *borders* of the local community, **two** *men* are helping to carry *one* long thing, a pole or plank or whatever.   [7 STROKES RANK 133]

317 肉 肉 meat   ▪️ borders 127 ◫ man (times 2) 311   ròu

This is a pictograph of a carcass cut open. Except for calligraphic flourishes intended to make it visually well-formed, scribes are careful to make this glyph bilaterally symmetric—that is, the right and left halves are the same, like in real life.

Perhaps the *borders* represent the borders—skin and hide—of the animal, and the *group of men* will be feasting on the innards, the *meat*.

肉 gets frequent use as a component in other graphs, but it often takes on an altered appearance in that role, namely '月'. Unfortunately, another common glyph—meaning 'moon' or 'month'—looks exactly the same! Oh, well... When 'meat' takes on its '月' guise, it often means 'body part'.

[6 STROKES RANK 1009]

318 内 内 **inside***   ▪️ meat 317 ◫ man 311 (altered)   nèi

In '*meat*', we dug within a carcass to get at the substance. In this character, the surface decoration is less, so we aren't digging quite to the same depth—just enough to get **inside** the body.   [4 STROKES RANK 175]

319 夅 夅 **to tower**   ☐ man (times 2) 311 ▪️ ear 82   sǒng

BF This pair of thugs **towers** over their intended victim. How can we tell? This poor guy's *ear* comes up only to the feet of the villainous *duo*.

[10 STROKES RANK 2163]

320 巫 巫 wizard   ▪️ labor, work 7 ☐ man (times 2) 311   wū

BF **Wizardry**, when done skillfully, appears to be the *work* of *several men*.

[7 STROKES RANK 2189]

321 坐 坐 **sit** ◼ earth, soil 9 ▦ man (times 2) 311   zuò

Two men **sit** back to back on a bench, backs up against the central backrest. Because they are drawn so small, we know the *two men* are **sitting** close to the *ground*.   [7 STROKES RANK 611]

322 闪 闪 **lightning** ◼ door 196 ◼ man 311   shǎn

BF "It was a dark and stormy night." Suddenly, a flash of **lightning** reveals a crouching *man* framed by the open *door*. Friend or foe?   [5 STROKES RANK 1113]

323 以 以 **use, take** ◼ mineshaft 135 (altered) ◻ dab 169 ◼ man 311   yǐ

Look at this environmentally-ignorant prat! We see *him* getting ready to throw a *bit* of garbage down the *mine*. He needs to **use** a garbage pail instead.   [4 STROKES RANK 23]

324 齿 齿 **tooth** ◼ stop! 181 ◼ receptacle 155 ◼ man 311   chǐ

BF A pictographic interpretation is best for this character, which shows a molar **tooth** on the upper jaw. The top part represents the **tooth**'s root, which *stops* the tooth from being pulled out of your mouth when you chew. The bottom '*receptacle*' component is the tooth itself. While the tooth's surface may be smooth, it is not flat. This tooth has some valleys in its exterior, and they have a shape like the character for '*man*'.   [8 STROKES RANK 1773]

325 合 合 **join; combine** ◼ man 311 ▭ one 2 ◼ mouth 41   hé

1 The 'joining' and 'combining' here refer to the pooling of efforts of a group of like-minded people, say. Recall, too, that nouns in Chinese can be either singular or plural. In this instance, it's helpful to regard the 'man' component as being plural—*many men* with only *one mouth*—a poetic description of worker solidarity, a **joining together**, if ever there was one.

2 The former narrative notwithstanding, this glyph looks just like a cozy little house—we see the roof, eaves, and body of the house from the side—that a weekend group of handymen built by **combining** their skills and efforts.   [6 STROKES RANK 171]

326 全 全 entire   ☐ man 311   ■ king 11   quá

According to the most enlightened theories of monarchy, it is the *ruler* who serves the **entire** *citizenry*, and not vice versa. Writing 'king' underneath 'man' helps underscore this relationship.   [6 STROKES RANK 124]

327 企 企 on tiptoe   ☐ man 311   ■ stop! 181   qǐ

BF Picture a fat *man*, a really fat *man* (that's why the man's legs are so far apart) trying to walk **on tippy-toes**. This is a somewhat precarious stance for this *man*, so he quickly comes to a complete *stop* to try to regain his balance.   [6 STROKES RANK 450]

328 舍 舍 give up   ☐ man 311   ■ tongue 225   shě

This verb 'to give up' is the same sense as 'abandon'. The most effective way for *someone* to **abandon** a claim to something is not by physical action, but by verbal means—swearing an oath in court, for example, or some other method which uses the *the tongue*.   [8 STROKES RANK 1344]

329 啥 啥 what? (dialect)   ☐ mouth 41   ■ give up 328   shá

Here we *abandon* proper grammar in favor of a dialectical utterance from our *mouth*. People may have trouble understanding this non-standard speech. **What** did you say?   [11 STROKES RANK 2082]

330 大 大 big   ■ man 311   ☐ one 2   dà

A standing *man* with outstretched arms, stretched to form a long *horizontal*, emphasizes the concept of **big**.   [3 STROKES RANK 17]

331 太 太 too (much)   ■ big 330   ☐ dab 169   tài

The '*dab*' draws attention to the *bigness* of something, thereby making it a marker of **excess**.   [4 STROKES RANK 240]

332 犬　犬　dog   ■ big 330　　☐ dab 169   quǎn

Look head-on into the face of your favorite **dog**. Here are the whiskers above the animal's dewlaps. One eye winks at you—what a joke life is!

[4 STROKES   RANK 2649]

333 天　天　**heaven**   ☐ one 2　　■ big 330   tiān

Heaven is *one* expanse above the great, *big* world.   [4 STROKES   RANK 78]

334 矢　矢　arrow   ☐ dab 169　　■ heaven 333   shǐ

BF Perhaps to early scribes who observed skilled archers letting fly their arrows, the arrow paths seemed so ethereal that this symbolism—which equated *heavenly dabs* with **arrows**—might have seemed fitting. We'll use either of those interpretations—'**arrow**' or '**slice of heaven**'—depending on context.   [5 STROKES   RANK 2811]

335 医　医　medical   ■ basket, box 152　■ arrow 334   yī
BF

1 In the throes of serious illness, the doctor who restores health via the application of **medicine** must often seem like a magician pulling a *bit of heaven* out of his little black *bag*.

2 **Medical** paraphernalia are metaphorically like *arrows* to the essence of a disease, to kill it dead, to the benefit of the patient.

[7 STROKES   RANK 482]

336 吴　吴　Kingdom of Wu   ☐ mouth 41　　■ heaven 333   wú

The ancient Kingdom of Wu lasted for about 60 years, starting in the year 222AD. At that time, there were two other competing kingdoms. Wu's territory was in the south of what has become modern China.

Chinese historians regard the ability to rule as a divine gift, a mandate from heaven. Here, the central *mouth* plays the role of a heavenly marker, showing that *heaven*'s mandate lies to the south—the location of **Wu**.

[7 STROKES   RANK 1135]

Unit 17

Notions and Trifles

337 夫 夫 **man (spiffy)** ■ big 330 ☐ one 2 fū

BF A *big* man (that is, an adult) with *one* horizontal hairpin in his hair symbolizes an adult **man**, at least in the ancient China in which men wore hairpins! We'll call him '**spiffy**' since the presence of this hairpin suggests dressing up. [4 STROKES RANK 377]

338 规 规 **rules and regulations** ■ man (spiffy) 337 ■ see 301 guī

BF *Men see* harmony when their world is governed by **rules and regulations**. [8 STROKES RANK 321]

339 头 头 **head** ■ dab (times 2) 169 ■ big 330 tóu

To remember this character, imagine rotating this drawing by 45 degrees or so to the right (in a clockwise direction). Look closely at the large crossed strokes. Don't they look like the four paws of a *big* forest creature? The small stroke at the lower right is the creature's tail, and the two remaining *dabs* become the eyes. This part of the animal, the **head**, is the most prominent part of this suggestive sketch. [5 STROKES RANK 147]

340 买 买 **buy** ☐ one 2 (altered) ■ head 339 mǎ

Some items for no good reason grab hold of you and won't let you go until you **buy** them—think designer sneakers, pet rocks, certain dolls, and so on. In this character, the horizontal '*one*' stroke has been altered to look like a hook. It signifies how *one* certain item hooks your imagination, the center of which is your *head*, and hangs on tight until you **buy** it. [6 STROKES RANK 758]

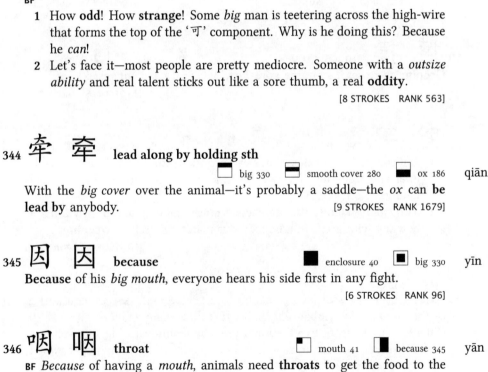

341 卖　卖　sell　　　　　　　　　⬜ ten 6　⬛ buy 340　　mài

"Buy low, sell high"—everyone knows this cliché. In this character, one '**sell**' equals *ten buy*'s, so a 'buy' is much lower than a 'sell'.

　　　Also, due to the stuff on top of 'sell' 卖, it seems higher than 'buy' 买.　　　　　　　　　　　　　　　　[8 STROKES　RANK 974]

342 实　实　solid, substantial　　　⬜ roof 247　⬛ head 339　　shí

BF The *roof* over this man's *head* makes him feel that his station in life is **solid and substantial**.　　　　　　　　[8 STROKES　RANK 100]

343 奇　奇　odd　　　　　　　　　⬛ big 330　⬛ can; may 60　　jī
BF

　1　How **odd**! How **strange**! Some *big* man is teetering across the high-wire that forms the top of the '可' component. Why is he doing this? Because he *can*!

　2　Let's face it—most people are pretty mediocre. Someone with a *outsize ability* and real talent sticks out like a sore thumb, a real **oddity**.
　　　　　　　　　　　　　　　　　　[8 STROKES　RANK 563]

344 牵　牵　lead along by holding sth

　　　　　　　　⬛ big 330　⬛ smooth cover 280　　⬛ ox 186　　qiān

With the *big cover* over the animal—it's probably a saddle—the *ox* can **be lead by** anybody.　　　　　　　　[9 STROKES　RANK 1679]

345 因　因　because　　　　　　　⬛ enclosure 40　⬛ big 330　　yīn

Because of his *big mouth*, everyone hears his side first in any fight.
　　　　　　　　　　　　　　　　　　[6 STROKES　RANK 96]

346 咽　咽　throat　　　　　　　　⬛ mouth 41　⬛ because 345　　yān

BF *Because* of having a *mouth*, animals need **throats** to get the food to the stomach.　　　　　　　　　　　　[9 STROKES　RANK 2031]

347 替 替 **for, on behalf of**   ▨ man (spiffy) (times 2) 337   ▧ speak 64   tì
Here are *two guys*, best friends for a long time. The guy on the left is making
a *speech* **on behalf of** his pal on the right.   [12 STROKES   RANK 1079]

348 扶 扶 **use a hand to support**   ▌ hand r 29   ▐ man (spiffy) 337   fú
This tall *man* has had a rough night of it (too much drinking, is it?)—he can
hardly remain upright. A kind passerby uses his *hand* to **support** him.
          [7 STROKES   RANK 1612]

349 莫 莫 **do not, not**   ▭ grass r 94   ▬ day, sun 63   ▬ big 330   mò
Big, tall *grasses* can obscure the *sun*. **Do not** let this happen, or the rest of
the garden plants will suffer.   [10 STROKES   RANK 955]

350 摸 摸 **touch, grope**   ▐ hand r 29   ▧ do not, not 349   mō
Groping is gross. It's putting your *hand* where it's *not* supposed to be.
          [13 STROKES   RANK 1367]

351 哭 哭 **weep**   ▨ mouth (times 2) 41   ▬ dog 332   kū
1 The components of this character form the features of a face assailed by
grief and **weeping**. The two "*mouths*" form eyes, from which a tear is
falling.
2 *Two mouths* signify the presence of much emotion, and nearby a *dog* is
howling with grief. In a human, this manifests itself as **weeping**.
          [10 STROKES   RANK 1210]

352 器 器 **vessel**   ▬ weep 351   ▨ mouth (times 2) 41   qì
BF The *four mouths* symbolize the noise that these many *mouths* can make! In
Chinese households of two thousand years ago, only valuable and well-used
cooking **vessels** can create a similar clatter.   [16 STROKES   RANK 441]

353 央 央 entreat   ■ man 311   ▭ one 2   ▣ towel 130 (altered)   yāng

BF The '*towel*' here is more of a ceremonial garment, perhaps a robe of office, draped around the shoulders of some official *man*, arms stretched wide, as he **entreats** his audience for donations.   [5 STROKES   RANK 800]

354 英 英 hero   ▭ grass r 94   ■ entreat 353   yīng

BF Here's a similar figure to §353, except now there's no *entreaty* going on. Instead, this man wears a ceremonial crown, made of *grass* or other decorative plant, to show the special status of this person (as was the custom in ancient Greece). Our guy is a **hero**!   [8 STROKES   RANK 371]

355 映 映 reflect, shine   ▯ day, sun 63   ■ entreat 353   yìng

The televangelist is *entreating* his followers to be generous with their donations. The television studios are hot—lights as bright as the *sun* shine on him. During close-ups, you can clearly see drops of sweat in their **reflection**.   [9 STROKES   RANK 1316]

356 弋 弋 arrow type   ■ big 330 (altered)   ▭ dab 169   yì

BF The **arrow** hit the *big* warrior in the left leg. He's just about to topple over. A *bit* of blood is flying away in the upper right of the picture.

Also: picture the **arrow** on its downward path. The arrow head points down to the right, and the aerodynamic feathered fins appear at the top.

[3 STROKES   RANK 4265]

357 式 式 model, standard   ▪ labor, work 7   ■ arrow type 356   shì

BF The boy is busy carving a **model** ship. It looks like hard *work* since he's using a sharp *arrow* as the carving tool.   [6 STROKES   RANK 303]

358 武 武 martial, military   ▯ correct 183 (altered)   ■ arrow type 356   wǔ

BF **Military** prowess and skill is all about discipline and knowledge of *correct* procedures, as well as practice with weapons, such as our fierce *arrow*.

[8 STROKES   RANK 501]

359 戈 戈 **halberd**   ■ arrow type 356   ◨ handle   gē

A **halberd** is a medieval combined spear and battle-ax. It's easy to imagine the diagonal as the main handle leading to the spear blade. The cross-strokes are the ax blades, and don't forget the drop of blood splashing in the air!

On the other hand, it may have suggested the kind of *arrow* we met in §356 to which a *handle* has been added. From *arrow* to **dagger** in one easy step!   [4 STROKES   RANK 1695]

360 找 找 **seek**   ▮ hand r 29   ▯ halberd 359   zhǎ•

Imagine **seeking** a lost treasure, something everybody wants. Use your *hand* to tightly hold your *sword*, which you need to repel the competition.

[7 STROKES   RANK 466]

361 我 我 I   ▮ hand r 29 (altered)   ▯ halberd 359   wǒ

I confidently hold my *sword* in my *hand* to symbolize the end of my training, and the introduction into the world of the new **me**.   [7 STROKES   RANK 9]

362 哦 哦 **chant softly**   ▯ mouth 41   ▮ I 361   é

I **chant softly** through my *mouth* so only I can hear *me*.

[10 STROKES   RANK 1913]

Unit 18

A Mighty Fortress...

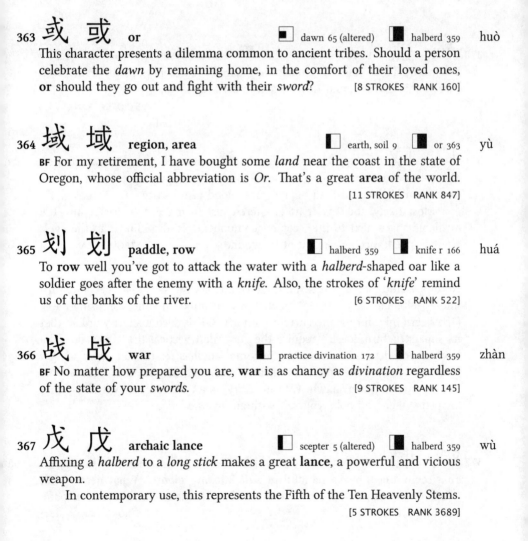

363 或 或 **or**   ◼ dawn 65 (altered)   ◼ halberd 359   **huò**

This character presents a dilemma common to ancient tribes. Should a person celebrate the *dawn* by remaining home, in the comfort of their loved ones, **or** should they go out and fight with their *sword*?   [8 STROKES   RANK 160]

364 域 域 **region, area**   ◼ earth, soil 9   ◼ or 363   **yù**

BF For my retirement, I have bought some *land* near the coast in the state of Oregon, whose official abbreviation is *Or*. That's a great **area** of the world.   [11 STROKES   RANK 847]

365 划 划 **paddle, row**   ◼ halberd 359   ◼ knife r 166   **huá**

To **row** well you've got to attack the water with a *halberd*-shaped oar like a soldier goes after the enemy with a *knife*. Also, the strokes of '*knife*' remind us of the banks of the river.   [6 STROKES   RANK 522]

366 战 战 **war**   ◼ practice divination 172   ◼ halberd 359   **zhàn**

BF No matter how prepared you are, **war** is as chancy as *divination* regardless of the state of your *swords*.   [9 STROKES   RANK 145]

367 戊 戊 **archaic lance**   ◼ scepter 5 (altered)   ◼ halberd 359   **wù**

Affixing a *halberd* to a *long stick* makes a great **lance**, a powerful and vicious weapon.

In contemporary use, this represents the Fifth of the Ten Heavenly Stems.   [5 STROKES   RANK 3689]

368 成 成　become, turn into　█ archaic lance 367　▣ fourth 25 (altered)　ché
Remember that the '*fourth*' component resembles a hook. With this villainous
hook and my *lance* I can **become** ruler of my village.　[6 STROKES RANK 59]

369 城 城　wall, city wall　▢ earth, soil 9　█ become, turn into 368　ché
The ancients were able take heaps of *earth* and *turn them into* cities and towns
by surrounding them with **walls**.　[9 STROKES RANK 413]

370 盛 盛　to fill, ladle　▬ become, turn into 368　▭ vessel, dish 110　ché
When you **ladle** some delicious and steaming chicken from the main soup
tureen, this divine liquid *turns into* a nourishing meal.
　[11 STROKES RANK 1142]

371 咸 咸　salty　█ archaic lance 367　▣ eye 78 (altered)　xiá
The young lance corporal was careless today. While playing with the *archaic
lance*, he carelessly pricked his *eye*. The blood tastes **salty**.

Most likely, the '*eye*' part is altered just to make it fit easier into the
available space next to the 'scepter' component. It also alludes to the eye's
altered appearance as a result of its wound.　[9 STROKES RANK 2525]

No one would blame you if the three characters 咸 'salty', 成 'become, turn
into' (§368), and 或 'or' (§363) melded in your mind into one, confusing mess.
(They certainly did for the current author!) '**Or**' is such a short word so that
its superstructure doesn't require the curvy left vertical the others do. The
hook attached to this vertical in '**become**' emphasizes its danger—if we get
too close to it, we **become** mincemeat. Remember, the part that looks almost
like an upside-down 'dawn' (旦) in '*salty*' is an altered *eye*, which is what
happens when you poke yourself with an *archaic lance*.

372 喊 喊　cry out　▢ mouth 41　█ salty 371　hǎn
That scoundrel threw a handful of *salt* into my *mouth*. What nerve! Salt
is acceptable in moderation, but so much of it makes me **cry out** in pain,
surprise, and disgust.　[12 STROKES RANK 1183]

373 戋 戋 **tiny, fragmentary**

▆ archaic lance 367 (altered)   ▆ archaic lance 367 (altered)   jiān

BF *Two archaic lances*, in the hands of superior soldiers, demolish each other in fairly short order. They reduce each other to piles of **fragments**.

[5 STROKES   RANK 6653]

374 尧 尧 **legendary emperor**

▆ tiny, fragmentary 373 (altered)   ▆ dollar 293 (altered)   yáo

This **legendary emperor** took the many *fragmentary monetary* systems in very ancient China which he altered and created one unified system of *currency*.

[6 STROKES   RANK 3264]

The ancient scribes, so I infer, were struck by the great beauty of trees. Tree components are among the most common in Chinese characters.

375 木 木 **tree**

■ big 330   ▯ scepter 5   mù

The Chinese have taken some artistic license with this glyph. The great roots at the bottom are juxtaposed to several branches at the top. There's nary a leaf or intervening segment of trunk in sight.   [4 STROKES   RANK 694]

376 林 林 **forest**

▯ tree (times 2) 375   lín

BF *Several trees* form a **forest**.   [8 STROKES   RANK 364]

377 森 森 **full of trees**

▭ tree 375   ■ forest 376   sēn

What with yet another *tree* added to the *forest*, we are simply **full of trees**.

[12 STROKES   RANK 1029]

378 本 本 **root or stem of plant**

■ tree 375   ▪ one 2   běn

The 'one' acts as a marker to mark the **root which develops into the trunk** of the *tree*.   [5 STROKES   RANK 92]

379 朱　朱　vermilion　　　　■ tree 375　▭ knife and mark　　zhū
BF Some vandal uses a *knife to scratch a small mark* on the mighty *tree*. Sap oozes out. It's a pretty **vermilion** color.　　　　[6 STROKES　RANK 1120]

380 珠　珠　pearl　　　　▮ king 11　▮ vermilion 379　　zhū
BF The *king* was precious in traditional Chinese society, and *vermilion* was a precious color in Chinese art. Fine **pearls** are precious stones which pulsate with life like a living being. If we place the living *king* next to *vermilion*, we get (or so it seemed to ancient scribes) a pair of components for '**pearl**'.　　　　[10 STROKES　RANK 1286]

381 未　未　have not yet　　　　■ tree 375　▯ one 2　　wèi
The forest elf **has not yet** climbed to the top of the *tree*. That tentative little marker in the form of '*one*' shows exactly where he stopped.　　　　[5 STROKES　RANK 385]

382 味　味　taste, flavor　　　　▮ mouth 41　▮ have not yet 381　　wèi
As food critic for a major metropolitan newspaper, it behooves you to do your job properly. Before deciding on the **taste** of the exciting new restaurant entrée, you need to carefully place a morsel in your *mouth*. You *have not yet* swallowed because you need to chew thoroughly to make sure all the component **flavors** are properly combined.　　　　[8 STROKES　RANK 844]

383 末　末　end, tip　　　　■ tree 375 (altered)　▭ one 2　　mò
The *one* extra cross-stroke is wider than its mate to emphasize that the upper part of the *tree*—the upper **end**, the **tip**—is the focus of the design.　　　　[5 STROKES　RANK 1164]

A few comments are in order regarding the characters 未 (§381) and 末 (§383). How *do* we tell them apart? They are almost identical, differing only in the relative lengths of the two horizontal strokes. The top of 未 looks like the character 土, 'earth' (§9); the tree is still in the soil—it *has not yet* been chopped down. The top of 末, on the other hand looks like 士, 'scholar' (§8). Naturally enough, the ancient scribes would have regarded scholarship as the 'tip', the *ne plus ultra*, of human achievement.

384 抹 抹 **put on, apply, smear**   ▮ hand r 29   ▮ end, tip 383   mǒ

You use the *tip* of your *hand* to **apply** make-up to your face.

[8 STROKES   RANK 2087]

385 杜 杜 **prevent**   ▮ tree 375   ▮ earth, soil 9   dù

BF *Trees* in the *earth* are useful natural barricades, **preventatives** for enemy attacks.

[7 STROKES   RANK 1277]

386 柜 柜 **cupboard**   ▮ tree 375   ▮ huge 18   guì

BF A **cupboard** is a *huge* piece of furniture made from a *tree*.

[8 STROKES   RANK 1994]

387 桂 桂 **cinnamon**   ▮ tree 375   ▮ earth, soil 9   ▮ earth, soil 9   guì

BF **Cinnamon** is a spice derived from a small evergreen *tree*. The two '*earth*' components together resemble an evergreen in profile, and also reminds us that a small tree keeps close to the earth.   [10 STROKES   RANK 1930]

388 果 果 **fruit**   ▮ field 57   ▮ tree 375   guǒ

BF The *field*-like shape grafted to the head of the *tree* isn't really a field, but is a ripe piece of **fruit** with odd stripes on its skin. It's a big piece of fruit, and so we need the strong root system of the tree to supply enough nutriments for its proper growth.   [8 STROKES   RANK 165]

Unit 19

Movers and Shakers

389 棵　棵　m for trees, cabbages, etc ⬜ tree 375　⬜ fruit 388　kē
A *tree* brought forth the *fruit* that we so enjoy. The harvest was so bountiful, that it was hard to **count it**. It helps to remember that fresh cabbage is also sweet! [12 STROKES RANK 2108]

390 查　查　check, investigate ⬜ tree 375　⬜ dawn 65　chá
There was a terrible racket out back last night! We have to wait for light of *dawn* to go out by the *tree* to **investigate** the cause. [9 STROKES RANK 459]

391 相　相　appearance ⬜ tree 375　⬜ eye 78　xiàn
BF You check the **appearance** of this picturesque *tree* by *eye*.
[9 STROKES RANK 152]

392 植　植　plant, grow ⬜ tree 375　⬜ straight, vertical 16　zhí
Look at all these *trees*—they're all so *straight and vertical*. Trees never look like that in nature. Clearly, they have been **planted** by some farmer.
[12 STROKES RANK 1124]

393 呆　呆　foolish, stupid ⬜ mouth 41　⬜ tree 375　dāi
The *mouth* on top of a *tree* looks like a child's puppet—head, arms, leg, and a vertical handle to hold—a Chinese bobble-head! Puppets are so endearing because of their **stupid** and **foolish** appearance. [7 STROKES RANK 1338]

394 束 束 **bundle, bunch**   ■ tree 375 (altered)   ▣ mouth 41   shù

Suppose our *tree* is an evergreen *tree* or something similar. It's time to cut it down and sell it as a Christmas or holiday tree. The strokes of the *'mouth'* suggest twine with which we tie it up to make a more convenient **bundle** of branches.   [7 STROKES   RANK 998]

395 困 困 **hard pressed**   ■ enclosure 40   ■ tree 375   kùn

BF The old farmer has an *enclosure* around his entire farm. As you see, there is only one *tree* there, so he and his family are **hard pressed** to survive, let alone make a living.   [7 STROKES   RANK 868]

396 操 操 **drill, exercise**   ▯ hand r 29   ▢ product 44   ▭ tree 375   cāo

The *hand* represents the staff sergeant leading the **drill**. Frequently, groups of soldiers practice in formation, shown here by the ordered *group of mouths*, and this is done outdoors, perhaps near a *tree*.   [16 STROKES   RANK 1173]

397 某 某 **certain, some**   ▭ sweet 103   ■ tree 375   mǒu

Most *trees* are bitter—sap, leaves, fruit, and so on. But the **certain** *trees* that have benefited mankind the most are those producing *sweet*, nutritious fruit.   [9 STROKES   RANK 517]

398 刺 刺 **thorn, splinter**   ▮ bundle, bunch 394 (altered)   ▮ knife r 166   cì

The *bundle* of trees has burst open. Some joker has cut the cords with his *knife*. The branches are sharp and wicked-looking. Watch out for the **splinters**!   [8 STROKES   RANK 1058]

399 析 析 **analyze**   ▮ tree 375   ▮ catty 118   xī

BF Any *wooden* furniture which is *unbalanced* is apt to crash to the ground, smashing itself into smithereens. With the little pieces all around, woodsmen can **analyze** the bits and see what went wrong.   [8 STROKES   RANK 1073]

400 闲 闲 idle   ■ door 196   ■ tree 375   xiá♦

I'm dying to go to work today, but the *tree* blocks my exit through the *door*. I'm forced to stay home today and sit **idle** in front of the TV all day! When my wife got back, I was so entranced by the TV, my wife thought I *was a tree*.   [7 STROKES   RANK 1529]

401 柏 柏 cypress   ▯ tree 375   ▯ white 201   bǎi

In Greek mythology, the **cypress** tree was associated with Hades, the god of the underworld. A *tree* striving toward the *white* light of the real world is a good emblem for this tree.   [9 STROKES   RANK 1596]

402 荣 荣 honorable   ▭ grass r 94   ▭ smooth cover 280   ■ tree 375   rón♦

BF The components suggest a *tree covered* in *grass* or other decorative vegetation, ornamentation appropriate in **honor** of someone.   [9 STROKES   RANK 993]

403 柱 柱 pillar, column   ▮ tree 375   ▯ master 220   zhù

Only the straightest, tallest, firmest of *trees* are chosen for their architectural suitability. What you might call *master trees* are appropriate for use in the construction of **pillars and columns**.   [9 STROKES   RANK 1691]

404 模 模 model, imitation   ▮ tree 375   ▯ do not, not 349   mó

BF When guys make wooden **models** of ships or airplanes, they *do not* use the whole *tree*.   [14 STROKES   RANK 689]

405 术 术 art, skill   ■ tree 375   ▢ dab 169   shù

BF It takes **artistry** to attack a big *tree*, carve away all the surplus wood (so to speak), and just leave a *small amount* of material in the shape of a beautiful statue, a stunning work of art.   [5 STROKES   RANK 328]

406 桌 桌 table   ▭ stand firm 173 (altered)   ▬ tree 375   zhuō

BF If my **table**, made from a *tree*, doesn't *stand firm* it's useless.

[10 STROKES   RANK 1193]

407 村 村 **hamlet** ⬛ tree 375 ⬜ inch 210 cūn

A **hamlet** stands in relation to a city as does an *inch*-long twig to a *tree*.

[7 STROKES   RANK 712]

408 椅 椅 **chair** ⬛ tree 375 ⬜ odd 343 yǐ

BF The *tree* must think it *odd* that its wood is used to make a **chair**, an artifact for supporting a type of animal (human) in a posture that is neither lying nor standing.   [12 STROKES   RANK 1663]

409 禾 禾 **rice or grain** ⬜ dab 169 ⬛ tree 375 hé

BF The *dab* at the top of the *tree* emphasizes the tiny scale of a plant. It's **grain**.   [5 STROKES   RANK 3587]

410 和 和 **and** ⬛ rice or grain 409 ⬜ mouth 41 hé

Harmony at the end of the day—*rice* **and** my *mouth* acting in unison to fill and to still my rumbling stomach. Heaven!   [8 STROKES   RANK 19]

411 香 香 **fragrant** ⬛ rice or grain 409 ⬛ day, sun 63 xiāng

Under the influence of the strong morning *sun*, the fresh-picked *rice* has an unmistakable **fragrance**.   [9 STROKES   RANK 776]

412 稿 稿 **cereal grain stalk** ⬛ rice or grain 409 ⬜ high 275 gǎo

BF Nature uses a **stalk of grain** to safeguard the *grain* for us, to keep it *high* off the ground, safe from predators and dirt.   [15 STROKES   RANK 1587]

413 科 科 **branch of study** ⬛ rice or grain 409 ⬜ cup-shaped 218 kē

BF *Rice grains* in a *cup* form interesting patterns, so interesting they form a separate **branch of study**.   [9 STROKES   RANK 277]

414 租　租　**rent**　　　■ rice or grain 409　　■ moreover 15　　zū

In long-gone days, the **rent** was paid in the form of agricultural produce. Here we see the actual **rent** payments symbolized by a portion of *grain*, and if we interpret '*moreover*' as a system of *shelves*, then we see *rice or grain* received as **rent** being stored in an appropriate bin, as a simple form of bookkeeping.　　　　　　　　　　　　[10 STROKES　RANK 1397]

Unit 20

Looking Good

415 种　种　**m for kinds**   ▮ rice or grain 409   ▯ middle 45   zhǒng

In a funny way, here is a picture of what happens when you try to feed a young, picky child. You've got some cereal *grain* for her. In the *middle* of eating it, she realizes it's the wrong **type**, so she shuts her mouth tight. Tough luck, mom!   [9 STROKES   RANK 57]

416 程　程　**rule, order**   ▮ rice or grain 409   ▯ appear 58   chéng

BF Piles of *grain*, which *appear* all the same, have a hypnotic effect. These piles nicely convey a sense of **rule** and of **order**.   [12 STROKES   RANK 314]

417 利　利　**advantage, benefit**   ▮ rice or grain 409   ▯ knife r 166   lì

It's to the farmer's **benefit** to use a *knife* or other sharp tool at the time of the *rice* harvest.   [7 STROKES   RANK 155]

418 莉　莉　**jasmine**   ▭ grass r 94   ▮ advantage, benefit 417   lì

BF The **jasmine** is a flower—a type of *vegetation*—with many associated *benefits*. It is, for example, the main ingredient in certain kinds of teas.   [10 STROKES   RANK 1878]

419 足　足　**foot**   ▭ mouth 41   ▮ man 311   ▯ foretell 170   zú

This profile of someone's foot shows toes pointing toward the right. The '*mouth*'-like portion at the top represents the cuff of a pant leg. The '*man*'-like part at the bottom is actually the lower part of the foot, the left stroke representing the ankle. The part that looks like a '*magic wand*' is part of the tongue and shoelaces of the shoe.   [7 STROKES   RANK 527]

420 捉 捉 to catch, capture ▮ hand r 29   ▮ foot 419   zhu▸

Quick, there goes that cute little rabbit! To **catch** or **capture** him, you need both your *hands* and *feet*. [10 STROKES RANK 1822]

421 走 走 to walk ▬ foot 419 (altered)   ▯ earth, soil 9   zǒu▸

Pounding the pavement is what **walking's** all about—you use your *feet* to cover lots of *ground*. [7 STROKES RANK 207]

422 赶 赶 rush ▮ to walk 421   ▮ dry 10   gǎn▸

The neurotic fellow out for a *walk* has a bad feeling. It's *dry* now, but rain clouds are darkening the sky. Best to **rush** home. [10 STROKES RANK 908]

423 赴 赴 go to, attend ▮ to walk 421   ▮ foretell 170   fù

Ever been to a company dinner or other shindig? Dreadful affairs. Indifferent food, boring speakers, everyone trying to suck up to the boss. To muster up the will power **to attend**, you need a push from your *magic wand* as you *walk* there. [9 STROKES RANK 1843]

424 楚 楚 clear ▮ forest 376   ▮ foot 419 (altered)   chǔ

BF I walk through the *forest* by *foot* to the famous hidden lake. The water is so **clear** it's fascinating to see the reflection of the tree in the surface (**clear**ly visible at the top of the character). From a certain angle—and this is what makes the lake so famous—it's not possible to distinguish between reality and reflection. [13 STROKES RANK 859]

425 夺 夺 seize ▭ big 330   ▪ inch 210   duó

It's not easy to **seize** something small. If we take something as small as an *inch*, for example, and make it *bigger*, then we can **seize** it with ease.

Alternatively, imagine a *big* man using his legs as pincers to **seize** and take hold of *inch*-long sticks between his thighs. [6 STROKES RANK 1199]

426 奋 奋 **act vigorously**   ☐ big 330 ◼ field 57   fèn

BF You really need to exert yourself, to **act vigorously** if you want to cultivate a *big field* properly.   [8 STROKES   RANK 1268]

427 失 失 **lose**   ☐ dab 169 ◼ man (spiffy) 337   shī

When you **lose** a game, you feel (at least temporarily) that you are just a *little bit* of the *person* you were before.   [5 STROKES   RANK 375]

428 知 知 **know**   ◼ arrow 334 ◼ mouth 41   zhī

Knowledge is power. Metaphorically speaking, expressing something you **know** is like letting fly an *arrow* from your *mouth*.   [8 STROKES   RANK 123]

429 智 智 **wit**   ☐ know 428 ◼ day, sun 63   zhì

BF When your friends and family feel that your expressions of *knowledge* sparkle like the *sun*, then you know you have been granted by the gods the gift of **wit**.   [12 STROKES   RANK 885]

430 贝 贝 **cowrie**   ◼ borders 127 ◼ man 311   bèi

BF The **cowrie**, a type of shell, served as an early form of money. This character often appears as a component, and when it does, we'll frequently ascribe a money-related meaning to it, such as 'valuable' or 'wealth'.

1 Here's a *man* overflowing the *borders* of his estate. This suggests a superfluity of possessions, an indicator of **wealth**.

2 Mollusks are the animals who manufacture **shells** and leave them behind for enjoyment (ours) after death (theirs). One well-known mollusk is the snail, but they all have a common structure—a fleshy foot protruding from its enclosing shell, and this glyph displays a representation of this structure.   [4 STROKES   RANK 1133]

431 则 则 **standard, norm**   ◼ cowrie 430 ◼ knife r 166   zé

BF Government muckety-mucks use a knife, symbolically, to create standards. For example, you can imagine the *knife* cutting a large amount of *money* into **standardized** subunits, much the way our Federal mint divides dollars into quarters, dimes, and nickels.   [6 STROKES   RANK 284]

432 贴　贴　**paste, stick to**　　▯ cowrie 430　▯ practice divination 172　　tiē

As a result of scrunching my *valuable cowrie shell* so it would fit here on the left, it developed a couple of cracks. I'm a good repairer, so people think I *practiced magic* when they see the shell after it's been fixed—it looks as good as new! But really, I just **pasted** some special strips over the cracks.

[9 STROKES   RANK 1454]

433 贲　贲　**hasten**　　▭ ten 6　▤ grass r 94　▤ cowrie 430　　bēn

BF Here's a person topped by an elaborate *shell*-shaped headdress made out of *grass* put under *ten*sion to give it form. (Wordplay alert!) She dare not **hasten**, or the whole thing will collapse around her.　[9 STROKES   RANK 4733]

434 喷　喷　**spurt, spout, gush**　　▯ mouth 41　▮ hasten 433　　pēn

BF A small boy's *mouth* has to *move fast* to capture the **gushing** water from the fountain. The '*hasten*' component helpfully looks like the spout of an ornate fountain.　[12 STROKES   RANK 1729]

435 赞　赞　**support, assist**　　▤ first (times 2) 300　▭ cowrie 430　　zàn

BF I made it a point to get to your presentation *first*. I was so early that this character is shown twice, to emphasize that I was able to help you set up on the platform, which looks like a giant *cowrie shell*. This is how I **support and assist** you.　[16 STROKES   RANK 1179]

436 质　质　**quality**　　▬ catty 118 (altered)　▮ cowrie 430　　zhì

The collector of *shells* assesses their **quality** by seeing how *unbalanced* they are.　[8 STROKES   RANK 404]

437 贵　贵　**expensive**　　▭ middle 45　▤ one 2　▤ cowrie 430　　guì

Imagine wearing a nice, **expensive** hat or headdress, which this character looks like. In detail, in the *middle* is *one* enormous *shell*—how chic!

[9 STROKES   RANK 873]

438 貫 贯 link up   ■ cowrie 430   ☐ field 57 (altered)   guàn

BF Hah—you just think it's a *field* over a shell! Actually, the top component is the top view of another *cowrie*. The extra-long horizontal line shows a string passing through this shell; it **links up** with the second shell whose profile we see on the bottom.   [8 STROKES   RANK 1478]

439 責 责 responsibility   ■ master 220 (altered)   ■ cowrie 430   zé

BF What happens when someone entrusts a *master* (of a house, firm, organization, whatever) with some money or other *valuable thing*? The master now incurs some **responsibility**, whether just to care for the valuable object or to do something with it.   [8 STROKES   RANK 535]

440 員 员 employee   ■ cowrie 430   ☐ mouth 41   yuán

BF Look at this character as a picture. Here's a broad-shouldered guy who developed those shoulder muscles in the warehouse as an **employee**.

     [7 STROKES   RANK 200]

Unit 21

A Time to Sow, a Time to Reap

441 贾 贾 **merchant**   ■ cowrie 430   □ west 291 (altered)   gǔ

This employee has a little extra decoration on his head, a *Western*-styled hat that makes him stand out. Who merits such special treatment? Why, it's the CEO of the firm, the head **merchant**.   [10 STROKES   RANK 2051]

442 损 损 **decrease, lose**   ■ hand r 29   ■ employee 440   sǔn

BF The major source of **decrease** in a merchant's inventory is the petty pilfering by *employees*. Whenever nobody's looking, they use their *hands* to help themselves to whatever they see.   [10 STROKES   RANK 911]

443 圆 圆 **round**   ■ enclosure 40   ■ employee 440   yuá

Everything in this character which looks square is really **round**! The *employee*'s head is not square—it's **round**. His shoulders are not square and broad, they're **round** and stooped in dejection from the constant same-old, same-old of his job. And he's trapped in the *enclosure* of his job, which is also **round**, to symbolize that he's always running around in circles.

[10 STROKES   RANK 1145]

444 页　页　page, leaf　　　☐ one 2　☐ dab 169　■ cowrie 430　　yè

1 Stand back and look at this character as if it were a sketch. The lower portion shows a lectern, attached to which (by a short chain) is an open book, comprised of many **pages**.

☐ one 2　☐ dab 169　▭ borders 127　▬ man 311

2 The **pages** of *one* book and its stories are like the *borders* of *one* country crammed with many *people*, so many that they are only separated from each other by a *small bit* of space.

3 The above diagrams notwithstanding, this character must have looked to ancient scribes like a stick figure of a **man**. The simplified head is connected by a short neck to broad shoulders themselves connected to arms held down at the side. A trim waist and two legs in motion rounds off this sketch. Sometimes, therefore, it pays to interpret this component, which appears in many other characters, as being a sketch of a *man*. The abbreviated head invites us to complete it with an additional component and so enhance and alter the meaning.　　[6 STROKES RANK 1128]

445 项　项　nape of neck　　　■ labor, work 7　■ page, leaf 444　　xiàng

BF It's hard *work* doing things on the back of your head, like trimming your ponytail. Therefore, the symbol for 'productive *labor*' perched jauntily at the **back of** this person's **neck** provides a perfect visual metaphor.

[9 STROKES RANK 571]

446 顶　顶　carry on your head　　　■ fourth 25　■ page, leaf 444　　dǐng

BF The ' 丁 ' part of this character (on the left) looks like a level surface, at the same level as the top of the head of the guy on the right. This level surface is a help to **carry things on the head**.　　[8 STROKES RANK 1000]

447 顽　顽　stupid, stubborn　　　■ dollar 293　■ page, leaf 444　　wán

BF Only a **stupid** person would pay a *dollar* for one *leaf* of a tree.

[10 STROKES RANK 2024]

448 颤 顫 **quiver, tremble**

□ cover 268 ■ return 42 ■ dawn 65 ▮ page, leaf 444   chà.

Dawn. Our playboy *man* is just *returning* home after a comprehensive night on the town and too much drinking. He would love to *cover* himself from the sharp night chill and from the effects of drinking—he's **trembling** violently.

[19 STROKES   RANK 1900]

449 颗 顆 **m for small, roundish things**   ▮ fruit 388 ▮ page, leaf 444   kē

Pieces of *fruit* are apt to be **small** and **round**ish, and so are *leaves* of trees (most of the time). The juxtaposition is therefore appropriate as a **measure word for beads, grains, and so on.**   [14 STROKES   RANK 1448]

450 卒 卒 **foot soldier**   □ cover 268 ▤ from 313 ▬ ten 6   zú

Here's a young **foot soldier** all dressed in military uniform—*cover* (that is, hat or helmet), protective goggles—and look, you can see me reflected in each of the lenses, shiny belt, and pants with the knife edge crease, making me look look like a '*ten*'.   [8 STROKES   RANK 2584]

451 醉 醉 **drunk**   ▮ new wine 303 ▮ foot soldier 450   zuì

Mix large amounts of *alcohol* together with one *foot soldier* and what's the result—public **drunkenness.**   [15 STROKES   RANK 1783]

452 吞 吞 **swallow, gulp down**   ■ heaven 333 (altered) ▬ mouth 41   tūn

He was very thirsty when he took that huge **swallow.** He opened his *mouth* so wide, I thought he would swallow *heaven* itself.   [7 STROKES   RANK 1797]

453 幕 幕 **stage curtain**   ■ do not, not 349 ▪ towel 130   mù

A **stage curtain** is a vast expanse of *cloth*, the purpose of which is to make sure your *do not* see the stage as the stagehands prepare for the next act.

[13 STROKES   RANK 1315]

454 墓 墓　tomb　　　　　■ do not, not 349　▪ earth, soil 9　　mù

A **tomb**—once you pass through the *earth* into it, you *do not* return.

[13 STROKES　RANK 1816]

455 奄 奄　castrate, spay　　　■ big 330　■ electricity 138　　yān

Well. When you apply *electricity* to the tender regions between this *big* man's legs, you **castrate** and cauterize this poor fellow in one fell swoop.

[8 STROKES　RANK 3462]

456 掩 掩　cover, hide　　　■ hand r 29　■ castrate, spay 455　　yǎn

The poor guy we met in §455 uses his *hand* over the *castrated* region to **cover** himself and **hide** his embarrassment.　[11 STROKES　RANK 1514]

457 仑 仑　order, coherence　　　■ man 311　■ ancient ladle 142　　lún

BF Young men are notorious for their crudeness and rowdiness. Don't even ask what they're doing with that soup *ladle*! But with maturity, these *men* find these tendencies transformed to ones of **order** and **coherence**.

[4 STROKES　RANK 2139]

458 顷 顷　in an instant　　　■ ancient ladle 142 (altered)　■ page, leaf 444　　qǐng

For some reason, you use a *spoon* to get rid of the yellow *leaves* on your lawn. But the wind catches them, and **in an instant** they're somewhere back on the ground.　[8 STROKES　RANK 2724]

459 柴 柴　firewood　　　■ this 233　■ tree 375　　chái

This tree has been chopped down to a small size, perfect for **firewood** this winter. The vertical strokes in '*this*' look like tongues of flame.

[10 STROKES　RANK 1981]

460 棍 棍　rod, stick　　　■ tree 375　■ elder brother** 149　　gùn

Using a piece of a *tree*, I tried carving a statue of my *elder brother*. His face is a tough one to imitate—the carving looked like a dull **stick** despite my best efforts—or maybe that's what I really think of him!　[12 STROKES　RANK 2255]

461 胃 胃 **stomach**   ■ field 57   ■ meat 317 (altered)   **wèi**
The **stomach** is a type of *meat* which, like a farmer's *field*, contains nutritious stuff.   [9 STROKES   RANK 1957]

462 刍 刍 **hay for fodder**   ■ man 311 (altered)   ■ boar's head 34 (altered)   **chú**
BF *Man* subdues the *wild boar* by providing **hay**.   [5 STROKES   RANK 4465]

463 争 争 **struggle**
   ■ man 311 (altered)   ■ boar's head 34 (altered)   ▯ scepter 5   **zhēn**
The **struggle** is between the *man* with a *stick* and a *wild boar*. It's not looking good for the man.   [6 STROKES   RANK 344]

464 睁 睁 **open (eyes)**   ■ eye 78   ■ struggle 463   **zhēn**
I hate the *struggle* every Monday morning between me and my *eyes*. My brain says 'open up!', while my heart and soul reply, 'stay shut'.   [11 STROKES   RANK 1963]

465 欠 欠 **owe, lack**   ■ man 311 (altered)   ■ man 311   **qiàn**
These two *men* are connected by a business relationship. The shorter fellow (on top) **owes** money to the other. While he **owes** this money, he **lacks** stature, at least temporarily.   [4 STROKES   RANK 1948]

466 翰 翰 **writing brush**
   ■ ten 6   ■ morning 70   ■ man 311   ■ feather, wing 123   **hàn**
BF Practicing Chinese calligraphy with a proper **writing brush** is demanding. The best time is *ten* in the *morning*. A *man* begins by picking up the **brush**, whose hairs are as fine as *feathers*.   [16 STROKES   RANK 1881]

Unit 22

A Time to Sew, a Time to Rip

467 挣 挣　**struggle, strive**　■ hand r 29　■ struggle 463　zhèng
You *struggle* using your *hands* as you **strive** through life.
[9 STROKES   RANK 1875]

468 换 换　**exchange, trade**　■ hand r 29　■ man 311 (altered)　■ entreat 353　huàn
The essence of **trade** is doing and talking, symbolized by a *hand* and a *man*
who *entreats* you to buy.　[10 STROKES   RANK 824]

469 唤 唤　**call, call out to**　□ mouth 41　■ man 311 (altered)　■ entreat 353　huàn
Why bother to **call out** to someone? You use your *mouth* to make the call
when you want to *entreat* a *man* to do something with you or for you.
[10 STROKES   RANK 1835]

470 兼 兼　**double, twice**　■ rice or grain (times 2) 409　▬ boar's head 34　jiān
BF Imagine using the *head of a huge, angry boar* to keep *two sheaves of grain*.
A **double** harvest?　[10 STROKES   RANK 1515]

471 题 题　**topic, subject, title**　■ is 184　■ page, leaf 444　tí
The **topic** of an article is what *is* on the *page*.　[15 STROKES   RANK 218]

472 万 万　**ten thousand**　□ one 2　■ man 311 (altered)　wàn
One good *man* is better than **ten thousand** of his middle-of-the-road col-
leagues.　[3 STROKES   RANK 322]

473 笑 笑 **laugh, smile** ▭ bamboo r 243   ■ heaven 333   xiào

The parts of *bamboo* look like eyes crinkled in laughter. The gods love laughter the best, and so **laughter** reaches *heaven* quicker than any prayer.

[10 STROKES   RANK 346]

474 丙 丙 **third in series** ▭ one 2   ■ inside* 318   bǐng

The downward '*borders*' component looks like a downward-pointing 'C', the **third** grade from the highest in school. This is the grade that *one* guy received after doing no work whatsoever.   [5 STROKES   RANK 2645]

475 越 越 **exceed** ◪ to walk 421   ◪ archaic lance 367 (altered)   yuè

BF An ancient bully, *walking about* with an *archaic lance* could take what he wanted from the cowering peasants and so **exceed** his current wealth.

[12 STROKES   RANK 440]

476 兔 兔 **rabbit** ▬ man 311 (altered)   ▬ mouth 41 (altered)   ▬ walking man 287   ⊡ dab 169   tù

A pictograph of a cute **rabbit**: the altered '*man*' component looks like two ever-so-cute ears atop a *mouth*-like head. All this surmounts powerful *legs* for quick hopping away from danger. Oh, and don't forget the cute *dab*-like tail.   [8 STROKES   RANK 2364]

477 免 免 **dismiss, fire, exempt** ■ rabbit 476   ▣ dab 169   miǎn

We **fired** the *rabbit*. I know that because the rabbit's *tail* has vanished.

[7 STROKES   RANK 755]

478 挽 挽 **draw, pull** ▮ hand r 29   ▮ dismiss, fire, exempt 477   wǎn

The rotten employee refused to leave the office even after being *fired*. I used my *hand* to forcibly **pull** him out and send him on his way.

[10 STROKES   RANK 2222]

479 晚 晚 **evening** ▮ day, sun 63   ▮ dismiss, fire, exempt 477   wǎn

BF When you *dismiss* the *sun*, you get **evening**.   [11 STROKES   RANK 641]

480 策　策　policy, plan, scheme

　　　　　　　　　　　　☐ bamboo r 243　　■ bundle, bunch 394 (altered)　　cè

BF The **plan** for the government was written on a *bundle* of *bamboo* scrolls.

[12 STROKES　RANK 714]

481 负　负　bear, carry on shoulders

　　　　　　　　　　　　☐ man 311 (altered)　　■ cowrie 430　　fù

This *man* is working for *money* for he is now old enough to **bear** responsibility for his own welfare.　　[6 STROKES　RANK 691]

482 入　入　enter, receive, take in　　■ man 311 (altered)　　rù

BF Although this looks like a *man* with a jaunty something or other on his head, think instead of a fledgling plant, whose roots force themselves down to **enter** the earth.　　[2 STROKES　RANK 210]

483 背　背　bear, shoulder　　☐ north 145　　■ meat 317 (altered)　　bēi

The '*meat*' represents a living body, **shouldering** an evenly divided load on its *north* end.　　[9 STROKES　RANK 787]

484 顿　顿　m for meals　　▮ stockpile, store up 150　　▯ page, leaf 444　　dùn

I've always been a healthy eater. Many *people stockpile* a great deal for **meals**.　　[10 STROKES　RANK 794]

485 鱼　鱼　fish　　☐ man 311 (altered)　　▮ field 57　　☐ one 2　　yú

1　Behold *one* **fish**, leaping out of the water and plunging back in. Up top, the forked tail, looking like a funny sort of *man*, flashes in the sunlight. The striped body, resembling the character for '*field*', is already re-entering the surface of the water.

2　The American Indians who practiced agriculture increased crop fertility by planting *one* **fish** with each seed. Here's a *man*, the farmer, in his *field*, inserting the poor **fish** below the surface of the soil.

[8 STROKES　RANK 852]

486 鲁 鲁 **stupid, dull, vulgar**   ☐ fish 485   ■ day, sun 63   lǔ

BF *Fish* swimming in the sea are marvels of grace and elegance. Remove them from their natural environment, and in the light of *day*, they look **dull** and **stupid**.   [12 STROKES   RANK 898]

487 宋 宋 **Song dynasty**   ☐ roof 247   ■ tree 375   sòng

This character, built up from an architectural component (*roof*) and material (*tree*) reminds us that the development of architecture and structural engineering was among the most important achievements of the **Song dynasty**.   [7 STROKES   RANK 990]

488 骨 骨 **bone**   ☐ boxy things   ■ meat 317 (altered)   gǔ

BF Those *boxy*, **bony** things atop a person's body represent the skeleton attached to the *meat*.   [9 STROKES   RANK 1036]

489 歌 歌 **song**   ▯ elder brother 62   ▯ owe, lack 465   gē

"There once was a fine *elder brother*
Who borrowed money from another.
The guy soon wanted it back
But bro' said, "Money I *lack*
But I know I can cadge from my mother."
How's that for an impromptu **song**?   [14 STROKES   RANK 1040]

490 晓 晓 **dawn, daybreak**   ▮ day, sun 63   ▮ legendary emperor 374   xiǎo

BF According to the story, this *legendary emperor* will rise with the *sun* to save his homeland, and so will appear at **dawn**.   [10 STROKES   RANK 1357]

491 赖 赖 **rely, depend on**   ▮ bundle, bunch 394   ▮ bear, carry on shoulders 481   lài

I'm too old to do this job any longer. I **rely** on my son to *carry* the heavy *bundles* on his shoulders.   [13 STROKES   RANK 1365]

492 吹　吹   blow, puff   ▮ mouth 41   ▯ owe, lack 465   chuī

If I **blow** too hard into a bagpipe (or other wind instrument), I will collapse. After such an effort, I surely *lack* the stamina to continue. Breath passes through the *mouth*.   [7 STROKES   RANK 1390]

Unit 23

Cleaning the Sewers

493 丧 丧 **mourning**   ☐ weep 351 (altered)   ◼ perish 269 (altered)   sān(

BF **Mourning** is the *weeping* for one who has *perished*.

[8 STROKES   RANK 1404]

494 箱 箱 **box, trunk, chest**   ◻ bamboo r 243   ◼ appearance 391   xiār

BF The **chest** was cunningly designed to have the *appearance* of *bamboo*.

[15 STROKES   RANK 1453]

495 趋 趋 **hasten, hurry**   ◼ to walk 421   ◼ hay for fodder 462   qū

BF The oxen *walk* home towards their *fodder* until they get a whiff of this delicious substance. Then, it's all I can do not to be dragged off my feet as they **hasten** to stuff themselves.   [12 STROKES   RANK 1486]

496 拖 拖 **pull, drag, haul**

◼ hand r 29   ◻ man 311 (altered)   ◼ also*, too* 140   tuō

This *man* uses *two* (sounds like '*too*') *hands* to **pull** the rickshaw.

[8 STROKES   RANK 1492]

497 欣 欣 **happy**   ◼ catty 118   ◼ owe, lack 465   xīn

BF My girl friend agreed to marry me. I'm giddy with **happiness**—and the giddiness *unbalances* me, as if I'm *lacking* self-control.

[8 STROKES   RANK 1523]

498 拟 拟 plan, intend
☐ hand r 29   ☐ mineshaft 135 (altered)   ☐ man 311   nǐ

The evil **plan** was to lure your girlfriend's new *boyfriend* to the edge of the *mineshaft*, and give a swift shove with your *hand*. How's that for melodrama?

[7 STROKES   RANK 1541]

499 贡 贡 tribute, gifts   ☐ labor, work 7   ☐ cowrie 430   gòng

BF Part of the *money* we all receive as wages from our *work* gets exacted from us as tax, a **tribute** to the various governments under which we serve.

[7 STROKES   RANK 1548]

500 寄 寄 send, mail, consign   ☐ roof 247   ☐ odd 343   jì

First-class stamps—what you use to **send** letters to a friend's *house*—often cost an *odd* number of cents.   [11 STROKES   RANK 1611]

501 耗 耗 consume, cost, dawdle
☐ tree 375   ☐ two 3 (altered)   ☐ hair 231   hào

The *two* pieces of antique *wood* were tied together with phony blond *hair*. This bundle of wood **cost** me a bundle, too.   [10 STROKES   RANK 1730]

502 菌 菌 mushroom ☐ grass r 94   ☐ enclosure 40   ☐ rice or grain 409   jùn

BF Inside the experimental *enclosure*, we sprinkle raw *grain* amongst the *grass*, just to see what happens. But they don't sprout—it's so moist that giant **mushrooms** grow instead.   [11 STROKES   RANK 1733]

503 赋 赋 endow, bestow   ☐ cowrie 430   ☐ martial, military 358   fù

The rebel *army* confiscates *money* for their warlords, and this is the source of their monetary **endowments**.   [12 STROKES   RANK 1747]

504 秩 秩 order*, sequence*   ☐ rice or grain 409   ☐ lose 427   zhì

BF The artist's latest masterpiece consists of an **orderly sequence** of *grains* glued to a mirror. The patterns are quite intricate; you could stare at them and *lose* yourself in the work.   [10 STROKES   RANK 1749]

505 捷 捷 victorious   ⬛ hand r 29   ⬛ to walk 421   ⬛ boar's head 34   **jié**

BF The **victorious** army *marches* in triumph, holding in their *hands* the heads of their enemies as if they were *boar's heads*.   [11 STROKES   RANK 1789]

506 盐 盐 salt   ⬛ earth, soil 9   ⬛ man 311 (altered)   ⬛ vessel, dish 110   **yán**

Workers of the world are the **salt** of the *earth*. I store some of that **salt** in a small *dish*, and set it on the table to season my meals.

[10 STROKES   RANK 1885]

507 柯 柯 ax handle   ⬛ tree 375   ⬛ can; may 60   **kē**

BF The *wooden* part of the ax is the **ax handle**. With a long, inflexible handle, I *can* do much more work than my neighbor.   [9 STROKES   RANK 1903]

508 棉 棉 cotton   ⬛ tree 375   ⬛ silk 206   **miá**

A certain *tree* (well, alright, it's a plant) provides *silk*-like fiber good for clothes. We call this **cotton**.   [12 STROKES   RANK 1967]

509 合 合 cozy house   ⬛ man 311   ⬛ one 2   ⬛ mouth 41

CMP We've already seen this component as a character in §325, but it's convenient, to treat it as a special component.

510 哈 哈 aha!   ⬛ mouth 41   ⬛ cozy house 509   **hā**

1 Here someone is sliding down the roof of our *cozy house*. How satisfying! You can hear this little imp saying '**aha**', a sound of satisfaction. Out of this imp's *mouth* comes '**aha**', a sound.

2 Imagine coming home after a stressful day at work to your nice, *cozy house*. How satisfying—an involuntary '**aha**' escapes your *mouth*.

[9 STROKES   RANK 713]

511 拾 拾 **pick up** ◾ hand r 29 ▢ cozy house 509 shí

(The definition refers to the act of picking something up from the ground.) After building this *cozy house*, it's necessary to use your *hands* to **pick up** all the building debris from the ground.

Also, it requires *manual* labor to keep the house tidy, inside and out, so it remains *cozy*. You always have **pick up** after kids, spouses, in-laws, guests, dogs, and so on. [9 STROKES RANK 1961]

512 答 答 **answer** ▢ bamboo r 243 ◼ cozy house 509 dá

Imagine joining the *bamboo* canes together to use as a primitive telephone system. From the inner sanctum of your *cozy house*, you could frame queries and receive **answers**. [12 STROKES RANK 559]

513 搭 搭 **build** ◾ hand r 29 ▢ answer 512 (altered) dā

1 The *hand* plucks the *answer* from the oracle, which encourages the **building** of a new temple.
2 In conjunction with a *hand*, the bit of grass above the cozy house is really another hand, as suggested in §29, but rotated by ninety degrees. A pair of hands working on the house are clearly engaged in **building**. [12 STROKES RANK 1842]

514 塔 塔 **pagoda** ◾ earth, soil 9 ▢ answer 512 (altered) tǎ

1 They've built the **pagoda** on a particularly fine lot of *earth*, which makes it a literal *answer* to our prayers.
2 It makes sense to consider the *answer* component to be a *decorated house*—the bit of grass on top provides the ornamental effect. In the *ground* of a building lot, we add some ornate decoration that looks made from grass or other vegetation to what started as an ordinary cozy house, and end up with a **pagoda**. [12 STROKES RANK 1030]

515 拿 拿 **take** ▢ cozy house 509 ◼ hand 27 ná

Here's a *hand* extending towards a *cozy house*—someone looking for a "hand out" is ready to **take** whatever they can from wherever they can. [10 STROKES RANK 645]

516 盒 盒 **small box** ⬜ cozy house 509 ⬛ vessel, dish 110 hé

BF A **small box** is a *vessel* that would be useful for storage in our *cozy house.* [11 STROKES RANK 2067]

517 命 命 **life, fate** ◧ cozy house 509 (altered) ▣ single ear 157 mìn

Here's one lucky guy. His **fate** has given him a loving family and this great *cozy house* to live in. But he knows this could all turn on a dime, so he cocks his *ear* to the wind (metaphorically speaking) to be on the lookout for anything that could trouble his fortune. [8 STROKES RANK 258]

518 夬 夬 **surprised man** ▌ man (spiffy) 337 ▯ unexpected mark

CMP That little vertical tweak is an *unexpected mark*—something the *man* had no idea was awaiting him. We'll use this component for a **surprised man.**

Unit 24

Bits and Bytes

519 块 块 **lump**   ■ earth, soil 9   ■ surprised man 518   kuài

While taking a walk on some unexplored *soil*, a *surprised man* trips over an unexpected clod of dirt, a **lump** of soil.   [7 STROKES RANK 793]

520 缶 缶 **dry mountainous bits**

   ■ dab 169   ■ dry 10   ■ mountain 21

CMP The bits and pieces of this component say it all.

521 缶 缶 **archaeological vessel**   ■ dry mountainous bits 520   fǒu

The clay found on tops of *dry mountains* was used in ancient times to create today's **archaeological vessels**.   [6 STROKES RANK 5328]

522 缺 缺 **be short of, lack**

   ■ dry mountainous bits 520   ■ surprised man 518   quē

Because of the *dry mountainous bits* to which the prisoners (a bunch of *men surprised* at this harsh sentence) have been exiled, there's a serious **shortage of** food. Everyone is slowly starving.   [10 STROKES RANK 875]

523 氵 氵 **water r**

CMP Drop a stone into a pool. The splashes feel good on a hot summer day. Here's three of those drops.

524 江 江 **river, Yangtze** ▌ water r 523 ▌ labor, work 7 jiān
A good **river** system helps a culture do *work*—transport goods, maintain communications, move people, and so on. It's no wonder that *water* plus *labor* comprised a **river** for the ancient scribes. (Nowadays, you're apt to see 'Yangtze' spelled according to pinyin rules as '**Yangzi**'.)
[6 STROKES   RANK 577]

525 汗 汗 **sweat** ▌ water r 523 ▌ dry 10 hàn
Sweat is *water* on our skin that, as it *dries*, keeps you cool.
[6 STROKES   RANK 1490]

526 汪 汪 **bow-wow** ▌ water r 523 ▌ king 11 wā
In my view, large, thoroughbred dogs—Newfoundlands, St. Bernards, mastiffs, and so on—are the *kings* of domesticated animals. But these big guys are messy and slobbery. You get *drops of liquid* all over you when these *kings* **bark**.
[7 STROKES   RANK 1876]

527 油 油 **oil** ▌ water r 523 ▌ let sb do sth 48 yóu
Fine **oil**, close to the consistency of *water*, *allows* you to do things (cook, keep machinery from seizing up, quiet noisy hinges, and so on) you couldn't do without this bit of grease.
[8 STROKES   RANK 948]

528 洁 洁 **clean** ▌ water r 523 ▌ lucky 56 jié
BF Believe it or not, *water* has feelings about what it's being used for. It doesn't care to water plants or to flush toilets, but it feels *lucky* if people use it for **cleaning**.
[9 STROKES   RANK 1531]

529 河 河 **river*** ▌ water r 523 ▌ can; may 60 hé
One characteristic of **rivers**: the flowing *water can* enable civilization (see §524).
[8 STROKES   RANK 574]

530 泪 泪 **tears** ▌ water r 523 ▌ eye 78 lèi
BF **Tears** are *water* that flows from the *eyes*.
[8 STROKES   RANK 1271]

531 泄 泄 **discharge gas or liquid** ▌ water r 523 ▌ generation 106   xiè

It looks like *water* flows through this complex mechanism on the right, one of our *generation's* most impressive inventions. Even so, it's so complicated that the **fluid** will **leak out** for sure.   [8 STROKES   RANK 2010]

532 汇 汇 **gather together** ▌ water r 523 ▌ basket, box 152   huì

There are some small chips of wood in the bottom of the basket, so small they fit between the basket reeds and are hard to gather. All I need do is pour *water* in the *basket*. The water floats the chips to the surface, where they clump together for easy **gathering**.   [5 STROKES   RANK 1187]

533 洞 洞 **hole, cavity** ▌ water r 523 ▌ same, similar 129   dòng

Water, drop by drop, works the *same* way on any stone surface. Eventually, it can wear a **hole** right through it.   [9 STROKES   RANK 1015]

534 活 活 **to live, alive** ▌ water r 523 ▌ tongue 225   huó

An ancient commentary on the nature of **life**? All you need is *water* to keep you going and a *tongue* to keep you talking!   [9 STROKES   RANK 219]

535 阔 阔 **wide, broad, vast** ▌ door 196 ▣ to live, alive 534   kuò

BF A young person, fresh out of college, is about to go out on her own. She looks out the *door* of her parents' house, where *life* beckons to her, a **wide** and **broad** canvas ready for her mark.   [12 STROKES   RANK 1675]

536 温 温 **lukewarm, to warm up** ▌ water r 523 ▌ day, sun 63 ▟ vessel, dish 110   wēn

Cold *water* in a *dish*. The summer *sun* shines on it all day. By evening, the water has **warmed up**.   [12 STROKES   RANK 867]

537 浩 浩   vast, grand   █ water r 523 █ tell 189   hào

BF The right, 'tell' component looks for all the world like a single-masted sailboat. How can you *tell* if the body of *water* your sailing on is **vast** enough for this vessel? If the sailboat doesn't sink, you're fine.

[10 STROKES   RANK 1864]

538 茫 茫   vast, without borders

█ water r 523   █ spike, sharp point 277 (altered)   mán

BF The ocean is **vast** and **borderless**. The shipwrecked sailor, floating hopelessly on the featureless *waters*, feels an ever present thirst pierce him like a *sharp spike*.   [9 STROKES   RANK 1951]

539 注 注   pour   █ water r 523 █ master 220   zhù

BF An empty cup requires you focus attention on it—its color, shape, workmanship, and so on. As soon as you **pour** anything into it, that focus shifts to the liquid inside. This liquid—*water*, tea, whatever—now dominates and becomes *master* of this situation.   [8 STROKES   RANK 492]

540 洗 洗   wash, bathe   █ water r 523 █ first 300   xǐ

Washing up and **bathing** are some things you do *first* when you get up. Of course, you use *water* in this process.   [9 STROKES   RANK 1247]

541 满 满   full, complete

█ water r 523 □ grass r 94 █ both, two 316   mǎn

I have *two* flowerpots outside. If I *water* them, flowers and *grasses* will **fill** them.

[Another meaning is 'Manchu'. The 满族—Mǎnzú—were a non-ethnic Chinese people that ruled China from the seventeenth century to the beginning of the twentieth. One class of officials in their empire were the 满大人—mǎndàrén—which came into English as 'mandarin' and lent its name in English for the modern standard Chinese language.]

[13 STROKES   RANK 436]

542 潜 潜 hide   ▌ water r 523   ▐▌ for, on behalf of 347   qián

BF Allan Quartermain (or is it James Bond?) submerges himself beneath *four-and-one-half* (sounds like *for, on behalf of*) feet of murky river *water*. This will effectively **hide** him from Dr. No, or Goldfinger, or whoever is the villain du jour.   [15 STROKES   RANK 1112]

543 漠 漠 desert   ▌ water r 523   ▐▌ do not, not 349   mò

BF A **desert** is a place where *water* is *not*.   [13 STROKES   RANK 1777]

544 润 润 moist, soft   ▌ water r 523   ▐▌ intercalary month 199   rùn

The ancients believed that the extra months added to the lunar calendar—the so-called *intercalary months*—to keep the length of the year more-or-less constant were particularly auspicious. For farmers, this meant a promise of additional *water* to keep their crops **moist** and healthy.

These are "**soft**" months—months that aren't always present.

         [10 STROKES   RANK 1369]

Unit 25

Clean Living

545 水 水 water — water r 523 (altered) — shuǐ

The graceful lines of 水 suggest the coming together of streams of **water**.

[4 STROKES   RANK 202]

546 益 益 benefit, advantage — water 545 (altered) — vessel, dish 110 — yì

BF Look at the *water* component—it appears sideways! But wait, maybe the *vessel* is sideways and the water is shown normal. Or maybe you, the reader, are sideways! This multiple point of view is **beneficial** in life, as it helps us keep an open mind.

[10 STROKES   RANK 649]

547 浅 浅 shallow, superficial — water r 523 — tiny, fragmentary 373 — qiǎn

Water in *tiny* amounts is the very definition of '**shallow**'.

[8 STROKES   RANK 1721]

548 湘 湘 Hunan province (abbrev) — water r 523 — appearance 391 — xiāng

The food in **Hunan province** is well-known for its spiciness. The tears running down your face after one of their authentic meals gives you a *watery appearance*.

[12 STROKES   RANK 2245]

549 录 录 record, write down

boar's head 34 (altered) — water 545 (altered) — lù

BF The ancients wasted nothing! Taking a *boar's head* and steeping it in *water* for several weeks, they created an ink that didn't fade. Moreover, they could easily remove bristles from the skin, and use these 'pens' to **record** tribal history.

[8 STROKES   RANK 919]

550 测 测   **to survey, measure**   ■ water r 523   ■ standard, norm 431   cè

One performs a **survey** to establish a *standard*. The most ancient surveys and measurements were of *water* levels (think of the ancient records of the Nile and its flooding), which explains the connection with *water*.

[9 STROKES   RANK 861]

551 酒 酒   **wine, liquor**   ■ water r 523   ■ new wine 303   jiǔ

After awhile, *new wine* absorbs humidity from the air, becoming more *watery* in the process—but it's still **wine!**   [10 STROKES   RANK 797]

552 池 池   **pool, pond**   ■ water r 523   ■ also*, too* 140   chí

BF What kind of body of *water* supports this odd contraption with the curved bottom, tall mast, and other stuff on a deck? The '*also*' component helps us visualize a small boat on a **pond.**   [6 STROKES   RANK 1709]

553 混 混   **confuse, mix up**   ■ water r 523   ■ elder brother** 149   hùn

Look—someone has thrown all the *brothers* into the *water*. Which one is the *eldest*? With all of them thrashing around, hair plastered down on their heads, it's too **confusing** to tell.   [11 STROKES   RANK 1137]

554 隶 隶   **belong to**   ■ boar's head 34 (altered)   ■ water 545 (altered)   lì

BF The *boar* is very **attached to** his face, but (being only a boar) he can only see it by glimpsing his *altered* reflection in the *water*.   [8 STROKES   RANK 1801]

555 泉 泉   **spring, fountain**   ■ white 201   ■ water 545   quán

BF A metaphorical image of a pristine mountain **spring** would be that of *white water*.   [9 STROKES   RANK 1641]

556 津 津 **ferry crossing** ▮ water r 523 ▮ pen, writing instrument 39   jīn

People put **ferry crossings** where the river is narrowest. Here's one crossing so convenient that it takes only a giant *pen* floating on the calm *waters* to **ferry** people across. Of course, pens are messy, but better 'ink' than 'sink'.   [9 STROKES   RANK 1353]

557 求 求 **request, entreat**

▮ water 545 (altered) ▯ dab 169 ▭ one 2   qiú

Something, some *little thing*, is floating on the surface of the *water*. It's my hat! It keeps drifting farther and farther away. Although it's only *one* inanimate object, I can't help **entreating** it to come back to me.

[7 STROKES   RANK 312]

558 球 球 **ball, sphere** ▮ king 11 ▮ request, entreat 557   qiú

The entire **globe** is ruled by the great *king* (or so he thinks). That means that any *request* he makes instantly gets carried out. He's having a **ball**!

[11 STROKES   RANK 628]

559 范 范 **pattern, model, example**

▭ grass r 94 ▮ water r 523 ▮ single ear 157 (altered)   fàn

BF The most famous *one-eared* painter of all time is Vincent van Gogh, who sliced one off in a fit of pique. And yet, even today, his techniques continue to inspire; he is a powerful role **model**. His colored areas, in which bits of colored *grass* swirl in *water* backgrounds, radiate bursts of energy.

[8 STROKES   RANK 705]

560 永 永 **forever, always** ▮ water 545 (altered) ▯ dab 169   yǒn

The marooned desert traveler could live **forever**, if only he had a *bit* of *water*.   [5 STROKES   RANK 842]

561 渔 渔 **fisherman** ▮ water r 523 ▮ fish 485   yú

A **fisherman** is a person who removes *fish* from the *water*.

[11 STROKES   RANK 1770]

562 污 污　**dirty, filthy, foul**　　■ water r 523　■ hand 27 (altered)　wū
BF Use *water* to wash your *hand* of dirt. Your *hand* is covered in so much
filth that its shape is distorted.　　　　　　　[6 STROKES　RANK 1405]

563 黎 黎　black, dark
　　　　　■ advantage, benefit 417　■ enter, receive, take in 482　■ water 545　lí
BF Is there an *advantage* to storing things that have *been placed in* buckets
of *water*? Probably not—the *water* provides a natural habitat for slime, crud,
and other unmentionables, so the result is a **black** and **dark** mess.
　　　　　　　　　　　　　　　　　　　　　[15 STROKES　RANK 1476]

564 滑 滑　**slippery, smooth, cunning**　　■ water r 523　■ bone 488　huá
The *bone* is very rough. If we dip it in *water*, it feels much **smoother**, at least
until the *water* dries.　　　　　　　　　[12 STROKES　RANK 1480]

565 沓 沓　**numerous, repeated**　　　■ water 545　■ speak 64　tà
BF The **repeated** gurgling sound in swift streams is like the *speech* of *water*.
　　　　　　　　　　　　　　　　　　　　　[8 STROKES　RANK 3806]

566 沃 沃　**fertile, rich**　　　■ water r 523　■ dab 169　■ big 330　wò
BF Crops that are *little* grow *big* with the addition of *water* which enhances
the natural **fertility** of the soil.　　　　　[7 STROKES　RANK 1808]

567 溃 溃　**burst, break through**　　■ water r 523　■ expensive 437　kuì
BF The raging *water* attacked the *expensive* seawall with gusto, finally **breaking through** with no care for the money involved.　　[12 STROKES　RANK 1916]

568 剥 剥　**to peel, shell, skin**　　■ record, write down 549　■ knife r 166　bāo
In medieval times, parchment was too valuable to discard after use. Instead,
scripes would **peel** away with a *knife* what had been *written down* to create
new writing space.　　　　　　　　　　　　[10 STROKES　RANK 1959]

569 ⟍ ⟍ **ice r**

CMP Drop a stone onto a block of ice. Not much happens, but if it's a heavy rock, some chips of ice may fly away. Here you see two.

570 冲 冲 **pour boiling water on** ▮ ice r 569 ▮▮ middle 45 chō

You can see foggy clouds of vapor above blocks of ice and steamy clouds near boiling water, which (perhaps) explains the connection between 'ice' and 'boiling water'. Were you to **pour a stream of boiling water** it would pass through the *middle* of a block of *ice*.   [6 STROKES RANK 702]

Unit 26

Fame and Fortune

571 决 决 **decide** ◧ ice r 569 ◨ surprised man 518 jué
The *man was surprised* by the amount of winter *ice* in New York City. This is not for him—he has **decided** to move to a warmer climate, and he'll be on the next plane to California. [6 STROKES RANK 273]

572 况 况 **situation** ◧ ice r 569 ◨ elder brother* 298 kuàng
BF We have a **situation** here. A piece of *ice* cut my *elder brother* in the head—you can see the two streams of blood running down his head.
[7 STROKES RANK 419]

573 减 减 **lower, reduce** ◧ ice r 569 ◨ salty 371 jiǎn
If you add *salt* to *ice*, you **reduce** the slipperiness of the mixture (at least you do after the ice melts). [11 STROKES RANK 857]

574 次 次 **time, occurrence** ◧ ice r 569 ◨ owe, lack 465 cì
I don't know about you, but on the *ice* I definitely *lack* stature. I fall several **times** while struggling to return to the safety and stability of solid ground.
[6 STROKES RANK 183]

575 茨 茨 **thatch** ⬒ grass r 94 ⬓ time, occurrence 574 cí
BF Any time a mouse falls from the ceiling and lands in the soup, it's *time* to replace the *grass* and straw in a **thatched** roof. [9 STROKES RANK 1936]

576 资 资 **money, expenses** ▢ time, occurrence 574 ■ cowrie 430 zī

BF Each *time* we get some *money*, we use it to pay off **expenses**.

[10 STROKES RANK 257]

577 冰 冰 **ice** ▢ ice r 569 ■ water 545 bīn

Well, what is there to say—when you add *ice* to *water* you get **ice**.

[6 STROKES RANK 1070]

578 净 净 **clean, net (price)** ▢ ice r 569 ▢ struggle 463 jìng

BF It's hard to keep **clean** in the winter. The water turns to *ice*, and the bitter cold makes simple washing a constant *struggle*.

[8 STROKES RANK 1377]

579 盗 盗 **steal, rob** ▢ time, occurrence 574 ▢ vessel, dish 110 dào

BF Each *time* I take a cookie from the cookie *jar*, I feel like I'm **robbing** my siblings.

[11 STROKES RANK 1619]

580 女 女 **standing woman**

CMP To me, this character signifies the nurturing that **women** seem best at. Arms outstretched in a protective manner, full-figured body, this is the essence of womanhood.

581 女 女 **woman** ■ standing woman 580 nǔ

[3 STROKES RANK 224]

582 娃 娃 **baby** ▢ woman 581 ▢ jade tablet 14 wá

BF The *woman*'s new *jade brooch* is the most beautiful, most expensive gift she's ever received. She can't keep her hands off it, and treats it like her **baby**.

[9 STROKES RANK 1833]

583 奸 奸 **evil, treacherous**   ▉ woman 581   ▉ dry 10   jiān

The **evil** scientist sent a heat ray to *dry* out the *woman's* cosmetics and
ointments. How **treacherous!**   [6 STROKES   RANK 1992]

584 妇 妇 **woman***   ▉ woman 581   ▉ boar's head 34   fù

BF In those ancient, benighted times, the prototypical *woman's* task was that
of sweeping the floor with *boar's head* bristles. Under this (outmoded) logic,
this was a perfect symbol for **woman.**   [6 STROKES   RANK 932]

585 如 如 **be like**   ▉ woman 581   ▉ enclosure 40   rú

A *woman* **is like** an *enclosure* in that she is the repository of so many sterling
characteristics.   [6 STROKES   RANK 67]

586 姑 姑 **paternal aunt**   ▉ woman 581   ▉ ancient 51   gū

BF That *ancient woman* is my dad's sister, my **paternal aunt.**

[8 STROKES   RANK 994]

587 姓 姓 **family name**   ▉ woman 581   ▉ give birth to 191   xìng

As soon as a *woman gives birth to* her child, it receives the **family name.**

[8 STROKES   RANK 1149]

588 妖 妖 **goblin, demon**   ▉ woman 581   ☐ dab 169   ▉ big 330   yāo

BF (Note well: the right component is *not* 'heaven' from §333. The top horizontal is a 'dab', not a bar.)   Look at that supernatural *woman!* She has
the power to make herself very *small* or super *large*.   She must be a **demon!**   [7 STROKES   RANK 1869]

589 姐 姐 **older sister**   ▉ woman 581   ▉ moreover 15   jiě

Here, the '*moreover*' component looks like a high stool, perfect for the *woman*
who's our **elder sister** who supervises when Ma's not home.

[8 STROKES   RANK 830]

590 要 要 **want, wish, request**   ▭ west 291 (altered)   ◼ woman 581   yào
'*West*' (where the sun sets) is a symbol of evening. Then, the working day is over, and this *woman* enjoys a quiet evening catering to her own **wishes**.

[9 STROKES   RANK 26]

591 耍 耍 **play (a role, tricks)**
▭ express add'l but contrasting info 83   ◼ woman 581   shu
The ancients considered the upper component to resemble a beard. A beard on a *woman*—talk about *contrasting information*! Obviously, she's **playing a role**.   [9 STROKES   RANK 2260]

592 妹 妹 **younger sister**   ◫ woman 581   ◫ have not yet 381   mè
BF We often picture a **younger sister** as a person who *has not yet* grown up to be a *woman*.   [8 STROKES   RANK 1185]

593 委 委 **listless, dejected**   ◼ rice or grain 409   ◼ woman 581   wě
BF The load of *grain* on this poor *woman*'s back is more than she can bear. No wonder she appears **listless** and **dejected**.   [8 STROKES   RANK 457]

594 矮 矮 **short of stature**   ◫ arrow 334   ◫ listless, dejected 593   ǎi
William Tell shot an *arrow* at the apple on his son's head, a duty imposed on him by the evil governor, and a task which made Tell very nervous and *dejected*. As every schoolboy knows, the child lived, partly because his **short stature** made the shot easier for his dad.   [13 STROKES   RANK 2027]

595 她 她 she   ◫ woman 581   ◫ also*, too* 140   tā
Human beings are human precisely because each one of us stores all our different traits in a single body, a single container, as it were. In this case we concentrate on one *woman*. **She** can be clever but *also* dumb, considerate but *also* selfish, outgoing but *also* shy, and so on and so on.   [6 STROKES   RANK 91]

596 母 母 **mother**   ■ woman 581 (altered)   ▣ two breasts   mǔ

BF A sketch of a *woman* which emphasizes her *two breasts* draws attention to her **motherly** qualities.   [5 STROKES   RANK 565]

Unit 27

Saving Face

597 舟 舟 **boat, ship** ⬚ dab 169 ■ mother 596 (altered) zhō

  1 The two dabs represent passengers crammed into this dugout, both manning the horizontal oar between them. In the interests of calligraphy, but not of seamanship, the south end seems to be left open to the elements!

  2 *Mothers* protect you from the evils of the world when you are *little*; **boats** protect you from the bruises and mishaps of the river.

[6 STROKES RANK 2224]

598 姿 姿 **looks, appearance** ▭ time, occurrence 574 ■ woman 581 zī

BF Each *time* a *woman* makes an **appearance**, she impresses the world with her grace, poise, bearing, and beauty. [9 STROKES RANK 1899]

599 姆 姆 **mother, nursemaid** ▊ woman 581 ▊ mother 596 mǔ

BF A *woman* acting like a *mother* is a **nursemaid**. [8 STROKES RANK 1061]

600 每 每 **every** ▬ man 311 (altered) ■ mother 596 měi

A *man* and his *mother* can do any and **every**thing, at least according to the mother. [7 STROKES RANK 359]

601 海 海 **sea** ▊ water r 523 ▊ every 600 hǎi

Every kind of *water*, from every part of the globe, empties into the **sea**.

[10 STROKES RANK 189]

602 梅 梅 plum flower or tree　　◼ tree 375　◻ every 600　　méi

The **plum** tree is a favorite one among the Chinese. It is thought that this *tree* encompasses within it *every* kind of arboreal virtue.　　[11 STROKES　RANK 1159]

603 嫌 嫌 dislike, mind　　◼ woman 581　◻ double, twice 470　　xián

If *two* people in a room **dislike** each other, the best way to calm things down is to send in a *woman* as mediator.　　[13 STROKES　RANK 1826]

604 安 安 rest content　　◻ roof 247　◼ woman 581　　ān

The essence of **resting content** is a house (whose *roof* is all we can see here) in which the *woman* of the house maintains order and calmness.

[6 STROKES　RANK 232]

605 案 案 record, file, law case　　◻ rest content 604　◼ tree 375　　àn

BF I *rest content* on the top of the tallest *tree* around, quietly **recording** the day's events in my diary. Meanwhile, some of my ex-students are **filing** down the base of the tree. Sooner or later I'm in for a nasty fall!

[10 STROKES　RANK 518]

606 按 按 press, push down, according to

◼ hand r 29　◼ rest content 604　　àn

It's a family gathering, and things are a little excited around now. **In accordance with** his standing as head of family, he uses his *hand* to make sure we all *rest content*.　　[9 STROKES　RANK 573]

607 威 威 power, might　　◼ archaic lance 367　▫ one 2　◼ woman 581　　wēi

BF Think of a legendary Amazon warrior as an example of a **powerful** and **mighty** person. *One woman* equipped with a powerful *archaic lance* is a force to reckon with.　　[9 STROKES　RANK 622]

608 舰 舰 **warship, naval vessel**   ▦ boat, ship 597   ▦ see 301   jiàr

Warships are always big and imposing. The idea is to scare your opponents when they *see* this scary *boat*. Maybe they can avoid battle altogether.

[10 STROKES   RANK 851]

609 毒 毒 **poison**   ▦ plentiful 12 (altered)   ▦ mother 596   dú

Ever hear of toxic *mother* syndrome? *Too much* of a *mother's* attentions can **poison** her child's existence.   [9 STROKES   RANK 947]

610 盘 盘 **dish, current market price**

▦ boat, ship 597   ▦ vessel, dish 110   pár

How do we get the picky child to eat? He is transfixed by the toy *boat* sailing in the *vessel* of cereal, and he eats! From now on, that's how I'll always envision a **dish**.   [11 STROKES   RANK 1049]

611 媒 媒 **matchmaker, go-between**

▦ woman 581   ▦ certain, some 397   mé*

BF The **matchmaker** traditionally matches a young *woman* with a very special *certain* someone.   [12 STROKES   RANK 1506]

612 ⺕ ⺕ **broom-like thing**

CMP We've seen broom-like things before (such as §§34 and 35), but this specially has a vertical handle to make the sweeping as ergonomic and easy as possible.

613 妻 妻 **wife**   ▦ broom-like thing 612   ▦ woman 581   qī

BF This character reflects the traditional view of a **wife** as a *woman* pushing a *broom*. With time, these traditional views will wither.

[8 STROKES   RANK 1076]

614 凄 凄 **chilly, sad**   ▌ ice r 569   ▌ wife 613   qī

BF Nothing is **chillier** (or **sadder**) than a sour marriage, the *wife* gone *icy* to her husband, and vice versa.   [10 STROKES   RANK 2352]

615 讠 讠 **speech r**

CMP This component refers to §270. As a radical in another character, it appears in this form.

616 计 计 **compute, calculate**   ▌ speech r 615   ▌ ten 6   jì

The act of *speaking* numbers to *ten* is a primitive form of **calculation**.   [4 STROKES   RANK 251]

617 订 订 **draw up, agree on**   ▌ speech r 615   ▌ fourth 25   dìng

The purpose of making a *speech* about issues that are put forth (sounds like *fourth*, get it?) on the table is to come to some sort of **agreement**. The form of '*fourth*' reminds me of a table-like platform.   [4 STROKES   RANK 1176]

618 语 语 **language**   ▌ speech r 615   ▌ me 81   yǔ

BF *My speech* is in *my* own native **language**.   [9 STROKES   RANK 493]

619 词 词 **word, term**   ▌ speech r 615   ▌ company 112   cí

A *company speech* often uses special **words** and **terms** that only other insiders understand.   [7 STROKES   RANK 959]

620 让 让 **allow**   ▌ speech r 615   ▌ on 175   ràng

If you **allow** someone to do something, it's because they made a convincing *speech* to you, and now the activity is *on*!   [5 STROKES   RANK 339]

621 诉 诉 **tell, relate**   ▌ speech r 615   ▌ scold, reprimand 177   sù

BF When we start **telling** stuff to our families, it often degenerates into a *speech* of *reprimand*.   [7 STROKES   RANK 595]

622 证　证　evidence, proof　　　■ speech r 615　■ correct 183　zh(

BF In those far-off days before forensic science and *CSI*, courtroom **evidence** often took the form of a *speech* by a reputed citizen giving their version of what was *correct*.　　　　　　　　　　　　　[7 STROKES　RANK 373]

Unit 28

Dogs and Cats

623 许 许 **allow, permit** ▮ speech r 615 ▮ noonish 188 xǔ
Authorities only **allow** political wannabees to stand up and make *speeches* at *noontime*. [6 STROKES RANK 263]

624 讨 讨 **discuss, study** ▮ speech r 615 ▮ inch 210 tǎo
The '*inch*' component derives from a truncated hand. Take note of your next animated **discussion**. I think you'll find that your *speech* is accompanied by lively *hand* motions as well. [5 STROKES RANK 833]

625 诗 诗 **poem, poetry** ▮ speech r 615 ▮ Buddhist temple 213 shī
Think of *Buddhist temples* as places so special that ordinary *speech* is simply inadequate. Devotees express themselves using inspired **poetry** instead. [8 STROKES RANK 906]

626 话 话 **dialect, vernacular** ▮ speech r 615 ▮ tongue 225 huà
The kind of *speech* that I really wrap my *tongue* around is my local **dialect**. [8 STROKES RANK 170]

627 认 认 **recognize, know** ▮ speech r 615 ▮ man 311 rèn
You **recognize** a *man* by his *speech*. [4 STROKES RANK 213]

628 误 误 **miss (due to delay)** ▮ speech r 615 ▮ Kingdom of Wu 336   wù
We were all enthralled by his *speech*, which seemed to proceed directly from his mouth and fly directly to heaven. '*Kingdom of Wu*' itself uses *mouth* and *heaven* (§§41 and 333). Alas, we were so engrossed we **missed** the last bus home!   [9 STROKES   RANK 854]

629 试 试 **test, try** ▮ speech r 615 ▮ model, standard 357   shì
He's **trying** like crazy to learn Mandarin Chinese, but every time he puts into *speech* the language *models* and pattern he's practiced, his Chinese friends break into hysterical laughter!   [8 STROKES   RANK 643]

630 诚 诚 **honest, sincere** ▮ speech r 615 ▮ become, turn into 368   ché
BF We all enjoy listening to people who are **honest** and **sincere** make *speeches*. Just by listening, we *become* uplifted.   [8 STROKES   RANK 1154]

631 谓 谓 **say, be called** ▮ speech r 615 ▮ stomach 461   wè
BF Perhaps those ancient scribes did have senses of humor. If so, we can imagine that the *speech*-like rumblings of a full *stomach* simulated **talking** and **calling**.   [11 STROKES   RANK 945]

632 论 论 **discuss, talk** ▮ speech r 615 ▮ order, coherence 457   lùn
People will lose patience with you and won't **talk** to you unless your *speech* possesses *coherence*.   [6 STROKES   RANK 205]

633 读 读 **read aloud, attend school** ▮ speech r 615 ▮ sell 341   dú
I'm a salesman. The quality of my *speech* is important, for the money I make from *selling* my product is for **going to college**.   [10 STROKES   RANK 752]

634 谋 谋 **work for, seek** ▮ speech r 615 ▮ certain, some 397   mó
Some politicians, such as President Bill Clinton, instinctively know how to best **work for** their goals. Without conscious thought, the *speech* they use is *certain* to convince their antagonists.   [11 STROKES   RANK 989]

635 课 课 **subject, course, class**   ▮ speech r 615   ▮ fruit 388   kè

Speeches directed at students produce *fruitful* results—this is an optimist's definition of a **course or class**. A more cynical observer regards it as a place where the stench of the lectures of hidebound professors land on student desks like masses of rotten *fruit*. What's your opinion?   [10 STROKES   RANK 1208]

636 勹 勹 **wrap**

CMP

1 See how the latch at the upper left of the radical has come undone? Place your stuff inside the strap and fix the latch—it's a **wrap**!
2 A person is bending over something, getting it ready for transport by **wrapping** it up.

637 匀 匀 **evenly divided**   ▮ wrap 636   ▮ two 3 (altered)   yún

BF A bundle, all *wrapped* up, is **evenly divided** into *two* parts.

[4 STROKES   RANK 2692]

638 均 均 **equal, even**   ▮ earth, soil 9   ▮ evenly divided 637   jūn

BF If you place seed in the *soil* in *evenly divided* groups, then the crop grows to the same **equal** height, more or less.   [7 STROKES   RANK 903]

639 句 句 **sentence**   ▮ wrap 636   ▮ mouth 41   jù

BF Your *mouth* produces words; by extension, one mouth represents a sequence of words. If you can *wrap* them up in grammatical and syntactical wrapping paper, you have a **sentence**.   [5 STROKES   RANK 707]

640 旬 旬 **period of 10 days, years**   ▮ wrap 636   ▮ day, sun 63   xún

BF '*Sun*' is a metaphor for a period of time, often a day. One such period of time gets *wrapped up* in one character. The period in question can refer either to ten days or ten years.   [6 STROKES   RANK 2332]

641 询 询 inquire   ■ speech r 615   ■ period of 10 days, years 640   xú▮

BF Listen to that pompous old fool **inquire** about the weather! He can't even do so clearly and directly. Rather, he views it a chance to make an annoying *speech*, so boring that it seems to last *ten days*!   [8 STROKES   RANK 1617]

642 勺 勺 spoon   ■ wrap 636   ■ dab 169   sha

BF The '*wrapper*' is really a distorted **spoon**. The latch of the wrapper is really an abbreviated handle, and the bowl-part has been emphasized in order to emphasize the spoon's contents—only a *drop* of Grandma's chicken soup is left.   [3 STROKES   RANK 3275]

643 的 的 of   ■ white 201   ■ spoon 642   de

'Of' appears in quotes, because this is a grossly simplified summary of the role that 的 plays in Chinese grammar. Perhaps the easiest way to remember this character is to squint somewhat at the components, and so observe that they form a stylized spelling of **de** using English letters. Anyway, this glyph occurs so often—no character is more frequent—you'll soon learn it regardless.

   [8 STROKES   RANK 1]

644 丐 丐 beg   ■ under 176   ■ wrap 636   gài

Those who **beg** are sometimes quite successful at their trade. You might never know it—after all, they keep their gains securely *under wraps*, under their tattered clothes.   [4 STROKES   RANK 2606]

645 与 与 give**   ■ spoon 642 (altered)   ▢ one 2   yǔ

Use *one spoon* to **give** a child their medicine.   [3 STROKES   RANK 108]

646 写 写 write   ▢ smooth cover 280   ■ give** 645   xiě

It's pouring rain. I **write** you a tender note, and as I *give* it to you, I *cover* it to protect it from the downpour.   [5 STROKES   RANK 448]

647 曷 曷 **how, why, when**   ▬ speech 270   ▬ beg 644 (altered)   hé

The *speech* of *beggars* can be wildly inventive, depending on the nature and credulity of their 'client'. Questions involving **how, why, and when** naturally flow out of their mouths.

  We'll use this component to represent a multitude of causes or sources.

[9 STROKES   RANK 5256]

648 揭 揭 **tear off, take off**   ▮ hand r 29   ▯ how, why, when 647   jiē

The '*how, why, when*' component looks like an ornate bottle, and the 'sun' at the top is a cork stuffed in to keep the many ingredients from evaporating. But someone's *hand* is at this cork, ready to **tear it off**.   [12 STROKES   RANK 1666]

Unit 29

Doing Something About the Weather

649 喝 喝 **to drink** ☐ mouth 41 ▮ how, why, when 647 hē
I need a **drink**. I love to pour the liquid through my *mouth*, and I don't care
how, why, or when I get it. [12 STROKES   RANK 983]

650 葛 葛 **kudzu vine** ☐ grass r 94 ▮ how, why, when 647 gé
Kudzu is the vine that devoured the American South. A voracious *grass*-like
plant that grows like lightning, so quickly you can't even begin to figure out
how, why, or *when* it managed to devour your entire garden.
[12 STROKES   RANK 1919]

651 渴 渴 **thirsty** ▮ water r 523 ▮ how, why, when 647 kě
All that ice cold *water*, splishing and splashing *all over the place* drives me
mad with **thirst**. [12 STROKES   RANK 1972]

652 歇 歇 **have a rest** ▮ how, why, when 647 ☐ owe, lack 465 xiē
How am I ever going to pay all my bills? *When* will I have enough money?
I *owe* so much! I need to **take a rest** before getting back to my accounts.
[13 STROKES   RANK 1828]

653 苟 苟 **thoughtless, careless** ☐ grass r 94 ▮ sentence 639 gǒu
BF After they mockingly flung *grass* clippings at me, the *sentences* that escaped
from my mouth made me blush later on. How **thoughtless** to let myself get
carried away! [8 STROKES   RANK 2886]

654 夕 夕   **romantic evening**

CMP Salute the appearance of the crescent moon with the advent of a **romantic evening.**

655 夕 夕   **evening, dusk**   ■ romantic evening 654 (altered)   xī
[3 STROKES   RANK 2003]

656 多 多   **many, much**   ■ evening, dusk (times 2) 655   duō

This character is especially useful. It suggests **many** as in the phrase 'many moons', 'many nights'. But it also suggests the passage of time, **much** time, *evening* upon *evening.*   [6 STROKES   RANK 61]

657 歹 歹   **evil, vicious**   ☐ one 2   ■ evening, dusk 655   dǎi

BF What does *one* need the cover of *dusk* for? Can't be good—must be something **evil** and **vicious.**   [4 STROKES   RANK 2905]

658 殖 殖   **propagate**   ▮ evil, vicious 657   ▯ straight, vertical 16   zhí

BF Winter is a necessary *evil*, killing plants but sparing their seeds. The seeds drop to the ground, and next spring sprout *straight* and tall, thereby **propagating** the species.   [12 STROKES   RANK 1438]

659 列 列   **arrange, line up**   ▮ evil, vicious 657   ▯ knife r 166   liè

The *evil* mugger used his *knife* to force the group of rock stars to **line up** for easy pickings.   [6 STROKES   RANK 500]

660 歼 歼   **annihilate**   ▮ evil, vicious 657   ▯ thousand 224   jiān

BF If you magnify *evil* thoughts by a *thousand*, you have the power to **annihilate** your enemies.   [7 STROKES   RANK 1815]

661 名 名　**personal name**　　■ evening, dusk 655　■ mouth 41　mí

BF In the *evening*, it's hard to see who's there. You use your *mouth* to identify yourself, which is the purpose of a **personal name**.　[6 STROKES RANK 203]

662 岁 岁　**years old**　　□ mountain 21　■ evening, dusk 655　suì

BF A young, strong person is mighty as a *mountain*. Gradually, they wind down until, in the *evening* of their life they are a shadow of their former selves. How do we measure this unfortunate transformation? Using their **years of age**.　[6 STROKES RANK 772]

663 罗 罗　**catch birds with a net**　　□ net r 107　■ evening, dusk 655　luó

BF What's the best way **to catch birds**? It's hard no matter how, but you increase the odds by using a *net* and waiting till *evening* when they rest, so they can't see you.　[8 STROKES RANK 392]

664 外 外　**outside, external**　　■ evening, dusk 655　■ foretell 170　wà

BF The day is pretty much done by *evening* time. To learn what's **outside** this time frame, we need a magic wand to *foretell* the future (or, we could just wait till tomorrow!).　[5 STROKES RANK 131]

665 够 够　**be enough**　　■ sentence 639　■ many, much 656　gòu

Many sentences are **enough** to get any point across.　[11 STROKES RANK 538]

666 残 残　**incomplete, deficient**　　■ evil, vicious 657　■ tiny, fragmentary 373　cán

BF When great *evil* is *fragmented* by the forces of good, the villain's plans become **deficient**.　[9 STROKES RANK 1150]

667 死 死　**die, pass away**　■ evil, vicious 657 (altered)　■ ancient ladle 142　sǐ

A great *evil* has befallen our leader, who has fallen down. That's him, upside-down, looking like a bent *spoon*. As a result, he **died**.　[6 STROKES RANK 317]

668 梦 梦 **dream**   ☐ forest 376   ■ evening, dusk 655 (altered)   mèng

Wandering in the *forest* at *evening* is scary. Things that look normal at noon take on an odd aspect when the light disappears. It's a nightmare **dream**scape.   [11 STROKES   RANK 865]

669 移 移 **change, alter**   ▌ rice or grain 409   ▐ many, much 656   yí

The great thing about *rice* and other *grains* is that there are *many* ways to **change** or **alter** them into good stuff to eat—flour, bread, cake, wraps, and so on.   [11 STROKES   RANK 880]

670 殊 殊 **different, special**   ▌ evil, vicious 657   ▐ vermilion 379   shū

BF The serial killer was nasty. His *evil* acts were always as *vermilion* bloody as possible, so everyone would know how **different** and **special** he was.

[10 STROKES   RANK 1191]

671 厂 厂 **cliff r**

CMP The cutaway section of a **cliff** looks just like this.

672 厂 厂 **factory**   ■ cliff r 671   chǎng

Imagine working in a nineteenth century **factory**—long hours, demeaning work, and negligible pay. Desperate workers climbed to the roof, and flung themselves off this man-made *cliff*.   [2 STROKES   RANK 963]

673 厅 厅 **public rooms, hall**   ☐ cliff r 671   ■ fourth 25   tīng

BF Here's a recurring dream sequence. I envision a high *cliff* into which are carved many rooms. Each room I enter is bigger and more magnificent than the one before it. Finally, the *fourth* one I enter is a vast **reception hall**, similar in size to the Rotunda in the U.S. Capitol building.   [4 STROKES   RANK 1217]

674 压 压 **press down**   ☐ cliff r 671   ■ earth, soil 9   ▪ dab 169   yā

Down from the top of the *cliff* comes a huge load of *earth* landing with a thud on the *little* guy who happened to be in the wrong place at the wrong time. The fallen earth **presses down down** on him, forever.   [6 STROKES   RANK 756]

Unit 30

One Door Closes, Another Opens

675 厌 厌 **loathe, detest** ☐ cliff r 671 ◼ dog 332 yài

BF Towards the end of his life, the rich old man grew to **detest** the entire world. He shuttered himself in a fortress-like mansion atop a *cliff*, and vicious *dogs* guarded the premises. [6 STROKES RANK 1633]

676 原 原 **original, unprocessed**

☐ cliff r 671 ◼ spring, fountain 555 (altered) yuá

BF Another image: an untouched mountain *spring*, gracefully jetting off some *cliff*, powerfully suggests something primeval, untouched, and **original** to nature. [10 STROKES RANK 193]

677 源 源 **source of river, fountainhead**

◼ water r 523 ◼ original, unprocessed 676 yuá

BF The **source of a river** is the part of the *waters* that is *original*. [13 STROKES RANK 670]

678 厉 厉 **harsh, severe, serious** ☐ cliff r 671 ◼ ten thousand 472 lì

BF As an example to the troops, the deserter was given a **harsh** and **severe** punishment. From the height of the *cliff*, in plain view of all other troops, he was given *ten thousand* lashes. [5 STROKES RANK 1339]

679 屵 屵 **high cliff** ☐ mountain 21 ◼ cliff r 671

CMP The *mountain* on top of the *cliff* emphasizes that it is a **high cliff**. This component is actually an extremely rare character, pronounced 'nàn'.

680 岸 岸 shore, coast   ▣ high cliff 679 ▣ dry 10   àn
High cliffs occur most often at the **shore**. The *dry part* next to the water is the **shore**.   [8 STROKES RANK 971]

681 广 广 shelter r   ▣ cliff r 671 ▢ dab 169
CMP *Cliffs* are so large and threatening. Here's a *little one*—quite cozy, really. Hollow out a little cave and crawl right in for instant **shelter**.

682 扩 扩 enlarge   ▣ hand r 29 ▣ shelter r 681   kuò
BF Why would you have a worker's *hands* toiling on our *house*? Most likely, it's to **enlarge** it.   [6 STROKES RANK 1051]

683 庙 庙 temple   ▣ shelter r 681 ▣ let sb do sth 48   miào
A **temple** provides a special kind of *shelter*. Even though there are strict codes of conduct, being there is such an uplifting and enlightening experience, that it feels like *you can do whatever you want*.   [8 STROKES RANK 1889]

684 店 店 shop   ▣ shelter r 681 ▣ practice divination 172   diàn
Originally, a **shop** was a special *shelter* for shamans and such to *practice divination*. Bit by bit, the fortuneteller or proprietor would supplement their income by furnishing tangible items people needed, until finally this purpose overshadowed the original one.   [8 STROKES RANK 1041]

685 庆 庆 celebrate   ▣ shelter r 681 ▣ big 330   qìng
BF Why this sudden need for a *big house*? We need the space for a lot of people. Everyone's coming to **celebrate**!

The sole difference between 厌 'loathe' (§675) and this character 庆 'celebrate' is the placement of the little 'dab' dot. In 'celebrate', the dot is nearer heaven, because celebration is a heavenly thing to do.

[6 STROKES RANK 1269]

686 广 广　**extensive**　　　　　　　■ shelter r 681　guǎ

The good thing about proper *shelter* is that it makes you feel protected against the elements. The mangiest, crumbiest cave feels like like an **extensive** castle to a person in need.　　　　　　　[3 STROKES　RANK 468]

687 庄 庄　**village**　　　■ extensive 686　■ earth, soil 9　zhu

BF It's not the houses that make a **village** a **village**, but how close to or spread out from each other they are. When houses are spread out *extensively* over the *earth*, we say we have a **village**.　　　[6 STROKES　RANK 1024]

688 座 座　**seat**　　　■ extensive 686　■ sit 321　zuò

An *extensive* bunch of people *sitting* in the same place—well, that must be a **seat**.　　　　　　　[10 STROKES　RANK 812]

689 庚 庚　**age**　　　■ extensive 686　■ big 330　■ man (spiffy) 337　gēn

Under the '*extensive*' part, '*big*' and '*man*' are superimposed. A small vertical stroke ties them together.

The *man* has finally reached sufficient *maturity* (='*big*' in Chinese) to go forth and perform *extensive* achievements. This is a fine symbol for one's chronological **age**.　　　　　　[8 STROKES　RANK 3072]

690 唐 唐　**Tang dynasty**　　　■ age 689 (altered)　■ mouth 41 (altered)　táng

The great **Tang dynasty** was a high point of Chinese civilization. The hallmark of this great *age* was the *verbal* arts, particularly poetry.

[10 STROKES　RANK 973]

691 廉 廉　**honest and upright**　　　■ shelter r 681　■ double, twice 470　lián

BF This contractor is one of the most **honest** workmen I've ever met. The *house* he built for us is super-strong because he *doubly* reinforced all the supports.　　　　　　[13 STROKES　RANK 1818]

692 康　康　healthy, peaceful, abundant

■ Tang dynasty 690 (altered)　■ water 545　　kāng

BF Under the enlightened rule of the *Tang dynasty*, throughout the land and even across the *water*, there was **abundant peace** and **health**.

[11 STROKES　RANK 900]

693 床　床　bed　　　　　　　■ shelter r 681　■ tree 375　　chuáng

People lay the mattress of their **bed** on a *wooden* frame inside their *shelter*.

[7 STROKES　RANK 1068]

694 麻　麻　hemp, pocked, pitted　　　■ shelter r 681　■ forest 376　　má

In a drying *shed* we dry raw fibers, a *forest* of them. The end product is flax and **hemp** we can spin into clothes.　　　[11 STROKES　RANK 1108]

695 摩　摩　rub　　　　■ hemp, pocked, pitted 694 (altered)　■ hand 27　　mó

BF Put that *hempen* glove on your *hand* and please **rub** my back! How soothing—and it scratches my back nicely, too.　　[15 STROKES　RANK 1162]

696 嘛　嘛　particle of persuasion

■ mouth 41　■ hemp, pocked, pitted 694　　ma

As is often true, '*mouth*' indicates a particle. The shy teen with the *pocked skin* problem needs more than a **particle of persuasion** to come along to the party.　　　　　　　　　[14 STROKES　RANK 1628]

697 疒　疒　sick　　　　　■ expelled matter　■ shelter r 681

CMP A **sick** person resting *at home* is in extremis, coughing, sneezing, *vomiting*, and what not.

698 癌 癌 **cancer**   ☐ sick 697   ■ product 44   ☐ mountain 21   ái

The beloved mother has become *sick*. The *three mouths* symbolize how closely her family huddles together for support. But they have a *mountain* of trouble to contend with, and are going to need a *mountain* of medical *products* before they're through, for the news is not good—it's **cancer**.

[17 STROKES   RANK 1799]

699 症 症 **disease**   ☐ sick 697   ■ correct 183   zh

BF Someone gets *sick*. With the *correct* diagnosis, we can identify the **disease** and prescribe proper treatment.   [10 STROKES   RANK 1258]

700 疾 疾 **disease***   ☐ sick 697   ■ arrow 334   jí

BF Perhaps for the ancient scribes, **disease** seemed to them to be like a dart or *arrow* which appeared from nowhere to strike you *sick* when you least expected it.   [10 STROKES   RANK 1273]

Unit 31

Four Legs Good, Two Legs Better

701 病 病 **disease, fall sick** ☐ sick 697 ◼ third in series 474   **bìng**
This is the *third* time this man has gotten *sick* in two weeks. Some chronic **disease** has gotten hold of him.   [10 STROKES RANK 427]

702 尸 尸 **dead body** ◼ enclosure 40 (altered)
CMP The *enclosure*-like bit at the top is the **body**, lying cold and **dead** on the bed. How can you tell it's dead? See the hand hanging down, extended at an unnatural angle.

703 尸 尸 **corpse** ◼ dead body 702 (altered)   **shī**
                                        [3 STROKES RANK 1517]

704 尺 尺 **ruler** ☐ corpse 703 ◼ measurement   **chǐ**
A popular notion in the old days—perhaps even now—is that a natural harmony exists between the dimensions of a human body. Here, we see a *measurement* made on a cooperative *corpse* in an effort to perform an analysis with a giant measuring device, a **ruler**.   [4 STROKES RANK 1474]

705 局 局 **bureau, office** ◼ ruler 704 (altered) ▣ mouth 41   **jú**
A government **office** is a place where far too many *rules* issue from the *mouths* of bureaucrats.   [7 STROKES RANK 483]

706 届 届 **a year's graduates** ☐ corpse 703 ◼ let sb do sth 48   **jiè**
At university, I worked so hard I thought I would become a *corpse*. Finally, *they let me* **graduate**.   [8 STROKES RANK 1522]

707 居 居 reside　　　　　　　　　　☐ corpse 703　◼ ancient 51　jū

The *ancient corpse* commands the respect of even the Communist officials, who will let it **reside** in its grave even though the prime location is needed for a party big-shot.　　　　　　　　　[8 STROKES   RANK 678]

708 据 据 occupy, seize　　　　　　　◼ hand r 29　☐ reside 707　jù

BF The *hand* represents the enemy occupier, come to your *residence* to **seize** the premises for themselves.　　　　　　　[11 STROKES   RANK 313]

709 剧 剧 play, drama　　　　　　　◼ reside 707　☐ knife r 166　jù

The set resembles the interior of a charming nineteenth century *residence*. A hooded figure silently enters from stage right, a wicked *knife* gleaming in the footlights. The **drama** begins, and the audience will be on the edge of their seats throughout!　　　　　　　　　[10 STROKES   RANK 909]

710 屈 屈 bend*　　　　　　　　　☐ corpse 703　◼ exit 22　qū

The *corpse* is being carried through the narrow *exit* to the hearse. (See how scrunched up the 'exit' appears in this character.) The person in life was quite fat, so it can't fit through the exit without **bending**.　[8 STROKES   RANK 1684]

711 刷 刷 brush, scrub　　☐ corpse 703　◼ towel 130　☐ knife r 166　shu

Corpse cleaning is a delicate art. The most important tools are *towels*, to **scrub** the corpse, and a *knife* to scrape off evidence of violence.
　　　　　　　　　[8 STROKES   RANK 1824]

712 卢 卢 gourd　　　　　　　　☐ foretell 170　◼ corpse 703　lú

BF With their eccentric, colorful, and entrancing appearance, **gourds** must have suggested themselves as aids to religious ceremonies. When dried and preserved, they represent the *corpses* of vegetables and can be used to *foretell* the future.　　　　　　　　[5 STROKES   RANK 1711]

713 尿 尿 urine   ☐ corpse 703   ☐ water 545   suī

With respect to medical matters, **urine** is a crucial bodily *fluid*. So much so, that if not eliminated pronto, the patient becomes a *corpse* in short order.

[7 STROKES   RANK 1877]

714 民 民 people, masses   ☐ ruler 704   ☐ one 2   mín

BF The **masses** usually find themselves serving *one ruler*.

[5 STROKES   RANK 113]

715 眠 眠 sleep, dormancy   ☐ eye 78   ☐ people, masses 714   mián

BF The *eyes* of the *people* never **sleep**!   [10 STROKES   RANK 1986]

716 尾 尾 tail   ☐ corpse 703   ☐ hair 231   wěi

The roadkill was the *corpse* of a fine raccoon. The body was left intact, but the wheels somehow stripped off all the fur, leaving *hair* only on its **tail**.   [7 STROKES   RANK 1282]

717 尼 尼 nun   ☐ corpse 703   ☐ ancient ladle 142   ní

BF Imagine that in ancient times, **nuns** prepared the *dead* for burial. Using *spoon*-like tools, they made the *corpses* appear as lifelike as possible as a service to the bereaved.   [5 STROKES   RANK 654]

718 呢 呢 particle with many uses   ☐ mouth 41   ☐ nun 717   ne

Nuns take vows of poverty, so the only thing they can own is a small and very special **particle with many uses**, sort of a multi-purpose tool. The '*mouth*' reminds us that particles originally served a purely verbal function.

[8 STROKES   RANK 383]

719 尽 尽 utmost, to the greatest extent   ☐ ruler 704   ☐ two 3   jǐn

The *two* marks beyond the end of the *ruler* emphasize our interest in things located **at the greatest extent**.   [6 STROKES   RANK 488]

720 泥 泥 **mud, clay**   ▮ water r 523   ▮ nun 717   ní
Because it was black, you couldn't tell the *nun*'s habit was plastered with dirt.
When she fell in the *water*, it formed a **muddy paste**.   [8 STROKES   RANK 1499]

721 尸 尸 **corpse with mark**   ▮ corpse 703   ▯ unexpected mark
CMP *Corpses* aren't always Hollywood clean and pretty. This one has an
unexpected mark.

722 声 声 **sound, voice**   ▮ scholar 8   ▮ corpse with mark 721   shē
Imagine a crazed *scholar* jumping down on a *corpse*, leaving a *mark*, and
forcing a bizarre **sound** to issue forth from the corpse's mouth.
    [7 STROKES   RANK 195]

723 眉 眉 **eyebrow**   ▮ corpse with mark 721   ▮ eye 78   méi
BF This *corpse* has been *marked* above the *eye*, to mark the location of the
eyebrow.   [9 STROKES   RANK 1460]

724 户 户 **door of house**   ▮ corpse 703   ▯ dab 169
CMP This component displays the left pane of a swinging **door**. The *bit* at the
top is the bolt in the hinge.

725 户 户 **door***   ▮ door of house 724   hù
Perhaps in some surreal Luis Buñuel-ian drama, someone uses a rigid *corpse*,
fastened on the floor and at the top, as the left-hand panel of a swinging
door.   [4 STROKES   RANK 801]

726 护 护 **protect**   ▮ hand r 29   ▮ door* 725   hù
BF The *door* **protects** the family against the thumping and knocking from the
hand of the crazed burglar.   [7 STROKES   RANK 529]

Unit 32

Let Your Fingers Do the Walking

727 启 启　**open up**　　　　☐ door* 725　■ mouth 41　　qǐ

BF *Doors* and *mouths* have one thing in common—they both **open up**.

[7 STROKES　RANK 1320]

728 扇 扇　**fan, leaf**　　　　☐ door* 725　■ feather, wing 123　　shàn

BF It's hot in China! As you enter through the *door*, the *feathers* of an old-fashioned hand-held **fan** provide some cooling relief.

[10 STROKES　RANK 1993]

729 扁 扁　**flat, crushed**　　　☐ door of house 724　■ book, booklet 134　　biǎn

The stupid contractor did such a poor job that one of the *doors* fell down on an old and valuable *book*, and **crushed** it to death!　[9 STROKES　RANK 1737]

730 篇 篇　**piece of writing**　　☐ bamboo r 243　■ flat, crushed 729　　piān

Although 'raw' *bamboo* appears naturally as rod-like giant stems, modern technology knows how to work it into *flat* forms, suitable for making floors and **writing surfaces**.　[15 STROKES　RANK 1008]

731 戶 戶　**door (alternate form)**　■ corpse 703　☐ one 2

CMP This alternate form displays the left panel of a swinging door. The *one* line at the top reminds us that a swinging **door** occupies many positions.

732 后 后 **behind**   ■ door (alternate form) 731 (altered)   ■ mouth 41   hò

BF Here the *mouth* represents a guy on audition in Hollywood. Oops—he didn't get the part. Don't let the *door* bang you on the **behind** on your way out.   [6 STROKES   RANK 48]

733 盾 盾 **shield**   ■ door (alternate form) 731 (altered)   ■ self 202   dù

A *door* painted with picture of the king him*self* makes a good **shield**.

[9 STROKES   RANK 1395]

734 所 所 **place**   ■ door (alternate form) 731   ■ catty 118   suǒ

His **place** is a real *cata*strophe. Worst is the *door*, furiously *unbalanced* and liable to bang you on the head at any minute.   [8 STROKES   RANK 54]

735 阝 阝 **hills**

CMP When you see this on the *left* of a character (as in 阡 and 防 and many more), it represents a range of **small hills**. To see the hills, just imagine rotating this radical to the left (clockwise) to see the soft pair of hills.

736 阳 阳 **sun**   ■ hills 735   ■ day, sun 63   yán

BF The **sun** peeks overs the *hills* at break of *day*.   [6 STROKES   RANK 650]

737 队 队 **team**   ■ hills 735   ■ man 311   duì

The **team** is lined up for inspection. Oops, I forgot my glasses, so when I look at the *men* on the team, their features are indistinct, and their heads look like a row of *hills*.   [4 STROKES   RANK 268]

738 阻 阻 **hinder, block**   ■ hills 735   ■ moreover 15   zǔ

BF Back in §15, we likened 且 to a sturdy pair of *bookshelves*. Imagine these shelves magnified to a large scale, and arranged in a long row. These shelves, together with the dense *hills* will surely **block** the invaders from entering our town!   [7 STROKES   RANK 1175]

739 阿   阿   **particle before names**   ▊ hills 735   ▊ can; may 60   ā

Chinese speakers use this particle to indicate familiarity (阿宝, 'A Bao') or to indicate some kind of relationship, often familial (阿大 'ā dà', the eldest; 阿哥 'ā gē' elder brother).

     When I return home after a trip, the sight of the distant *hills* near my home *can* fill me with a welcome sense of **familiarity**.   [7 STROKES   RANK 471]

740 啊   啊   **phrase suffix**   ▊ mouth 41   ▊ particle before names 739   a

Chinese scribes often use the *mouth* radical to draw interjections and particles, perhaps to suggest an exhalation of breath on an occasion that's slightly out of the ordinary. 阿 has many alternate pronunciations. All of them, including the main one treated here, refer to interjections.   [10 STROKES   RANK 753]

741 陆   陆   **land, continent**

              ▊ hills 735   ▊ earth, soil 9   ▊ mountain 21   lù

BF How might we characterize a **continent**? By the presence of *hills, mountains*, and *land*.   [7 STROKES   RANK 675]

742 院   院   **courtyard**   ▊ hills 735   ▊ finish, complete 296   yuàn

BF From the comfort and beauty of my Chinese **courtyard**, I sit contemplating the scenic *hills*, visible in the distance, until the period of meditation is *completed*.   [9 STROKES   RANK 338]

743 陶   陶   **pottery**   ▊ hills 735   ▊ wrap 636   ▊ archaeological vessel 521   táo

BF Out in the *hills* beyond town, the archaeologists dug deeply to find some old *wrapped pots* which appear to be some of the most ancient example of **pottery** known.   [10 STROKES   RANK 1601]

744 隔   隔   **separate, impede**

              ▊ hills 735   ▊ cauldron for meat or cereal 279   gé

The *hill* tribesman threatened to **impede** our progress by tossing us into their huge *stew pots*. We ran for our lives!   [12 STROKES   RANK 1319]

745 阝 阝 **town**

CMP When the component that's identical to 'hills' of §735 appears on the *right* of a character, as in 邦 and 那 and many others, it represents the skyline of a **town**.

　How to distinguish this component from §735? Imagine 'reading' a character from left to right, from distant to near to you, as if the glyph represented a land- or townscape. The hills are in the distance, while the **town** is right up close.

746 邦 邦 **nation state**　　　■ plentiful 12 (altered)　■ town 745　　bān

BF Prosperous **nations** are formed from confederations of *towns* whose thriving economies—their goods are *plentiful*—bids fair for the future.

[6 STROKES　RANK 1363]

747 帮 帮 **to help**　　　■ nation state 746　■ towel 130　　bān

You'll never believe how I lost track of time right before my dinner party the other day! The doorbell rang as I was getting out of the shower, wrapped in nothing but a *towel*. What a *state* I was in. Boy, did I need **help** that night!

[9 STROKES　RANK 769]

748 邮 邮 **to post, mail**　　　■ let sb do sth 48　■ town 745　　yóu

The central **post** office is in mid-*town*. I'll stop in quickly to buy some stamps (which look like the left component), which will *allow me* to send out some important mail.

[7 STROKES　RANK 1652]

749 耶 耶 **interrogatory particle**　　　■ ear 82　■ town 745　　yē

Things in the *town* are so noisy, I did not *hear* your question. **What did you say?**

[8 STROKES　RANK 1174]

750 厶 厶 **private**

CMP This gentle profile shows someone's big, fat nose! Don't stick your nose in my business—it's **private**!

　We'll frequently use this component to represent a **snobbish person** or **busybody**, or sometimes just a **nose**.

751 云　云　cloud　　　　　　　　　⬛ two 3　⬛ private 750　　yún

Here are *two* snobs, each trying to outdo the other in keeping their *nose* in the **clouds**.　　　　　　　　　　　　　[4 STROKES　RANK 692]

752 坛　坛　altar　　　　　　　　　⬛ earth, soil 9　⬛ cloud 751　　tán

Here's how **altars** are supposed to work: You pile raw animal parts on the *earth*, get them burning vigorously, and the denser the resulting *clouds* of smoke, the more appreciative will be the deity.　　[7 STROKES　RANK 1806]

Unit 33

Here and There

753 会　会　**meet, assemble**　　☐ man 311　　■ cloud 751　　huì

In my experience, **meetings** are huge wastes of time. *Clouds* of *people* mill about, accomplishing nothing! Most of their talk takes the form of *clouds* of obfuscation.　　[6 STROKES　RANK 29]

754 去　去　**go**　　■ earth, soil 9　　■ private 750　　qù

One good example of "**going**" is death—departure from this earth. For then you will end up in a *private* place within the *earth*.　　[5 STROKES　RANK 64]

755 至　至　**to, until**　　☐ one 2　　■ private 750　　■ earth, soil 9　　zhì

Some*one*'s *nose* on the *ground*—nothing further happens **until** this guy picks himself up and brushes himself off.　　[6 STROKES　RANK 267]

Beginners could be forgiven for confusing the characters 去 (§754) and 至 (§755). Both combine the 'private' and 'earth' components, but in different orders. Both are so common that you can't help but get them right, at least in the long run. But what of the short run? As a memory aid, focus on the bottom. For 至, soil is something we till—sounds like 'until'. For 去, remember that 'private' looks like someone's nose, and keep in mind the stupid rhyme 'the nose goes'.

756 到　到　**arrive**　　■ to, until 755　　☐ knife r 166　　dào

I need to **arrive** at the office for a crucial job interview, and I'm really nervous. *Until* I get there, my emotions are on a *knife* edge.　　[8 STROKES　RANK 22]

757 室 室 **room**＊   ☐ roof 247 ▉ to, until 755   shì

BF I'm not really home, safe in my **room**, *until* I am under my own *roof.*

[9 STROKES   RANK 708]

758 罷 罷 **stop, cease**   ☐ net r 107 ▉ go 754   bà

The *net* that these practical jokers threw over my head as I was *going* to class, made me **stop** dead in my tracks.   [10 STROKES   RANK 1305]

759 摆 摆 **place, put, arrange**   ▉ hand r 29 ▉ stop, cease 758   bǎi

You use your *hand* to shove around all the jigsaw puzzle pieces, but you *stop* when they're all **arranged** nicely.   [13 STROKES   RANK 1158]

760 却 却 **now (storytelling)**   ▉ go 754 ☐ single ear 157   què

Actually, this is one of those small words that often occurs with other small words to connote some adverbial meaning.

    Now that the story has begun, I'm all *ears* as the events *go* on to their thrilling conclusion.   [7 STROKES   RANK 287]

761 丢 丢 **lose, misplace**   ☐ dab 169 ▉ go 754   diū

We **lose** stuff when *little bits* of pieces somehow *go* astray.

[6 STROKES   RANK 1639]

762 法 法 **method**   ▉ water r 523 ▉ go 754   fǎ

BF A great advance in the history of mankind is the development of **methods** of using *water*. Using water to *go* places, such as over water wheels, was a landmark in technology.   [8 STROKES   RANK 65]

763 予 予 **give**＊   ▉ private 750 (altered) ▉ fourth 25   yǔ

BF The bottom '*fourth*' component resembles a clenched fist which has rammed into some guy's *nose* with such force that the scribes write it upside-down. The attacker **gave** his victim some serious health concerns.

[4 STROKES   RANK 925]

764 野 野 open country   ■ inside 71 ■ give* 763   yě

BF When I'm out in **open country**, I have to go back *inside* right away. All that wildlife *gives* me hay fever!   [11 STROKES   RANK 845]

765 舒 舒 relax   ■ give up 328 ■ give* 763   shū

BF As a student of Eastern meditation, I know I achieve **relaxation** if I *give up* worldly cares and *give* in to the harmony of the universe.

[12 STROKES   RANK 1459]

766 县 县 county   ▬ moreover 15 ▬ private 750   xià

Think of a **county** as a government entity which stores its own records, *privately*, in long series of '*moreover*'-like bookshelves.

[7 STROKES   RANK 877]

767 台 台 platform, stage   ▬ private 750 ▬ mouth 41   tái

Why, look at the speaker there on the **platform**. He's positioned so that you really can only see his *nose* and *mouth*.   [5 STROKES   RANK 388]

768 抬 抬 raise, lift   ■ hand r 29 ■ platform, stage 767   tái

I **lift** the luggage onto the train *platform* with my *hands*.

[8 STROKES   RANK 1386]

769 治 治 manage, administer   ■ water r 523 ■ platform, stage 767   zhì

BF Think back to the many student demonstrations in the late '60s–early '70s. The authorities often **managed** to control them by standing on a raised *platform* and shooting streams of *water* at the students from hoses.

[8 STROKES   RANK 274]

770 胎 胎 fetus, baby   ■ meat 317 (altered) ■ platform, stage 767   tāi

The leftmost component often receives the interpretation of '*meat*'. Nine o'clock, Monday morning, and a sad case to present to these med students. This *flesh* on the teaching *stage* was someone's **baby** a short time ago.

[9 STROKES   RANK 1984]

771 允　允　**permit, allow**　　　□ private 750　■ walking man 287　**yǔn**

BF You will have to **allow** me my own interpretation of this character: I see a *nose* with the characteristic fold of the upper lip underneath it which reminds us, in the talkativeness of this person which leads to excessive motion of the upper lip, as a *walking man*.　　　　　　　　　　　[4 STROKES　RANK 1443]

772 充　充　**fill, full**　　　□ cover 268　■ permit, allow 771　**chōng**

BF If we *cover* the huge pile of *permit* applications, we realize that there are far too many to **fill**.　　　　　　　　　　　[6 STROKES　RANK 690]

773 勾　勾　**cross out**　　　■ wrap 636　■ private 750　**gōu**

Somebody *wrapped* that snob's *nose*. It looks likes he's been **rubbed out**.　　　　　　　　　　　[4 STROKES　RANK 2034]

774 沟　沟　**trench, groove**　　　■ water r 523　■ cross out 773　**gōu**

Imagine some catastrophic flooding somewhere. In an effort to cancel or *cross out* these *waters*, the authorities have dug a series of **trenches**.　　　　　　　　　　　[7 STROKES　RANK 1610]

775 幺　幺　**youngest**　　　□ private 750 (altered)　■ private 750　**yāo**

BF Two aunties stick their pointy *noses* in close to see the adorable new baby—the **youngest** addition to the family!　　　　[3 STROKES　RANK 4505]

776 玄　玄　**incredible**　　　□ cover 268　■ youngest 775　**xuán**

BF The family across the street behaves like they're in a Victorian melodrama. Something is **incredibly** wrong with their *youngest*, so they try to *cover* up his existence.　　　　　　　　　　　[5 STROKES　RANK 1717]

777 畜　畜　**livestock**　　　■ incredible 776　■ field 57　**chù**

BF The farmer's *field* is an *incredible* mess—filthy, smelly, and ugly. But that's what you get when you keep your **livestock** there.　　　[10 STROKES　RANK 2030]

778 蓄 蓄 **store, save up**   ☐ grass r 94   ■ livestock 777   xù

BF Winter is coming. If I don't **store** hay and *grass* now, the *livestock* will starve to death during those cold months.   [13 STROKES   RANK 1985]

Unit 34

Animate and Inanimate

779 兹 兹 **now, at present**   ■ incredible (times 2) 776   zī

BF There's no time like the **present**—or, to put it another way, nothing is as *incredible* as **now**.   [9 STROKES RANK 1781]

780 滋 滋 **sprout, spurt**   ■ water r 523   ■ now, at present 779   zī

The three dots of the *water* component plus the two dots of the *double 'incredible'* suggest—at least visually—that there's lots of water around. At home, that might mean that water is **spurting** from a burst pipe, and it's happening *now*! In the fields, the abundant water helps ensure that the crops will **sprout**.   [12 STROKES RANK 1931]

781 瓜 瓜 **melon**   ■ cliff r 671   ■ private 750   ■ curvey stripe   guā

The juicy **melons** we buy in the summer have skins marked with *curvy stripes* and odd designs suggesting *noses*, mountains, and *cliffs*. These patterns suggests the random pattern of the striping.   [5 STROKES RANK 1827]

782 始 始 **begin, start**   ■ woman 581   ■ platform, stage 767   shǐ

BF This famous *female* chef is getting ready for a demonstration of her art. It takes forever to get her equipment up on the *stage*, so that—finally—she can **begin**.   [8 STROKES RANK 381]

783 屋 屋 **house, room**   ■ corpse 703   ■ to, until 755   wū

BF The kindly old man died unexpectedly in his **room**. The landlord let the *corpse* lie there *until* the funeral even though he was anxious to re-rent it.   [9 STROKES RANK 863]

784 握 握 hold, grasp, shake hands ▮ hand r 29 ▮ house, room 783   wò
So shaken was I by his death that I had to use my *hand* to **hold** onto the
walls of the *room* to keep from falling down.   [12 STROKES RANK 1032]

785 承 承 bear, hold, undertake
▬ water 545 (altered) ▮ hand 27 (altered) ▯ private 750 (altered)   ché
BF I **undertake** a *private* commission for the government. The valuable ship-
ments must be *privately* transported by *hand*. The easiest way to accomplish
this is via river, canal, or other body of *water*.   [8 STROKES RANK 639]

786 预 预 in advance ▮ give* 763 ▮ page, leaf 444   yù
BF If you *give* a little something to the *page*, you can get into the reception
in advance of everyone else. What a coup!   [10 STROKES RANK 647]

787 层 层 layer, story, floor ▮ corpse 703 ▮ cloud 751   cén
The elevator in my building is out of order! By the time I walked up to my
apartment on the top **story**, I felt like a *corpse*, even though my head was in
the *clouds* that I could easily see from my windows.   [7 STROKES RANK 699]

788 构 构 construct, form ▮ tree 375 ▮ cross out 773   gòu
BF For the neighborhood church, we were able to **construct** a *cross out* of
wood (ouch!).   [8 STROKES RANK 511]

789 序 序 order, sequence ▮ shelter r 681 ▮ give* 763   xù
BF The homeless people all line up at the *shelter*. We will *give* them food in
the **order** in which they came.   [7 STROKES RANK 836]

790 私 私 selfish, personal, private ▮ rice or grain 409 ▮ private 750   sī
BF What! The Communist leaders are keeping all the *grain* harvest for their
personal and *private* use. How unjust—and how **selfish**!
    [7 STROKES RANK 1023]

791 购 购   **buy, purchase**   ▮ cowrie 430   ▮ cross out 773   gòu

I have my shopping list in one hand, and my *money* in the other. Each time I **buy** something on the list, I *cross out* the item.   [8 STROKES   RANK 1078]

792 矣 矣   **marks completed action**   ▯ private 750   ▮ arrow 334   yǐ

This character represents a Chinese particle, dating from classical times, which marks the completion of an action. Grammatically, it functions similar to modern 了, 'le'.

Imagine the '*private*' component as a concrete barrier, against which the flying *arrow* collides and stops. Its **action is completed.**

     [7 STROKES   RANK 2069]

793 埃 埃   **dirt, dust**   ▮ earth, soil 9   ▮ marks completed action 792   āi

BF At life's end, the *completion of my activity* on this *earth*, my body turns into **dust.**   [10 STROKES   RANK 1121]

794 幻 幻   **fantasy**   ▮ youngest 775   ▮ place of refuge 111   huàn

BF My *youngest* child was always prone to odd, **fantastic/** dreams. He always woke up screaming, and needed his mother's *comforting arms* to soothe him back to sleep.   [4 STROKES   RANK 1417]

795 幽 幽   **remote, secluded**   ▮ mountain 21   ▮▮ youngest (times 2) 775   yōu

BF The two '*youngest*' components look like a brush disguising the *mountain* pass and keeping everything **remote** and **secluded.**   [9 STROKES   RANK 1636]

796 灬 灬   **fire r**

CMP These are several of the little blue **flames** on a gas burner.

Fire uses up resources and things—by burning them to a crisp—so we will sometimes use this meaning.

797 点 点 dot ▪ practice divination 172 ▪ fire r 796   diǎ

The fortune teller failed to *foretell* the *fire* that would break out during the night, and the family's vast possessions were reduced to **dots**.

[9 STROKES   RANK 128]

798 然 然 correct, so ▪ meat 317 (altered) ▪ dog 332 ▪ fire r 796   rán

BF Some ancient scribe must have been a gourmand with peculiar tastes. His favorite dish, *meat* of *dog*, must be roasted on a *fire* for it to be **correctly** done. [12 STROKES   RANK 55]

799 烈 烈 strong, intense ▪ arrange, line up 659 ▪ fire r 796   liè

BF To start a *fire* in the fireplace or barbecue, carefully *arrange* the charcoal bricks. The better you do this, the more **intense** will be the fire!

[10 STROKES   RANK 802]

800 庶 庶 numerous

▪ shelter r 681 ▪ horned animal 100 ▪ fire r 796   shù

BF Picture a brutal blizzardy night, out west in cattle country. These *cows* are normally ornery, but on such a vicious evening, they're happy to take advantage of the *shelter* the barn provides. They warm themselves by a large *fire*. You know the weather's bad because these cold cattle are so **numerous**.

[11 STROKES   RANK 3016]

801 席 席 mat ▪ numerous 800 (altered) ▪ towel 130   xí

BF A **mat** is a *cloth* on the ground where *numerous* people gather to sit and relax. [10 STROKES   RANK 894]

802 燕 燕 swallow bird

☐ horned animal 100   ▬ north 145 (altered)   ▪ mouth 41   ▬ fire r 796   **yàn**

BF Here's a parent **swallow** returning to feed her fledglings. Look, there they are, the four hungry dots each with a *burning* appetite. That's not an *animal* up top, but rather their distinctive tail. Compared with other birds, their wings appear short and stubby, but the bird's natural habitat is way up *north*, so it's no wonder its wings resemble the '*north*' component. We use an open *mouth* to represent the bird's compact body.   [16 STROKES   RANK 1705]

803 黑 黑 black   ☐ staring through window   ▬ earth, soil 9   ▬ fire r 796   **hēi**

The war is over. *Staring through the window* at the devastation is wrenching. *Fire* has ripped into the *earth*, and **blackened** it.   [12 STROKES   RANK 519]

804 默 默 silent, keep silent   ■ black 803   ☐ dog 332   **mò**

BF The *black dog* was **silent** all night long, proving that the burglar must have been a member of the household, known to the dog.   [16 STROKES   RANK 1031]

Unit 35

Stop and Go

805 墨 墨 **ink, ink stick** ⬛ black 803 ⬛ earth, soil 9 mò
Scribes use a *black, earth*-like substance to make **ink**.

[15 STROKES RANK 1493]

806 杰 杰 **outstanding person, hero** ⬛ tree 375 ⬛ fire r 796 jié
BF A *tree* surviving a raging *conflagration*? It must be truly outstanding, and, by analogy, refers to a **outstanding person**. [8 STROKES RANK 1129]

807 纟 纟 **silk r**
CMP Somehow, these are **silk** threads twisted together.
  Chinese weavers are skilled artisans, and sometimes we wish to emphasize the structure of their work. We would then use a complicated form of this radical, 糸.

808 乡 乡 **township** ⬛ silk r 807 (altered) xiā
A certain level of industrialization is necessary to transform the raw *silk* cocoons into the kind of thread that can be woven into clothes. The alteration in the *silk* radical symbolizes the alteration that applies to the cocoon. Typically, you need to be in a **town** to find artisans with the proper skills to do this. [3 STROKES RANK 922]

809 丝 丝 **silk*** ⬛ silk r (times 2) 807 sī
See how the two *silk* threads are joined at the bottom strokes to yield superior strength to the resulting **silk** fabric. [5 STROKES RANK 1026]

810 红 红 **red** ▊ silk r 807 ▊ labor, work 7   hóng

The Chinese people love a certain bright orangey **red** color. If a *silk* garment is to be properly seductive, to do its *work*, it must be that color.

[6 STROKES   RANK 502]

811 纽 纽 **button** ▊ silk r 807 ▊ hideous 37   niǔ

BF In the very old days, a piece of poorly-woven *silk*—silk that was too *hideous* for any other use—was pressed and knotted together to make a **button**.

[7 STROKES   RANK 1767]

812 组 组 **section, group** ▊ silk r 807 ▊ moreover 15   zǔ

The spoiled rich kids fling their *silk* shirts on the *bookcase*. *Moreover*, they let the maid pick up this **group** of shirts and bring it to the laundry.

[8 STROKES   RANK 358]

813 结 结 **tie, knit, knot, weave** ▊ silk r 807 ▊ lucky 56   jié

High-quality Chinese gift stores display and sell some of the most intriguing and entrancing decorative **knots** I have ever seen. Made of *silk*, they symbolize good *luck*.

[9 STROKES   RANK 236]

814 细 细 **thin, slender** ▊ silk r 807 ▊ field 57   xì

Think here of the newly sprouted wheat in a farmer's *field*. At first, these shoots resemble *silk* threads, they are so **fine** and **slender**.

[8 STROKES   RANK 597]

815 纠 纠 **correct, rectify** ▊ silk r 807 ▊ speak up! 92   jiū

BF Fancy officials, all dressed up in their *silk* gowns, can intimidate ordinary citizens. One honest soul has discovered an error in the proclamation, and *speaks up* in an effort to **rectify** the situation.

[5 STROKES   RANK 1723]

816 绳 绳 rope   ■ silk r 807   ■ tadpole 136   sh∢

Silk threads by themselves are pretty weak. But make a paste of *tadpole* bodies, smear it on the silk, and—presto—you have a strong **rope**.

[11 STROKES   RANK 1983]

817 纵 纵 vertical   ■ silk r 807   ■ from 313   zò◗

BF You test the quality of *silk* thread by holding it taut so it extends *from* top to bottom—**vertically**.

[7 STROKES   RANK 1236]

818 纳 纳 accept, receive   ■ silk r 807   ■ inside* 318   nà

BF In the ancient world, odd pieces of *silk* served as receipts for important items. That is, the writing *inside* the scrap of *silk* showed that the owner had **received** the item in question in good condition.

[7 STROKES   RANK 684]

819 给 给 give   ■ silk r 807   ■ cozy house 509   gěi

The sight of my freshly pressed *silken* dressing gown waiting for me in my *cozy house* always **gives** me a tiny frisson of pleasure no matter how often this happens.

[9 STROKES   RANK 180]

820 约 约 ask, invite   ■ silk r 807   ■ spoon 642   yu∢

Your host is wearing his best *silk* suit, and uses a *spoon* as a symbolic 'welcome' to his home. How could you ask for a better **invitation** than this?

[6 STROKES   RANK 424]

821 药 药 medicine   ■ grass r 94   ■ ask, invite 820   yào

Especially in olden times, **medicine** was created out of *grasses* and other herbal components. These potions were *invitations* to get better.

[9 STROKES   RANK 662]

822 绕 绕 wind, coil   ■ silk r 807   ■ legendary emperor 374   ràc

News flash: they've just discovered the mummified body of the *legendary emperor* Yao. It was preserved by means of masses of *silk* thread, which were **coiled** around the royal corpse.

[9 STROKES   RANK 1485]

823 绘 绘 **draw, paint**   ▮ silk r 807   ▮ meet, assemble 753   huì

BF There's a bunch of strange guys who *meet* to practice strange artistic techniques. They use *silk* threads to **paint** pictures, which have a strangely rich appearance.   [9 STROKES   RANK 1809]

824 统 统 **gather, unite**   ▮ silk r 807   ▮ fill, full 772   tǒng

BF The embroidery project is going to take all of my attention. All the *silk* threads completely *fill* my hand as I **gather** them together to begin the project.
                                                    [9 STROKES   RANK 264]

825 绿 绿 **green**   ▮ silk r 807   ▮ record, write down 549   lǜ

The ministers *recorded* the proclamation in gold letters on *silk* brocade. Alas, the gold was false, and the characters soon turned **green**.
                                                    [11 STROKES   RANK 1088]

826 经 经 **warp (fabric)**
                             ▮ silk r 807   ▮ man 311 (altered)   ▮ labor, work 7   jīng

The **warp** are those threads in the making of cloth that form parallel tracks in the cloth. Perpendicular to them run threads going over and under them to create the fabric.

Thus, the **warp** of the *silk* cloth provides channels up and down around which an active *man* (see the cartoonish horizontal stroke on his head which indicates action or movement) scurries doing all kinds of *work*.
                                                    [8 STROKES   RANK 62]

827 纯 纯 **pure, unmixed**   ▮ silk r 807   ▮ electricity 138 (altered)   chún

Silk can conduct *electricity* (believe it or not) as long as the wire is **pure** silk.   [7 STROKES   RANK 1125]

828 素　素　**plain, simple, quiet**　　☐ plentiful 12 (altered)　■ silk r 807　　sù

BF There's something ironic in a character meaning '**plain**' being so visually complex! But perhaps that's the point...

Lots of elegant dresses use *silk* in an understated way (and '*silk*' is indeed on the underside of the character) to create **plain** but elegant clothes.

[10 STROKES   RANK 661]

829 系　系　**academic department**　　☐ dab 169　■ silk r 807　　xì

Life in **academic college departments** is funny. The politics is convoluted and brutal, a *bit* like complex *silken* embroidery but of far less value.

[7 STROKES   RANK 216]

830 线　线　**thread, string, wire**　　■ silk r 807　☐ tiny, fragmentary 373　　xià

When you take *silk* and shred it into *fragmentary* bits, you get silk **thread**.

[8 STROKES   RANK 430]

Unit 36

A Picture is Worth One Thousand Words

831 续 续　**continue, extend, replenish**

◫ silk r 807　◻ sell 341 (altered)　xù

The *silk*worms in the *cell*ar (sounds like '*sell*er') are thriving. They multiply and **replenish** themselves, escape from their tanks, and crawl up the walls and into our bedrooms. It's awful!　　　　[11 STROKES　RANK 552]

832 率 率　**rate, proportion**

◻ cover 268　◼ silk r 807　▪▪ strings　◧ scepter 5　lǜ

Pay attention to the piece of *silk* at the center of this glyph. It's surrounded by all kinds of marks representing frayed threads. The *silk* hasn't been hemmed, and gradually, at a slow **rate**, the threads unravel.　　　　[11 STROKES　RANK 625]

833 索 索　**search, demand, exact**

▭ market 273 (altered)　▬ silk r 807　suǒ

BF I **search** the entire *market* for the best *silk*, comparing quality and price, so I can **exact** the best deals.　　　　[10 STROKES　RANK 805]

834 编 编　**weave, plait**

◫ silk r 807　◻ flat, crushed 729　biān

The best way to deal with a bunch of *silk* threads is to **weave** them into a *flat* piece of fabric.　　　　[12 STROKES　RANK 858]

835 紫 紫　**purple**

◫ this 233　◫ silk r 807　zǐ

In the old days, it was tough to impart a rich **purple** color to cloth. *This* color was special, and used only for special garments, such as those made from *silk*.　　　　[12 STROKES　RANK 1646]

836 累 累 pile up, accumulate   ☐ field 57   ■ silk r 807   lěi
BF Use threads of *silk* to tie together the products of our *fields* as they **accumulate** in a good year.   [11 STROKES   RANK 1323]

837 绩 绩 merit, accomplishment   ▌ silk r 807   ▐ responsibility 439   jì
BF The student **merits** the *silk* robes of an accomplished scholar by virtue of her *responsibility* and diligence.   [11 STROKES   RANK 1547]

838 衤 衤 clothing r
CMP A favorite gown has been hung in the closet (waiting its turn for the next regal occasion), and it's a little crushed as a result, as you can see.

839 衣 衣 clothing   ■ clothing r 838 (altered)   yī
BF Imagine a favorite **gown** hung on a hanger, just after it's come back from the cleaners. The lines suggest the lines of this fine garment. Look sharp to see the stylish collar (the dab shows the position of the head) surmount the flowing sleeves and the drape of the body of the gown.   [6 STROKES   RANK 725]

840 袖 袖 sleeve   ▐ clothing r 838   ▐ let sb do sth 48   xiù
BF Imagine that *clothes* originally took the form of table cloth-like garments draped over a person's head. It was hard to maneuver in them until some fashion genius created **sleeves** which *allowed people to do whatever they wanted.*   [10 STROKES   RANK 1686]

841 表 表 external, surface   ◳ hair 231 (altered)   ■ clothing 839 (altered)   biǎ◖
BF When *hair* appears on an article of *clothing* (say a fur coat), it appears on the **external surface**.   [8 STROKES   RANK 177]

842 展 展 expand, develop   ◰ corpse 703   ▐ clothing 839 (altered)   zhǎ◖
An ugly traffic accident. We **spread** some *clothes* over the *corpse* out of respect for both the victim and the other people at the accident site.   [10 STROKES   RANK 275]

843 农 农 **agriculture**   ■ clothing 839 (altered)   nóng

BF Scholars speculate that **agriculture** was the first accomplishment of civilization. By altering the fruits and vegetables that early farmers cultivated, it became possible to create warm and durable *clothing.*   [6 STROKES   RANK 465]

844 浓 浓 **dense, thick**   ■ water r 523   ■ agriculture 843   nóng

That's how you get fields **dense** with crops—practice *agriculture* and use plenty of *water.*   [9 STROKES   RANK 1585]

845 补 补 **mend, patch**   ■ clothing r 838   ■ foretell 170   bǔ

I'm a guy, and so don't have a clue how to **patch** *clothes.* As far as I'm concerned, somebody takes a *magic wand* and waves it over the tear to make it go away.   [7 STROKES   RANK 944]

846 裁 裁 **cut, cut cloth**

              ■ earth, soil 9   ■ clothing 839   ■ halberd 359   cái

There's no time to waste, so I use my *halberd* to make *clothes,* and I throw the scraps on the *ground.* That's how real men **cut cloth!**

                                             [12 STROKES   RANK 1203]

847 裂 裂 **split, divide up**   ■ arrange, line up 659   ■ clothing 839   liè

The volunteers have *lined up* the used *clothing* in neat piles, and are ready to **divide** it **up** among the worthy poor.   [12 STROKES   RANK 1317]

848 衰 衰 **decline, wane, feeble**

              ■ clothing 839 (altered)   ■ day, sun 63 (altered)   shuāi

BF Look how gaudy this guy's *clothes* are—so much so that the *sun* seems to shine out of it. As men's clothes get more outrageous, so does civilization **decline.**   [10 STROKES   RANK 1702]

849 哀 哀 **sorrow, lament**   ▰ clothing 839 (altered) ▭ mouth 41   āi
BF At times of mourning or other great **sorrow**, you wear special types of *clothing* and, with your *mouth*, you **lament**.   [9 STROKES   RANK 1751]

850 袁 袁 Yuan Shikai
▭ earth, soil 9   ▰ mouth 41   ▰ clothing 839 (altered)   yu
Yuan Shikai (袁世凯), first President of the Republic of China (1912–15), declared himself Emperor in 1916. The normal glyph for 'imperial robes' 袞 shows traditional intricacy, especially on the top. Lines are clean and spare in the twentieth century, as you see here. Think of **Yun Shikai**'s imperial aspirations, the cleaner lines of the *robes* being *grounded* in edicts issuing from his *mouth* to justify the renewal of royalty.   [10 STROKES   RANK 1755]

851 己 己 **self* r**
CMP BF This character looks like a backwards 's', which stands for '**self**'.
  Also: like life itself, the line segments of 己 constantly change direction. A life history of one**self** in miniature.   [3 STROKES   RANK 162]

852 己 己 **self***   ▰ self* r 851   jǐ
BF   [3 STROKES   RANK 162]

853 己 已 **already**   ▰ self* 852 (altered)   yǐ
BF Compared to the previous panel, we see here that the topmost of the open spaces are about to close up. The course of life has **already** been charted.
    [3 STROKES   RANK 117]

854 岂 岂 **how could it be?**   ▭ mountain 21   ▰ self* 852   qǐ
He has a *mountain* of troubles weighing him down. His whole *self* is enmeshed in these difficulties. **How can it be that** he will ever get out of this mess?   [6 STROKES   RANK 1726]

855 记 记 **remember**   ▮ speech r 615   ▮ self* 852   jì

Speaking to our*self* over and over helps to **remember** stuff—shopping lists, speeches, material for tests, and so on.   [5 STROKES   RANK 306]

856 纪 纪 **historical record**   ▮ silk r 807   ▮ self* 852   jì

BF On a piece of *silk* brocade, an artisan has woven an intricate pattern signifying the **historical records** of many people—many *selves* and their historical accomplishments.   [6 STROKES   RANK 584]

Unit 37

Time Waits for No Man

857 包 包 **wrap, envelope** ☐ wrap 636 ■ self* 852 (altered) bā◄

Wrapping yourself tightly in a warm winter cloak, say, emphasizes the concepts of **wrapping** and **enveloping**. [5 STROKES RANK 454]

858 泡 泡 **blister, bubble** ▮ water r 523 ▮ wrap, envelope 857 pà◄

A **blister** is a bit of *water wrapped* up in your skin. [8 STROKES RANK 2000]

859 弓 弓 **bow (weapon)** ■ self* 852 (altered) gō◄

Many weapons of war, especially in ancient times, required teamwork to use—think of cannon, catapults, and so on. One **weapon** that could be worked by a soldier him*self* was the **bow**. [3 STROKES RANK 2229]

860 起 起 **rise** ▮ to walk 421 ▮ self* 852 qǐ

Imagine taking a *walk* on a steamy summer day after a drenching rain. The '*self*' component looks like a wisp of vapor, a cloud of steam **rising** from the pavement from the heat of the day. [10 STROKES RANK 75]

861 配 配 **join together** ▮ new wine 303 ▮ self* 852 pèi

"Now we **join together** this couple in the bonds of holy matrimony." In celebration, let's raise the glass of *wine* to toast the happy couple, who are now committed to treating the other as they would them*selves*.

[10 STROKES RANK 738]

862 危 危　danger, imperil

■ cliff r 671　　▢ man 311 (altered)　　▢ self* 852 (altered)　　wēi

BF A deranged *man* near the edge of a *cliff* **imperils** him*self*.

[6 STROKES　RANK 826]

863 脆 脆　fragile, brittle　▮ boat, ship 597 (altered)　　▮ danger, imperil 862　cuì

Because it is **fragile** and **brittle**, the *boat endangers* all our lives.

[10 STROKES　RANK 1976]

864 宛 宛　bent　▢ roof 247　▮ evening, dusk 655　▢ self* 852 (altered)　wǎn

BF *Evening*, at *home*. The person him*self* is in bed, in a slumped and relaxed position while sleeping. That's why the body is **bent**.　[8 STROKES　RANK 2528]

865 仓 仓　barn, storehouse　　▢ man 311　▬ self* 852 (altered)　cāng

BF That's not a *man*—it's the broad roof of a **barn** to **store** food and stuff for your*self* and your family.　[4 STROKES　RANK 1882]

866 苍 苍　dark green　　▢ grass r 94　▬ barn, storehouse 865　cāng

BF This character takes its meaning from the color of the wilted *grass* in a well-stocked *barn* that peaks out of the windows. From a distance, it appears **dark green**.　[7 STROKES　RANK 1728]

867 舱 舱　shipboard cabin or hold

▮ boat, ship 597　▢ barn, storehouse 865　cāng

BF The part of a *boat* dedicated to *storing* stuff is the **cabin**.

[10 STROKES　RANK 1846]

868 抢 抢　pillage, loot　　▮ hand r 29　▮ barn, storehouse 865　qiǎng

After the riot, the *barn* doors gaped open. The mob could not contain itself. The villagers used their *hands* to **pillage** and **loot** whatever they could.

[7 STROKES　RANK 1412]

869 创 创　**initiate, inaugurate**　　■ barn, storehouse 865　□ knife r 166　chɯ
To celebrate the **inauguration** of the new *barn*, the town mayor has been
invited to step forward and cut the ribbon with a *knife*.

[6 STROKES   RANK 635]

870 枪 枪　rifle, gun　　■ tree 375　□ barn, storehouse 865　qiā
A long *barn* makes a perfect **rifle** range. Stand at one end with your **rifle**
and shoot at the *tree* at the other end.　　[8 STROKES   RANK 874]

871 导 导　**guide, lead**　　□ already 853 (altered)　■ inch 210　dǎ
BF A road only an *inch* wide is *already* in place. It will be an effective conduit
or **guide** because generations of hobbits have maintained it properly.

[6 STROKES   RANK 343]

872 引 引　**lead, guide**　　■ bow (weapon) 859　□ scepter 5　yǐn
The king with his royal *scepter* together with his chief *bow*man **lead** the
people to victory.　　[4 STROKES   RANK 479]

873 厄 厄　**trapped in difficult situation**
　　■ cliff r 671　■ self* 852 (altered)　è
Here *I* am, near the edge of a high *cliff*, **trapped** as a maniac tries to push
me off.　　[4 STROKES   RANK 2407]

874 顾 顾　**attend to, look after**
　　■ trapped in difficult situation 873　■ page, leaf 444　gù
I was *trapped in a difficult situation* but I tripped over the *pages* of an open
book, regained my balance, and was able to **attend to** the situation and fix
it.　　[10 STROKES   RANK 815]

875 袍 袍　**robe, gown**　　■ clothing r 838　■ wrap, envelope 857　páo
BF A **robe** is an article of *clothing* that *wraps* you from head to toe.

[10 STROKES   RANK 2324]

876 抱 抱 **hold or carry in arms**   ⬛ hand r 29   ⬛ wrap, envelope 857   bào

When you **hold** or hug that special someone, you *enfold* them with your *hands*.   [8 STROKES   RANK 1122]

877 马 马 **horse r**

CMP This is such a lovely character, especially in its traditional form

馬

which clearly shows the head, mane, back, legs, and tail tucked back underneath the body.

878 马 马 **horse**   ⬛ horse r 877   mǎ

[3 STROKES   RANK 276]

879 玛 玛 **agate**   ⬛ king 11   ⬛ horse 878   mǎ

BF **Agates** are gemstones characterized by a flowing, banded appearance. The bands can be splendid looking, almost *kingly* in some specimens. In others, the flowing shapes of the bands reminded the scribes (perhaps) of the flowing images of the mane of a *horse* in full gallop.   [7 STROKES   RANK 1248]

880 骂 骂 **curse, abuse**   ⬛ mouth (times 2) 41   ⬛ horse 878   mà

Watch two merchants. All you can see of them here are their two *mouths* as they review the detail of a recent sale of a *horse*. The left guy purchased a *horse*, but the right one delivered a mule. Listen as they **curse** and **abuse** each other.   [9 STROKES   RANK 1449]

881 吗 吗 **yes or no?**   ⬛ mouth 41   ⬛ horse 878   ma

Getting your kids to answer questions with a simple **'yes' or 'no'** is thankless. I scream from my *mouth* until I'm *hoarse* (sounds like '*horse*').

[6 STROKES   RANK 453]

882 驻 驻 halt, stay   ■ horse 878   ■ master 220   zh

You know when someone's *mastered* the art of riding a *horse* when they're able to command it to **halt**, and it obeys.   [8 STROKES   RANK 1288]

Unit 38

Prophet and Profit

883 骑 骑 **ride or sit astride**   ■ horse 878   ■ odd 343   qí
Sitting astride a *horse* is an *odd* way to pass the time. After a while, it strains your muscles.   [11 STROKES RANK 1398]

884 冯 冯 **ford a stream**   ■ ice r 569   ■ horse 878   píng
BF Winter. The river is frozen solid, but we must cross it. General Washington needs to receive our message to plan the campaign. Using my trusty *horse* to carry me, we break through the *ice*, **ford the stream**, and deliver the crucial message.   [5 STROKES RANK 1719]

885 鸟 鸟 **bird**   ■ horse 878 (altered)   niǎo
Here's another beautiful character, which, to a beginner's eyes, superficially resembles 'horse' (§878). In the traditional form, you can make out the components of a peacock-like fowl

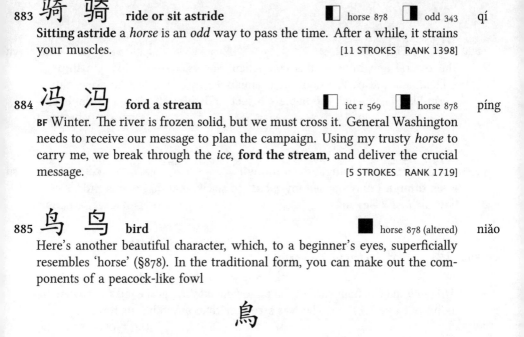

which shows the fancy feathered head, the claws below, and the long tail feathers.   [5 STROKES RANK 1263]

886 乌 乌 **crow**   ■ bird 885 (altered)   wū
BF We see a **crow** as an eyeless *bird*. The absence of eyes emphasizes the jet-black-ness of the creature, no contrast anywhere.   [4 STROKES RANK 1244]

887 鸣 鸣 **bird or animal cry**   ■ mouth 41   ■ bird 885   míng
A **bird call** is produced through the *mouths* of *birds*.   [8 STROKES RANK 1680]

888 岛 岛 island   ■ bird 885 (altered) ■ mountain 21 dǎ

The typical **island** at the time when people first designed these characters was formed by an undersea *mountain* sticking up and inhabited by nothing but *birds*.   [7 STROKES   RANK 798]

889 鸿 鸿 wild swan   ■ river, Yangtze 524 ■ bird 885 hó

BF One of the grandest of *river birds* is the **wild swan**.

[11 STROKES   RANK 1924]

890 虫 虫 insect   ■ mouth 41 ▯ scepter 5 ■ worm ch

The central apparatus of this component shows a *scepter*-like pin through a *mouth*-shaped cork, a tool often employed by naturalists to skewer their *worm*-like specimens. The hapless **insect** finds himself pinned to the board.

[6 STROKES   RANK 1287]

891 虽 虽 although, even though   □ mouth 41 ■ insect 890 suì

Even though I only opened my *mouth* to speak, and that only a little, somehow an *insect* flew in.   [9 STROKES   RANK 504]

892 强 强 strong, powerful

      ■ bow (weapon) 859 ■ although, even though 891 qiá

Although the chieftain carried the huge *bow* into the peace talks, we knew he didn't need it. As it was, he was **stronger** than any other man there.

[12 STROKES   RANK 292]

893 妈 妈 mom   ■ woman 581 ■ horse 878 mā

A true **mother** is a *woman* who would protect her child against herds of stampeding *horses*.   [6 STROKES   RANK 750]

894 骗 骗 **deceive, swindle**   ■□ horse 878   ■■ flat, crushed 729   piàn
The city slicker bought the *horse* without examining it close up. It turned
out to be an inflatable doll, looking good from a great distance. But in a few
hours, and from close up, when all the air leaked out, the so-called animal
was *flat*. The city slicker had been **swindled**.   [12 STROKES   RANK 1503]

895 融 融 **melt, thaw**   ■□ cauldron for meat or cereal 279   □■ insect 890   róng
The freezing soldiers stuffed ice into the *cauldron* for **melting** to get some
drinking water. They found the water loaded with *insects* they couldn't see
when the ice was still frozen.   [16 STROKES   RANK 1225]

896 蛋 蛋 **egg**   ■□ foot 419 (altered)   ▬■ insect 890   dàn
Birds aren't the only creatures who lay **eggs**. While on safari a few years
back, some nasty *insect* used my *foot* as a nesting territory, and presented me
with a wicked parasitic disease.   [11 STROKES   RANK 1387]

897 蛇 蛇 **snake, serpent**   ■□ insect 890   ■□ it 249   shé
To many people, a **snake** is the essence of creepy-crawliness. For many
people, *it* engenders primeval disgust as do many *insects*.
                                                       [11 STROKES   RANK 1689]

898 犭 犭 **dog r**
CMP This component pictures the family **dog** curled up in front of the fireplace,
and viewed from above. The main curve represents Fido's body in repose, his
tail tucked up against him. The front pair of legs is attached to his ears, and
the stroke representing his hind legs completes the sketch.

899 狱 狱 **prison, jail**   ■□ dog r 898   ■■ speech r 615   □■ dog 332   yù
BF Here's man, someone capable of *speech*, surrounded by two *dogs*, both big
and fierce. In the old days, this was what served as a **prison**.
                                                       [9 STROKES   RANK 1597]

900 独 独　alone, only　　　　　　■ dog r 898　■ insect 890　dú

The pathetic-looking homeless person smells like a *dog* and is covered with *insects*. Phew! No wonder he or she is all **alone**.　　　[9 STROKES　RANK 627]

901 犯 犯　violate, offend, commit crime

　　　　　　　　　　　　　　■ dog r 898　■ single ear 157 (altered)　fàn

That *dog* ripped my *ear* off! I am **violated** and **offended**.

　　　　　　　　　　　　　　　　　　[5 STROKES　RANK 767]

902 狂 狂　mad, crazy, conceited　　　■ dog r 898　■ king 11　kuá

Dogs can be **mad**. People who are **mad** often think they are the *king*. That's what *dog*, *king*, and **madness** have in common.　　[7 STROKES　RANK 1147]

903 狗 狗　dog*　　　　　　　　■ dog r 898　■ sentence 639　gǒu

A **dog** is one of the few animals that is *dog*-gone smart enough to learn the meanings of simple *sentences*.　　　　[8 STROKES　RANK 1281]

904 貌 貌　appearance, aspect

　　　　　■ dog r 898 (altered)　■ white 201　■ elder brother* 298　mà

BF The component on the left—a *dog* gone wild—is by itself a very rare character denoting 'wild beast' (or sometimes 'legless worm'!). Since it's so rare, we'll just remember it as a dog with an emphasis on the teeth. Anyway, my *older brother* turned *white* as a sheet in its presence—his **appearance** changed dramatically.　　　　　　　　　　[14 STROKES　RANK 1595]

905 猫 猫　cat　　　　　　　　■ dog r 898　■ seedling 97　mā

Believe it or not, the Chinese view the **cat** as a *dog*-like animal. In former days, the **cat** was not housebound, but wandered freely throughout the *seeded* fields, looking for mice, moles, and other farm pests.　　[11 STROKES　RANK 1673]

The heart is apparently an especially important organ to the Chinese. It occurs as a component in not one but two forms.

906 心 忄 heart (fat)

CMP This is the first of those two forms, and occurs when this component appears on the bottom of characters. As in Western prose and poetry, we'll often equate the **heart** with an emotion or emotional event.

907 心 心 heart   ■ heart (fat) 906 (altered)   xīn

The central curve suggests the actual **heart**, surrounded by three gouts of blood.   [4 STROKES   RANK 90]

908 志 志 aspiration   ☐ scholar 8   ▬ heart (fat) 906   zhì

Scholarly accomplishments were punishingly difficult to achieve in ancient China, so much so that it becomes easy to interpret *scholarly emotion* as **aspiration**.   [7 STROKES   RANK 542]

Unit 39

Less is More

909 悲 悲 sad, sorrow   ▢ not 13   ■ heart (fat) 906   bēi

Sadness and **sorrow** are prime examples of *negative emotions*.

[12 STROKES   RANK 1166]

910 忠 忠 loyal   ▢ middle 45   ■ heart (fat) 906   zhō

BF *Central* to all the *emotions* is **loyalty**.   [8 STROKES   RANK 1322]

911 闷 闷 stuffy, muggy   ■ door 196   ◧ heart 907   mē

A giant *heart* threatens to fill up the *doorway*. It keeps growing and expanding! Any more of this, and you'll be smothered in the room. As it expands, the moist tissue gives off lots of water vapor, so everything feels **stuffy** as well.   [7 STROKES   RANK 1830]

912 息 息 breath, news   ▢ self 202   ■ heart (fat) 906   xī

BF In ancient times, one's **breath** was the exhaust (so to speak) of *one's own heart-felt emotion*.   [10 STROKES   RANK 428]

913 媳 媳 daughter-in-law   ▌ woman 581   ▌ breath, news 912   xí

BF Family relations are emotion-laden connections. A *female relation* that causes the *breath* of a senior family member to increase in intensity might well be a **daughter-in-law**.   [13 STROKES   RANK 2393]

914 忘 忘 **forget**   ☐ perish 269 ■ heart (fat) 906   wàng

Forgetting is metaphorically akin to the *perishing* of *emotion*. The 'perish' bit looks like a heavy anvil, hammering down on the heart to shrink it.

[7 STROKES   RANK 1056]

915 态 态 **attitude**   ☐ too (much) 331 ■ heart (fat) 906   tài

BF That guy's got a real **attitude**. It's as if there's *too much emotion* leaking out of his *heart.*   [8 STROKES   RANK 528]

916 恩 恩 **kindness, favor**   ☐ because 345 ■ heart (fat) 906   ēn

Because the gods in heaven have *hearts*, they will grant us blessings and **favors**.   [10 STROKES   RANK 888]

917 嗯 嗯 **how come? why?**   ▯ mouth 41 ☐ kindness, favor 916   ňg

Our *mouth* expresses **wonderment** about the sudden unexpected *kindness and favor* that fell our way.   [13 STROKES   RANK 2042]

918 患 患 **trouble, disaster**   ☐ strung together 46 ■ heart (fat) 906 huàn

BF When several *emotions* are *strung together*, this may be a sign of **trouble**. How so? **Disaster** brings with it a plethora of emotions. It may help to view the '*strung together*' component as a couple of weights attached to a sharp spear. An enemy is attacking your *heart*, and only **trouble** or **disaster** will follow.   [11 STROKES   RANK 1249]

919 思 思 **think, consider**   ■ field 57 ■ heart (fat) 906   sī

BF An alien *field*, which has somehow come to life, pounds on my *heart* repeatedly to try to kill me. I have to **think** real hard if I want to save myself.   [9 STROKES   RANK 298]

920 忌 忌 **envy, be jealous**   ■ self* 852 ■ heart (fat) 906   jì

BF A *heart* concerned only with the *self* easily **envies** others, since there is no room for generosity of feeling.   [7 STROKES   RANK 1922]

921 慧 慧 intelligence, wisdom   ▣ broom 36   ▣ heart (fat) 906   hu

BF It takes a good deal of **intelligence** to create a *broom* using an animal *heart*.

    The '*broom*' component itself looks like some kind of Rube Goldberg device that only someone possessed of extraordinary **wisdom** and **intelligence** could create.   [15 STROKES   RANK 1505]

922 惑 惑 confuse   ▣ or 363   ▣ heart (fat) 906   hu

BF For me, choosing the perfect wife is so *emotional*—I don't know if I should choose my childhood sweetheart *or* the girl I met in graduate school. I'm so **confused!**   [12 STROKES   RANK 1600]

923 想 想 think, believe   ▣ appearance 391   ▣ heart (fat) 906   xiǎ

It's amazing how often Chinese embed charming metaphors into their characters. For example, here we see the (metaphorical) *appearance* of a *heart* as a **thought** or **belief**.   [13 STROKES   RANK 99]

924 悬 悬 suspend, hang   ▣ county 766   ▣ heart (fat) 906   xu

The *county* bigwig has his private clothes rack in his office. He is so forthright and outgoing it's as if he **hangs** his *heart* there each day.

        [11 STROKES   RANK 1879]

925 感 感 feel, sense   ▣ salty 371   ▣ heart (fat) 906   gǎr

Pouring *salt* on a wound is a famous way of increasing **feeling**, albeit in a negative sense. Here, the open wound is on some one's *heart*.

        [13 STROKES   RANK 243]

926 愿 愿 sincere, honest   ▣ original, unprocessed 676   ▣ heart (fat) 906   yuᵃ

BF What *emotion* do you feel when you visit a *pristine* mountain spring? Whatever it is, it's sure to be **honest** and **sincere**.   [14 STROKES   RANK 598]

927 慈 慈 **compassionate, kind** ▨ now, at present 779 ▨ heart (fat) 906   cí

BF Major religions teach that at *any moment*, one's goal should be to be full of an *emotion* which is **compassionate, kind,** and loving.

[13 STROKES   RANK 1487]

928 惠 惠 **kind, benevolent, gentle**

▨ insect 890 ▨ two 3 ▨ heart (fat) 906   huì

BF I saved *two insects* from the fly swatter. What *emotion* is that? Great **benevolence.**   [12 STROKES   RANK 1524]

929 怨 怨 **blame, reproach, reprove**

▨ evening, dusk 655 ▨ self* r 851 (altered) ▨ heart (fat) 906   yuàn

Lying in bed at *night* is the worst—you're prey to all sorts of thoughts and *emotions* in which you **blame** *yourself* for everything wrong in your life.

[9 STROKES   RANK 1637]

930 忄 忄 **heart (skinny)**

CMP This is the second of the '**heart**' components, which scribes use whenever a 'heart' component appears on the left. Imagine the bottom curve of §906 stretched taut and combining with one of the drops of blood. The remaining two drops suggest the bloody nature of this organ.

931 悟 悟 **realize** ▨ heart (skinny) 930 ▨ me 81   wù

It took me a long time to **realize** that the *heart* inside *me* is the source of the real me.   [10 STROKES   RANK 1668]

932 怔 怔 **panic-stricken** ▨ heart (skinny) 930 ▨ correct 183   zhēng

BF After a **panic attack**, the *heart* has to *correct* its rhythms.

[8 STROKES   RANK 2191]

933 性 性 **nature, character** ▨ heart (skinny) 930 ▨ give birth to 191   xìng

The *heart gives birth to* the true **nature** and **character** of someone.

[8 STROKES   RANK 122]

934 怕　怕　**to fear, be afraid**   ■ heart (skinny) 930   □ white 201   pà

My wife awoke last night from a terrible nightmare, all **in fear**. It's a dreadful *emotion*—her face was *white*.   [8 STROKES   RANK 631]

Unit 40

Curves and Straightaways

935 忙 忙 **busy**   ▮ heart (skinny) 930   ▮ perish 269   **máng**

When you're truly **busy** your *heart* is working so furiously it's in danger of *perishing*.   [6 STROKES RANK 827]

It's easy to confuse this character 忙 with 忘 (§914) since both combine 亡 (§269) with one or the other forms of 'heart'. But the 'f' in 'forget' is like the 'f' in 'fat'—'forget' uses the 'fat' heart. Coldy efficient executives, 'busy' all the time, are in real danger of crowding emotion out of their lives completely. In 忙, the skinny 'heart' at the left will soon be pushed off the page to perish (or so it appears).

936 快 快 **fast**   ▮ heart (skinny) 930   ▮ surprised man 518   **kuài**

A badly *surprised man* finds his *heart* beating wildly—very **fast**. It takes a couple of minutes for him to regain control.   [7 STROKES RANK 366]

937 懂 懂 **understand, know**   ▮ heart (skinny) 930   ▮ director 229   **dǒng**

You fully **understand** the issue when your *heart* is able to *direct* your behavior.   [15 STROKES RANK 1211]

938 恰 恰 **exactly, properly**   ▮ heart (skinny) 930   ▮ cozy house 509   **qià**

It's been a rough day at the office. At night, returning to my *cozy house*, my *heart* beats calmly at the welcome sight of an environment which is **exactly** what my soul needs.   [9 STROKES RANK 1308]

939 愤 愤 anger ▮ heart (skinny) 930 ▮ hasten 433   fèi

BF **Anger** is often the result of *emotion* that develops with too much *haste*. If we force ourselves to stay calm in a stressful situation, we can more easily control angry feelings.   [12 STROKES   RANK 1508]

940 惯 惯 accustomed, used to ▮ heart (skinny) 930 ▮ link up 438   gu

Becoming **accustomed to** something is the process of regarding something as usual and ordinary which at first would have been unusual and special. Imagine *linking* your *heart* to this new something to reign in your emotion and so become **accustomed** to it.   [11 STROKES   RANK 1226]

941 悔 悔 regret, repent ▮ heart (skinny) 930 ▮ every 600   hu

BF Shoulda, woulda, coulda. **Regret** is an *emotion* that *every*body feels.   [10 STROKES   RANK 1853]

942 恒 恒 permanent ▮ heart (skinny) 930 ▮ speak 64 ▮ one (times 2) 2   héi

BF That *speech* of love was so sincere that it carved not one but *two marks* on my *heart*. You weren't toying with my emotions—our love is a **permanent** state.   [9 STROKES   RANK 1764]

943 爿 爿 chopped wood ▮ tree 375 (altered)

CMP In keeping with its meaning of **chopped wood**, it's helpful to regard this component as the elaborated left half of 木 '*tree*' (§375).

944 臧 臧 lucky, good ▮ chopped wood 943 ▮ archaic lance 367 ▮ subject of a ruler 17   zāi

BF The battle rages to the right and left! The loyal *subject* finds himself in the midst of the melee. Suddenly, a huge *lance* plunges towards his neck, to be stopped at the last instant by a *piece of wood* that happened to get in the way. What **luck**—he lives to tell the story.   [14 STROKES   RANK 4304]

945 藏 藏 **hide, conceal**   ▢ grass r 94   ▮ lucky, good 944   cáng

BF The *lucky* guy found a pile of gold coins someone lost. He used a pile of *grass* to **hide** his treasure.   [17 STROKES   RANK 907]

946 𧾷 𧾷 **foot r**   ▢ mouth 41   ▮ stop! 181

CMP This is a distorted version of 'foot' (§419), which Chinese scribes use whenever '**foot**' appears as a left ingredient for characters like 趴, 趾, and plenty more.

There are some folks about whom it is said they are so dumb that they cannot walk and talk at the same time. Here's one of them. Since they're using their *mouth*, they come to a complete *stop*. They are now standing still on their **feet**.

947 跃 跃 **leap, jump**   ▮ foot r 946   ▢ dab 169   ▮ big 330   yuè

BF Whenever you **jump**, you use your *feet* to leave the ground for a *small bit* of time. You try to **jump** as *high* as you can.   [11 STROKES   RANK 1516]

948 距 距 **be apart or away from**   ▮ foot r 946   ▮ huge 18   jù

With one step of his *foot*, our *huge* man from §18 quickly **moves away from** the jeering crowds.   [11 STROKES   RANK 1202]

949 跌 跌 **fall, tumble**   ▮ foot r 946   ▮ lose 427   diē

While using your *feet* to walk, run, or dance, if you *lose* your balance, you can take a nasty **tumble**.   [12 STROKES   RANK 1590]

950 跑 跑 **run**   ▮ foot r 946   ▮ wrap, envelope 857   pǎo

I have a lot of chores to do, and very little time. I use my *feet* to *wrap* them up by **running** from one place to the next.   [12 STROKES   RANK 864]

951 践 践 **trample, tread upon**   ▮ foot r 946   ▮ tiny, fragmentary 373   jiàn

BF The neighbor's teenagers **trampled** all over my garden with their huge, Doc Martens-shod *feet*, destroying the *tiny* sprouts.   [12 STROKES   RANK 1578]

952 踏 踏 **step on, tread, stamp**

▮ foot r 946　▮ numerous, repeated 565　tà

What does a *foot* do *repeatedly*? It **steps** and **stamps**, that's what.

[15 STROKES RANK 1753]

953 亻 亻 **man r**

CMP Here's the squished form of 人 (§311). In this form, it fits into the character square while leaving room for other stuff.

954 仁 仁 **benevolence**

▮ man r 953　▮ two 3　rér

One of the most ideal feelings between *two men* is **benevolence**.

[4 STROKES RANK 1360]

955 什 什 **what**

▮ man r 953　▮ ten 6　she

We've found it's a good idea to visualize abstract words like 'what' by means of well-known concrete phrases that use these words. '**What** the hell!?'—we'll use this as our tag phrase for 什. For me, 'hell' is spending eternity with the *ten men* closest to me in life, and that's how we'll remember this character.

[4 STROKES RANK 156]

956 任 任 **assume a post**

▮ man r 953　▮ scholar 8　▯ dab 169　rèr

The right component of 任 is not the 'king' of §11! Look closely—the middle horizontal is longer than its upstairs and downstairs neighbors.

Here in the West, academic appointments work differently from 'regular' jobs. As he **assumes a new post**, the administration views this *man* as a *little bit* of a genuine *scholar*. He will receive re-appointments (and ultimately tenure) if he displays scholarly growth.

[6 STROKES RANK 186]

957 佳 佳 **fine, beautiful**

▮ man r 953　▮ jade tablet 14　jiā

We see a *person* contemplating a *jade tablet* because it's so **fine** and **beautiful**.

[8 STROKES RANK 1583]

958 估 估   estimate   ▮ man r 953   ▮ ancient 51   gū

   1 One of *man*'s *ancient* skills is learning to **estimate** the value of goods.

   2 One of your favorite summer jobs in college was the year you worked
      in the pawnshop downtown. You had to learn to accurately **estimate** or
      appraise every *old* and worthless thing brought in by any *man*.

                                   [7 STROKES   RANK 1326]

959 仲 仲   **2nd in seniority**   ▮ man r 953   ▮ middle 45   zhòng

I get the sense that this character originated at a time when small groups
typically consisted of three things. The **second** *man* in a group of siblings,
say, was apt to be the *middle* in age.   [6 STROKES   RANK 1706]

960 伸 伸   stretch, extend   ▮ man r 953   ▮ express 47   shēn

Here's a *man* who's so sure of himself he's not afraid to *express* his opinion
in any social setting, and thereby **extend** himself.   [7 STROKES   RANK 1161]

Unit 41

Mighty Fine

961 伍 伍 5-man squad   ▯ man r 953   ▯ five 19   wǔ

The components perfectly describe this meaning. The squad in question was part of the ancient armies of China.   [6 STROKES   RANK 1472]

962 何 何 denotes interrogation   ▯ man r 953   ▯ can; may 60   hé

Men are the ones with all the *ability*—at least that was the received wisdom for centuries. Now modern science has turned that statement on its head. In the same way, when you turn a statement on its head, you get a **question**.   [7 STROKES   RANK 229]

963 侍 侍 serve, wait upon   ▯ man r 953   ▮ Buddhist temple 213   shì

BF *Men* who work in religious *Buddhist temples* do so to **serve** God.   [8 STROKES   RANK 1871]

964 荷 荷 carry a burden   ▭ grass r 94   ▮ denotes interrogation 962   hè

BF Here comes someone **carrying a** strange **burden** on their back. *What* is it? *Where* are they going? *Why* are they even bothering with it? It's a load of *grass* or hay.   [10 STROKES   RANK 1427]

965 但 但 but   ▯ man r 953   ▯ dawn 65   dàn

You've heard the expression "down but not out." Well, here we have a *man* still lingering over his morning washing up and breakfast when he should be on his way to work—it's *dawn*, **but** he's not out!   [7 STROKES   RANK 95]

966 佰 佰 **hundred (fraudproof)** ▢ man r 953 ▇ hundred 203 **bǎi**

Gather *one hundred men*, and group them together. They will check each other and ensure each stays honest. The '**fraudproof**' part relates to the maintaining of honesty among a group of merchants.   [8 STROKES   RANK 5437]

967 宿 宿 **stay overnight** ▢ roof 247 ▇ hundred (fraudproof) 966 **sù**

BF I can sleep anywhere. Just put a *roof* over my head, and I cheerfully get *one hundred* winks. I'm always calm in these situations; you might call me *fraughtproof* (sounds like '*fraudproof*'). I prefer to **stay overnight** so as to better enjoy the company of others.   [11 STROKES   RANK 1752]

968 缩 缩 **contract, shrink** ▢ silk r 807 ▢ stay overnight 967 **suō**

I let my *silk* underwear *stay overnight* in the washtub. Is anyone surprised that the garments **shrunk**? Now they're too tight to be comfortable!

[14 STROKES   RANK 1304]

969 仙 仙 **immortal** ▢ man r 953 ▢ mountain 21 **xiān**

BF One feature of any landscape seems eternal and **immortal**—*mountains*. By comparing a *man* to a *mountain*, the anonymous Chinese artist illustrates **immortality**.   [5 STROKES   RANK 1255]

970 伯 伯 **father's elder brother** ▢ man r 953 ▢ white 201 **bó**

BF **Older brothers** can be vicious to their siblings. One *man* so tormented his younger brother that the brother turned *white* with fear every time the boy saw his older brother. The boy, now a father himself, never forgot those feelings.   [7 STROKES   RANK 821]

971 付 付 **pay** ▢ man r 953 ▢ inch 210

▢ man r 953 ▢ hand 27 (altered) ▫ dab 169 **fù**

This character shows a *hand* (a variant of §27) handing over *a little something* to he *man* on the left. That's what it means to **pay** something to someone.

[5 STROKES   RANK 820]

972 咐 咐 **to instruct, exhort** ▫ mouth 41   ▪ pay 971   fù

BF I *pay* a tutor to **instruct** me. The '*mouth*' part shows him delivering his lecture as loudly as possible. I *pay through* the nose, and must *pay* attention as well. [8 STROKES   RANK 2093]

973 府 府 **mansion**   ▫ shelter r 681   ▪ pay 971   fǔ

BF To buy a **mansion**, you have to *pay* and *pay* for this luxurious type of *shelter*. [8 STROKES   RANK 417]

974 附 附 **add, attach**   ▪ hills 735   ▪ pay 971   fù

We are so **attached** to the picturesque *hills* outside town that we are glad to *pay* extra taxes and fees to keep them pristine and beautiful for us and future generations. [7 STROKES   RANK 923]

975 促 促 **to urge**   ▪ man r 953   ▫ foot 419   cù

When *men* get **urges** to go to specific places, they use their *feet* to get them there. Of course, nowadays, we use cars, trains, and planes to scratch those itchy **urges**, but this was not so in the days of the scribes. [9 STROKES   RANK 1102]

976 仆 仆 **fall forward**   ▪ man r 953   ▫ foretell 170   pū

BF The clumsy magician has a tendency to **fall forward** especially after drinking too much, but here's magic to the rescue! He uses his powers to *foretell* the situation and right himself. [4 STROKES   RANK 1812]

977 件 件 **m for items, things, etc**   ▪ man r 953   ▪ ox 186   jiàr

Nowadays, groups of items might well include things like 'luggage' or 'designer shirts'. But in ancient times, things were of more immediate use, things like 'cuts of meat'. Here, in fact, some *man* is about to divide up a freshly-slaughtered *ox* preparatory to counting out the **pieces** for distribution. [6 STROKES   RANK 250]

978 们 们 **plural marker**   █ man r 953   █ door 196   men

People naturally gather around gates and *doorways* in hopes of picking up bits of news or handouts of food, to buy and sell stuff, and so on, so this is a good way to show **the idea of many things**.   [5 STROKES RANK 13]

979 信 信 letter   █ man r 953   █ speech 270   xìn

Today there are a million ways to communicate with someone not directly in front of you. Not so in the olden days. Then, a **letter** was the main way of capturing a *person's speech* in a permanent way.   [9 STROKES RANK 176]

980 住 住 to live   █ man r 953   █ master 220   zhù

Where is *man* the *master* of his domain? Why, where he **lives**, of course!

[7 STROKES RANK 309]

981 伟 伟 **great, imposing**   █ man r 953   █ leather 115   wěi

BF A *man* appropriately decked out in *leather* garments and shoes appears very **imposing**.   [6 STROKES RANK 1107]

982 俩 俩 two (colloquial)   █ man r 953   █ both, two 316   liǎ

This means almost the same thing as **both** or *two*, but it tends to be spoken whenever there are *two people* involved.   [9 STROKES RANK 1574]

983 代 代 **take the place of**   █ man r 953   █ arrow type 356   dài

I've been waiting for hours on line, and then this *man* comes up to me holding a sharp *arrow* in a very threatening manner. Sure enough, he wants **to take my place** in line.   [5 STROKES RANK 174]

984 伐 伐 cut down   █ man r 953   █ halberd 359   fá

In times of peace, *men* use their *swords* to **cut down** trees and crops.

[6 STROKES RANK 1810]

985 俄　俄　Russian　　　　　　　　　　　■ man r 953　■ I 361　é
Russian *men* are very *egotistical*.　　　　　　[9 STROKES　RANK 975]

986 休　休　to rest　　　　　　　　　　　　■ man r 953　■ tree 375　xiū
BF A *person* leans against a *tree* to get a bit of **rest**.　[6 STROKES　RANK 1082]

Unit 42

Sooner or Later

987 保 保 **protect, defend** ◨ man r 953 ◨ foolish, stupid 393 bǎo

BF A *man* might try to use a *foolish* puppet to deceive the enemy into thinking that there are more men than there are. That's a well-known ploy to **defend** a settlement. [9 STROKES RANK 266]

988 堡 堡 **fortress** ◨ protect, defend 987 ◨ earth, soil 9 bǎo

BF In olden days, **fortresses** were lines of *protection* and *defense* constructed from giant walls of *earth*. [12 STROKES RANK 1521]

989 体 体 **body*** ◨ man r 953 ◨ root or stem of plant 378 tǐ

BF The **body** is the *root* of a *man* or *woman*'s physical essence. [7 STROKES RANK 149]

990 例 例 **example, instance** ◨ man r 953 ◨ arrange, line up 659 lì

Why is this *man* so busy *lining things up*? They are jelly beans from a new bag of candy, and they show off all the **examples** of colors and flavors of the jelly beans. [8 STROKES RANK 547]

991 倒 倒 **topple, fall over** ◨ man r 953 ◨ arrive 756 dǎo

It's midnight, and I watch this tableau from the safety of my bedroom window. An odd, caped *man* has chased some other *man* down the street in a threatening manner. Indeed, as this *man arrived* at the safety of his house, he **fell over** from an excess of anxiety. (At this, the caped *man* ran away.) [10 STROKES RANK 608]

992 隹 隹   short-tailed bird   ▮ man r 953   ▮ master 220   zh▸

This pictograph is both a component and a very low frequency independent character. **Short-tailed birds** include pigeons, crows, and the like.

It's easy to confuse the right part with 主, 'master' (§220). But note carefully: '*master*' has only three horizontals, while '**bird**' has four! **Birds** fly over *masters*, so they deserve a 'higher' rank, and the additional chevron emphasizes this.   [8 STROKES   RANK 5837]

993 堆 堆   to heap up   ▮ earth, soil 9   ▮ short-tailed bird 992   du̇

Birds rarely perch on the *ground*. The only way this could happen is if the *soil* was **heaped up** to fool the bird into thinking of it as a perch.

[11 STROKES   RANK 1370]

994 推 推   push   ▮ hand r 29   ▮ short-tailed bird 992   tuī

Geese are becoming a positive nuisance in many parts of the United States, and courageous people in public parks often use their *hands* on these *short-tailed birds* in order to **push** their way through a flock.

[11 STROKES   RANK 505]

995 唯 唯   only, alone   ▮ mouth 41   ▮ short-tailed bird 992   wé

Many years ago, in London's Hyde Park I was fascinated to watch patient men who had, after a fashion, trained the wild pigeons there. Standing stock still, and teaching the *short-tailed birds* to use their hand as a perch, these avian trainers got one *bird* at a time—one bird **alone**—to peck seeds from the lips of their *mouths*.   [11 STROKES   RANK 1094]

996 崔 崔   lofty   ▮ mountain 21   ▮ short-tailed bird 992   cuī

BF When the *short-tailed bird* flies to the top of the *mountain*, it takes a **lofty** flight path.   [11 STROKES   RANK 2552]

997 催 催   to urge*   ▮ man r 953   ▮ lofty 996   cuī

We **urge** *lofty* behavior upon our *friend* before things get too out of hand.

[13 STROKES   RANK 2064]

998 霍 霍 **suddenly, quickly** ▢ rain 85 ▣ short-tailed bird 992 huò
Suddenly—with no warning—the flock of *short-tailed birds* flying overhead *showers* you with their filthy droppings.   [16 STROKES   RANK 1442]

999 准 准 **standard, criterion** ▮ ice r 569 ▣ short-tailed bird 992 zhǔn
BF *Birds* worthy enough of being kept on *ice* conform to a certain **standard**.
      [10 STROKES   RANK 379]

1000 惟 惟 **way of thought, -ism**
▮ heart (skinny) 930 ▣ short-tailed bird 992 wéi
This guy is a real *bird*-brain. He's so enthusiastic about *bird*-watching and all things pertaining to *birds* (especially those with *short tails*), that his entire **way of thinking** is organized into bits of *emotion* which flutter around inside him like *birds*.   [11 STROKES   RANK 1856]

1001 焦 焦 **burnt, scorched** ▣ short-tailed bird 992 ▭ fire r 796 jiāo
BF The best example of something being **burnt** or **scorched**—in a good sense—is the notion of a large and *short-tailed bird* being slow roasted over a *fire* for dinner.   [12 STROKES   RANK 1554]

1002 瞧 瞧 **look at** ▯ eye 78 ▣ burnt, scorched 1001 qiáo
When you *scorch* or *burn* something, you darken its color. This rich dark color reminds me of your beautiful, smoking hot *eyes* whenever I **look at** them.   [17 STROKES   RANK 1551]

1003 集 集 **gather, collect** ▣ short-tailed bird 992 ▭ tree 375 jí
BF A flock of *short-tailed birds* sits on a *tree*. If we could sneak up on them without alerting them, we could **gather** them by the dozens!
      [12 STROKES   RANK 406]

1004 雇 雇 **employ** ☐ door of house 724 ◼ short-tailed bird 992 gù

Jobs can seem constricting and confining, just like solitary confinement in prison. Others regard themselves in their **employment** as caged *short-tailed birds* with the only way out firmly blocked by the *door.*

[12 STROKES   RANK 1817]

1005 雁 雁 **wild goose**

☐ high cliff 679 ⊔ man r 953 ◼ short-tailed bird 992 yàn

How do birds fly in China? Not in a v-formation, for they don't have this letter! In China, they say that migrating birds fly in a 人-shape (§311). The Chinese therefore see **wild geese** as a flock of *short-tailed birds* launching themselves in 人-formation from a higher *cliff.*   [12 STROKES   RANK 2553]

1006 鷹 鷹 **eagle** ☐ wild goose 1005 (altered) ◼ bird 885 yīng

Scribes emphasize the nobility and grandeur of the **eagle** by illustrating the *bird*-ness of the *wild goose.*   [18 STROKES   RANK 1927]

1007 伏 伏 **bend over** ◻ man r 953 ☐ dog 332 fú

The only way the *man* can pet the cute *doggie* is if he **bends over** to do it.   [6 STROKES   RANK 1389]

1008 停 停 **stop, pause** ◻ man r 953 ◻ pagoda 514 tíng

1 When the *man*, a typical tourist, first encountered the beautiful *pagoda*, its beauty and grace forced him to **stop** in his tracks.

2 Here's a *man* in such a religious trance that he bumps his nose on the *pagoda* that he was coming to pray in. That forced him to **stop!**

[11 STROKES   RANK 693]

1009 仰 仰 **look up** ◻ man r 953 ◻ head held high 160 yǎng

A *man* who is *holding* his *head high* is **looking up**.   [6 STROKES   RANK 1368]

1010 值 值 **to be worth**   ▮ man r 953   ▮ straight, vertical 16   zhí
Here's a silly image. If you want to buy a person, you go to a *person* store, where all the available people are hung neatly on the walls, all *straight* and *vertical*. Trying to make a selection? Check the labels next to each piece of merchandise—it tells you exactly how much each **is worth**!

[10 STROKES   RANK 600]

1011 侧 侧 **inclined to**   ▮ man r 953   ▮ standard, norm 431   cè
People who do *normal* stuff all the time are **inclined** to keep on doing it.

[8 STROKES   RANK 1220]

1012 侦 侦 **to spy**   ▮ man r 953   ▯ foretell 170   ▮ cowrie 430   zhēn
BF How do you **spy** on someone? The *man* here can *foretell* the person's actions with a device made from a *cowrie shell*.   [8 STROKES   RANK 1479]

Unit 43

Silence is Golden

1013 侯 侯 **archery target**

      ■ man r 953   □ cover 268 (altered)   ■ arrow 334   hó▸

BF A *man* shooting an *arrow* into the air. A *covering*—perhaps a roof or a tree, but most likely the **archery target**—stops it. The change on the top of '*cover*' makes the dab look like a handle, so it's easy to move the **target**.

    More commonly, this character refers to a **marquis**, a Chinese nobleman. Perhaps only noblemen with the leisure their class afforded them were able to practice archery.   [9 STROKES RANK 1756]

1014 候 候 **time, season**   ■ archery target 1013   ▮ path   hòʋ

BF "**Time** flies like an arrow." Well, here's that arrow's *path*, unfortunately very short, cut short by the *archery target*, perhaps a metaphor for death itself.   [10 STROKES RANK 341]

1015 他 他 **he**   ■ man r 953   ■ also*, too* 140   tā

Human beings are human precisely because we each one of us store all our different traits in a single body. In this case we concentrate on one *man*. **He** can be clever but *also* dumb, considerate but *also* selfish, outgoing but *also* shy, and so on and so on.   [5 STROKES RANK 10]

1016 化 化 **change, transform**   ■ man r 953   ■ ancient ladle 142   huà

The one constant thing in a person's life is **change**. Hooking a symbol like '*ancient ladle*' to a *man* emphasizes the **changes** and **transformations** that are ever present.   [4 STROKES RANK 178]

1017 花 花   **blossom, flower**   ☐ grass r 94   ■ change, transform 1016   huā

The most amazing *transformation* in the plant kingdom, in my opinion, is to observe how a *green plant changes* as it develops a beautiful, fragrant **blossom**.   [7 STROKES   RANK 410]

1018 华 华   **glory, splendor**   ■ change, transform 1016   ■ ten 6   huá

Note that the '*ten*' is slightly altered—the cross-stroke is much nearer the top of the vertical than is usual, as if to resemble a stage for all to see the *transformation* to take place. What merits such display? Something **glorious** will ensue, and everyone deserves to see it.   [6 STROKES   RANK 412]

1019 货 货   **goods**   ■ change, transform 1016   ■ cowrie 430   huò

This character encompasses half of a freshman economics course. *Wealth* supports the *transformation* of resources into **goods** and commodities that you can sell to create even more *wealth*!   [8 STROKES   RANK 818]

1020 伦 伦   **human relationship**   ■ man r 953   ■ order, coherence 457   lún

BF In a healthy **human relationship**, one *person* brings *order* to the life of the beloved, and vice versa.   [6 STROKES   RANK 970]

1021 倾 倾   **incline, lean**   ■ man r 953   ■ in an instant 458   qīng

Here's a *man* just walking along, minding his own business. Suddenly, he trips over a ladle hidden by leaves (see §458) and *in an instant* he finds himself **leaning** forward at a dangerous angle. Will he fall or regain his balance?   [10 STROKES   RANK 1260]

1022 侵 侵   **invade**   ■ man r 953   ■ broom* 133 (altered)   qīn

BF The 'towel' component in §133 has been altered to look like the character 又 'hand', quite different from the 'hand' 手 of §27. (We'll discuss this second 'hand' many units ahead, but in the meantime think of a hand in the form of a closed fist.) Perhaps the fist emphasizes the aggressive action of the *man*, who is preparing to **invade** the domain of a *broom* handler. Apparently, sweeping is a very territorial occupation. Who knew?   [9 STROKES   RANK 1086]

1023 依 依 **count on, depend on**   ☐ man r 953   ☐ clothing 839   yī

BF The *man* over there was so nicely dressed in smart *clothing* that we instinctively knew we could **count on** him for assistance.   [8 STROKES   RANK 568]

1024 似 似 **seem, appear**   ☐ man r 953   ☐ use, take 323   sì

BF During Mardi Gras, *men use* unusual costumes to **appear** to be something they are not.   [6 STROKES   RANK 431]

1025 谁 谁 **who**   ☐ speech r 615   ☐ short-tailed bird 992   shu

An owl is a *bird* with a very *short tail* whose cry sounds like *speech*. The owl calls out "Hoo, hoo—**who, who**."   [10 STROKES   RANK 648]

1026 维 维 **fiber, hold together**   ☐ silk r 807   ☐ short-tailed bird 992   wé

BF I've trained my little *short-tailed bird* to fly back and forth carrying lightweight *silk* threads each time. Gradually we build up the strength of the composite **fiber** until such time as we can pull the two sides and **hold them together** with this length of **fiber**.   [11 STROKES   RANK 520]

1027 偏 偏 **inclined to one side**   ☐ man r 953   ☐ flat, crushed 729   piā

The safe fell out the window, and a *man* was *crushed* to death. Now he is **inclined to one side**—in fact, his head points backwards.   [11 STROKES   RANK 1204]

1028 售 售 **sell***   ☐ short-tailed bird 992   ☐ mouth 41   shu

BF The market is falling! The price of chicken is plummeting, as you see here—that's why the *short-tailed bird's mouth* is on the bottom. If we don't **sell** now, for whatever we can get, we'll lose everything!   [11 STROKES   RANK 1114]

1029 符 符 **tally, symbol, sign**   ☐ bamboo r 243   ☐ pay 971   fú

In ancient China, absent computers, shopkeepers **tallied** purchases via **marks** on small slices of *bamboo* so customers (and clerks) knew how much to *pay*.   [11 STROKES   RANK 1205]

1030 债 债 **debt**   ■ man r 953 ■ responsibility 439   zhài
Paying off **debt** is a *man*'s primary *responsibility*.   [10 STROKES   RANK 1223]

1031 袋 袋 **pouch, bag, pocket** ■ take the place of 983 ■ clothing 839   dài
Pockets help *take the place of* bulky *clothing*.   [11 STROKES   RANK 1310]

1032 贷 贷 **loan, borrow** ■ take the place of 983 ■ cowrie 430   dài
A **loan** *takes the place of* your own *money*.   [9 STROKES   RANK 1605]

1033 腐 腐 **rotten, putrid, stale** ■ mansion 973 (altered) ■ meat 317   fǔ
BF One of the workmen left a *ham* sandwich in one of the rooms of the
mansion they worked in. They only realized it, days afterwards, when the
stench of **rotting** *meat* filled the house.   [14 STROKES   RANK 1576]

1034 彳 彳 **left step** ■ dab 169 ■ man r 953
CMP Let's interpret this radical as a '*little man*', the metaphor being applied to
the left side of the person. For most people, this is the weaker, and smaller,
side.
    Imagine a person in front of you facing left. Although the heel of the
foot is missing, this component clearly shows the **left foot**. The dab suggests
the presence of the right foot, just visible next to it.
    Since the ancients associated the left with weakness, this component also
has the meaning 'walk slowly'.

1035 行 行 **firm, business** ■ left step 1034 ■ one 2 ■ fourth 25   háng
Stare for a bit at the right hand '*one fourth*' assembly. See how it is a
mirror image—sorta kinda—of '*left step*'? Starting a **business** is a complicated
procedure. Prudent entrepreneurs proceed carefully, *step* by *step*. Finally,
when everything comes together, as the steps do here, are they ready to
commence operations.   [6 STROKES   RANK 53]

1036 得 得　**verbal particle**　▮ left step 1034　▢ dawn 65　▮ inch 210　de

As a grammatical particle, we Chinese speakers use this word to show how some action is carried out.

The '*left step*' conveys the idea of action. We (figuratively) need to wait for *dawn* until there's enough light to show us the the result of the action. Then, with the proper lighting, we can measure to the *inch* the nature of change to the verb. [11 STROKES RANK 39]

1037 征 征　**go on a journey**　▮ left step 1034　▮ correct 183　zhē

BF **Setting off on a journey**, particularly in the pre-automobile era of human history, involved literally taking *steps* toward your goal following the *correct* path. [8 STROKES RANK 739]

1038 懲 懲　**punish, discipline**　▭ go on a journey 1037　▮ heart (fat) 906　chē

BF Proper **discipline** is a *journey* filled with *emotion*. You keep your children (for example) on the proper path. [12 STROKES RANK 1821]

Unit 44

A Slice of Life

1039 德 德 **Germany**
⬛ left step 1034 ⬛ ten 6 ⬛ net r 107 ⬛ one 2 ⬛ heart (fat) 906   dé

BF This character puts me in mind of the **German** military getups common in nineteenth century operetta. Soldiers goose*stepping to the left*, capped by ornate helmets with tall '*ten*'-shaped (that is, cross-shaped) ornaments, while a *net*ful of fabric weighted down by medals festoons their *single heart*.

[15 STROKES   RANK 256]

1040 律 律 **law, rule**   ⬛ left step 1034 ⬛ pen, writing instrument 39   lǜ

BF Imagine that the '*left step*' is a symbol of regulation, in that all citizens march to the same step. **Laws**, written and recorded with *pens*, help **rule** society.   [9 STROKES   RANK 526]

1041 往 往 **in the direction of, toward**

⬛ left step 1034 ⬛ king 11 (altered)   wǎng

When you *march* as confidently as a *king* **in the direction** of your destination, you'll get there sooner rather than later.   [8 STROKES   RANK 369]

1042 待 待 **stay**   ⬛ left step 1034 ⬛ Buddhist temple 213   dāi

We have earlier imagined a *Buddhist temple* as a place to enter and seek refuge. In this character, this process is made more explicit. A petitioner *steps* forward into the *temple*, preparing to **stay** for some time.

[9 STROKES   RANK 673]

1043 徒 徒 **disciple, pupil, follower**   ▮ left step 1034   ▮ to walk 421   tú

BF In antiquity, 'left' is associated with clumsiness, shadiness, ineptitude, and other sinister attributes. So the *left steps* of a young person associated with the confident skillful *walking* of a Master is a way to refer to a **disciple** or **pupil** who still has a lot to learn from their teacher.   [10 STROKES RANK 1060]

1044 径 径 **path, track**

▮ left step 1034   ▮ man 311 (altered)   ▮ labor, work 7   jìn

BF *Men* taking their *steps* in the same place every day to do the same *work*; that's how **paths** get worn in the forest.   [8 STROKES RANK 1307]

1045 御 御 **control, manage**   ▮ left step 1034   ▮ unload, take sth off 241   yù

BF Effective bosses **manage** their work *step* by *step*, and make sure to *offload* each task properly.   [12 STROKES RANK 1381]

1046 循 循 **follow, abide by**   ▮ left step 1034   ▮ shield 733   xú

BF I am happy to **follow** Hercules into battle. He's got the *shield*, and he bears the brunt of the fighting, while I *step* behind him in the relative calm there.   [12 STROKES RANK 1744]

1047 ⸯ ⸯ   **eight (v)**

CMP The 'v' stands for *variant*.

When used as a component, the next character 八 comes out as ⸯ . It's as if the praying hands of the next panel relax immediately after the photo is snapped. In this relaxed pose, the finger tips point downward, as we see in this variant form.

1048 八　八　eight　　　　　　　　■ eight (v) 1047 (altered)　　bā

Hands in prayer exert a strong pull for artists and photographers. Imagine here that some aspiring photographer attempts to capture hands in prayer from the side. Unfortunately, his own hands slip, and he only captures the upper portion of the pose. What we see are **eight** fingers in profile. Chinese scribes often associate '**eight**' with the concept of 'abundance', and on occasion, we will too.

　　The number eight has a special significance for Chinese people. In the Cantonese language, the pronunciation of 八 makes it sound like a word meaning 'rich' or 'abundant', so '**eight**' too becomes lucky. This happy connotation has since spread to Mandarin-speaking regions as well.

[2 STROKES　RANK 451]

1049 兑　兑　exchange, convert　　□ eight (v) 1047　　■ elder brother* 298　　duì

When *a lot* of *elder brothers*—representing the best of several clans—gets together, you can bet there will be plenty of words **exchanged** between them.　　[7 STROKES　RANK 2424]

1050 悦　悦　pleased　　■ heart (skinny) 930　　□ exchange, convert 1049　　yuè

BF Normally, people are dull and placid, but if we *convert* to something positive, then we will be **pleased**, a positive *emotion*.　　[10 STROKES　RANK 1995]

1051 阅　阅　read, review　　■ door 196　　■ exchange, convert 1049　　yuè

BF When the discussion group meets to **review** a book, it always leads to a noisy *exchange* of views. The *doorway* reminds us that we observe a view through it.　　[10 STROKES　RANK 1489]

1052 说　说　speak, talk　　■ speech r 615　　□ exchange, convert 1049　　shuō

If you don't mind a slightly highfalutin' image, the **speaking** you do with someone else involves *exchanging speech* between you.　　[9 STROKES　RANK 24]

1053 总 总 always, anyway

◻ eight (v) 1047　◼ mouth 41　◼ heart (fat) 906　zǒ

Every language has little words that appear all the time in speech in many contexts. They've all got many different meanings—like English 'just' or 'anyway'—that sharpen the speaker's expressions in any of several ways. 总 plays such a role in Chinese. An *abundance* of *verbal* aspects makes the speaker's *emotion* clear to his listener.　[9 STROKES   RANK 228]

1054 聪 聪 intelligent

◼ ear 82　◼ always, anyway 1053　cō

BF You've got to be **intelligent** to use your *ear* to identify the proper context and meaning of '*anyway*'.　[15 STROKES   RANK 1669]

1055 具 具 tool, utensil

◼ eye 78 (altered)　◼ eight 1048　jù

BF *I* (sounds like '*eye*') become *abundantly* productive with the proper **tool**.　[8 STROKES   RANK 391]

1056 惧 惧 to fear, dread

◼ heart (skinny) 930　◼ tool, utensil 1055　jù

BF The evil overseer walks around with a heavy *tool* in his hand, threatening the slaves for the slightest infraction. It led to an *emotional* climate of **fear and dread**.　[11 STROKES   RANK 1616]

1057 俱 俱 entirely

◼ man r 953　◼ tool, utensil 1055　jù

Wasn't it Archimedes who said "Give me a lever and I will move the world" (or something like that)? Here's a *man* with a *tool*, and as a result he's **entirely** on his own.　[10 STROKES   RANK 1909]

1058 真 真 real

◻ ten 6　◼ tool, utensil 1055　zh

With only one or two *tools* at hand, my weekend projects come out looking amateurish and crummy. But with *ten tools* at my disposal, the results look **real**.　[10 STROKES   RANK 204]

1059 慎　慎　**cautious, careful**　　　■ to fear, dread 1056 (altered)　☐ ten 6　　shèn
BF When you've been *frightened* by the same thing *ten* times in a row, you learn a degree of **caution**.　　　　　　　　　　　　[13 STROKES   RANK 1765]

1060 谷　谷　**cereal, grain**　　　☐ eight 1048　■ man 311　▪ mouth 41　　gǔ
BF Look closely at the grim face of a murderer—squinty eyes; large, ugly nose; and a huge, unsightly mouth. He shovels food into that *mouth* at the breakfast table as if this is his last meal. A **cereal** killer for sure. (Outrageous wordplay alert!)　　　　　　　　　　　[7 STROKES   RANK 1095]

1061 俗　俗　**vulgar**　　　▮ man r 953　▮ cereal, grain 1060　　sú
BF The *man* with the '*cereal*' face looks **vulgar**.　　[9 STROKES   RANK 1354]

1062 六　六　**six**　　　☐ dab 169　▭ one 2　■ eight 1048　　liù
Something flat, like the horizontal stroke for '*one*' suggests something level, perhaps an even number. The *eight* on the bottom suggests an even number having some relation to *eight*. Finally, the *dab* on top suggests an even number which is slightly smaller than eight, a number like **six**.　　[4 STROKES   RANK 478]

1063 小　小　**small**　　　■ eight 1048　▯ hooked stick 24　　xiǎo
The '*eight*' stands for the abundance, the fortune that I earned by my own efforts. Here comes someone with a *stick-like* weapon to try to take a part of it from me in outright robbery. What started as abundance ends up as something **small**.　　　　　　　　　　　[3 STROKES   RANK 83]

1064 示　示　**show, indicate**　　　■ two 3　■ small 1063　　shì
BF Young mothers can be awful. Here's one with *two little* ones that she's forever **showing** off.　　　　　　　　　　[5 STROKES   RANK 425]

Unit 45

Looking Good

1065 际 际 **border, boundary** ▮ hills 735 ▮ show, indicate 1064   jì
BF The distant *hills show* the country's **borders**.   [7 STROKES   RANK 423]

1066 标 标 **to mark, label** ▮ tree 375 ▮ show, indicate 1064   biā
In those ancient days before felt-tip markers and embedded microchips, we would have **marked** our stuff using *wooden* sticks to *show* what belongs to us.   [9 STROKES   RANK 473]

1067 禁 禁 **prohibit** ▮ forest 376 ▮ show, indicate 1064   jìn
Despoilers of the environment, beware! As you gaze over the fence, the *forest shows* you its plentiful resources, but you are **prohibited** from touching them.   [13 STROKES   RANK 986]

1068 票 票 **ticket** ▮ west 291 (altered) ▮ show, indicate 1064   pià
You need a **ticket** to see a *show* in London's *West* End (equivalent to the Broadway theater district in New York City).   [11 STROKES   RANK 910]

1069 漂 漂 **drift, float** ▮ water r 523 ▮ ticket 1068   pià
The path of true love is rarely straight. On the way to a concert, the couple in front bursts into a loud argument. No concerts today! In the *water*, there are their *tickets*, **floating** forlornly in the current.   [14 STROKES   RANK 1568]

1070 尖 尖 **point, tip** ▮ small 1063 (altered) ▮ big 330   jiā
The **point** or **tip** is where something *little* becomes *bigger and bigger* as you move away from it. (Think of a mountain top.)   [6 STROKES   RANK 1321]

1071   尘   尘   **dust, dirt**   ▭ small 1063 (altered)   ▣ earth, soil 9   chén

BF **Dust** and **dirt** form when nature pulverizes *earth* to form *small* particles.

[6 STROKES   RANK 1718]

1072   你   你   **you**   ▮ man r 953   ▭ man 311 (altered)   ▣ small 1063   nǐ

Ready for a lesson in visual perspective? Suppose I am speaking to you—that's me, the *man* there on the left. **You** appear to be a *smaller person* because **you** are standing farther away.   [7 STROKES   RANK 32]

1073   余   余   **surplus, remainder**

▭ man 311   ▣ show, indicate 1064 (altered)   yú

When *men* get interested in *showing off* their possessions, we know they have a **surplus** at their command—they no longer are worried about sheer survival. To emphasize this, ancient scribes stuck a surplus stroke in the '*show*' component.   [7 STROKES   RANK 729]

1074   斜   斜   **oblique, slanting**

▮ surplus, remainder 1073   ▮ cup-shaped 218   xié

I hold my *cup-shaped* cup and tea spills out. At first, I thought there was a *too much* in the cup, but it was me being clumsy—I was holding the cup so it **slanted**.   [11 STROKES   RANK 1786]

1075   涂   涂   **smear, apply**   ▮ water r 523   ▮ surplus, remainder 1073   tú

At a restaurant, for example, waiters are always pouring *water* into glasses. There's always *extra* water, and by the end of the meal, it's **smeared** and spread over the entire table.   [10 STROKES   RANK 1735]

1076   茶   茶   **tea**   ▭ grass r 94   ▣ surplus, remainder 1073 (altered)   chá

The top horizontal of the '*surplus*' component is missing—so we can regard this component as representing something that is not *extra* but is essential. Perhaps the ancients regarded **tea** as a type of *grass*, so this character represents an essential herb, exactly how tea fanatics regard this brew to this day.   [9 STROKES   RANK 1272]

1077 京 京 **capital city**   ☐ cover 268   ▦ mouth 41   ▬ small 1063   jīu

BF Picture yourself as a country cousin in the **capital** for the first time. You *cover* your *mouth* in astonishment. All the monumental buildings, statues, well-dressed strollers, and so on make you feel so *small*.

[8 STROKES   RANK 566]

1078 凉 凉 **cool**   ▌ ice r 569   ☐ capital city 1077   liáₙ

Ever been to *capital city* in mid-winter? It's perceptibly warmer than the surrounding countryside. When it's *icy* in the 'burbs, it's merely **cool** in the *capital*.

[10 STROKES   RANK 1581]

1079 惊 惊 **startle, to alarm**   ▌ heart (skinny) 930   ☐ capital city 1077   jīⁿ

The country cousin in his country's *capital* is very ill at ease. His *emotions* are getting a fierce workout, as a succession of unexpected sights continually **startles** him.

[11 STROKES   RANK 659]

1080 添 添 **increase**

   ▌ water r 523   ▮ heaven 333   ▪ small 1063 (altered)   ◣ dab 169   tiāₙ

It looked like a *little something* fell from *heaven*, but it was a coconut from the tall palm tree by the pool. The little boy *watered* it faithfully, and it sprouted and **increased** in height rapidly.

[11 STROKES   RANK 1859]

1081 雀 雀 **sparrow**   ☐ small 1063   ▬ short-tailed bird 992   qu

BF A **sparrow** is a good example of a *small* but annoying *short-tailed bird*.

[11 STROKES   RANK 2331]

1082 截 截 **cut off, sever**   ▌ sparrow 1081 (altered)   ☐ halberd 359   jié

Prepare for a bloody story: The delinquent took the *sparrow* and his *sword* and **cut off** its head. That's why the '*sparrow*' component is altered.

[14 STROKES   RANK 1552]

1083 景 景 **view, scene**　　　　☐ day, sun 63　■ capital city 1077　**jǐng**

BF By *light of day*, nothing surpasses the spectacle and the **view** of any major or *capital city*.　　　　　　　　　　　　　[12 STROKES　RANK 814]

1084 琼 琼 **fine jade**　　　　☐ king 11　■ capital city 1077　**qióng**

BF We've established, back in §221, a connection between jade and the monarchy. The *capital* is the best part of the *king's* domain, so no wonder this character refers to **fine jade**.　　　　　　[12 STROKES　RANK 2205]

1085 掠 掠 **plunder**　　　　☐ hand r 29　■ capital city 1077　**luè**

BF The government officials who infest a country's *capital* always seem to have their *hands* out for fees, bribes, or worse. It's legal **plunder**!

[11 STROKES　RANK 1868]

1086 只 只 **only**　　　　■ mouth 41　■ eight (v) 1047　**zhǐ**

Imagine something in *abundance* (perhaps a plate piled high with rice) being funneled into someone's *mouth*. But a person can **only** eat so much.

As a result of this interpretation, we'll sometimes fix the meaning of '**restricted amount**' when 只 appears as a component.　　[5 STROKES　RANK 97]

1087 积 积 **amass, accumulate**　　☐ rice or grain 409　☐ only 1086　**jī**

Picture a small pile of *grain*. The pile contains a fixed and *restricted amount*. However, if we acquire lots and lots of piles, we will have **amassed** valuable property.　　　　　　　　　　　　　[10 STROKES　RANK 728]

1088 职 职 **duty, job**　　　　☐ ear 82　☐ only 1086　**zhí**

BF A guy with big jug *ears* has a strange **job**—he *only* has to scoop up leaves with them.　　　　　　　　　　　　　[11 STROKES　RANK 616]

1089 识 识 **know, recognize**　　☐ speech r 615　☐ only 1086　**shí**

How can you **recognize** a friend, even in the dark? *Only* when they *speak* is this task possible.　　　　　　　　　[7 STROKES　RANK 340]

1090 织　织　**weave**　　　　　■ silk r 807　■ only 1086　zh

At the time scribes were standardizing the form of Chinese characters, **weaving** was still so new as to be that era's "hi tech"-nology. As such, its early use was restricted *only* to the use of *silk* thread.　　　[8 STROKES　RANK 578]

Unit 46

Twenty-four/Seven

1091 公 公　public affairs　　　□ eight 1048　■ private 750　　gōng
BF *Eight private* things all at once—it's not possible to keep them all *private*.
Before you know it, everything's **public**.　　　[4 STROKES　RANK 115]

1092 讼 讼　litigation　　　‖ speech r 615　‖ public affairs 1091　　sòng
BF Even in ancient times, when personal *speech* was used in the context of
public affairs it was subject to **litigation**.　　　[6 STROKES　RANK 1862]

1093 其 其　his, her, its, theirs　　　□ eye 78 (altered)　□ eight 1048　　qí
You know how your eyes get big when you look with envy at someone else's
jewelry, fancy car, or trophy spouse? Someone's *eyes* are growing round
and large—the eyes are overflowing their usual borders—at the sight of *the
abundance* that belongs to their best friend. If you are truly so envious
of **their** material achievement, then how strong a friendship can it really
be?　　　[8 STROKES　RANK 85]

1094 甚 甚　very, extremely　　　■ his, her, its, theirs 1093　□ mineshaft 135　　shèn
Noble families accumulated a lot of junk over the generations, junk which
they nevertheless tried to hide when the revolution came. They tried storing
their stuff down an old, abandoned *mineshaft*, but there was an **extreme**
quantity of stuff, **too** much to fit.　　　[9 STROKES　RANK 626]

1095 堪 堪　can, may　　　‖ earth, soil 9　‖ very, extremely 1094　　kān
The *earth* is *very* helpful to us as we try to make a living in this cold world.
By virtue of its fertile bounty, we **can** survive.　　　[12 STROKES　RANK 1811]

1096 斯 斯 refined ■ his, her, its, theirs 1093   ▢ catty 118   sī
BF There's something about *their* stuff that's *unbalanced*. Hardly genteel, hardly **refined**.   [12 STROKES   RANK 168]

1097 基 基 base, foundation
■ his, her, its, theirs 1093 (altered)   ▣ earth, soil 9   jī
1 BF In ancient, barbarous cities, people used the *property* of those conquered in war as *soil* to serve as the **foundations** of *their* own buildings.
2 This character shows an Eiffel Tower-like structure, whose **base** rests on the *earth*.   [11 STROKES   RANK 280]

1098 穴 穴 cave, den, hole   ▢ roof 247   ■ eight 1048   xu
The topmost *roof* emphasizes the sheltering quality of a **cave**, but it's useful to interpret the strokes of the '*eight*' in a visual manner—sloping walls which limit the space and suggest a claustrophobic interior.   [5 STROKES   RANK 1940]

1099 探 探 look for, explore
■ hand r 29   ▢ cave, den, hole 1098 (altered)   ■ tree 375   tà
Picture the *hand* holding a lantern up, so as to see better. We proceed from the depths of *caves* to the tops of *trees* as we **look for** our elusive goal. But we do the *caves* first; that's why 'caves' appears on top of 'tree'.
[11 STROKES   RANK 917]

Sometimes the topmost dab is left off when 穴 appears as a component, either for reasons of space or because it's not necessary to emphasize the middle of the roof. Compare §§1098 and 1099.

1100 深 深 deep
■ water r 523   ▢ cave, den, hole 1098 (altered)   ■ tree 375   sh
Imagine a body of *water* so **deep** that it encompasses the depths of *caves* to the highest *tree*. Watch out—you could drown in such **deep** *water*.
[11 STROKES   RANK 401]

1101　火　火　fire　　　　　　　　　■ man 311　▣ eight (v) 1047　　huǒ
It's impossible not to be struck by the elemental reaction of a *man* to a roaring
fire. He stands in surprise, arms raised in awe.　　　[4 STROKES　RANK 433]

1102　炎　炎　scorching hot　　　　　　　　　　■ fire (times 2) 1101　　yán
BF *Two fires* yield **scorching hot** conditions.　　　[8 STROKES　RANK 1324]

1103　淡　淡　bland, weak　　　　■ water r 523　■ scorching hot 1102　　dàn
Go ahead, pour *water* onto that *scorching hot* pan. After the steam clears,
the degree of heat will be much **weaker** than it was.
　　Also, the average of cool *water* with something *scorching hot* is a much
more **bland** condition.　　　[11 STROKES　RANK 1293]

1104　灭　灭　extinguish　　　　　　　□ one 2　■ fire 1101　　miè
If you put *one* lid on a *fire*, it's **extinguished**.　　　[5 STROKES　RANK 953]

1105　灵　灵　clever, sharp　　　□ boar's head 34　■ fire 1101　　líng
A scene from your worst nightmare—in front of you, an enraged wild *boar*
is charging you. But behind you rages an out-of-control forest *fire*. What to
do? You'll need every dose of **cleverness** and **sharpness** to get out of this
one.　　　[7 STROKES　RANK 734]

1106　伙　伙　partner, mate　　　　■ man r 953　■ fire 1101　　huǒ
BF No matter how well-matched you are with your **partner** or **mate**, there
will be *fiery* fights between you and that *person*.　　　[6 STROKES　RANK 1047]

1107　灯　灯　lamp, light　　　　　■ fire 1101　■ fourth 25　　dēng
You put—carefully and safely—a bit of *fire* on top a high *platform*, and you
get a **lamp**.　　　[6 STROKES　RANK 1115]

1108 烟 烟 smoke ▌ fire 1101 ▌ because 345 yā

Because of *fires*, there's always **smoke**! [10 STROKES RANK 967]

1109 烦 烦 vexed, annoyed ▌ fire 1101 ▌ page, leaf 444 fá

BF Most *people* regard **vexatious** feelings as being *fire*-like.

[10 STROKES RANK 1253]

1110 秋 秋 autumn ▌ rice or grain 409 ▌ fire 1101 qi

BF **Autumn** is a fun time now that the harvest work is complete. Of course, we harvest the *grain*, but there's time for gathering 'round the *fire* for singing and snuggling. [9 STROKES RANK 1151]

1111 愁 愁 worry about ▬ autumn 1110 ▬ heart (fat) 906 ch

As a child, my *emotion* in *autumn*, at the start of the new school year, was **worry about** the new term. [13 STROKES RANK 2113]

1112 炉 炉 stove ▌ fire 1101 ▌ door of house 724 lú

BF The *fire* on the other side of the *door*, safely imprisoned inside the **stove**, provides toasty warmth on a bitter winter day. [8 STROKES RANK 1980]

1113 关 关 shut, close ▢ eight (v) 1047 ▬ heaven 333 gu

Dealing with the public in a busy store is no picnic. By the time the day ends, you've had it. Once you lock up and **close** the store, it feels *a lot* like *heaven*. [6 STROKES RANK 127]

1114 联 联 allied (forces), joint (effort) ▌ ear 82 ▌ shut, close 1113 liá

BF Nobody's perfect. But when you **ally** yourself with someone, you *shut* your *ears* to their negative aspects.

[12 STROKES RANK 356]

1115 郑 郑　**serious, earnest**　　　■ shut, close 1113　█ town 745　zhèng

BF New Year's Eve. They *closed* the whole *town* for some **serious** partying.

[8 STROKES RANK 1132]

1116 光 光　light, ray　　　▬ fire 1101 (altered)　▬ walking man 287　guāng

1 Unless a *fire* is out of control, it stays put. But this character shows an aspect of *fire* which *travels*. The part of fire which travels wherever it can are the **rays of light** it emits.

2 Another way to think of this character: The horizontal line represents the horizon of the sea, which partly cuts off the setting or rising sun. The curved lines on the bottom show the reflection of the sun's **rays** in the water, and we can think of the strokes above the horizon as **rays** emanating from the sun itself.　　　[6 STROKES RANK 290]

Unit 47

Keeping Up

1117 业 业 **trade, industry**　　　　■ a machine　■ eight (v) 1047　　yè

BF The assembly of horizontal and vertical struts represents some factory *machine*, the tools of some **industry**. You can think of the pair of dabs as a wish for *abundance*, or as sparks thrown off by the manufacturing process.

[5 STROKES　RANK 130]

1118 恋 恋 **feel attached to**

□ dab 169　■ trade, industry 1117 (altered)　■ heart (fat) 906　liàn

BF The scribes are using the component for '*trade*' upside-down, and the opposite of 'business' is 'pleasure'. A *dab* of glue attaches this pleasure to the *heart*, symbolizing a **feeling of attachment**.　　[10 STROKES　RANK 1464]

1119 亚 亚 **inferior**　　　■ trade, industry 1117　□ one 2　yà

A country relying on only *one industry* will have an **inferior** economy.

[6 STROKES　RANK 420]

1120 恶 恶 **evil**　　　■ inferior 1119　■ heart (fat) 906　è

Evil is an *inferior* kind of *emotion*.　　[10 STROKES　RANK 792]

1121 显 显 **appear, be obvious**　　□ day, sun 63　■ trade, industry 1117　xiǎ

Most technological advances work by taking an existing technique and expanding upon it. Every so often, though, someone creates something truly innovative. It's as if someone shines a bright light, bright as the *sun*, on an existing *industry* to discover something which, in hindsight, **appears obvious**.　　[9 STROKES　RANK 469]

1122 湿　湿　**wet, damp**　　　■ water r 523　　■ appear, be obvious 1121　　shī
When a silk dress gets **wet**, the location of the *water* spot is *obvious*.

[12 STROKES　RANK 1743]

It's easy to forget whether the 日 component goes above or below in §§1121 and 1122. With 显, the 'sun' goes up top, as befits a guiding light or lamp. In 晋, on the other hand, it's better to think about how the '日' contains within it the outline of the doorway through which we pass, and so belongs on the bottom.

1123 晋　晋　**enter, advance**　　　■ inferior 1119　■ day, sun 63　　jìn
When you **enter** a building, you block the *sun* and become *inferior* to it.

[10 STROKES　RANK 1645]

1124 普　普　**general, universal**　　□ eight (v) 1047　■ enter, advance 1123　　pǔ
BF If something—a custom, expression, fad, and so on—*advances* into the front ranks of culture to the point where it can be found *abundantly*, then it is **general** or **universal**.　　　[12 STROKES　RANK 630]

1125 严　严　**strict**　　　■ inferior 1119　■ cliff r 671　　yán
The mountain-climbing instructor is so **strict** that she'll only allow us to attempt climbing *inferior cliffs*. Hiss, boo!　　[7 STROKES　RANK 545]

1126 盖　盖　**cover***　　□ eight (v) 1047　■ king 11　■ vessel, dish 110　　gài
The silversmith created a **cover** for the costly *vessel* that featured *several kings* cavorting in strange costumes.　　[11 STROKES　RANK 1052]

1127 米　米　**rice**　　　■ tree 375　□ eight (v) 1047　　mǐ
The presence of *eight* different strokes in all different directions is supposed to suggest **rice** grains scattered all over the floor.　　[6 STROKES　RANK 575]

1128 来 来 **come** ■ rice 1127 ▭ one 2 lá

When the unexpected guest **comes**, you need to prepare *one* additional portion of *rice* for the meal.   [7 STROKES   RANK 15]

1129 粗 粗 **coarse** ▯ rice 1127 ▯ moreover 15 cū

The shelves of '*moreover*' provide a place to sort grains of *rice*. But rice grains are small, and this method only works for very **coarse** grains.

[11 STROKES   RANK 1414]

It's easy to mistake 粗 'coarse' with 租 'rent' (§414), especially since the left components of both refer to rice or grain. But 禾 typically refers to crops, portions of which can be remitted as rent. The character 米, on the other hand, usually refers to prepared food, which can definitely be described as coarse, and is not suitable for rent.

1130 莱 莱 **fallow fields** ▭ grass r 94 ■ come 1128 lá

BF Consider a **fallow field**. In the fallow state, it brings no food or wealth to the family, so they can't wait for crops—even *grass*—to *come* to this field.

[10 STROKES   RANK 1196]

1131 糟 糟 **spoiled** ▮ rice 1127 ▯ plaintiff and defendant 105 zā

Someone stole my *rice*, and by the time I got to court, after all the sparring between *plaintiff and defendant*, it was too late. The *rice* had **spoiled**.

[17 STROKES   RANK 1918]

1132 断 断 **break, snap, cut**

▯ mineshaft 135 (altered) ▯ rice 1127 ▯ catty 118 dū

As the vehicle approached the mine, something **snapped**. As a result, a whole load of *rice* fell off the *unbalanced* car and down the *mineshaft*.

[11 STROKES   RANK 434]

1133 料 料 **stuff** ▮ rice 1127 ▯ cup-shaped 218 liā

BF A prime example of **stuff** is a *cup* of *rice*.   [10 STROKES   RANK 557]

1134 类　类　kind, type, class　　　　　　　■□ rice 1127　■ dog 332　lèi
(Note the dog's eye merges with the lower right grain of rice.) Here are two prototypical **types** of organisms in the vegetable and animal kingdoms—*rice* and blind *dogs* (that's why there are no eyes!).　　　　[9 STROKES　RANK 311]

1135 奥　奥　profound, abstruse
　　　　　　　　　■ safe house, security 265　■ rice 1127　■ big 330　ào
BF Here's a remote part of your *safe house*. A *big* pile of *rice* lies undetected because it's so dark and obscure. In this way, the Chinese symbolize something **abstruse** and **profound**.　　　　　　　[12 STROKES　RANK 972]

1136 噢　噢　oh! (surprised understanding)
　　　　　　　　　■ mouth 41　■ profound, abstruse 1135　ō
The cry of **surprised understanding** involuntarily proceeds from your *mouth*. You finally understand the *abstruse* point that the professor was trying to explain.　　　　　　　　　　　　　　　[STROKES　RANK 2347]

1137 娄　娄　trouble, blunder　　　　　　■ rice 1127　■ woman 581　lóu
BF In the deeply misogynistic society of ancient China, it was surely a male scribe who designed a character in which **trouble** was not only ascribed to *women*, but compared in number to grains of *rice*.　　[9 STROKES　RANK 4052]

1138 楼　楼　multi-story building　　　　■ tree 375　■ trouble, blunder 1137　lóu
In **buildings with more than one story**, it's easy for a young suitor to climb a *tree* to get into *trouble*. There's a great risk of discovery!
　　　　　　　　　　　　　　　　　　　[13 STROKES　RANK 876]

1139 尚 尚 still, yet   ▨ eight (v) 1047   ▮ to face 266   sh

The word 'still' can divide time into two periods: When he fired the gun, it was **still** raining. Here, the firing of the gun marks a boundary in time, up to which it was raining. Afterwards, well, we don't yet know.

The '*eight*' represents abundance, and the vertical stroke divides it in two. Time up to a point is known—it is the future that's unknown and scary. The open end of the '*facing*' component seems to point away from what's known. Thus, in this metaphorical and slightly convoluted manner, we see that this character represents 'still'. (Perhaps it's better to just memorize it!)

When we encounter this character as a component, we'll ascribe one of several meanings to it. We might interpret it as a 'dividing point' or a 'sharp boundary'. Sometimes, the 'borders' subcomponent (see §127) will often imply that one part of our interpretation contains the other part.

[8 STROKES   RANK 878]

1140 堂 堂 **room for a special purpose**   ▭ still, yet 1139   ▮ earth, soil 9   tá

BF Here's a *division* between the general outdoors—the *earth*—and the indoors (everything which isn't outdoors). A **room has a special purpose**—to shelter us from the elements.   [11 STROKES   RANK 980]

1141 掌 掌 **palm of the hand**   ▭ still, yet 1139   ▮ hand 27   zh

BF The **palm of the hand** is the part that actually holds things. This character represents a *boundary* of the *hand* between the fingers, which can hold things but will easily drop them, and the **palm**, which holds things well but can't grab.   [12 STROKES   RANK 890]

1142 常 常 often   ▭ still, yet 1139   ▮ towel 130   ch

BF Despite the visual decomposition, this looks to me like a hanging man (see §131) on a makeshift gallows. I've **often** thought that this is a ghastly fate to be avoided at all costs!   [11 STROKES   RANK 187]

Unit 48

Not So Fast!

1143 党 党 **political party**   ■ still, yet 1139   ▬ son 288   dǎng
A group of men (all of whom are somebody's *sons*) gather together in opposition to those whose opinions are *various and different*. Thus is born a **political party**.   [10 STROKES   RANK 411]

1144 赏 赏 **admire**   ■ still, yet 1139   ▬ cowrie 430   shǎng
BF *Shells* have the *potential* of becoming beautiful jewelry, engendering **admiring** glances from all.   [12 STROKES   RANK 1450]

1145 倘 倘 **if, in case**   ▮ man r 953   ▮ still, yet 1139   tǎng
The *man* on the left is short-hand for all things human—affairs, events, possessions, and so on. The '*still, yet*' component implies division. For human affairs, the division is between true and false or between happened and not (yet) happened—in other words, the same relation as determined by **if** or **in case of**.   [10 STROKES   RANK 2118]

1146 幸 幸 **luck, good fortune**   ▬ earth, soil 9   ■ eight (v) 1047   ▬ dry 10   xìng
BF This is an easy character to remember if you imagine it originated in a wet and marshy part of China. A person with *land* which is both *abundant* and *dry* is blessed with **good fortune**.   [8 STROKES   RANK 902]

1147 羊 羊 **sheep**   ▬ eight (v) 1047   ▬ three 4   ▯ scepter 5   yáng
I don't care what the diagram shows—here's the skin of a fat, plump **sheep**. From top down, we see the two ears, the face, the four legs, and the tail.   [6 STROKES   RANK 1337]

1148 美 美   **beautiful**   ■□ sheep 1147 (altered)   ■■ big 330   m
For a farmer, there's no sight more **beautiful** than a *big*, plump *sheep*. (Here, the sheep's tail has been docked.)   [9 STROKES   RANK 151]

1149 善 善   **good, kind**   ■■ sheep 1147 (altered)   ■■ speech 270   sh
Sheep are well-known as gentle animals, and a person whose *speech* is like a *sheep* is sure to be **good** and **kind**.   [12 STROKES   RANK 749]

1150 洋 洋   **vast**   ▌ water r 523 ▌ sheep 1147   yá
BF Think of a sponge in the shape of a *sheep*. You place it in *water*, it soaks up liquid, and the *sheep* grows till it becomes **vast** in size.   [9 STROKES   RANK 803]

1151 样 样   **appearance***   ▌ tree 375 ▌ sheep 1147   yà
BF In agrarian settings, what counted most towards a landowner's peace of mind was the proper **appearance** of wealth—agriculture, symbolized by a *tree*; and livestock, represented by a *sheep*.   [10 STROKES   RANK 88]

1152 详 详   **detailed**   ▌ speech r 615 ▌ sheep 1147   xiǎ
BF Imagine that a *sheep* gets to make a *speech* for a change. Sheep, being sheep, would copy each other's speech slavishly, down to the last **detail**!   [8 STROKES   RANK 1439]

1153 拳 拳   **fist**   ⊞ eight (v) 1047 ■□ man (spiffy) 337 ■□ hand 27   qu
This sketch shows part of a *hand* knocking down some other *man*, shaking loose a *couple of drops* of blood or sweat in the process. Only the **fist** is capable of this power.   [10 STROKES   RANK 1784]

1154 兰 兰   **orchid**   ⊡ eight (v) 1047 ■■ three 4   lán
The **orchid** is a flower with an *abundance* of positive attributes, which is why it's such a special flower. Fragrance, brilliant color, and long-lastingness are its *three* most important qualities.   [5 STROKES   RANK 642]

1155 拦 拦 **to bar or block**   ▮ hand r 29   ▮ orchid 1154   lán

We see someone's *hand*, intent on cutting off and stealing a rare *orchid* specimen. At the last moment, its beauty captivates him, and **bars** him from this destructive deed.   [8 STROKES   RANK 1996]

1156 烂 烂 **rot, fester**   ▮ fire 1101   ▮ orchid 1154   làn

Why would anyone want to cook an *orchid*? Nevertheless, you can imagine that applying *heat* to an *orchid* or other fine flower accelerates the processes of decay and **rot**.   [9 STROKES   RANK 1754]

1157 金 金 **gold**   ▮ entire 326   ▮▮ eight (v) 1047   jīn

BF In time of war, you want to transform all your wealth to a form which makes it easy to move. That's difficult—you've been very successful and you own a lot. The solution that worked centuries ago and which works now is to convert your *entire* fortune, all your *abundance*, into **gold**.

[8 STROKES   RANK 260]

1158 乎 乎 **huh?**   ▯ eight (v) 1047   ▮ in; at; to 26   hū

乎 is an interrogatory particle, capable of expressing interrogation, surprise, surmise, or admiration. The character 于, an old friend from §26, has an *abundance* of *prepositional meanings*, so it's reasonable to combine these two characters to form this particle. Which meaning do you want??

[5 STROKES   RANK 458]

1159 呼 呼 **exhale**   ▯ mouth 41   ▮ huh? 1158   hū

Expressions of *surprise or surmise* are often accompanied by puffs of air as we **exhale** from our *mouth*.   [8 STROKES   RANK 843]

1160 平 平 **flat, level, even**   ▯ eight (v) 1047   ▮ dry 10   píng

When there is *a lot* of *dry*, arid land, the wind and weather can blow away all the high points, and fill in all the low points, so that the landscape turns into something **flat**, **level**, and perfectly **even**.   [5 STROKES   RANK 215]

1161 苹 苹 **apple**　　□ grass r 94　■ flat, level, even 1160　　píɪ

BF Legend has it that William Tell shot an **apple** off his son's head with an arrow. Good thing the boy's head was sufficiently *flat* and *level* to keep the apple from rolling off into the *grass* before his dad could shoot it!

[8 STROKES   RANK 2478]

1162 评 评 **comment, criticize**　　■ speech r 615　■ flat, level, even 1160　　píɪ

BF It's amazing that people who deliver the most devastating **criticism** often deliver the *speech* with their verdict in a very *flat* affect.

[7 STROKES   RANK 809]

1163 萍 萍 **duckweed**　　□ water r 523　■ apple 1161 (altered)　　píɪ

BF Although the components are subtly altered in comparison with the previous panel, nevertheless they somehow suggest an *apple* that grows in the *water*. In this case, the surprising item is **duckweed**, which primarily provides nutrition for ducks, but can also be gathered and eaten by people, like an *apple*.

[8 STROKES   RANK 2478]

1164 半 半 **half, semi**　　■ eight (v) 1047　■ two 3　□ scepter 5　　bàɪ

Here is *two* of something, cut in **half** by a *scepter* or other mighty stick. The force of the blow is so severe that *many* chips fly in the air.

It's easy to confuse the two characters 平 (§1160) and this character 半. The top vertical of 平 is *flat*, like its definition. The flying chips at the top of 半 represent a fraction of the original object; '**half**' is also a fraction.

[5 STROKES   RANK 513]

1165 伴 伴 **companion, partner**　　■ man r 953　■ half, semi 1164　　bàɪ

A *person* is only *half* a soul without their life **partner** by their side.

[7 STROKES   RANK 1298]

1166 单 单 **single, sole**　　□ eight (v) 1047　■ first in a series 50　■ one 2　　dāɪ

BF The '*first*' and '*one*' emphasize the singularity of a certain someone. The *abundance* is his **alone**—he doesn't have to share.

[8 STROKES   RANK 389]

1167 首　首　**head, leader**　　☐ eight (v) 1047　☐ one 2　▊ self 202　shǒu

BF There's *a lot of* something on the flat top surface of *one's self*. It must be hair. What else appears of the tops of heads? In these ancient times, when Chinese characters were becoming developed, imagine that only **leaders** and **heads** of state had the privilege of wearing and displaying long, flowing locks.　　　　　　　　　　　　　　　　　　　[9 STROKES　RANK 481]

1168 豆　豆　**bean**　　☐ one 2　▊ mouth 41　▊ eight (v) 1047　☐ one 2　dòu

This slightly surreal depiction shows a bowl of steaming **beans**. The bottom horizontal is the table top, and the dabs of the '*eight*' both suggest the profile of the bowl and the *abundance* within. With accurate perspective, the *mouth* of the bowl should really be elliptical. The smaller horizontal that tops the character suggests the high level of beans within the bowl, or perhaps rising steam.　　　　　　　　　　　　　　　　　　　[7 STROKES　RANK 1793]

Unit 49

Hills and Dales

1169 喜 喜 **like, happy** ☐ ten 6　▬ bean 1168　▪ mouth 41　xǐ

BF Some people just can't get enough *beans*. For those unusual few, they **like** nothing more than to shovel *ten* bowls of *beans* into their *mouths*.

[12 STROKES　RANK 668]

1170 嘻 嘻 **giggle** ☐ mouth 41　▮ like, happy 1169　xī

When you are *happy*, the sound from your *mouth* might well be a contented **giggle**.

[15 STROKES　RANK 2432]

1171 短 短 **short, brief** ▮ arrow 334　▮ bean 1168　du

An *arrow* made out of *beans* isn't very good (it's not worth beans!). If you can shoot it at all, it will only go a **short** distance.

[12 STROKES　RANK 889]

1172 曾 曾 **once, formerly**

☐ eight (v) 1047　▤ twin windows　☐ eight (v) 1047　▬ day, sun 63　cé

To me, the *twin dabs* at the top look like a pair of eyes, whose reflections appear in *twin windows*. It's miserable outside—the eyes also resemble drops of rain on the glass—and the poor child imprisoned inside imagines a vision of the *sun* that **formerly** shone all the time.

[12 STROKES　RANK 463]

1173 增 增 **increase, add** ▮ earth, soil 9　▮ once, formerly 1172　zē

Nowadays, nobody's making land. By and large, what you see is what there is. But in *former* days, eons ago, this wasn't true. Due to violent geological processes, the *earth* was **increasing**.

[15 STROKES　RANK 446]

1174 僧 僧 **monk**　　　■ man r 953　■ once, formerly 1172　　sēng

BF Many religions postulate multiple lifetimes of a soul. This character suggests that a *former* existence of a *man* was as a **monk**.

[14 STROKES   RANK 2013]

1175 兽 兽 **wild beast**　　□ eight (v) 1047　■ field 57　■ one 2　■ mouth 41　　shòu

BF There's a herd, a veritable *abundance*, of these frightening **wild beasts** in the *field*. *One* of them notices me, and immediately threatens me with its open *mouth*.

[11 STROKES   RANK 1602]

1176 墙 墙 **wall**　　■ earth, soil 9　■ earth, soil 9　■ eight (v) 1047　■ return 42　　qiáng

BF In ancient days, **walls** were built out of heaped *earth*. What were they protecting? Perhaps the *abundant* harvest from the *earth*, or the men of the tribe, *returning* from raiding forays of their own.

[14 STROKES   RANK 1212]

1177 夹 夹 **place in between**　　■ man (spiffy) 337　□ eight (v) 1047　　jiā

This character illustrates itself in two ways: (1) 夫 is between the two dabs of '*eight (v)*', and (2) these dabs are **between** the two horizontals of 夫. Metaphorically, *people* are the source of *abundance*, and *abundance* is the source of *people*.

[6 STROKES   RANK 1758]

1178 侠 侠 **heroic**　　■ man r 953　□ place in between 1177　　xiá

BF So many *people* have gathered to celebrate some *man*'s **heroic** achievements that Times Square is packed beyond belief. Everyone is *placed in between* everyone else.

[8 STROKES   RANK 1216]

1179 立 立 **erect, stand**   ☐ cover 268   ■ eight (v) 1047   ☐ one 2   lì

  1 A *man* (altered from the usual; here constructed from '*cover*' and '*eight (v)*') is **standing** on *one* horizontal surface.

  2 This character reminds me of the house of cards that I struggled to **erect** on rainy weekends of my childhood. 立 shows a view from the side of just a portion of this house! The *cover* controls the *abundance* of cards on the *horizontal surface* and keeps them **standing up**.

[5 STROKES   RANK 197]

1180 拉 拉 **pull, draw, tug**   ■ hand r 29   ☐ erect, stand 1179   lā

What does the *hand* near the puppet have to do to keep it *standing*? It **tugs** and **pulls** at it.   [8 STROKES   RANK 324]

1181 啦 啦 **indication of excitement, doubt**

☐ mouth 41   ■ pull, draw, tug 1180   la

Expressions of excitement and doubt are indications of increased emotional *tension*. The '*mouth*' indicates the **expressive** nature of this character, since the mouth is the ordinary vehicle for expression.   [11 STROKES   RANK 1194]

1182 部 部 **part, section**   ☐ erect, stand 1179   ■ mouth 41   ■ town 745   bù

It's easy to recognize the tourist **section** of *town*. Past generations have *erected* many impressive monuments in the various city squares, each of which looks like a big *mouth*.   [10 STROKES   RANK 84]

1183 位 位 **m for persons (polite)**   ■ man r 953   ☐ erect, stand 1179   wèi

Formal occasions generally demand that *people* do more *standing* than at a casual occasion, where people are slouching and chatting. So '*people stand*' represents this **formal counting word**.   [7 STROKES   RANK 182]

1184 妾 妾 **I (woman's form)**   ☐ erect, stand 1179   ■ woman 581   qiè

Roll call. All you *women*, when you hear your name, *stand* up, and shout out, "Here **I** am!"   [STROKES   RANK 3242]

1185 接 接 **come close to**　　　　■ hand r 29　□ I (woman's form) 1184　jiē

"**Come close** to *me*, so *I* can hold your *hand*," said my 97-year-old grandmother.　　　　　　　　　　　　　　　　　　　　　　　　[11 STROKES   RANK 247]

1186 童 童 **child**　　　　　　　□ erect, stand 1179　▬ inside 71　tóng

BF The only kind of person who can *stand* up *inside* a small closet or other
confined space are **children**.　　　　　　　　　　　　[12 STROKES   RANK 1229]

1187 撞 撞 **run into, collide**　　　　■ hand r 29　□ child 1186　zhuàng

Imagine *children* running around in a frenzy, and definitely not looking where
they're going. An adult uses her *hand* as a human 'bumper' to avoid **collision**.
　　　　　　　　　　　　　　　　　　　　　　　　　　　[15 STROKES   RANK 1540]

1188 商 商 **trade, business**

　　　　　□ erect, stand 1179　▬ borders 127　▬ eight 1048　▬ mouth 41　shāng

BF Here, the *border* symbolizes your house, and the '*eight mouths*' inside
are your big family, always hungry. If you are *upright* in your **business**
dealings, you will prosper and your family will eat. Notice how, in the
interests of efficiency, the bottom stroke of 'erect, stand' coincides with the
top of 'borders'.　　　　　　　　　　　　　　　　　　[11 STROKES   RANK 402]

1189 音 音 **sound**

　　　　□ cover 268　▬ eight (v) 1047　▬ one 2　▬ speak 64　yīn

BF This character represents the operation of a microphone, shown standing
on end. At the bottom, you see where the **sound** enters the mechanism,
as someone *speaks*. The microphone's guts amplifies this sound as it passes
through a special *horizontal* membrane, making it appear more *abundant*, so
every*one* can hear, as it passes outward through the *cover*.
　　　　　　　　　　　　　　　　　　　　　　　　　　　[9 STROKES   RANK 540]

1190 暗 暗 **dark, dim**　　　　■ day, sun 63　■ sound 1189　àn

Here you see '*sound*' crowding out the *sun*. This is what happens when it gets
dark—the realm of sight diminishes in importance, while listening achieves
prominence.　　　　　　　　　　　　　　　　　　　　[13 STROKES   RANK 829]

1191 意 意 **idea, meaning**   ■ sound 1189   ■ heart (fat) 906   yì

BF This character expresses a metaphorical meaning for **idea** or **meaning** as the '*sound*' of an *emotion*.   [13 STROKES   RANK 104]

1192 竞 竞 **compete, contend**   ▢ erect, stand 1179   ■ elder brother* 298   jìn

BF Among families, sibling rivalry—especially among boys—is a major source of intense energy. If the *elder brother stands firm*, he usually wins the **competition**.   [10 STROKES   RANK 1100]

1193 竟 竟 **in the end**   ▢ sound 1189   ■ walking man 287   jìn

Think of a nineteenth-century platoon of soldiers. To the stirring *sound* of bagpipes, these *walking men* march to battle. **In the end**, this tactic is successful, and the soldiers win.   [11 STROKES   RANK 706]

1194 境 境 **boundary**   ▮ earth, soil 9   ▮ in the end 1193   jìn

BF No matter how extensive are your territories and *land*, if you keep on traveling, *in the end* you will reach its **boundary**.   [14 STROKES   RANK 582]

Unit 50

Clever Ducks

1195 培 培 **bank up with earth**

▌ earth, soil 9 ■ erect, stand 1179 ▪ mouth 41 **péi**

Banking involves taking *earth*, and making it *stand up* in heaps. Why? To increase fertility, and so to put more food in your *mouth*.

[11 STROKES RANK 1152]

1196 端 端 **end, extremity**

▌ erect, stand 1179 ■ mountain 21 ▪ express add'l but contrasting info 83 **duān**

BF Refer back to §89. A giant *stands erect*, and we see examples of his **extremities**. His head is level with the tops of *mountains*, while his weight forces his feet underground, where a few of his *toes* are wedged below the surface of the soil. [14 STROKES RANK 916]

1197 倍 倍 **-fold**

▌ man r 953 ■ erect, stand 1179 ▪ mouth 41 **bèi**

A *man* who is scrunched down so you can only see his *mouth* but who then takes the trouble to *stand* up, multiplies his apparent height several**fold**. [10 STROKES RANK 1392]

1198 章 章 **chapter, section**

■ sound 1189 ▪ ten 6 **zhāng**

BF The *sound* here is music. Western musical compositions often occur in many parts; 'ten' is a stand-in for 'many'. The parts of a musical composition could be the verses, movements, variations, and so on that form the **sections** of the composition. [11 STROKES RANK 539]

1199 站 站 **stop, station**   ▮ erect, stand 1179   ▮ practice divination 172   zh▸

Regardless of the visual decomposition, this character looks to me like someone has stuck a marker (that's the vertical portion on the right) into a bucket (that's the mouth on the lower right) of cement which has been allowed to harden. Nothing will budge it. Where it *stands erect*, that's the landmark for other vehicles to **stop**.   [10 STROKES   RANK 544]

1200 辛 辛 **hardworking**   ▭ erect, stand 1179   ▬ ten 6   xī▸

BF A worker *standing up* for *ten* hours or more is genuinely **hardworking**.
[7 STROKES   RANK 1463]

1201 辞 辞 **diction**   ▮ tongue 225   ▮ hardworking 1200   cí

While learning Chinese, your *tongue works hard* to get the **diction** right.
[13 STROKES   RANK 1469]

1202 亲 亲 **relatives**   ▬ erect, stand 1179   ▬ show, indicate 1064 (altered)   qī▸

BF Pardon a play on words, but **relatives** are often people whom you can't *stand*! Here, the 'stand' part and the 'show' part share the central horizontal bar; you often *share* stuff with relatives. Also, we often *reveal* personal details with relatives that we wouldn't dream of telling anyone else. The 'show' part is altered slightly, in that the central hook extends all the way up to this central stroke. Sometimes, because they're **relatives**, they give you a little extra, a little more than you deserve.   [9 STROKES   RANK 362]

1203 新 新 **new**   ▮ relatives 1202   ▮ catty 118   xī▸

The acquisition of **new** *relatives*—by marriage, say—often leads to a sense of *unbalance* as pecking orders need to be re-affirmed and re-fought.
[13 STROKES   RANK 161]

1204 帝 帝 **emperor***   ▭ erect, stand 1179 (altered)   ▬ towel 130   dì

BF In the presence of the **emperor**, one must *stand especially straight* and put on special decorative *cloths*. We stand on a special platform, and that's why the platform of the '*stand*' component is slightly fancier than normal.
[9 STROKES   RANK 612]

1205 竭 竭   make the utmost effort

██ erect, stand 1179   ██ how, why, when 647   jié

BF The team is depending upon you **to make the utmost effort**! You *stand up* and approach the starting line. Your senses reel. The pressure mounts, as the crowd's shouts seem to come from *all over the place*.   [14 STROKES   RANK 1987]

1206 啻 啻   not only

██ emperor* 1204   ██ mouth 41   chì

BF The *emperor* is making a long-awaited and highly infrequent appearance before the people. Is he man or god? He makes his appearance, and it's clear he's all-too-human. **Not only** is his body like those of other men, but there's something wrong with his *mouth*—it hangs lower in his face than normal.   [12 STROKES   RANK 4249]

1207 滴 滴   drip

██ water r 523   ██ not only 1206 (altered)   dī

Not only is the *water* radical part of this glyph, but the character also makes reference to the three **drops**. The 'towel' part is extended, in case we need a towel to wipe up the watery mess. Moreover, the extra horizontal bar inside the towel makes us think that the towel is "ancient" (§51). I guess we're using an old towel for clean up.   [14 STROKES   RANK 1896]

1208 蒂 蒂   base of fruit

██ grass r 94   ██ emperor* 1204   dì

BF We have to rely, yet again, on metaphor and analogy. In the same way that the **base of a fruit** is the part on which it rests or is supported, so too is the *emperor* the person on whom the empire is supported and reliant. The bit of *grass* up top reminds us that fruit is part of the vegetable kingdom, and the analogy extends to a member of this kingdom (fruit).

[12 STROKES   RANK 1429]

1209 南 南   south

██ ten 6   ██ borders 127   ██ eight (v) 1047   ██ dry 10   nán

States or countries are regions delimited by *borders*. This character makes reference to *ten* of these states, with special attention to the ones with *abundant dryness*. For an empire like China, which is in the Northern Hemisphere, the *abundantly* hot states are the ones in the **south**.   [9 STROKES   RANK 307]

1210 喃 喃 mumbling   ■ mouth 41   ■ south 1209   ná

BF Northern people are full of their own special prejudices, often regarding people from southern tropical regions as doing things slowly, perhaps in response to the killing heat they live with. Language is the worst. The *mouth* sounds of these *southerners* seem like **mumbling** to intolerant Northern ears.   [12 STROKES   RANK 2233]

1211 献 献 offer, donate   ■ south 1209   ■ dog 332   xià

In America, it's hot down *south*. So *south* plus *dog* equals 'hot dog'. I'm famous for my hot dogs. Next time we have a barbecue, come on over—I'd like to **offer** you one.   [13 STROKES   RANK 1192]

1212 兴 兴 prosper   ■ six 1062   ■ eight (v) 1047   xīn

You **prosper** when things flourish and grow, most often in the context of business. Here's an example—*six* things become *eight*.   [6 STROKES   RANK 531]

1213 举 举 to lift   ■ prosper 1212 (altered)   ■ dry 10 (altered)   jǔ

The altered 'dry' component suggests land that was formerly *dry* but now isn't. The farmer's fortunes are therefore about to *prosper*. This should **lift** his spirits.   [9 STROKES   RANK 586]

1214 尊 尊 honor, venerate   ■ eight (v) 1047   ■ new wine 303   ■ inch 210   zūn

A lot of *wine*—poured into tiny, *inch*-high cups—is a symbol of the **honor** and **respect** due to our great master upon his retirement. *Gānbēi!*   [12 STROKES   RANK 1134]

1215 奈 奈 how can one help?   ■ big 330 (altered)   ■ show, indicate 1064   nài

BF The altered 'big' partially obscures a background sketch of someone in clear distress, for we see the wrinkled brow and the tears coursing down each side of her nose. The person in front is clearly sympathetic. He stands there, legs spread out, arms outstretched toward the grief stricken woman, and begs to be of service. **How can he help?**   [8 STROKES   RANK 1624]

1216 慕　慕　admire*

☐ grass r 94　　☰ day, sun 63　　■ big 330 (altered)　　☐ small 1063 (altered)　　mù

Here's a person I can really **admire**. Why? Well, he's a prosperous farmer, plenty of *grass*, and a permanently *sunny* disposition. Furthermore, he's *big*-hearted and generous—to an exaggerated extent—to those who have *much less* than he.　　　　　[14 STROKES　RANK 1990]

1217 窝　窝　nest, lair　☐ cave, den, hole 1098　☰ mouth 41　■ inside* 318　　wō

What's a **nest** anyway but a *cave or lair inside* of which gape the many open *mouths* of the fledgelings.　　　　[12 STROKES　RANK 1962]

1218 薛　薛　marsh grass

☐ grass r 94　■ to heap up 993 (altered)　■ hardworking 1200　　xuē

BF Work in the swamps is sweaty and tough. Harvesting the **marsh grass** demands *hard work* to *heap up* the cut *grass* for gathering. Notice how severely 堆 'heap up' has been altered so as to fit inside the character comfortably.　　　　[16 STROKES　RANK 1953]

1219 空　空　empty　　■ cave, den, hole 1098　■ labor, work 7　　kōng

A good example of **empty** is a *cavernous* factory room, **empty** of ongoing *work*.　　　　[8 STROKES　RANK 272]

1220 腔　腔　body cavity　　■ meat 317 (altered)　☐ empty 1219　　qiāng

The part of a *body* that is *empty* is a—**body cavity**.　　[12 STROKES　RANK 1914]

Unit 51

Animal, Vegetable, and Mineral

1221 产　产　**give birth to***　⬛ erect, stand 1179 (altered)　⬛ cliff r 671　chǎ
Midwives and mothers compare the trauma of **giving birth** to another awful situation, that of someone *standing* on a *clifftop* preparing to throw themselves off.　　　　　[6 STROKES　RANK 159]

1222 辨　辨　**distinguish between**
⬛ hardworking 1200 (altered)　⬛ divider　⬛ hardworking 1200　biài
Police lineup. Two *hardworking*-looking guys are separated by a curved *divider* (see the little doorknob on its left?) on one side. Can you **distinguish** between the innocent bystander and the perpetrator?
　　　　　[16 STROKES　RANK 1910]

1223 胖　胖　**fat, stout, plump**　⬛ meat 317 (altered)　⬛ half, semi 1164　pàı
The person who regularly eats a portion of *meat* followed by *half* of another is bound to get **fat**.　　　　　[9 STROKES　RANK 1893]

1224 鉴　鉴　**reflect, mirror**　⬛ inspect, supervise 237 (altered)　⬛ gold 1157　jiàı
Note that in the '*inspect*' portion on top, the bloody vessel has been abbreviated to a single bloody dot.
　　　If we *inspect* a sheet of *gold*, our image will **reflect** off its surface.
　　　　　[13 STROKES　RANK 1655]

1225 款 款 clause in document

▪ scholar 8   ▪ show, indicate 1064   ▪ owe, lack 465   **kuǎn**

In China, we use *scholars* to help draw up contracts. With their special knowledge of grammar, they *show* what the other party *owes* us in each of the **contract clauses**.   [12 STROKES   RANK 807]

1226 耀 耀 bright, dazzling

▪ light, ray 1116   ▪ feather, wing 123   ▪ short-tailed bird 992   **yào**

BF The *shine* from the *feathers* of a beautiful *bird* can be **bright** and **dazzling**.   [20 STROKES   RANK 1804]

1227 尔 尔 you, thou

▪ man 311 (altered)   ▪ small 1063   **ěr**

Suppose I am speaking to you. **You** appear to be a *smaller man* because **you** are standing away from me.   [5 STROKES   RANK 220]

1228 算 算 calculate, compute

▪ bamboo r 243   ▪ tool, utensil 1055 (altered)   **suàn**

Bamboo is so soft it isn't useful for many *tools*. But you can make beads from it to create an abacus for **calculating** prices and so on.   [14 STROKES   RANK 403]

1229 容 容 allow, tolerate   ▪ roof 247   ▪ cereal, grain 1060   **róng**

The hippy parents (relics of the 1960s) were very **tolerant**. Under their *roof*, their kids were so messy that *grain* started growing in the filth!   [10 STROKES   RANK 442]

1230 裕 裕 abundant   ▪ clothing r 838   ▪ cereal, grain 1060   **yù**

BF The wedding was so lavish, they threw *rice* like it was water. I kept finding *grains* in my *clothes* for months, that's how **abundant** everything was.   [12 STROKES   RANK 2023]

1231 肖 肖 **like, similar to**   ⬜ small 1063 (altered)   ⬛ meat 317 (altered)   xiā

BF The '*meat*' here refers to an animal or person, and we are supposed to marvel at how a *small animal*—the young of the species—is **similar to** its parents.   [7 STROKES   RANK 2019]

1232 削 削 **pare, peel with knife**   ⬛ like, similar to 1231   ⬜ knife r 166   xiā

With a deftly wielded *knife*, you make a piece of shapeless wood *look like* something else by means of skillful **peeling away** of the wood.   [9 STROKES   RANK 1794]

1233 消 消 **disappear, vanish**   ⬜ water r 523   ⬛ like, similar to 1231   xiā

Water is *like* a magic potion (sometimes). Used properly, it can make stains **vanish!**   [10 STROKES   RANK 439]

1234 悄 悄 **quiet, silent**   ⬛ heart (skinny) 930   ⬜ like, similar to 1231   qiā

BF **Quiet**ness is a lot *like* a subdued *emotion*.   [10 STROKES   RANK 1434]

1235 稍 稍 **slightly, somewhat**   ⬛ rice or grain 409   ⬜ like, similar to 1231   shā

All *grains* look *similar* to one another because the *grains* of each species are **somewhat** alike.   [12 STROKES   RANK 1373]

1236 除 除 **remove, do away with**   ⬜ hills 735   ⬛ surplus, remainder 1073   chu

During boom times, there's plenty of *surplus*, so much so that we have to **remove** it to the uninhabited parts of the *hills* so it's not in the way.   [9 STROKES   RANK 464]

1237 谈 谈 **talk, chat**   ⬜ speech r 615   ⬛ scorching hot 1102   tán

What do we **chat** about when we **chat**? We don't waste time *talking* about anything but the *hottest* of topics.   [10 STROKES   RANK 474]

1238 称　称　**call to, name**　　■ rice or grain 409　　■ you, thou 1227　　chēng
I **called out** to *you*, but *you* didn't hear, so I threw some *rice* your way to get your attention (as if at a wedding).　　[10 STROKES　RANK 449]

1239 突　突　**dash forward**　　▢ cave, den, hole 1098　　■ dog 332　　tū
BF The thieves tried to sneak up on the banker's house. They failed to take the *dog* into account. Out from his *den*, he **dashed forward** to grab the lead robber by the seat of his pants.　　[9 STROKES　RANK 484]

1240 乐　乐　**glad to, enjoy**　　■ show, indicate 1064 (altered)　　lè
When people **enjoy** life, they can't help *showing* this emotion on their faces, and, indeed, in every action. On the left, the extra curvy stroke connecting the horizontals represents a crinkle line around the eyes that you see around genuinely **happy** people.　　[5 STROKES　RANK 619]

1241 继　继　**continue, succeed, follow**
　　■ silk r 807　　▢ mineshaft 135　　▢ rice 1127　　jì
BF The construction material was a strange mixture of *silk* and *rice*. Don't laugh—up to now, the repair of the *mineshaft* had gone fitfully forward, but now with this new stuff, we can **continue** and finish it in no time.
　　　　　　　　　　[10 STROKES　RANK 655]

1242 弹　弹　**flick, pluck, play instrument**
　　■ bow (weapon) 859　　▢ single, sole 1166　　tán
I know the left part is a *weapon*, but its bends are suggestive of two fingertips reaching over to a *single* guitar string to **pluck** it.　　[11 STROKES　RANK 632]

1243 您　您　**you (formal)**　　■ you 1072　　■ heart (fat) 906　　nín
In **formal** situations, my greeting to **you** is one of respectful *emotion*.
　　　　　　　　　　[11 STROKES　RANK 726]

1244 寅 寅 3–5am   ☐ roof 247   ■ man 311 (altered)   ☐ crossed hands   yíı

Strictly speaking, proceeding from the top down, you write this character using the following sequence of components: *roof* (§247), *one* (§2), *let somebody do something* (§48), and *eight* (§1048). It's hard to create one narrative using all these, so it's better to hark back to the historical development of this character, which depicts a reclining *man* under the *roof* of his house. We know he's reclining because his *hands* are *crossed* on his chest. This especially restful period of slumber most often occurs very early in the morning, between **3–5am.**   [11 STROKES   RANK 3422]

1245 演 演 perform, play, act   ■ water r 523   ■ 3–5am 1244   yǎ

The rain *water* that leaked on my head *very early this morning*, waking me out the best sleep I've had in a long time, caused me to jump out of bed and dance around in surprise and shock. Early morning dog walkers peering through my windows thought I was rehearsing for a **play.**   [14 STROKES   RANK 715]

1246 税 税 tax, duty   ■ rice or grain 409   ■ exchange, convert 1049   sh

The government forces you to deal with the devil. You give them a portion of your earnings—a **tax**—which would have been in the form of *rice or grain* way back when, and, *in exchange*, the government provides you with services.

[12 STROKES   RANK 781]

Unit 52

A Veritable United Nations

1247 宗 宗 **clan, sect, faction** ☐ roof 247 ■ show, indicate 1064 zōng

BF People of like mind or tradition—those belonging to the same **clan** or faction—often *show* their common bond by hanging out together in the same place, under the same *roof.* [8 STROKES RANK 727]

1248 综 综 **summing up, aggregate**

☐ silk r 807 ■ clan, sect, faction 1247 zōng

BF I use strong *silk* rope to tie up all the *sect* members, forming one giant **aggregate** which the police can easily **round up.** [11 STROKES RANK 1425]

1249 踪 踪 **footprint, trace, tracks**

☐ foot r 946 ■ clan, sect, faction 1247 zōng

BF Marching on *foot* along with the rest of your *clan* leaves plenty of **footprints.** [15 STROKES RANK 1532]

1250 控 控 **accuse, charge** ☐ hand r 29 ■ empty 1219 kòng

BF You were supposed to keep track of my money. But now your *hand* is *empty.* I **accuse** you of stealing it! [11 STROKES RANK 780]

1251 登 登 **scale, climb** ■ stop! 181 (altered) ■ bean 1168 dēng

I had to *stop* and catch my breath when I got to the huge hill of *beans.* It was my task to **climb** this monster. [12 STROKES RANK 817]

1252 松 松 pine tree   ■ tree 375 ■ public affairs 1091   sō

People engaged in *public affairs* are supposed to be upright like a **pine tree**, so a good symbol for the **pine** is a juxtaposition of '*tree*' with '*public affairs*'.

[8 STROKES   RANK 895]

1253 炮 炮 cannon, firecracker   ■ fire 1101 ■ wrap, envelope 857   pà

The aftermath of *firing* a **cannon** is the noise and smoke which *envelopes* you.

[9 STROKES   RANK 914]

1254 脱 脱 shed, take off   ■ meat 317 (altered) ■ exchange, convert 1049   tuō

Here's my recipe for **shedding** weight. Simply eat more *meat* and protein, and *exchange* the fat for muscle!

[11 STROKES   RANK 943]

1255 鲜 鲜 fresh, new   ■ fish 485 ■ sheep 1147   xiā

Don't eat either the *fish* or the *mutton* unless they're very **fresh**.

[14 STROKES   RANK 958]

1256 辟 辟 law   ■ dead body 702 ■ mouth 41 ■ hardworking 1200   pì

Surely I've been *working too hard*. The *dead body* against the wall has just opened its *mouth* and started talking to me. This is against all natural **law**!

[13 STROKES   RANK 2140]

1257 壁 壁 wall, cliff, rampart   ■ law 1256 ■ earth, soil 9   bì

BF The *earth* upholds the city, symbolized by its *laws*. What *earth* formation does that? A high **cliff**.

[16 STROKES   RANK 1380]

1258 填 填 fill in, stuff   ■ earth, soil 9 ■ real 1058   tiá

That teddy bear isn't *real*. He might look it, because they use space-age *sand* to **stuff** him.

[13 STROKES   RANK 1970]

1259 欲 欲   wish, desire, want   ▮ cereal, grain 1060   ▯ owe, lack 465   yù

BF Breakfast time, and the **desire** for a bowl of nourishing *cereal* becomes strong. Oops, we're *fresh out* of cereal. It's going to be a long day...

[11 STROKES   RANK 1045]

1260 萨 萨   Buddha, kind-hearted person

▯ grass r 94   ▮ hills 735   ▮ give birth to* 1221   sà

BF The *hills* and the *grass* and all the other qualities of Mother Nature contribute to the *birth* of major religious figures like the **Buddha**.

[11 STROKES   RANK 1046]

1261 烧 烧   burn, cook, run a fever

▮ fire 1101   ▯ legendary emperor 374   shāo

When a *legendary emperor* died, the courtiers used a huge pyre of *fire* to **burn** the body. Otherwise, the king's dreadful disease would spread throughout the court and the country.   [10 STROKES   RANK 1201]

1262 障 障   obstruct, hinder   ▯ hills 735   ▮ chapter, section 1198   zhàng

BF The invaders will have a tough time capturing us. Nature has divided the *hills* into *sections* which **obstruct** and **hinder** the enemy's progress.

[13 STROKES   RANK 1237]

1263 徐 徐   slowly, gently   ▮ left step 1034   ▮ surplus, remainder 1073   xú

I am *walking* to market to sell the *surplus* we grew on our farm this year. It's a heavy load, and forces me to walk **slowly**.   [10 STROKES   RANK 1313]

1264 尝 尝   taste, experience, ever

▬ still, yet 1139 (altered)   ▬ cloud 751   cháng

The '*still, yet*' part indicates a transition. In this case, from good times to not-so-good times—hence, the *cloud*. What a life-altering **experience** these adverse situations can be!   [9 STROKES   RANK 1621]

1265 偿 偿 **compensate, repay**

　　　　　　　　　　　　■ man r 953　　■ taste, experience, ever 1264　　　chǎ

BF The piper must always be paid. This *man*'s unfortunate *experience* requires some sort of **compensation**.　　　　　　　　[11 STROKES　RANK 1329]

1266 灾 灾 **disaster, calamity**　　　□ roof 247　■ fire 1101　　zāi

BF The *roof* is on *fire*! Help us put it out, and avoid a **disaster**!

　　　　　　　　　　　　　　　　　[7 STROKES　RANK 1349]

1267 辩 辩 **argue, dispute, debate**

　　　　　　　　　　　■ hardworking (times 2) 1200　■ speech r 615　　bià

Two of my *best workers* are really getting into it, and *words* are flying about. I hope the **argument** doesn't get out of hand.　　　[16 STROKES　RANK 1355]

1268 崇 崇 **respect, adulate**　　■ mountain 21　　■ clan, sect, faction 1247　　chó

Here, '*mountain*' is a stand-in for the direction in which our thoughts move, and when the whole *clan* tends towards these lofty feelings, it indicates **respect** and **adulation**.　　　　　　　　[11 STROKES　RANK 1482]

1269 煤 煤 coal　　　　　■ fire 1101　□ certain, some 397　　mé

In the old days, we needed a *certain* something to keep the winter *fires* well stoked. That something was **coal**. (Nowadays, it's money!)

　　　　　　　　　　　　　　　　　[13 STROKES　RANK 1740]

1270 衮 衮 **imperial robes**

　　　　　■ cover 268　　■ public affairs 1091　　■ clothing 839 (altered)　　gǔ

BF Official events for those in *public affairs* require special *clothing* and a very fancy head *cover*. These conditions define the **imperial robes** of old.

　　　　　　　　　　　　　　　　　[10 STROKES　RANK 4843]

1271 滚 滚 **roll, turn, scram!**   ■ water r 523   ■ imperial robes 1270   gǔn
At the height of the religious ceremony, the emperor tripped and **rolled** down
the ornate steps by the altar. His *imperial robes* had soaked up sacrificial
blood, and the gory *liquid* flew off in drops during this ghastly journey.

[13 STROKES   RANK 1542]

1272 燃 燃 **burn, ignite**   ■ fire 1101   ■ correct, so 798   rán
When we use *fire* in the *correct* manner, it becomes a useful resource by which
we **ignite** stoves and furnaces. Otherwise, it rages out of control, becoming
harmful rather than helpful.   [16 STROKES   RANK 1553]

Unit 53

Looking on the Bright Side

1273 澳 澳 **bay, cove** ▢ water r 523 ▢ profound, abstruse 1135 ào
BF An *abstruse* point is apt to be deep; a **bay** is a deep body of *water*.

[15 STROKES   RANK 1627]

1274 尉 尉 **military official** ▢ corpse 703 ▢ show, indicate 1064 ▢ inch 210 wè
BF The **military official** remembered this grisly scene, repeated all too often during the great rebellion: gunfire *showing* a *corpse*, *inch*-long knife wounds piercing the body.

[11 STROKES   RANK 2126]

1275 慰 慰 **console, comfort** ▢ military official 1274 ▢ heart (fat) 906 wè
BF After witnessing the awfulness of war first hand, the *military official*'s next job was to show *compassion* and attempt to **console** the grieving widows and orphans.

[15 STROKES   RANK 1632]

1276 陪 陪 **accompany** ▢ hills 735 ▢ erect, stand 1179 ▢ mouth 41 pé
The *hill* people are notoriously shy. When they come to town, they *stand* together and keep their *mouths* shut. They always **accompany** one another.

[10 STROKES   RANK 1664]

1277 赔 赔 **compensate, pay for** ▢ cowrie 430 ▢ erect, stand 1179 ▢ mouth 41 pé
When you damage your neighbor's lawnmower, you *stand up* like a man, open your *mouth*, and give the guy *money* to **compensate** him for the damage.

[12 STROKES   RANK 1734]

1278 誉　誉　**reputation, fame**　　　■□ prosper 1212　　□■ speech 270　　yù

BF *Prosperity* and proper *speech* augment a person's **reputation**.

[13 STROKES   RANK 1676]

1279 欺　欺　**deceive, cheat**　　　■□ his, her, its, theirs 1093　　□■ owe, lack 465　　qī

BF I made *them* believe that they *owed* me money, but it was a fraud—I **cheated** them.

[12 STROKES   RANK 1699]

1280 粒　粒　**grain, granule, pellet**　　　■□ rice 1127　　□■ erect, stand 1179　　lì

BF Someone threw *rice* on the floor where I was *standing* in my bare feet. I could feel each and every **grain**—oh, the pain!

[11 STROKES   RANK 1714]

1281 峡　峡　**gorge, canyon**　　　□■ mountain 21　　□■ place in between 1177　　xiá

BF To early explorers, **gorges** and **canyons** were picturesque valleys nestled *between mountains*.

[9 STROKES   RANK 1727]

1282 粹　粹　**pure*, unmixed***　　　■□ rice 1127　　□■ foot soldier 450　　cuì

BF The prince (disguised as a *soldier*) went to the wedding. The guests threw filthy *rice* at him, but it all rolled off, because he was so **pure**.

[14 STROKES   RANK 1736]

1283 糖　糖　**sugar, sweets, carbs**　　　■□ rice 1127　　□■ Tang dynasty 690　　táng

In the collective Chinese memory, nothing was **sweeter** than life during the *Tang dynasty*. Chinese **candy** tends to be in separate pieces, sprinkled with *rice* flour to keep it from sticking together.

[16 STROKES   RANK 1746]

1284 弥　弥　**full, overflowing**　　　■□ bow (weapon) 859　　□■ you, thou 1227　　mí

When *you* hold your giant *bow* and stand in the doorway, you fill it to **overflowing**.

[8 STROKES   RANK 1785]

1285 丿 彡 **feathers**

CMP You can imagine these **feathers** in a wing, upswept to catch the wind. **Feathers** have other uses—dusting, writing, drawing—and can be suggestive of other growths on living creatures, such as hair and bristles, and maybe fingernails and shells.

1286 珍 珍 **precious thing**   ■ king 11   ■ man 311   ■ feathers 1285   zh▸

BF In this and other characters, '*man*' straddles '*feathers*', perhaps to suggest to readers the concept of "human feathers." Of course, people don't grow feathers, so this must be a poetic expression of decorative things that grow from someone's body. In all likelihood, this represents a head of hair, but not just anybody's hair—rather, an impressive, Beethovenian or Einsteinian mop.

This character paints a picture of luxuriant hair on the head of a *king*. This was a **precious thing** to the citizens in those days.

[9 STROKES   RANK 1314]

1287 须 须 **beard, must**   ■ feathers 1285   ■ page, leaf 444   xū

What are those wispy, whiskery, *feathery* things adjacent to a *man's face*? Why, his **beard**, of course!   [9 STROKES   RANK 444]

1288 趁 趁 **take advantage of**
■ to walk 421   ■ man 311   ■ feathers 1285   ch▸

Here's a *man* (the king, perhaps, from §1286) *walking around* and in danger of tripping over his long, *luxuriant hair*. The Royal Tonsorial Parlor is part of his stroll—he'd better **take advantage** of this opportunity to get a haircut.

[12 STROKES   RANK 2109]

1289 穆 穆 **respectful, dignified**
■ rice or grain 409   ■ silk 206 (altered)   ■ feathers 1285   m▸

BF Here's our special suit for this **respectful and dignified** occasion. Of course we use *silk*, tastefully accoutered with some *feathers* for decoration. Since the harvest is the source of our prosperity, we cram our pockets full of *grain* to throw in a celebratory manner at the end of the ceremony.

[16 STROKES   RANK 1683]

1290 影 影 **shadow, reflection**   ▮ view, scene 1083   ▯ feathers 1285   yǐng

BF We're shooting a movie. There's a typical urban *view*, and notice how high the sun is in the sky—the *feathery* **shadows** are clearly visible.

[15 STROKES   RANK 390]

1291 彭 彭 **surname of Peng**   ▯ ten 6   ▮ bean 1168   ▯ feathers 1285   péng

This character simply represents **a particular family name**, and has no other meaning so far as I can tell. How can we fix it in our minds forever?

Beans are notorious for the gassiness they induce; the *feathery* vapor trails on the right suggest the gas tracks from *ten* bowls of *beans*. The cook's plea: "**P**lease **e**at our **n**orthern **G**arbanzos," and those initials spell 'peng'. The rising second tone suggests the buoyant properties of gas.

[12 STROKES   RANK 1501]

1292 參 参 **take part in, participate**

▯ private 750   ▮ big 330 (altered)   ▮ feathers 1285   cān

BF They'll only let me **take part in** the gang if I show true dedication. I need to wear something that's *private* and very meaningful to me, like the *big* bunch of pink *feathers* I dance around in when nobody's watching.

[8 STROKES   RANK 507]

1293 诊 诊 **diagnose**   ▮ speech r 615   ▯ man 311   ▮ feathers 1285   zhěn

BF My ideal doctor is a *man* whose hands on my body are like *feathers*. He *speaks* his **diagnosis** calmly and in measured tones, no matter how serious.

[7 STROKES   RANK 1401]

1294 惨 惨 **miserable, wretched**

▮ heart (skinny) 930   ▯ take part in, participate 1292   cǎn

It's *emotional* to *take part in* so many office parties. It makes me **miserable**—celebrating other people's promotions, but never my own.

[11 STROKES   RANK 1530]

1295 彦 彦 **accomplished, talented**

◧ cliff r 671   ◰ erect, stand 1179   ◼ feathers 1285   yà

BF His talents make him *stand out* from the crowd, figuratively as if he were *standing* atop a *cliff*, the *feathers* indicative of the elegance of his **accomplishments.**   [9 STROKES   RANK 2559]

1296 颜 颜 **color**

◨ accomplished, talented 1295   ◨ page, leaf 444   yà

BF Upon receiving compliments on his *talents*, his *face* flushed deeply with embarrassment, turning (it seemed) every **color** of the rainbow.

[15 STROKES   RANK 1545]

1297 丱 丱 **contented cows**

◼ horned animal 100   ◲ one 2

CMP Imagine a long line of **contented cows** all resting their heads on the rail of their pens. Here's a snapshot of this bucolic scene—there's only room to show *one* of these *horned animals.*

1298 昔 昔 **former times, past**

◻ contented cows 1297   ◼ day, sun 63   xī

BF An aging bull ruminates on his **past** life. All *day* long, it was his sole job to ensure that the *cows stayed contented.*   [8 STROKES   RANK 2388]

Unit 54

Tomorrow is Another Day

1299 措 措 **arrange**　　　　　▮ hand r 29　　▮ former times, past 1298　　cuò

BF Things that have been neatly **arranged** *some time ago* somehow always get messed up, seemingly by themselves. We need to use our *hands* carefully to set them back in order.　　　　　　　　　　[11 STROKES　RANK 1148]

1300 借 借 **borrow or lend**　　　　　▮ man r 953　　▮ former times, past 1298　　jiè

The *man* **loaned** me money some time *past* when I was in real need of it. Now he needs my repayment as someone else needs to **borrow** it.

[10 STROKES　RANK 984]

1301 惜 惜 **cherish, value highly**

▮ heart (skinny) 930　　▮ former times, past 1298　　xī

BF People **cherish** things and other people who have been with them a long time. In this way, an *emotion* tied to something well-known from *former times* arises.　　　　　　　　　　[11 STROKES　RANK 1512]

1302 共 共 **together**　　　　　▮ contented cows 1297　　▮ eight 1048　　gòng

There's an *abundance* of *cows contentedly* resting in their barn. Domestic animals somehow learn to act **together**.　　[6 STROKES　RANK 330]

1303 供 供 **supply, feed**　　　　　▮ man r 953　　▮ together 1302　　gōng

For effective deployment of a large group of *men* acting *together* (think of an army), you need **to supply** and **feed** these hungry guys. Remember, an army travels on its stomach!　　　　　　　　　　[8 STROKES　RANK 550]

1304 洪 洪 vast, grand (water)   ▮ water r 523   ▮ together 1302   hó

BF When several great rivers or other flowing bodies of *water* come *together*, the result is a **vast**, flood-like expanse.   [9 STROKES RANK 1350]

1305 黄 黄 yellow

▮ contented cows 1297   ▮ field 57 (altered)   ▮ eight 1048   hu

It's harvest time, and the farmer reviews his status. The *cows are contented*, the *fields* have produced an *abundance*, and all is right with the world. While green is the prominent color in the spring and summer, now is the time when **yellows** and browns hold sway.   [11 STROKES RANK 561]

1306 横 横 horizontal stroke   ▮ tree 375   ▮ yellow 1305   hé

A newly-cut *tree* looks *yellow* if the woodsman **cuts** it **horizontally** so you can see the bright inner material.   [15 STROKES RANK 1330]

1307 谨 谨 careful, cautious

▮ speech r 615   ▮ animal hide 101   ▮ earth, soil 9   jǐn

Chinese people behaved **carefully** and **cautiously** during the Cultural Revolution. The result of one wrong or misunderstood *speech*, and they would have to *hide* (different word, but the same sound as in '*animal hide*') in the *earth* to escape the fury of the Red Guards!   [13 STROKES RANK 1917]

1308 典 典 canon, dictionary   ▮ together 1302   ▮ borders 127   di

BF Masses of words bound *together* within the '*borders*' of a single book constitute a **dictionary**.   [8 STROKES RANK 1044]

1309 恭 恭 respectful   ▮ together 1302 (altered)   ▮ small 1063 (altered)   gō

BF Here are several scholars *together* for the first time. Despite their eminence, they show as much **respect** to the *least* of them (who's very funny-looking) as to the mightiest.   [10 STROKES RANK 1742]

1310　巷　巷　lane, alley　　　　　　■ together 1302　　■ single ear 157　　xiàng

BF This old-fashioned **alley** is so narrow that we can't pass through it *together*. If we do, there's only room for a *single ear*—the other gets scraped off on the walls of the buildings.　　　　　　　　　　　　　　　　[9 STROKES　RANK 2399]

1311　港　港　harbor, port　　　　　　■ water r 523　　■ lane, alley 1310　　gǎng

BF A **harbor** is the *water* equivalent of a *lane*, for it leads vessels to the city in an orderly manner.　　　　　　　　　　　　　　　　[12 STROKES　RANK 927]

1312　暴　暴　sudden and violent, savage

　　　　　　　　　　　■ day, sun 63　　■ together 1302　　■ water 545　　bào

"Nature red in tooth and claw...," quoth the poet. So it is appropriate for aspects of nature—*sun* and *water*—act *together* to illustrate the **sudden violence** of which nature is capable.　　　　　　　　　　　　[15 STROKES　RANK 1028]

1313　爆　爆　explode, burst, quick-fry

　　　　　　　　　　　■ fire 1101　　■ sudden and violent, savage 1312　　bào

Fire and *sudden violence*—the very definition of an **explosion**.

　　　　　　　　　　　　　　　　　　　　　　　[19 STROKES　RANK 1243]

1314　赛　赛　compete, game, competition

　　　　　　　　　　　□ roof 247　　■ together 1302 (altered)　　■ cowrie 430　　sài

Competitions like the Olympic **Games** are meant to transcend political differences. All teams gather *together* under one *roof* to **compete**. The fact that 'together' is altered reminds us that the contestants who participate might not normally be found *together* in the same room! The nature of the **game** is such that while the prize for winning might be money, it just as well might be something symbolic, like a *seashell*.　　　　　[14 STROKES　RANK 1064]

1315 塞 塞 fill, stuff in

☐ roof 247   ▬ together 1302 (altered)   ▬ earth, soil 9   sā

Let's work *together* to throw *soil* into this large abandoned *house*. Thereby, we **fill** the house up so it can serve as a barricade to the enemy.

[13 STROKES   RANK 1080]

1316 寒 寒 cold, glacial

☐ roof 247   ▬ together 1302 (altered)   ▬ ice r 569 (altered)   há

BF It's so **cold** outside, that even as we huddle *together* under the *roof*, *ice* coatings have formed all around us.   [12 STROKES   RANK 1297]

1317 戴 戴 wear, put on (clothes)

▮ halberd 359 (altered)   ☐ ten 6   ▪ field 57   ▪ together 1302   dà

This character forms a schematic for what the well-dressed soldier would have **worn** in ancient, scribal times. The left shows us the clothing part of the costume—tall helmet at the top resembles '*ten*', and the tight tunic and smart trousers reminded someone of '*field*' and '*together*'. An out-sized *sword* on the right completes the sketch.   [17 STROKES   RANK 1228]

1318 翼 翼 wing, flank

▬ feather, wing 123   ☐ field 57   ▬ together 1302   yì

BF All of a sudden, *feathers* started raining down on the big corn*field* across the street. The feathers are huge and stay *together* in a big pile. They must come from the **wing** of a huge bird!   [17 STROKES   RANK 1294]

1319 腊 腊 sausage   ▮ meat 317 (altered)   ▮ former times, past 1298   là

BF Remember the boar we butchered *some time ago*? We took the *meat* and made delicious **sausages** from it.   [12 STROKES   RANK 1497]

1320 籍 籍　**books, works**

　　　　　　　◼ end, tip 383　◼ former times, past 1298　▢ bamboo r 243　jí

BF Ever see pictures of '**books**' from *ancient* China?　They were made of *bamboo* strips cut from the *tips* of the plant, and sewn together.

[20 STROKES　RANK 1579]

1321 猎 猎　**hunt, chase**　　　◼ dog r 898　◼ former times, past 1298　liè

BF In *times past*, there was great reliance on *dogs* to help conclude a successful **hunt**.　[11 STROKES　RANK 1687]

1322 采 采　**distinguish, differentiate**　　▢ dab 169　◼ rice 1127

CMP Despite the visual decomposition you see here, the origin of this character is as a claw mark. In former times, it was important—crucial!—to be able to **differentiate** between the various animals of the forest on the basis of traces they left behind. In this case, the strokes going every which way must have suggested the stylized print of a claw.

1323 番 番　**kind**　　◼ distinguish, differentiate 1322　◼ field 57　fān

Fields contain many kinds of crops, each needing *different* care. As a result, it's important to *distinguish* between the **kinds** of crops in the various *fields*.

[12 STROKES　RANK 1452]

1324 播 播　**sow, broadcast**　　◼ hand r 29　◼ kind 1323　bō

I use my *hand* to throw the different *kinds* of seed into a field, which is exactly what **sowing** is.　[15 STROKES　RANK 1275]

Unit 55

Power of Suggestion

1325 悉　悉　**know, learn**　▢ distinguish, differentiate 1322　■ heart (fat) 906　**xī**
BF The most basic type of **learning** involves *distinguishing* between different
emotions—know thyself! 　　　　　　　　　　[11 STROKES　RANK 1428]

1326 翻　翻　**turn over, cross over**
　　　　　■ distinguish, differentiate 1322　■ field 57　▮ feather, wing 123　**fā**
After all these years as a farmer, I still can't *differentiate* between a well-
plowed *field* and a marsh land covered with *feathery* grass. As a result, it's
hard for me **cross over** to the other side. 　　　[18 STROKES　RANK 1027]

1327 钅　钅　**gold r**
CMP This is just a squished-up form of '*gold*' (§1157).

1328 锦　锦　**brocade**　　　　　▮ gold r 1327　▮ silk 206　**jǐ**
BF Brocade is a luxurious fabric made of *silk* shot with *gold* or other shiny
metallic thread. 　　　　　　　　　　　　　[13 STROKES　RANK 1947]

1329 锐　锐　**sharp, acute**　　　▮ gold r 1327　▮ exchange, convert 1049　**ru**
BF The **sharp** businessperson is the one who can profitably *convert* his goods
into *gold*. 　　　　　　　　　　　　　　　[12 STROKES　RANK 1851]

1330 销　销　**melt metal**　　　▮ gold r 1327　▮ like, similar to 1231　**xiā**
If you put all different pieces of *gold* into the kiln, they all become *similar*
shapeless lumps after the **metal melts**. 　　　[12 STROKES　RANK 904]

1331 钱　钱　**money, coins**　　◧ gold r 1327　▢ tiny, fragmentary 373　　qián
Gold becomes convenient when you chop it up into many *tiny* but standard-ized units. These bits, like **coins**, become useful as **money**.

[10 STROKES　RANK 603]

1332 错　错　**bad, wrong, mistaken**
◧ gold r 1327　▢ former times, past 1298　　cuò
In *former times* this country's money was made out of *precious metal*, but now our coinage is debased and **bad**.　　　[13 STROKES　RANK 638]

1333 铁　铁　**iron**　　　　◧ gold r 1327　▢ lose 427　　tiě
The *gold* bars somehow became spoiled, as if they were living things. Grad-ually, they *lost* their color—and their value.　Now, they're just **iron** in-gots.　　　　　　　　　　　　　　　　　　　[10 STROKES　RANK 779]

1334 钟　钟　**bell, clock, time**　　◧ gold r 1327　▢ middle 45　　zhōng
The *metal* item that was of central importance in ancient China was the **bell**, located in the *middle* of the town square. It marked **time**, tolled for important events, and represented authority and prosperity.　　[9 STROKES　RANK 905]

1335 镇　镇　**trading center, garrison post**　◧ gold r 1327　▢ real 1058　　zhèn
That **trading post** is so tiny it looks fake, but don't be fooled—it's *real*! The soldiers take their job of guarding the *gold* very seriously.

[15 STROKES　RANK 1002]

1336 针　针　**needle, pin, injection**　◧ gold r 1327　▢ ten 6　　zhēn
The '*gold*' here really stands for any fine metal, and the '*ten*' refers—more or less—to its shape. Also, in the old days, you needed one *gold* coin to buy *ten* **needles**—that's how costly they were to manufacture.

[7 STROKES　RANK 1116]

1337 镜 镜 **mirror** ■ gold r 1327 ▮ in the end 1193   jìŋ

BF The myth of the pot of *gold* at *the end of* the rainbow endures as a **mirror** of a universal desire for easy money. [16 STROKES RANK 1251]

1338 钻 钻 **drill, bore** ▮ gold r 1327 ▯ practice divination 172   zu

Prospecting—**drilling** for *gold*—is a little like *practicing divination*. You hope for the best, but you never know what you'll find. [10 STROKES RANK 1724]

1339 铜 铜 **copper** ■ gold r 1327 ▮ same, similar 129   tó

Many metals—especially when newly minted and untouched by tarnish—are so bright and shiny as to appear *similar* to *gold*. **Copper** is prominent among this group. [11 STROKES RANK 1772]

1340 ⺌ ⺍ **small (v)**

CMP

1 In the same way that 'eight' and other components have two variants, so too does '**small**' (§1063).

2 However, here's another interpretation that's also useful. The two ticks on the end signify abundance, and the vertical in the middle splits or divides this abundance. Sometimes we can interpret this component as meaning 'potential', a potential for abundance. At other times, this represents the destruction or diminution of something plentiful.

1341 当 当 **work as, become** ▬ small (v) 1340 ▬ boar's head 34   dā

You use this verb in the sense of becoming as in 'I want to **become** (to **work as**) an astronaut'. This character shows a seed just sprouting out of the layered ground, another way to interpret the *boar's head*. Tentatively, it spreads out a few *small* leaves, to mark the transition as it **becomes** a plant from a seed. The tiny leaves symbolize the **potential** abilities of the young plant. [6 STROKES RANK 71]

1342 挡 挡 **ward off, block**　　　　■ hand r 29　　▥ work as, become 1341　　dǎng

A *hand* approaches our sprouting seed. Some vicious child likes uprooting these seedlings for the fun of it! He will **block** its *becoming* a real plant, and so destroy its potential.　　　　　　　　　　[9 STROKES   RANK 1933]

1343 锁 锁 **lock up, lock**

■ gold r 1327　　▤ small (v) 1340　　▥ cowrie 430　　suǒ

The sound of engaging a **lock** is similar to that of a bunch of *small shells* jingling together. Of course, the **lock** itself is made of *metal*.　　　　　　　　[12 STROKES   RANK 1558]

1344 档 档 **files, archives**　　　　■ tree 375　　▥ work as, become 1341　　dàng

BF I feel like I have *become* a *tree*, because I pile up **files** all day long, creating stacks of paper which become as hard and unyielding a the *trees* they once were.　　　　　　　　　　　　　　[10 STROKES   RANK 1787]

1345 𭕄 ⺍ **hands raised high**

CMP We only see three upraised arms, but the topmost curve, almost horizontal, suggests the presence of hands, and many more arms, in the background.

1346 摇 摇 **shake, wave**

■ hand r 29　　▢ hands raised high 1345　　▣ dry mountainous bits 520　　yáo

Here are a group of heroes stranded on a *desert-dry mountain*. Everybody **waves** all their *hands* (all of which are *raised high*) vigorously in the attention to attract attention.　　　　　　　　　　[13 STROKES   RANK 940]

1347 妥 妥 **appropriate, proper**　　■ hands raised high 1345　　▣ woman 581　　tuǒ

The cowering *woman* in front is comforted by the *raised hands* of her loved ones that all is secure and **proper**.　　　　　　　　[7 STROKES   RANK 1840]

1348 采　采　pick, gather　　　　　▢ hands raised high 1345　　■ tree 375　　cǎ

The best fruit sits high on the *tree*. *Hold your hands high* in order to **pick** those succulent plums.　　　　　　　　　　[8 STROKES　RANK 585]

1349 菜　菜　dish, course, veggies　　　▢ grass r 94　　■ pick, gather 1348　　cà

Vegetables are personally *gathered* by great chefs for their mouthwatering **dishes**.　　　　　　　　　　[11 STROKES　RANK 1266]

1350 彩　彩　colorful　　　　　　■ pick, gather 1348　　▢ feathers 1285　　cǎ

BF The main reason to *gather feathers* is because they are so bright and **colorful**.　　　　　　　　　　[11 STROKES　RANK 1177]

Unit 56

A Bird in the Hand

1351 佥 佥 **together, unanimous**

■ cozy house 509 (altered)   ▬ hands raised high 1345   qiān

BF The crucial meeting takes place in this *cozy house*. They vote on the motion. Everybody *raises their hands*. The motion carries—it's **unanimous!**

Although a low frequency character in its standalone incarnation, it appears as a component in other characters.   [7 STROKES   RANK 5613]

1352 险 险 **dangerous**   ■ hills 735   ■ together, unanimous 1351   xiǎn

We formed a search party so we would go all *together* to the *hills*. It's too **dangerous** to go by yourself.   [9 STROKES   RANK 672]

1353 应 应 **ought**   ■ extensive 686   ■ hands raised high 1345 (altered)   yīng

The members *raise their hands* to affirm an *extensive* list of motions, a list of all the things we **ought** to do.   [7 STROKES   RANK 144]

1354 剑 剑 **sword, saber**   ■ together, unanimous 1351   ■ knife r 166   jiàn

A **saber** is a kind of *knife*. What kind? Well, when the intellectuals in the party *raise their hands* to vote on something, the warlord makes one mighty swing of his **saber** and chops off all their hands!   [9 STROKES   RANK 869]

1355 检 检 **check, examine**   ■ tree 375   ■ together, unanimous 1351   jiǎn

Infestations of *trees* by insects are increasingly common. If you group the *trees together*, then they are much easier to **examine**.   [11 STROKES   RANK 731]

1356 验 验   **examine, check**   ▮ horse 878   ▮ together, unanimous 1351   yi
In the old days, the days of the Wild American West, buying a *horse* was a serious craft. Until you build up skill, you need to get all your friends *together* to help you **examine** the the *horse* you're thinking of buying.

[10 STROKES   RANK 534]

1357 签 签   **sign one's name**   ▯ bamboo r 243   ▮ together, unanimous 1351   qi
In ancient times, people only **signed their name** at special occasions. Most often, it signaled *unanimous agreement.* Pens for signing were made out of *bamboo.*

[13 STROKES   RANK 1254]

1358 夫 夫   **mighty tree**
CMP You know this is a **mighty tree**, a conifer, because of the Christmas-tree profile and the three levels of branches, each loaded with pine needles.

1359 春 春   **spring (season)**   ▮ mighty tree 1358   ▮ day, sun 63   ch
BF Imagine this Kodak moment. The *mighty tree* dominates the foreground, showing off its new foliage. They are lit up by the rays of the *sun*, which is still low in the sky to indicate the moderate weather of **spring**.

[9 STROKES   RANK 921]

1360 奏 奏   **memorialize the emperor**
▮ mighty tree 1358   ▮ heaven 333   zo
It's from the ramparts of the extraordinary **monument to the emperor** (think: pyramids, Sphinx) that we see the *mighty tree* as symbol of homage to the son of *heaven.*

[9 STROKES   RANK 1543]

1361 秦 秦   **Qin (dynasty)**   ▮ mighty tree 1358   ▯ rice or grain 409   qi
It is thought that the **Qin** dynasty gave its name to the word 'China'.
    The **Qin** first brought modernity to Chinese civilization—more than two millennia ago. A centralized government made possible a countrywide program of public works, symbolized by this *mighty tree*, and helped guarantee supplies of food and *grain* to all citizens throughout the country.

[10 STROKES   RANK 1394]

1362 湊 湊 **assemble**   ◼ ice r 569   ◼ memorialize the emperor 1360   còu
Everyone had to **assemble**, even on this *icy* day, to *memorialize the emperor.*
[11 STROKES   RANK 2193]

1363 奉 奉 **give, present**   ◼ mighty tree 1358   ◼ ceremonial sword   fèng
The solemnity and majesty of the moment are emphasized by holding the
ceremony outside, beneath our *mighty tree.* The king **presents** the *ceremonial
sword* to the patriot.   [8 STROKES   RANK 1382]

1364 寿 寿 **longevity**   ◼ mighty tree 1358 (altered)   ◼ inch 210   shòu
The *mighty tree* is in danger of toppling over—lightning has destroyed the
right support system of its great trunk. Wise forest rangers merely need to
insert a one *inch* slab of wood to preserve the supports, and to safeguard the
longevity of the tree.   [7 STROKES   RANK 1615]

1365 卷 卷 **egg roll, roll up**
   ◼ spring (season) 1359 (altered)   ◼ single ear 157 (altered)   juǎn
It's messy as we make the year's first batch of **egg rolls**; the dabs up on top
emphasize this mess. The kitchen is still dark—it's only very early *spring*—so
the 'sun' between the curved supports is gone. We roll the wrapper in the
shape of the spiral folds of a person's *ear.*   [8 STROKES   RANK 1016]

1366 圈 圈 **pen, sty**   ◼ enclosure 40   ◼ egg roll, roll up 1365   juàn
The pigs are in their **pen**, quietly waiting for dinner. Tonight it's their favorite—slightly stale *egg rolls*—that get tossed into the *enclosure.*
[11 STROKES   RANK 1366]

1367 泰 泰 **peace, quiet**   ◼ mighty tree 1358   ◼ water 545   tài
BF What could be more **peaceful** than a **quiet** spot in the country, the sound
of wind whistling through *mighty trees* while *water* gurgles and splashes in
a nearby brook.   [10 STROKES   RANK 1318]

1368 籌 籌 **tally, counter**   ☐ bamboo r 243   ■ longevity 1364   ch

Bamboo plant have such *longevity* that you can use them as **tallies** of the passage of historical events (new governments, the occurrence of eclipses and earthquakes, and so on).   [13 STROKES RANK 1677]

1369 ⼍ ⼍ **time's arrow**

CMP This right-pointing arrow is a bit stylized, because the upper part of the arrow point is only sketched in.

1370 今 今 **today, current**   ■ man 311   ■ time's arrow 1369   jī

The flow of time is often likened to the flight of *time's arrow*, flying from the left (the past) to the right (the future). Here, the legs of a *man* attempt to pinion time's flight right now, **today**.   [4 STROKES RANK 336]

1371 贪 贪 **corrupt, venal**   ☐ today, current 1370   ■ cowrie 430   tā

The only way the government worker gets the *wealth* that he craves *today* is if he is thoroughly **corrupt**.   [8 STROKES RANK 1874]

1372 念 念 **read aloud**   ■ today, current 1370   ■ heart (fat) 906   ni

When a skilled reader **reads aloud**, she conveys her *current emotion*.
[8 STROKES RANK 477]

1373 令 令 **season**   ■ today, current 1370   ☐ dab 169   lín

BF A *little bit* of *today*—that is, today, plus the few weeks before and after—comprise a **season**.   [5 STROKES RANK 378]

1374 玲 玲 **exquisitely made**   ▮ king 11   ▮ season 1373   lín

BF The **exquisitely made** jewelry in view on noble ears, fingers, and limbs announces the beginning of the social *season*—when the *king* and other royals begin the round of fancy balls and such.   [9 STROKES RANK 1855]

1375 零　零　**zero**　　　　　　　　▢ rain 85　　◼ season 1373　　líng

During the *rainy season*, there's absolutely **nothing** to do, except wait for better weather.　　　　　　　　　　　　　　[13 STROKES   RANK 1342]

1376 齢　齢　**age, years**　　　　　　▯ tooth 324　　▯ season 1373　　líng

BF Imagine we're in the middle of *tooth season*, the time when teeth fall out of our mouths like rain from the heavens. This is a problem for older people (at least it used to be, in times of poor public health) after the passage of many **years**.　　　　　　　　　　　[13 STROKES   RANK 1510]

Unit 57

Whatever You Say

1377 领　领　**neck**　　■ season 1373　■ page, leaf 444　lǐ

BF The **neck** is a *seasonal* body part *on top of a person*. That is, sometimes you see it (warmer weather), and sometimes you don't (cooler times).

[11 STROKES　RANK 329]

1378 冷　冷　**cold**　　■ ice r 569　■ season 1373　lě

When it's the '*ice*' *season*, it's sure to be bitter **cold**.　　[7 STROKES　RANK 700]

1379 怜　怜　**sympathy, pity**　　■ heart (skinny) 930　■ season 1373　lí

BF *Heart season* is the time of year when you display **sympathy** and **pity** for your fellow man. Hopefully, this '*heart season*' runs all year long.

[8 STROKES　RANK 1599]

1380 吟　吟　**chant, recite**　　■ mouth 41　■ today, current 1370　yí

Today's sounds always sound fresh and new. In a few years, they are as outdated as religious **chanting**.　　[7 STROKES　RANK 2015]

1381 含　含　**keep in the mouth**　　■ today, current 1370　■ mouth 41　há

You **keep in your mouth** what's *currently* in your *mouth*.

[7 STROKES　RANK 937]

It's easy to confuse 吟 and 含 (§§1380 and 1381). But 吟 'chant, recite' refers to actual production of sound, and the sound travels further with the mouth part 口 on the side. With the mouth aimed down, as in 含, no one would hear anything.

1382 琴 琴 **zither-like instrument**

█ king (times 2) 11   ▬ today, current 1370   qín

Zithers are folk-instruments with many rows of strings and frets, which the *two kings* resemble. Think of the bottom component as a pick (like a guitar pick) to pluck the strings to make music.   [12 STROKES   RANK 1701]

1383 铃 铃 **bell**   █ gold r 1327   █ season 1373   líng

Bells constructed out of *fine metal* are *seasonal* items that hang outside to make beautiful music when soft breezes blow.   [10 STROKES   RANK 1969]

1384 邻 邻 **neighbor, neighborhood, neighboring**

█ season 1373   █ town 745   lín

BF In ancient times, rich folk wandered from country to *town*, and back, depending on the *season*. In *season*, you could depend on having a **neighbor** in *town*, otherwise the city house was a lonely place indeed.

[7 STROKES   RANK 1659]

Small, diagonal strokes are common.

1385 石 石 **stone r**

CMP The level surface with the sloping downward edge represents the profile of a **stone** cliff.

1386 石 石 **stone, rock**   ▬ stone r 1385   shí

BF The things at the bottoms of cliffs tend to be monstrous **stones** and boulders. The 'mouth' component is a big *rock*, not a mouth.   [5 STROKES   RANK 414]

1387 碧 碧 **green jade**   █ emperor 207 (altered)   ▬ stone, rock 1386   bì

BF We saw in §207 that we could think of an *emperor* as a 'white king', with these elements stacked vertically. Here, to accommodate a crowded character square, these components are juxtaposed to each other horizontally.

What kind of *stone* would appeal to the *emperor*? Why, **green jade**, of course—China's royal gem.   [14 STROKES   RANK 2165]

1388 岩 岩 cliff, crag　　　　　■ mountain 21　■ stone, rock 1386　　yi

BF The salient quality of a **cliff** is the abrupt and sudden contrast between the high ground on one side of the cliff and the low ground on the other. This character emphasizes the contrast in terrain—the high *mountain* on top next to the big *rock* resting on the ground below.　　　　[8 STROKES   RANK 1423]

1389 碰 碰 touch, bump

■ stone, rock 1386　■ enter, advance 1123 (altered)　☐ eight (v) 1047　pe

The '*enter*' component on the right is missing the 'sun' that belongs at the bottom. The *stone* rolled into the cave, and destroyed the *sunlamp* when it **bumped** into it! The '*abundant*' dabs up top represent pieces of debris flying all over the place.　　　　[13 STROKES   RANK 1371]

1390 碎 碎 broken　　　　　■ stone, rock 1386　■ foot soldier 450　su

The force of the bomb blast dropped a *stone* on the *soldier*. Only his helmet was **broken**.　　　　[13 STROKES   RANK 1420]

1391 碍 碍 hinder, obstruct

■ stone, rock 1386　☐ day, sun 63　☐ one 2　■ inch 210　ài

We're trapped in the mine! Peering up, we can only see *one inch* of the *sun* over the horizon. By its light, we see the huge *stone* that **hinders** our escape.　　　　[13 STROKES   RANK 1437]

1392 矿 矿 ore　　　　　■ stone, rock 1386　■ extensive 686　ku

Extensive supplies of an important kind of mineral or *stone* is what **ore** is.　　　　[8 STROKES   RANK 1385]

1393 碗 碗 bowl　　　　　■ stone, rock 1386　■ bent 864　wa

Waterproof things were few and far between in ancient times. That's why a peculiar *bend* in a small *rock* would have been so valuable—it would have served as a leak proof **bowl**.　　　　[13 STROKES   RANK 1939]

1394 础　础　base*, foundation*　　■ stone r 1385　□■ exit 22　　chǔ
BF The component that means '*exit*' has a structural appearance—it looks like
it could hold stuff. Perhaps it does, and it holds large amounts of *stone*, which
act as a strong and solid **base** or **foundation** to this building.

[10 STROKES   RANK 1014]

1395 磨　磨　polish, wear down, pester
　　　　　■ hemp, pocked, pitted 694 (altered)　　■■ stone, rock 1386　　mó
Go ahead, wrap some *linen* cloth around a hefty *stone*. You'll find it makes
a great **polishing** tool. With patience, it **wears down** the roughest blemish.
It reminds me of the way my kids **pester** when they want something—they
simply **wear** me **down**.　　　　　　　　[16 STROKES   RANK 1537]

1396 码　码　number　　■ stone, rock 1386　□■ horse 878　　mǎ
Stones got lodged in the *horse*'s hoof. We **counted** every step back to town.

[8 STROKES   RANK 1345]

1397 磁　磁　porcelain　　■ stone, rock 1386　□■ now, at present 779　　cí
BF *At present*, no one eats out of hollowed *stones*. Everything is now **porcelain**
or china!　　　　　　　　　　　　　　　[14 STROKES   RANK 1771]

1398 了　了　le r
CMP 了 is the supreme example of an important Chinese word which defies
easy translation. By great good fortune, it's so common that you'll soon learn
how to recognize and draw it.

1399 了　了　le　　　　　　　■ le r 1398　　le
One of the important uses of this common word is to signal a sudden 'change
of state' (refer to your favorite textbook for a more leisurely and meaningful
discussion), suggested by the twists and turns of this squiggly character. We'll
use it to signify a sudden, significant change.　　[2 STROKES   RANK 5]

1400 亨 亨 **smooth**   ☐ cover 268   ☴ mouth 41   ▬ le 1399   hē

A roof (*cover*) over your head, food to keep your *mouth* happy, and *changes* for the better mean life is finally becoming **smooth** for you.

[7 STROKES   RANK 2146]

1401 哼 哼 **hum, croon**   ▮ mouth 41   ☐ smooth 1400   hē

The sound from your *mouth* when things are going *smoothly* is apt to be a **humming** or **crooning**.   [10 STROKES   RANK 1966]

1402 子 子 **son, child**   ▮ le 1399   ⊟ one 2   zǐ

BF There is no *change* in life so sudden as the birth of *one* **child**.

[3 STROKES   RANK 37]

Unit 58

Big Doings

1403 享 享 **enjoy**   ■ smooth 1400   ▣ one 2   xiǎng

When *one* thing after another goes *smoothly*, then I sit back and **enjoy** life.

[8 STROKES   RANK 1227]

Here again is the case of two characters, those in §§1400 and 1403, that can be confused. Both 'smooth' and 'enjoyable' are adjectives that apply to life, but 'enjoyable' conveys a little bit *more* than just 'smooth'. The character 享 'enjoy' contains *one* more stroke than 亨 'smooth'.

1404 仔 仔 **animal young**   ■ man r 953   ■ son, child 1402   zǐ

BF A *man* takes his *son* to the zoo, where their favorite exhibits feature the **animal young**.

[5 STROKES   RANK 1572]

1405 好 好 **good, OK**   ■ woman 581   ■ son, child 1402   hǎo

No scene better suggests a sense of **good**ness than a *woman* together with her *child*.

[6 STROKES   RANK 82]

1406 李 李 **plum**   ▣ tree 375   ■ son, child 1402   lǐ

BF The ancient Chinese considered **plums** to be the most important of fruits. As a result, the *offspring* of orchard *trees* were often **plums**.

[7 STROKES   RANK 472]

1407 季 季 season*   ▪ rice or grain 409   ▪ son, child 1402   jì

BF At the start of one **season**, the *grain*, which is the *offspring* of last year's crop, is still unripe. But by **season's** end, it has ripened and matured.

[8 STROKES   RANK 1279]

These two glyphs—李 'plum' and 季, §§1406 and 1407—have meanings that can get jumbled. The little 'dab' atop 季 suggests immaturity, and you need an entire season for the crop to fully ripen.

1408 俘 俘 capture, take prisoner   ▪ man r 953   ▪ hands raised high 1345   ▪ son, child 1402   fú

BF Young soldiers—so young they seem like *children*—have *raised their hands* in surrender to the *man* who has **captured** them.   [9 STROKES   RANK 2057]

1409 浮 浮 float   ▪ water r 523   ▪ hands raised high 1345   ▪ son, child 1402   fú

The small *child* has fallen into the *water*. General panic! All the other swimmers gather round, *hands held high*, to keep him out of harm's way. But not to worry—children naturally **float** in water.   [10 STROKES   RANK 1462]

1410 孙 孙 grandson   ▪ son, child 1402   ▪ small 1063   sū

BF A **grandson** is like a *son*, but the filial relationship has been diluted—made *small*—by the intervening generation.   [6 STROKES   RANK 995]

1411 孟 孟 eldest among brothers   ▪ son, child 1402   ▪ vessel, dish 110   m

BF Which *child* sits at the head of the table by the *dishes* of food? The **eldest among them**, by virtue of his status and superior strength and growth.

[8 STROKES   RANK 1575]

1412 孔 孔 hole, aperture   ▪ son, child 1402   ▪ mineshaft 135   kǒ

Holes in the ground that mark old *mineshafts* are quite dangerous, especially for puppies and *children*.

This character also stands for **Confucius**.   [4 STROKES   RANK 1289]

1413 孤 孤 **solitary, isolated** ▮ son, child 1402 ▮ melon 781 gū

BF The *boy* is gorging himself on a *melon*, and he is making such a sloppy pig of himself that no one sits near him. He has become **solitary** and **isolated**.

[8 STROKES RANK 1334]

1414 郭 郭 **outer city wall**

▮ high 275 (altered) ▮ son, child 1402 ▮ town 745 guō

BF The *town* protects its *children* and other vulnerable people by means of something *high*—the massive **outer city wall**. [10 STROKES RANK 1813]

1415 字 字 **character, word** ▯ roof 247 ▮ son, child 1402 zì

You want a **character**—I'll give you a **character**. It's my *son*. At age forty-two, he still lives under my *roof*! (And when is he going to get married?)

[6 STROKES RANK 393]

1416 疑 疑 **doubt, suspect**

▮ ancient ladle 142 ▮ arrow 334 ▯ son, child 1402 (altered) ▮ stop! 181 (altered) yí

BF Using a *ladle* as an *arrow*, his *son* seriously expects that he will be able to *stop* danger. I **suspect** he's a little bit nuts. [14 STROKES RANK 698]

1417 疗 疗 **cure, treat illness** ▮ sick 697 ▮ le 1399 liáo

BF One of the functions of the '*le*' character is to signal a change of state. Thus, if someone starts out *sick*, and then there is a *change in the state* of their health, they must be **cured**! [7 STROKES RANK 949]

1418 猛 猛 **fierce, valiant** ▮ dog r 898 ▮ eldest among brothers 1411 měng

In a litter of puppies, the *eldest* among these *dogs* has been observed to secure his position by **fierce** behavior towards his siblings. [11 STROKES RANK 1157]

1419 厚 厚 **thick, deep, profound**

☐ cliff r 671   ▪ day, sun 63   ▪ son, child 1402   h

The college freshman stands on top of the *cliff*, pondering how different words like '*son*' and '*sun*' sound alike yet have different meanings. How **profound**, or so he thinks.

[9 STROKES   RANK 1235]

1420 凝 凝 **congeal, curdle**   ☐ ice r 569   ☐ doubt, suspect 1416   n

Early on, I began to *doubt* you still loved me. When you poured *ice* cubes down my back at the party, my suspicions **congealed** into knowledge.

[16 STROKES   RANK 1631]

1421 丿 丿 **action path**

CMP The presence of this element suggests a **path** along which something important happened. Sometimes, it suggests just the **action** itself.

1422 么 么 **huh? what?**   ▪ action path 1421   ▪ private 750   m

BF A fly or worm or something is tracing an *action path* along my neighbor's *nose*. **What** the heck is it?

[3 STROKES   RANK 63]

1423 长 长 **long, length**

▬ one 2   ☐ scepter 5 (altered)   ▪ action path 1421   ▪ action path 1421 (altered)   ch

The *scepter* is the back wall of a room, and the *horizontal* represents a **long** mirror bisecting it. A ray of light from the mirror travels to the upper right. The lower half of this vision is a mirror image of the upper half. It's well known that a mirror in a room increases the apparent **length** of the room.

[4 STROKES   RANK 109]

1424 勿 勿 **do not**   ▪ action path (times 3) 1421   ☐ place of refuge 111   w

There's a lot of *activity* going on, and it is all **not permitted**. Everything is restricted to the *place of refuge* in order to circumscribe the activity.

[4 STROKES   RANK 2563]

1425 豕 豖 **pig, boar**   ☐ one 2   ■ do not 1424 (altered)   ☐ gaping jaws   shǐ

BF The **boar** is *one* animal you *do not* want to take for granted. They have foul tempers, they can be vicious, and their temperament can turn on a dime. Those *gaping jaws* help emphasize this warning!   [7 STROKES   RANK 4953]

1426 家 家 **home**   ☐ roof 247   ■ pig, boar 1425   jiā

Most of the people who live in my **home** under my *roof* are such *pigs!*
                                                         [10 STROKES   RANK 56]

1427 易 易 **easy**   ▢ day, sun 63   ■ do not 1424   yì

BF My *son* (sounds like '*sun*') *does not* do anything all day long! Life is **easy** for him.   [8 STROKES   RANK 461]

1428 物 物 **thing, matter**   ▌ ox 186   ☐ do not 1424   wù

BF Imagine an immigrant speaking, someone whose English is not quite up to snuff. "**Nothing**'s the **matter**—*do not ox* me again!" Many foreigners pronounce 'ask' like '*ox*'.   [8 STROKES   RANK 142]

Unit 59

Not So Fast!

1429 东 东 **east** ■ show, indicate 1064 (altered) ⬜ action path 1421 dō
As the sun ascends in the **east**, its rays *indicate* the *action path* that it traces
in the sky. [5 STROKES RANK 194]

1430 车 车 **car** ◧ east 1429 (altered) ■ ten 6 ch
In the old days, how would you have gotten from California to New York?
You climb in your **car**, and head *east*. In *ten* days, more or less, you'll be
bucking crowds in Times Square.
   Also: 车 shows the outline of the front of your new, fire-engine red
Lexus, seen from above. The car's hood is on the left. The horizontals represent the wheels on the right and left. The front right door is open, and if you
look inside, you'll see the front row of bucket seats (that's the vertical line)
neatly bisected in two. [4 STROKES RANK 361]

1431 军 军 **military** ⬜ smooth cover 280 ■ car 1430 jū
BF Put a strong, weapons-resistant *cover* on a *car*, and you've converted it to
military use. [6 STROKES RANK 102]

1432 辉 辉 **brightness, splendor** ▌ light, ray 1116 ▌ military 1431 hu
BF In the old days, before 'imperialism' became a dirty word, one presumed
that the metaphorical *light* from *military* exploits brought **brightness** and
splendor to the reigning monarch. [12 STROKES RANK 1623]

1433 浑 浑 muddy ▮ water r 523 ▮ military 1431 hún

Military vehicles are big and heavy. After a rainstorm, this heaviness churns up a lot of earth, which mixes with rain *water* to create dismal, **muddy** conditions. [9 STROKES RANK 1991]

1434 挥 挥 brandish ▮ hand r 29 ▮ military 1431 huī

It's the heat of battle. With your *hand*, you seize a *military* flag, **brandish** it in the face of the enemy, and lead your troops to victory. [9 STROKES RANK 742]

1435 辈 辈 lifetime ▯ not 13 ▮ car 1430 bèi

BF I remember those horrible years BDL—before driving license. *Not* having a *car* at my disposal made every day seem a **lifetime**! [12 STROKES RANK 1477]

1436 辆 辆 m for vehicles ▮ car 1430 ▮ both, two 316 liàng

That squished *car* on the left is so small it only fits *two* people. It must be a sports car, a classic Corvette—the standard by which all such cars are **measured**. [11 STROKES RANK 1375]

1437 斩 斩 behead ▮ car 1430 ▮ catty 118 zhǎn

Talk about gruesome! One the *car's* wheels came off during highway driving. The car became *unbalanced*, and in a freak accident, the driver was **beheaded**. [8 STROKES RANK 2463]

1438 渐 渐 gradually ▮ water r 523 ▮ behead 1437 jiàn

The rat's body lay in the *water* with only the head exposed. Due to the action of bacteria in the water, the flesh was rapidly decomposing. **Gradually**, these natural causes resulted in the separation of the head from the body—a sort of natural *beheading*. [11 STROKES RANK 870]

1439 暂 暂 **temporarily**　　　　　　☐ behead 1437　■ day, sun 63　　zà

Our ancient forebears always created gods to represent natural phenomena. In those times, if '*day*' was thought of as a handsome god, then night would have seemed like a *beheading* of this god. Fortunately, this was only **temporary**—*day* always returned the next morning.　　　　　　[12 STROKES   RANK 1325]

1440 辑 辑 **compile, edit**　　　■ car 1430　☐ mouth 41　■ ear 82　　jí

BF The author travels in his *car* all over, conducting interviews to get material for his next blockbuster. For the sake of efficiency, he works on his material while driving, talking to himself (that's why the *mouth* is so close to the *ear*) to **edit** and **compile** this material while on the road.　　　[13 STROKES   RANK 1362]

1441 轻 轻 **light, agile**

　　　　　■ car 1430　☐ man 311 (altered)　■ labor, work 7　　qī

The small horizontal tick on top of '*man*' is an example of comic-book art—it represents swiftness and speed. Some *man* in his *car* is able to finish his *work* with seeming **agility** because the work was so **light**.　　　[9 STROKES   RANK 460]

1442 必 必 **must**　　　　　■ heart 907　■ action path 1421　　bì

A *heart's action* is something that **must** happen—otherwise you die.

　　　　　　　　　　　　　　　　　　[5 STROKES   RANK 248]

1443 秘 秘 **secret**　　　　■ rice or grain 409　■ must 1442　　m

BF Something that *must* be done is a requirement. The government requisitions large amounts of *grain*, but keeps the amount **secret**, so the enemy won't know the scale of preparation.　　　　　　[10 STROKES   RANK 896]

1444 瑟 瑟 **rustling sound**　　　■ king (times 2) 11　■ must 1442　　sè

It's a solemn moment as a *pair of kings* from neighboring states gather to sign a treaty. It *must* be signed! No one dares make noise to interrupt the proceedings—only the **rustling sounds** of the rulers' robes can be heard.　　　　　　[13 STROKES   RANK 1694]

1445 乍 乍 **suddenly**   ⬛ action path 1421 ⬛ a ladder   zhà
Here's a brief example of an unexpected and **sudden** change of motion. Here you are, climbing a *ladder* when you **suddenly** slip and fall down. The *action path* shows the trajectory of your descent.   [5 STROKES   RANK 2914]

1446 作 作 **to do, make**   ⬛ man r 953 ⬛ suddenly 1445   zuò
A *man* climbing up and down a *ladder* is bringing supplies up to the roof **to do** repairs.   [7 STROKES   RANK 49]

1447 昨 昨 **yesterday**   ⬛ day, sun 63 ⬛ suddenly 1445   zúo
BF You're having such a good time with old college friends you haven't seen in twenty years that you hardly notice the passage of time. The *sun* has long since gone down, and this great day is *suddenly* just another **yesterday**.   [9 STROKES   RANK 1475]

1448 炸 炸 **explode, burst**   ⬛ fire 1101 ⬛ suddenly 1445   zhà
What is especially dangerous when you are playing with *fire*? Something can *suddenly* happen, like an **explosion** that you never expect.   [9 STROKES   RANK 976]

1449 怎 怎 **how, why**   ⬛ suddenly 1445 ⬛ heart (fat) 906   zěn
BF The '*suddenly*' part looks like a *ladder*. Imagine a perky *heart* attempting to fix the roof. Suddenly, the *ladder* breaks and falls on the *heart*, quashing it flat. The broken ladder looks like a 'Y' (sounds like **why**).   [9 STROKES   RANK 382]

1450 弟 弟 **younger brother**
⬛ sheep 1147 ⬛ bow (weapon) 859 ⬛ action path 1421   dì
BF In ancient hunter societies, **younger brothers** had to prove themselves by accomplishing a successful *action*, such as using their *bow* to capture someone else's *sheep*.   [7 STROKES   RANK 816]

1451 第 第 ordinal prefix

⬚ bamboo r 243   ⬛ younger brother 1450 (altered)   d‹

In hierarchical societies, it's important to list *younger brothers* in **order**. In those days, people died often and unexpectedly, so an orderly bequeathing of family assets was crucial. If you've ever stared at a length of *bamboo* for any amount of time, you'll appreciate the connection. These stalks are divided quite clearly into **order**ly and regular sections.   [11 STROKES   RANK 114]

1452 不 不 no!   ⬛ under 176   ⬛ action path 1421   b‹

Here's one way to make sure an *action* will **not** go to completion—make sure it stays *under*ground, or otherwise *under* the radar.

It also looks like an upside-down wineglass, complete with upside-down stirrer. This is definitely **not** the way to get drunk!   [4 STROKES   RANK 4]

1453 杯 杯 cup   ⬛ tree 375   ⬛ no! 1452   b‹

BF The crafts person has used *wood* to create this upside-down **cup**. **Cups** made from *wood* should *not* be made this way!   [8 STROKES   RANK 1396]

1454 坏 坏 spoiled, bad   ⬛ earth, soil 9   ⬛ no! 1452   h‹

In ancient days, people thought that vapors emanating from the *earth* had a **bad** and harmful effect, rendering everything that was too close to the soil *not* good.   [7 STROKES   RANK 832]

Unit 60
Slow Down and Smell the Flowers

1455 环 环 **encircle**　　　　　　　█ king 11　█ no! 1452　huán

The *king* takes his cup, which we *know* (sounds like '*no*') got overturned on the table, and supports it by **encircling** it with his hands.

　　It's easy to mistake the two characters in §§1454, 1455 for each other—坏 versus 环. If you've ever bought food and stored it for later use, you know that you have to keep it off the ground, for ground contact promotes spoilage. In olden times, the circle was considered to be the most perfect of geometric forms, so much so that it sometimes received holy or royal status, so it's easy therefore to associate '*king*' with '**encircling**'.　　　　[8 STROKES　RANK 681]

1456 否 否 **negate**　　　　　　　█ no! 1452　█ mouth 41　fǒu

When you use your *mouth* to say *no*, you are **negating** an opinion.

[7 STROKES　RANK 620]

1457 怀 怀 **state of mind**　　　█ heart (skinny) 930　█ no! 1452　huái

'*Heart*' is a visual synonym for 'emotion', and here it's next to an *overturned cup*. The cup restrains *emotion* and sets the stage for a sober **state of mind**.

[7 STROKES　RANK 762]

1458 在 在 **located at**

　　　　　█ one 2　█ scepter 5　█ earth, soil 9　█ action path 1421　zài

The '*one*' and '*scepter*' mark out a **location** in the *earth* which you get to by following the *path of action*.　　　　[6 STROKES　RANK 6]

1459 存 存 store, preserve

▭ one 2 ⬚ scepter 5 ▪ son, child 1402 ▪ action path 1421   cú

Observe the *action path* of a car, starting from a fixed structure and terminated by *one scepter*-like obstacle, resulting in the death of the young driver. The three strokes seem to cradle and **preserve** the image of the *child*, much as the bereaved parents will **store** the precious memories of their *son*.

[6 STROKES   RANK 384]

1460 者 者 -er   ▭ earth, soil 9 ▪ day, sun 63 ▬ action path 1421   zh

(This cryptic definition refers to certain verbs which comes directly in front of it. '-er' is the same thing as 'one who...'.) You need to apply *action* to bring something from under the *earth*—a metaphor for unformed and chaotic—to the light of *day*—a metaphor for a fully finished activity. This is the job of **someone who performs an activity**, a perform-**er**.   [8 STROKES   RANK 103]

1461 都 都 all   ▯ -er 1460 ▯ town 745   dō

All kinds of people *able to do* **all** kinds of things can always be found in large *towns* and cities.   [10 STROKES   RANK 68]

1462 著 著 write, compose   ▯ grass r 94 ▪ -er 1460   zh

Paper was one of the great discoveries of ancient China, developed long before its production began in the West. Made from *grass* and other vegetable matter, the components in 著 refer to an *active process* which uses this vegetable matter invention, namely **writing** on paper.   [11 STROKES   RANK 777]

1463 署 署 government office   ▯ net r 107 ▪ -er 1460   sh

Despite his most conscientious efforts, the civil servant in his **government office** finds all his *actions* trap him in an entangling *net* of bureaucratic red tape.   [13 STROKES   RANK 1379]

1464 赌 赌 bet, gamble   ▮ cowrie 430 ▯ -er 1460   dǔ

Some scribe once thought that *wealth* fosters one major *activity*—**gambling**. Is this evidence of ancient Chinese cynicism?   [12 STROKES   RANK 2037]

1465 孝 孝 **filial**   ▬ earth, soil 9   ▬ action path 1421   ▬ son, child 1402   xiào

BF Filial responsibility is the duty of a *child* who helps ensure that order and security is transformed out of *earthly* chaos by means of uplifting *actions*.

[7 STROKES   RANK 2116]

1466 看 看 **look at, see**   ▬ three 4   ▪ eye 78   ▮ action path 1421   kàn

My *eyes* are very sensitive to sunlight. In this character, a hand shades my *eyes* so I'll better be able to **see** into the distance (stage right). The additional horizontals represent my hair flapping in the breeze, and the curve shows the *action path* of my arm.   [9 STROKES   RANK 76]

1467 才 才 **indicates sth just happened**

▬ hand 27 (altered)   ▬ action path 1421   cái

Top of the ninth, tie score—a fly ball is headed out of the park; we see the *path it takes*. It looks like another win for the Yankees. But wait—**something surprising just happened!** The rookie outfielder sticks his *hand* up, catches the fly, and the batter is out! It's anybody's ballgame as we head into overtime. Notice that the scribes use an abbreviated form of '*hand*', appropriate perhaps when we abbreviate the *action path* of the baseball.

Sometimes, the vividness of this character will suggest a person engaged in dancing, jumping, or some other active performance.

[3 STROKES   RANK 235]

1468 团 团 **round, circular**

▬ enclosure 40   ▬ indicates sth just happened 1467   tuán

Remember, the surrounding *enclosure* is really **round**—it just looks square because writing brushes don't do well with actual **circles**! To me, the 'action path' (§1421) of the 才 part makes this component so vivid that I see an active man inside the *enclosure* grappling with its **round** shape, maybe trying roll it down the street, like a young child in a tire.   [6 STROKES   RANK 405]

1469 闭 闩 shut*, close*   ■ door 196   ▣ indicates sth just happened 1467   bì

Ow-the *door just* **shut** on my toe! That's me in the middle, dancing in pain.
Keep the distinction between the two lookalikes 囝 and this one, 闭. The first means circle, which the outer enclosure clearly suggests. The '*door*' component occurring in this character is an old friend by now.

[6 STROKES   RANK 1267]

1470 财 财 wealth, riches

■ cowrie 430   ▢ indicates sth just happened 1467   cá

BF The heavy *shell just* fell on my head! I was in the hospital for weeks. The successful lawsuit made me **rich**.   [7 STROKES   RANK 680]

1471 材 材 timber   ▮ tree 375   ▢ indicates sth just happened 1467   cá

BF One minute, it's a noble, living *tree*. The next minute, it fell and *just* missed this guy who is dancing in fright. In the blink of an eye, a majestic *tree* has become just another piece of **timber**.   [7 STROKES   RANK 952]

1472 牙 牙 tooth*   ■ indicates sth just happened 1467 (altered)   ⬚ one 2   yá

The 'action path' (§1421) shows here the inner surface of *one* sharp canine **tooth** pointing up; the hooked vertical forms the outer surface of the tooth, and the hook is the root of the tooth anchored in the animal's jaw (not drawn). The point of the **tooth** has *just* penetrated the juicy slab of meat, the layer drawn at the top.   [4 STROKES   RANK 997]

1473 呀 呀 ah!, oh!   ▮ mouth 41   ▢ tooth* 1472   yá

That's your flesh that the canine *tooth* is embedded in. Out of your *mouth* comes expletives like **oh** and **ah**, among others less printable.

[7 STROKES   RANK 929]

1474 雅 雅 elegant   ▮ tooth* 1472   ▮ short-tailed bird 992   yǎ

Imagine strutting your stuff with an **elegant** necklace made from the *teeth* of *birds*.   [12 STROKES   RANK 1139]

1475 少 少 **few, little** ◻ small 1063 ◼ action path 1421 **shǎo**
The character 小 (§1063) refers to relative size, whereas this current character 少 refers to relative numbers of things. It's easy to keep straight—we use tools to perform an *activity*, and tools are counted rather than measured.

[4 STROKES   RANK 233]

1476 吵 吵 **quarrel, make noise** ◻ mouth 41 ◼ few, little 1475 **chǎo**
We **quarrel** using our *mouth*, and if we're any good at it, we end up with *few* close friends.

[7 STROKES   RANK 2040]

1477 妙 妙 **wonderful** ◼ woman 581 ◼ few, little 1475 **miào**
In contrast to ancient thinking, *women* have *few* natural disadvantages. This makes them **wonderful!**

[7 STROKES   RANK 1250]

1478 省 省 **economize, be frugal** ◻ few, little 1475 ◼ eye 78 **shěng**
Spending only a *few* dollars is to **be frugal**. Turn **economize** into a verb by adding a couple of *eyes*, sounds like '-ize', a verb suffix, and we've got it!

[9 STROKES   RANK 666]

1479 沙 沙 **sand** ◼ water r 523 ◻ few, little 1475 **shā**
Look in the *water*. See those *little*, granular particles? That's **sand**.

[7 STROKES   RANK 848]

1480 莎 莎 **katydid** ◻ grass r 94 ◼ sand 1479 **shā**
BF People who study insects consider **katydids** another name for "long-horned grasshopper," and the *grass* radical up top looks a little horn-like. Common species in North America are quite small, almost like grains of living *sand* in a sea of *grass*.

[10 STROKES   RANK 2125]

Unit 61

Buy Now, Pay Later

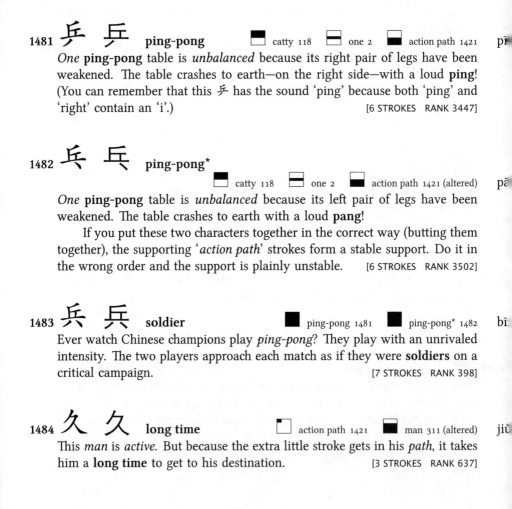

1481 乒 乒 **ping-pong**　⬜ catty 118　🔲 one 2　⬛ action path 1421　　pī

One **ping-pong** table is *unbalanced* because its right pair of legs have been weakened. The table crashes to earth—on the right side—with a loud **ping**! (You can remember that this 乒 has the sound 'ping' because both 'ping' and 'right' contain an 'i'.)　　　　　　　　　　　　　　[6 STROKES　RANK 3447]

1482 乓 乓 **ping-pong***

　　　　　⬜ catty 118　🔲 one 2　⬛ action path 1421 (altered)　　pā

One **ping-pong** table is *unbalanced* because its left pair of legs have been weakened. The table crashes to earth with a loud **pang**!

If you put these two characters together in the correct way (butting them together), the supporting '*action path*' strokes form a stable support. Do it in the wrong order and the support is plainly unstable.　　[6 STROKES　RANK 3502]

1483 兵 兵 **soldier**　⬛ ping-pong 1481　⬛ ping-pong* 1482　bī

Ever watch Chinese champions play *ping-pong*? They play with an unrivaled intensity. The two players approach each match as if they were **soldiers** on a critical campaign.　　　　　　　　　　　　　　[7 STROKES　RANK 398]

1484 久 久 **long time**　⬜ action path 1421　⬛ man 311 (altered)　jiǔ

This *man* is *active*. But because the extra little stroke gets in his *path*, it takes him a **long time** to get to his destination.　　　　[3 STROKES　RANK 637]

1485 片　片　slice, flake

■ action path 1421　⬛ weight atop slices　⬛ place of refuge 111 (altered)　　piàn

This character shows a Renaissance courtier in profile. Ramrod posture, one leg slightly behind him, while the other is bent at the knee. He holds a tray of **flaky** pastries, with a *weight on top* of the **slices** to keep them all from sliding off as he offers them to the visiting princess.　　[4 STROKES　RANK 455]

1486 卑　卑　low, inferior　　⬛ white 201　⬛ action path 1421　⬛ ten 6　　bēi

BF A brief *action* sequence: you're using a *white*-tipped hammer to pound a spike (in the shape of the Chinese numeral *ten*) till it's **low** in the ground.

[8 STROKES　RANK 2059]

1487 牌　牌　plate, tablet　　⬛ slice, flake 1485　⬛ low, inferior 1486　　pái

BF A *slice* of metal placed close to the surface would look *low* if the surface were horizontal. It is a **tablet** inscribed with important information.

[12 STROKES　RANK 1261]

1488 將　将　handle a matter

⬛ slice, flake 1485 (altered)　⬛ evening, dusk 655　⬛ inch 210　　jiāng

My spouse has never figured out how to barbecue meat, and it always comes out almost like charcoal! I **handle the matter** tactfully by *slicing* the meat, which is dark as *night*, into small, *inch*-like pieces which I force myself to swallow.　　[9 STROKES　RANK 132]

1489 刀　刀　knife　　⬛ place of refuge 111　⬛ action path 1421　　dāo

The *place of refuge* is disturbed by the *action* of the intruder. The brave hero used his **knife** to save us all.

　　This component expands the slim **knife** of §166, but it's still the same **knife**.　　[2 STROKES　RANK 1067]

1490 分　分　divide, separate　　⬛ eight 1048　⬛ knife 1489　　fēn

The '*eight*' at the top used to be a whole man (§311) until someone sliced him open with a *knife*. Now he's **divided** it into **separate** pieces.

[4 STROKES　RANK 79]

1491 方　方　square, direction

　　　　　　　　⬚ cover 268　■ action path 1421　⬚ place of refuge 111　fā

1 This stylized plow emphasizes the importance of this tool to the ancient economy. The furrows precisely change **direction** and the resulting pattern of a **square** field impressed ancient scribes.

2 See how the *action* extends at the end and over the *place of refuge*? The *cover* provides a restraint to make sure that the **direction** of our motion stays within a particular **square**.　　　　　　　　[4 STROKES   RANK 60]

1492 力　力　strength　　　　　　　■ knife 1489 (altered)　lì

The handle of the *knife* has been altered to emphasize the **strength** you need to force the blade deep into the bowels of… Well, you fill in the rest.

Take care not confuse this character with 刀 in §1489.

　　　　　　　　　　　　　　　　[2 STROKES   RANK 106]

1493 为　为　do, accomplish　　　■ strength 1492　⬚ cut marks　wè

With the *strength* of his arms, the thug had made the *cutting marks* with his knife, and realized that he had **accomplished** the killing deed.

　　　　　　　　　　　　　　　　[4 STROKES   RANK 18]

1494 动　动　move　　　■ cloud 751　■ strength 1492　dò

The essence of **movement**, particularly in the Chinese systems of exercise, is to appear light as a *cloud* yet perform with controlled *strength*.

　　　　　　　　　　　　　　　　[6 STROKES   RANK 73]

1495 川　川　river　　　■ action path 1421　⬚ scepter (times 2) 5　ch

BF The flowing water runs between the two banks of the river. Here, the left bank has a curved path not present on the right.　　[3 STROKES   RANK 1109]

1496 顺　顺　in the direction of　　■ river 1495　■ page, leaf 444　sh

Envision a *river* full of *leaves*. All the leaves flow **in the direction of** the current—a dramatic sight.　　　　　　　　[9 STROKES   RANK 938]

1497 荒 荒 **desolate** ▢ grass r 94 ▬ perish 269 ▬ river 1495 (altered)   huāng
Read the components from the bottom up: The action of the flooded *river*
causes the our house to *perish*. There's slimy *grass* and gook all over. The
desolation is total.   [9 STROKES   RANK 1328]

1498 慌 慌 **panic, nervous** ▌ heart (skinny) 930 ▌ desolate 1497   huāng
My *heart* palpitates madly in the presence of great *desolation*. I have become
nervous to the point of **panic**, for what will become of us?
                                                           [12 STROKES   RANK 1650]

1499 州 州 **state, province** ▬ river 1495 ▬ eight 1048 ▢ dab 169   zhōu
We'll use the '*river*' as a metaphor for natural resources. This character
shows an area so large that parts possess *abundant* resources, while other
parts possess *very little*. A region so vast forms a separate **state**.
                                                            [6 STROKES   RANK 721]

1500 洲 洲 **continent** ▌ water r 523 ▌ state, province 1499   zhōu
Water surrounds a group of *states*—this defines a **continent**.
                                                            [9 STROKES   RANK 701]

1501 步 步 **step**
▬ stop! 181 ▬ few, little 1475 (altered) ▬ action path 1421   bù
A **step** starts with a *stop* (so to speak), followed by a *small* amount of *action*
on your part.   [7 STROKES   RANK 349]

1502 涉 涉 **wade, ford** ▌ water r 523 ▌ step 1501   shè
BF The verb '**wade**' refers to *steps* you take in the *water*.
                                                           [10 STROKES   RANK 1239]

1503 亦 亦 also, too

◻ cover 268   ▓ small 1063 (altered)   ▯ action path 1421   yì

1 A *little* kid is running down the *path* after the big kids, arms swinging from his sides. "Hey, wait for me! I want to come, **too!**"

2 As kids, some of us loved collecting lightning bugs and trapping them live in a *covered* but *small* bottle. A few of them could co-exist peacefully, but if there were **too** many, some of them made a bee-line to the *cover* as an *action* to escape. The 'too' we highlight in this narrative is, to be sure, the wrong meaning, but it is the right word.   [6 STROKES   RANK 886]

1504 赤 赤 red, be flushed

▬ earth, soil 9   ▬ small 1063 (altered)   ▯ action path 1421   ch

This is silly, but here I am dressed up in a bizarre party costume, and this is my hat. A pile of *earth* from which a bunch of roots dangle rests on the hat brim. No wonder my face is all **flushed** in embarrassment!.   [7 STROKES   RANK 1660]

1505 赫 赫 awe-inspiring

▓ red, be flushed (times 2) 1504   hè

Two people with the same party hat at the same party? **Awesome**, dude.

[14 STROKES   RANK 1346]

1506 老 老 old   ▬ earth, soil 9   ▬ action path 1421   ▬ hair 231 (altered)   lǎ

On our life *path* back into the grave's *earth*, one prominent change is in our *hair*, which whitens as we get **old**.   [6 STROKES   RANK 179]

Unit 62

In the Blink of an Eye

1507 轮 轮 **wheel, wheel-like** 　■ car 1430　■ order, coherence 457　lún
BF It's the **wheels** that bring *order* to a *car*.　　　　[8 STROKES　RANK 1096]

1508 匆 匆 **hasty** 　■ spoon 642　■ action path (times 2) 1421　cōng
BF I've got to take this *spoonful* of medicine. I move too **hastily** and the medicine streams off the spoon's edge, in two *action paths*.

It's very tempting to see this character as 勿 'do not' (§1424) with some sort of dab-like stroke. If this composition is more to your liking, then fine.
　　　　　　　　　　　　　　　　　　　　　　　　[5 STROKES　RANK 1622]

1509 俞 俞 **consent** 　□ join; combine 325　■ boat, ship 597 (altered)　■ river 1495 (altered)　yú
BF Well, I *combined* the materials to construct a small *boat* to travel the *river*. It wasn't the best ever built, but my Master **consented** to give me credit for it.　　　　　　　　　　　　　　　　　　　　[9 STROKES　RANK 3251]

1510 愉 愉 **happy, joyful** 　■ heart (skinny) 930　■ consent 1509　yú
BF I am **happy** over my Master's *consent* and the accompanying *emotions* of **joyfulness**.　　　　　　　　　　　　　　　[12 STROKES　RANK 1982]

1511 吻 吻 **kiss** 　■ mouth 41　■ do not 1424　wěn
A **kiss** is often an unwanted overture. In such cases, *do not* bring your lips near your beloved's *mouth*.　　　　　　　　[7 STROKES　RANK 1973]

1512 扮 扮 dress up as, disguise as

▮ hand r 29   ▮ divide, separate 1490   bà

The best **disguises** are those created out of everyday materials. In preparation, we watch a *hand separate* articles of clothing in preparation for the ultimate outfit.   [7 STROKES   RANK 1974]

1513 乃 乃 so, therefore   ▮ action path 1421   ▮ bow (weapon) 859 (altered)   nǎ

Words like '**so**' and '**therefore**' refer to results. If I use my *bow* to take *action*, results will follow.

When it appears as a component, we may let it represent '**results**'.   [2 STROKES   RANK 1165]

1514 隽 隽 handsome, talented

▬ short-tailed bird 992   ▬ so, therefore 1513   ju

BF I need to impress this really **handsome** guy I am dating, *so therefore* I bought him a pet *bird*.   [10 STROKES   RANK 4236]

1515 携 携 carry, take along

▮ hand r 29   ▮ handsome, talented 1514 (altered)   xi

I **take along** by *hand* the *handsome* little boy. Too bad his behavior doesn't match his appearance.   [13 STROKES   RANK 1964]

1516 套 套 sheath, cover   ▬ big 330   ▮ long, length 1423 (altered)   tà

BF As my grandmother used to say, every pot has a **cover**. That is, the **cover** matches the container exactly in terms of *size* and *length*, among other attributes. The alterations to the '*long, length*' component look very similar to the traditional form.   [10 STROKES   RANK 1091]

1517 象 象 elephant

▢ man r 953 (altered)   ▢ eye 78 (altered)   ▬ pig, boar 1425   xi

What an animal! Vaguely *pig*-like in form, with huge *eyes* at a funny angle that fix you with almost human expressiveness, and so big that a *man* can ride on top—now that's an **elephant**.   [11 STROKES   RANK 300]

1518 豫 豫 **pleased, content** ▯ give* 763 ▯ elephant 1517 yù

BF That's me—the guy on the back of the *elephant*, and the *elephant* is *giving* me the ride of my life. I am **pleased** and **content** at the novelty of it all.

[15 STROKES RANK 1956]

1519 像 像 **resemble** ▯ man r 953 ▯ elephant 1517 xiàng

Some readers may be old enough to remember *elephant* jokes. Why does a *man* **resemble** an *elephant*? They both walk on two legs—except for the *elephant*. (This would have gotten big belly laughs in 1963.)

[13 STROKES RANK 294]

1520 旁 旁 **side** ▭ erect, stand 1179 (altered) ▬ square, direction 1491 páng

BF To my eyes, the '*square*' on the bottom looks like a football lineman plowing into an opponent *standing* firm against him. Something's got to give, though, and one of them will get shunted to the **side**. [10 STROKES RANK 981]

1521 膀 膀 **upper arm, shoulder** ▯ meat 317 (altered) ▯ side 1520 bǎng

BF In a human, the *side* of the *carcass* comprises the **upper arm** or **shoulder**.

[14 STROKES RANK 1941]

1522 卯 卯 **early morning** ▬ head held high 160 ▯ action path 1421 mǎo

(This is the fourth of the so-called Earthly Branches, and refers to the time period 5–7AM.)

At this time of the day, **so early in the morning**, it's only the pillow that *holds my head high*, and it's a struggle to perform any meaningful *action*.

[5 STROKES RANK 3926]

1523 留 留 **retain, stay** ▭ early morning 1522 (altered) ▬ field 57 liú

To **retain** ownership of your *fields*, you have to start work every day very *early in the morning*.

[10 STROKES RANK 554]

1524 溜 溜 slide, glide, sneak off   ▯ water r 523   ▮ retain, stay 1523   liū

No crops grow in the winter. Starting in January, I allow my fields to *retain* *water* which soon freezes so friends can **skate** and **glide** across the surface.

[13 STROKES   RANK 1923]

1525 贸 贸 commerce, trade

▯ early morning 1522 (altered)   ▬ cowrie 430   m

BF "The *early* bird catches the worm." **Trade** with *money* starts *very early* in the day.   [9 STROKES   RANK 1092]

1526 肠 肠 intestines   ▮ meat 317 (altered)   ▯ easy 1427 (altered)   ch

During dissections in biology lab, all the organs looked the same to me, except for the **intestines**. They were by far the *easiest* part of the *body* to identify, by virtue of their ropiness.   [7 STROKES   RANK 1921]

1527 汤 汤 soup   ▮ water r 523   ▮ easy 1427 (altered)   tā

Soup is *easy* to make. Hot *water* is the main ingredient, and then add whatever else is at hand.   [6 STROKES   RANK 1618]

1528 扬 扬 raise, wave   ▮ hand r 29   ▮ easy 1427 (altered)   yá

BF **Waving** is an *easy* activity for a *hand*. That's why it's one of the first things babies do.   [6 STROKES   RANK 1084]

1529 杨 杨 poplar   ▮ tree 375   ▮ easy 1427 (altered)   yá

BF **Poplars** are particularly *easy trees* to cultivate and grow. Because it's *easy* to grow and looks so good in the garden, the **poplar** has become quite **popular**!   [7 STROKES   RANK 1062]

1530 扔 扔 throw, toss   ▮ hand r 29   ▮ so, therefore 1513   rē

One of the easiest ways to get *results* is to use your *hand* to **throw** something at your professor!   [5 STROKES   RANK 1905]

1531 库　库　**warehouse, storehouse**　☐ shelter r 681　☐ car 1430　kù
Nowadays, **warehouse** stores are so vast and cavernous that employees use special *cars* to drive around the expansive *structure*.　[7 STROKES　RANK 1097]

1532 加　加　**add, increase**　☐ strength 1492　☐ mouth 41　jiā
Ever been to a kid's birthday party? The *stronger voices* are, they more they **add** to the festivity of the occasion.　[5 STROKES　RANK 166]

Unit 63

One World, One Dream

1533 劣 劣　inferior, low quality　　▮ few, little 1475　　■ strength 1492　　liè
A product possessing *few strengths* is certainly of **low quality**.
[6 STROKES　RANK 1902]

1534 芬 芬　sweet smell, fragrance　　▮ grass r 94　　■ divide, separate 1490　　fē
BF Why do freshly-mowed lawns smell so **fragrant**? It has to do with the
action of the lawnmower blades, which thresh and *separate* the stalks of *grass*
and so release one of the great smells of summer.　　[7 STROKES　RANK 1890]

1535 纷 纷　numerous, confused　　▮ silk r 807　　▮ divide, separate 1490　　fē
BF I forgot to hem the *silk* handkerchief I was making as a gift. When my
rotten little brother came along and cut it with a scissors, it *separated* into
its **numerous** component threads.　　[7 STROKES　RANK 1181]

1536 妨 妨　hinder, impede　　▮ woman 581　　▮ square, direction 1491　　fá
BF The beggar *women* constantly surround rich gentlemen on their *way* home
and **hinder** their progress.　　[7 STROKES　RANK 1873]

1537 架 架　put up, prop up　　▮ add, increase 1532　　■ tree 375 (altered)　　jiǎ
If you make a contraption by *adding* pieces of *wood* together, you'll be able
to **prop up** something heavy.　　[9 STROKES　RANK 846]

1538 嘉 嘉 excellent, praise

☐ ten 6   ▬ bean 1168   ☐ add, increase 1532   jiā

BF In ancient schools, beans were a reward for good work. The more beans you got, the better your grade. If the teacher *added ten beans* to your grade, you knew your performance was truly **excellent**.   [14 STROKES   RANK 1845]

1539 宾 宾 guest, visitor

☐ roof 247   ▬ soldier 1483   bīn

BF In the old days, the most notorious of **guests** were *soldiers* which the government forced you to shelter under your *roof*.   [10 STROKES   RANK 1534]

1540 劫 劫 rob, plunder

▮ go 754   ▮ strength 1492   jié

BF When soldiers *go out* of their camps intending to use their *strength*, it can only be for one purpose—to **rob** and **plunder**.   [7 STROKES   RANK 1825]

1541 驾 驾 harness, draw a cart

☐ add, increase 1532   ▬ horse 878   jià

All you have to do is *add* some special equipment to the *horse*, like a **harness**, and you can use the animal to **draw a cart**.   [8 STROKES   RANK 1567]

1542 贺 贺 congratulate

▬ add, increase 1532   ▬ cowrie 430   hè

BF When are **congratulations** called for? From a Chinese point of view, sudden *increase* in *wealth* is one such occasion.   [9 STROKES   RANK 1690]

1543 张 张 stretch, expand

▮ bow (weapon) 859   ▮ long, length 1423   zhāng

BF How does a *bow* manage to change its *length*? It **stretches** and **expands** under the care of a skillful archer.   [7 STROKES   RANK 318]

1544 涨 涨 rise (water, prices)

▮ water r 523   ▮ stretch, expand 1543   zhǎng

Figuratively, the *waters* of the river '*expand*' when the water level **rises**.   [10 STROKES   RANK 1803]

1545 契 契 contract, legal agreement

◨ plentiful 12   ◳ knife 1489   ■ big 330   qì

BF A **contract** in our modern world is a document stipulating conditions for the *mutual benefit* of the two sides to an agreement. What form would **contracts** have taken in pre-literate societies? Perhaps a *knife* would mark the conditions on some permanent surface, and people would agree to make this the permanent record for important (*'big'*) **legal agreements.**

[9 STROKES   RANK 1819]

1546 场 场 gathering place, field   ■ earth, soil 9   ◳ easy 1427 (altered)   ch

It's *easy* to set up open-air fairs and markets on wide-open expanses of *earth*. Such **fields** became **gathering places** which gave rise to markets.

[6 STROKES   RANK 249]

1547 另 另 other, another   ◻ mouth 41   ■ strength 1492   lì

Poor people often curse the existence of destitute relatives. "**Another** *mouth* to feed! I'll need all my *strength* to earn more money." [5 STROKES   RANK 489]

1548 别 別 do not, must not   ■ other, another 1547   ◳ knife r 166   bi

There are two kitchen *knives* on the counter. One is dull, the *other* is deadly sharp. Whatever you do, **do not** play around with the sharp one.

[7 STROKES   RANK 222]

1549 切 切 cut, slice   ■ seven 137   ◳ knife 1489   qì

That expensive set of *seven knives* makes precision **slicing** and **cutting** a breeze.   [4 STROKES   RANK 337]

1550 办 办 do, manage, set up   ▮ strength 1492   ◻ eight 1048   bà

The '*eight*' that should have been at the top represents something that's indivisible, and the task at hand is to split it in two. With the application of great *strength*, we can **do** this.   [4 STROKES   RANK 367]

1551 功　功　**merit, achievement**　　■ labor, work 7　■ strength 1492　　gōng

By virtue of my *hard work* and my *strength* of will, I received the highest award for **meritorious achievement**.　　[5 STROKES　RANK 452]

1552 召　召　**call, convene**　　■ knife 1489　■ mouth 41　　zhào

Every family is different in their own way. A had a friend once whose mother tapped a *knife* against the teeth in her *mouth* when she wanted to **call** the whole family together.　　[5 STROKES　RANK 1214]

1553 招　招　**beckon, enlist**　　■ hand r 29　■ call, convene 1552　　zhāo

Figuratively speaking, the recruiter waves his *hand* towards you to **enlist** you to join the *call* to serve your country.　　[8 STROKES　RANK 941]

1554 昭　昭　**clear, obvious**　　■ day, sun 63　■ call, convene 1552　　zhāo

BF They *convened* the meeting early in the *day*, because in the bright light it would be **clear** who the troublemakers were.　　[9 STROKES　RANK 2190]

1555 照　照　**shine, illuminate**　　■ clear, obvious 1554　■ fire r 796　　zhào

The *fire* reflected in the *obviously* valuable antiques in the room **shone** fiercely and emphasized the richness of the furnishings.　　[13 STROKES　RANK 443]

1556 绍　绍　**connect, introduce**　　■ silk r 807　■ call, convene 1552　　shào

BF *Silk* threads are like cords **connecting** the parties who have been *called* together for a group wedding in some exotic religious cult. Think of it, until now these potential mates have never even been **introduced**.

[8 STROKES　RANK 1234]

1557 超　超　**overtake, surpass, super-**

■ to walk 421　■ call, convene 1552　　chāo

BF Yeesh—I just found out about the **super**-important meeting that's been *called*. I have to *walk* fast so I can **overtake** everyone else and get the seat closest to my boss.　　[12 STROKES　RANK 754]

1558 陈　陈　**put on display**　　　　　　　■ hills 735　■ east 1429　ch

BF The sun rises in the *east*, vividly lighting up the special landscaping on the *hills* that we've **put on display**.　　　　　　[7 STROKES　RANK 525]

Unit 64

Life is Like a Dream

1559 历 历 **experience** ☐ cliff r 671 ☐ strength 1492 lì

BF The terrorists almost succeeded in throwing me off the *cliff*. I held on by my fingertips, and used all my *strength* to pull myself up to safety. What an **experience!** [4 STROKES RANK 480]

1560 房 房 **house** ☐ door of house 724 ☐ square, direction 1491 fáng

BF I went into my **house** through the front *door* to see a giant *square* box aligned in the *direction* pointing to the moon. [8 STROKES RANK 512]

1561 防 防 **guard, defend against** ☐ hills 735 ☐ square, direction 1491 fáng

BF Giant *square hills* are the best **defense against** hordes of marauding enemies. Because of their *square*ness, there are no gaps when lined up next to each other. [6 STROKES RANK 548]

1562 密 密 **thick, dense, intimate**

☐ roof 247 ☐ must 1442 ☐ mountain 21 mì

The forest cover on the *mountain*side is so lush that it forms a *roof*-like cover overhead and makes it well-nigh impassable. We *must* persevere through the **dense** and **thick** vegetation, for we need to reach the command camp by nightfall. [11 STROKES RANK 591]

1563 苏 苏 **revive, Suzhou** ☐ grass r 94 ☐ do, manage, set up 1550 sū

BF The old fool *managed* to run into a lamp post and knock himself out cold. A wandering healer threw some aromatic *grass* over him and managed to **revive** him. [7 STROKES RANK 590]

1564 助 助 help, assist, aid   ▮ moreover 15   ▮ strength 1492   zì

You can **help** yourself to whatever you want—even if it's not yours—as long as you have *more (over) strength* than anyone else.   [7 STROKES   RANK 607]

1565 男 男 male   ▬ field 57   ▬ strength 1492   ná

BF Only **men** have the *strength* to plow a *field*.   [7 STROKES   RANK 602]

1566 仍 仍 still, yet, again and again

▮ man r 953   ▮ so, therefore 1513   ré

At first, the task looks impossible. But a *man* tries it **again and again**, and *therefore he* achieves the proper *result*.   [4 STROKES   RANK 601]

1567 勉 勉 strive to, do with effort

▬ dismiss, fire, exempt 477   ▮ strength 1492   m

BF The new hire exerted great *strength* to counter the allegations which led to his *dismissal*. He did **strive** to retain his position.   [9 STROKES   RANK 2078]

1568 伤 伤 injure, wound

▮ man r 953   ▭ man 311 (altered)   ▬ strength 1492   sh

Two men doing something that involves great *strength*. It must be a fight, and one *man* is trying his best to **injure** the other *man*.   [6 STROKES   RANK 660]

1569 初 初 at first   ▮ clothing r 838   ▮ knife 1489   ch

BF **At first** you need to use your *knife* to cut the cloth and make *clothing*.   [7 STROKES   RANK 667]

1570 劳 劳 toil   ▬ grass r 94   ▬ cover 268   ▬ strength 1492   lá

BF One needs great *strength* to haul dried *grass* into the hut and to create a thatched *roof*. All in all, too much **toil** is required.   [7 STROKES   RANK 679]

1571 协 协   harmonize, cooperate, assist

▮ ten 6   ▮ do, manage, set up 1550   xié

BF Only with **cooperation** and inter-personal **harmony** can *ten* people *manage* to finish the job.   [6 STROKES   RANK 735]

1572 胁 胁   coerce, force   ▮ meat 317 (altered)   ▮ do, manage, set up 1550   xié

BF I use a rotting, stinking piece of *meat* as a club by which I *manage* to get my way, as I **force** you to do what I want you to do.   [8 STROKES   RANK 1494]

1573 阵 阵   battle array   ▮ hills 735   ▮ car 1430   zhèn

The insurgents have been training for months! Down from the *hills* roll their *chariots*, all in perfect **battle array**.   [6 STROKES   RANK 788]

1574 邪 邪   evil, odd   ▮ tooth* 1472   ▮ town 745   xié

BF From afar, *towns*, with their jagged profiles, can look like a mouth full of rotten *teeth*, and are frequent metaphors for **evil** and depravity.   [6 STROKES   RANK 1539]

1575 穿 穿   penetrate, pierce   ▢ cave, den, hole 1098   ▮ tooth* 1472   chuān

The *cavity* in my *tooth* was hurting me. The dentist said it was so big, it threatened to **pierce** the *tooth*, and then where would I be?   [9 STROKES   RANK 785]

1576 份 份   share, portion   ▮ man r 953   ▮ divide, separate 1490   fèn

Let's take that *man*'s money. We can *divide* it into equal amounts, so we each get a **share**. Let's do it fast, before the cops get here!   [6 STROKES   RANK 784]

1577 弯 弯   bent, curved, crooked   ▢ also, too 1503   ▮ bow (weapon) 859   wān

Imagine *two* (sounds like 'too') *bows* lying in a heap. What a tangled mess of **bent** wood!   [9 STROKES   RANK 1662]

1578 湾 湾 **gulf, bay**　　　⬛ water r 523　⬛ bent, curved, crooked 1577　w

BF A sharply *bent* section of coast enclosing a body of *water* defines a **bay**.

[12 STROKES   RANK 855]

1579 忽 忽 **suddenly***　　　⬛ do not 1424　⬛ heart (fat) 906　h

BF *Don't* scare me like that. My *heart* is beating wildly. It's your **sudden** (and unwanted!) kiss that did it to me.　　　[8 STROKES   RANK 912]

1580 输 输 **transport, convey**　　　⬛ car 1430　⬛ consent 1509　s

BF My parents *consented* for me to use the *car* to **transport** all my friends to the dance.　　　[13 STROKES   RANK 939]

1581 勒 勒 **bridle, rein in**　　　⬛ animal hide 101　⬛ strength 1492　lè

BF Trying to **rein in** my horse, I used too much *strength*—in fact, I killed him! Now he's just glue and *hide*.　　　[11 STROKES   RANK 966]

1582 载 载 **write down, year**

⬛ earth, soil 9　⬛ car 1430　⬛ halberd 359　z

Did you see that!? That crazy guy attacked the new *car* with a big *sword*, which was so sharp that the front end fell to the *ground*—and it was this **year**'s model, too. Then the attacker got back into his vehicle and drove off, but not before I **wrote down** his plate number.　　　[10 STROKES   RANK 977]

1583 练 练 **practice, train, drill**　　　⬛ silk r 807　⬛ east 1429 (altered)　li

I **practice** my Chinese martial arts every morning. Wearing *silk* pajamas, I face *east* for this daily regimen.　　　[8 STROKES   RANK 1005]

1584 炼 炼 **smelt, refine**　　　⬛ fire 1101　⬛ east 1429 (altered)　li

The blowing wind forces the *fire* to travel *east*. What a disaster! The *fire* is so hot it **smelts** the metal in all the houses it destroys.　　　[9 STROKES   RANK 1763]

Unit 65

Stopping and Starting

1585 诸　诸　**all, various**　☐ speech r 615　☐ -er 1460　zhū

The big thing about *speech* is that you can *use it* to express **all** kinds of meanings.　[10 STROKES　RANK 1021]

1586 猪　猪　**hog, pig**　☐ dog r 898　☐ -er 1460　zhū

Believe it or not, a **pig** shares many positive *abilities* with a *dog*. It's loyal, smart, trainable, long-lived—and you can eat it, too.　[11 STROKES　RANK 1762]

1587 绪　绪　**matter's beginning**　☐ silk r 807　☐ -er 1460　xù

BF Imagine that the **beginning of important matters** was commemorated by a small but precious token, such as a piece of worked *silk*. Such a gift was entrusted only to a person *capable of carrying out the duty*.

[11 STROKES　RANK 1413]

1588 训　训　**lecture, train, teach**　☐ speech r 615　☐ river 1495　xùn

A qualified **lecturer** or **teacher** is one whose *speech* flows like a *river*.

[5 STROKES　RANK 1022]

1589 访　访　**visit, call on, seek**　☐ speech r 615　☐ square, direction 1491　fǎng

BF I need to **visit** my cousin. I *speak* to the old gent in the *square* to see if I'm on the right track.　[6 STROKES　RANK 1037]

1590 蒙 蒙   **cheat, hoodwink**

☐ grass r 94   ☐ smooth cover 280 (altered)   ■ pig, boar 1425 (altered)   m

Feral *pigs* are smart and strong. We have to **hoodwink** them to catch them. Here's one that's already been trapped. It's in a deep pit, topped by a *reinforced cover*. A layer of *grass* fooled the animal into walking over it.   [13 STROKES   RANK 1039]

1591 鬼 鬼   **ghost, spirit**

■ white 201   ■ action path 1421   ■ mineshaft 135   ■ private 750   g

In European traditions, a **ghost** is this big *white* thing, with long smokey limbs capable of all kinds of *action*. Generally, you only "see" them when it's as dark as possible, like the darkness of a *mineshaft*. Of course, the most horrifying **ghosts** of all are one's *private* ghosts.   [9 STROKES   RANK 1042]

1592 软 软   **soft, pliant**   ■ car 1430   ■ owe, lack 465   ru

Softness and **pliability** had better be qualities that *cars lack*!   [8 STROKES   RANK 1043]

1593 秀 秀   **to flower, put forth ears of grain**

■ rice or grain 409   ■ so, therefore 1513   xi

BF Springtime: time to plant the *grain*. Autumn: the *result* is **ears of grain**, ripe for harvesting.   [7 STROKES   RANK 1136]

1594 诱 诱   **guide, lead, induce**

■ speech r 615   ■ to flower, put forth ears of grain 1593   yǒ

BF *Speaking* with *flowery* phrases **induces** the electorate to vote you into office.   [9 STROKES   RANK 1707]

1595 魔 魔   **devil, evil spirit, monster**

■ hemp, pocked, pitted 694 (altered)   ■ ghost, spirit 1591   m

BF The *ghost* wore a *linen* cape to frighten people. Why does it have to be linen? It's so hard to clean and iron! I'll have to work double-hard to keep it fresh and pressed. This *ghost* is truly an **evil spirit**.   [20 STROKES   RANK 1180]

1596 刃 刃 blade edge   ■ knife 1489 ▫ mark   rèn

BF The *mark* on the *knife* emphasizes its "business end"—the **blade edge**.

[3 STROKES   RANK 2700]

1597 忍 忍 bear, endure, forbear   ▭ blade edge 1596 ■ heart (fat) 906   rěn

That noisy couple down the hall is in a dreadful, toxic relationship. She loves
her man dearly, but he never spends his nights with her. It's like a *knife* in
her *heart* that she must **endure!**   [7 STROKES   RANK 1127]

1598 梁 梁 bridge, roof beam

▫ water r 523   ▭ blade edge 1596 (altered)   ■ tree 375   liáng

BF The way to cross *water* (in ancient times) was to use a knife's *blade edge*
or other such tool to work a *tree* into the architectural elements out of which
they could build a **bridge**.   [11 STROKES   RANK 1416]

1599 蒋 蒋 surname; Chiang Kai-Shek

▭ grass r 94   ■ handle a matter 1488   jiǎng

Chiang Kai-Shek (Cantonese pronunciation) was the head of the Republic of
China from 1928 through 1975. His name in Mandarin is Jiǎng Jièshí, which
accounts for the relatively high frequency of this word. 蒋 appears not to
have any other meaning.

Chiang Kai-Shek achieved prominence by virtue of his leadership and
capability in *handling matters*. The *grass* laurels he wears on top demonstrate
the honor accorded him by the Chinese people.   [12 STROKES   RANK 1172]

1600 彻 彻 thorough, penetrating

■ left step 1034   ▌▌ ancient ladle 142   ▫ knife 1489   chè

BF To get the maximum **penetrating** power of floor stain you need to *stomp*
on it, mash it with a *spoon*, and cut it with a *knife*.   [7 STROKES   RANK 1240]

1601 仿 仿 **imitate, copy, resemble**

▮ man r 953   ▯ square, direction 1491   fǎ

This character seems to show a *man* trying to **imitate** a dancer. Outstretched arms, bent legs, but something is not quite right. He looks like he's collapsing on the ground—not the proper *direction* at all.   [6 STROKES   RANK 1259]

1602 彖 彖 **determine, make a judgment**

▯ mutual 20 (altered)   ▮ pig, boar 1425   tu

BF Watch out for *pigs*! A *mutual* friend got in one's way at dinner time, and suffered severe lacerations and other alterations. He **determined** then and there—never trust a *pig* on its way to the dinner bowl.

[9 STROKES   RANK 6434]

1603 缘 缘 **reason*, cause***

▮ silk r 807   ▯ determine, make a judgment 1602   y

BF The **reason** that judges wear *silk robes* is this: it's more impressive when they *render judgment*.   [12 STROKES   RANK 1274]

1604 奶 奶 **breast*, milk***   ▮ woman 581   ▯ so, therefore 1513 (altered)   n

In olden times, it must have seemed that the inevitable *result* of a *mature woman* was childbirth and **breastfeeding**.   [5 STROKES   RANK 1278]

1605 偷 偷 **steal, pilfer**   ▯ man r 953   ▮ consent 1509   tō

A *man* who takes things without the owner's *consent* is guilty of **stealing**.

[11 STROKES   RANK 1284]

1606 愈 愈 **the more—the more**   ▮ consent 1509   ▯ heart (fat) 906   y

The **more** I *consent* to go out with her, **the more** I feel a growing *emotional* attachment. Where will it end?   [13 STROKES   RANK 1301]

1607 穷 穷 **impoverished, exhausted**

☐ cave, den, hole 1098   ■ strength 1492   qióng

The hike was so **exhausting** we used our last reserves of *strength* to crawl
into the *cave*.   [7 STROKES   RANK 1343]

1608 魂 魂 **soul, spirit, mood**   ▮ cloud 751   ▯ ghost, spirit 1591   hún

Chinese *ghosts* are more solid than ours. A particularly "*cloudy*" ghost serves
as a **spirit** or **soul**.   [13 STROKES   RANK 1348]

1609 劲 劲 **vigor, energy**

▮ man 311 (altered)   ▰ labor, work 7   ▯ strength 1492   jìn

The *man* does his *work* using great *strength*, showing great **vigor** and **energy**.
                                                    [7 STROKES   RANK 1358]

1610 贫 贫 **poor**   ☐ divide, separate 1490   ■ cowrie 430   pín

BF When *money* is *divided* among many people, nobody gets enough, and
nobody is happy. Everybody stays **poor**.   [8 STROKES   RANK 1359]

Unit 66

Big Doings

1611 荡 荡 **swing, shake, wash away** □ grass r 94 ▪ soup 1527 d

By error, they put loco*weed* in the *soup*. Anybody who ate it began to **shake** for a short bit. [9 STROKES RANK 1424]

1612 矛 矛 **lance, pike, spear** ▪ give* 763 ▪ action path 1421 n

Our umpteenth-great-grandfather was off on a hunt. "*Give* it to 'em good! We need plenty of *action* to bring home the bacon. May your **spear** fly true!" [5 STROKES RANK 1441]

1613 柔 柔 **soft, supple, gentle** ▫ lance, pike, spear 1612 ▪ tree 375 r

BF The woodsman uses his *spear* to pound the hardwood *tree* to make it **soft** enough to work with. [9 STROKES RANK 1573]

1614 励 励 **encourage, exhort** ▪ harsh, severe, serious 678 ▪ strength 1492 lì

BF "Everyone thinks the clods on the other team are *harsh* and *severe*. But you guys can do it. Combine your *strength* and you'll win." With these shouts of **encouragement**, we know we can win! [7 STROKES RANK 1468]

1615 券 券 **ticket, certificate** ▪ eight (v) 1047 ▪ man (spiffy) 337 ▪ knife 1489 q

The rock concert is all sold out. Some thug has approached a *man* with **tickets**; watch the *drops* of sweat fly off his face. The mugger uses a *knife* to rob the *man* of his **tickets**. [8 STROKES RANK 1481]

1616 粉　粉　powder　　　　■ rice 1127　□ divide, separate 1490　　fěn

Start with *rice*, and now keep *dividing* it into ever smaller particles. Soon enough, you'll end up with a handful of **powder**, suitable for makeup or cooking.　　　　　　　　　　　　　　　　　　　[10 STROKES　RANK 1498]

1617 豪　豪　super-talented person

□ high 275 (altered)　■ pig, boar 1425　　háo

BF A *pig* as part of a character for a talented fellow? Well, in Chinese tradition, *pigs* and *boars* are fat, prosperous, and happy. A person with *high* levels of *pig*ness is apt therefore to have **superior talents**. After all, they named a Chinese year after the *pig*!　　　　　　　　　　　[14 STROKES　RANK 1513]

1618 储　储　store up, save　■ man r 953　□ speech r 615　■ -er 1460　　chǔ

BF A *person* who **saves up** their lifetime experiences doesn't hesitate to draw upon them to make a point. Such a *person* makes a fine *speak-er*.

[12 STROKES　RANK 1526]

1619 勃　勃　flourishing, thriving

■ ancient 51 (altered)　■ son, child 1402　□ strength 1492　　bó

BF If the family environment is *strong*, *children* get a chance to grow *old* in **thriving** health.　　　　　　　　　　　　　　　　[9 STROKES　RANK 1533]

1620 频　频　frequently, repeatedly　　■ step 1501　□ page, leaf 444　　pín

Walking around—taking *step* after *step*—and reading, where you keep turning *page* after *page*, are examples of **repetitious** activities.

[13 STROKES　RANK 1535]

1621 伪　伪　false, fake, bogus　　　■ man r 953　□ do, accomplish 1493　　wěi

BF When *men* claim they've *done* something, but they haven't, those claims are **bogus**! The dotted diagonal line that's part of '*do, accomplish*' emphasizes the unreality, the **false**ness of the deed.　　　　　[6 STROKES　RANK 1556]

1622 勤 勤 diligent, hardworking

☐ hide 542   ☐ earth, soil 9   ☐ strength 1492   qí

It takes **diligence** and *strength* to lay the raw *hide* on the *earth* and work it until it's fully cured, flexible, and usable.   [13 STROKES   RANK 1565]

1623 幼 幼 young

☐ youngest 775   ☐ strength 1492   yè

BF As **young** creatures grow in skills, they continually test their *strength*, and that of their parents.   [5 STROKES   RANK 1577]

1624 芳 芳 fragrant, virtuous (name)

☐ grass r 94   ☐ square, direction 1491   fā

BF The *right kind* of *grasses* are those with **fragrant** flowers.   [7 STROKES   RANK 1586]

1625 帐 帐 curtain, canopy

☐ towel 130   ☐ long, length 1423   zł

BF You form a **curtain** from a *long* piece of *towel.*   [7 STROKES   RANK 1603]

1626 辖 辖 have jurisdiction over

☐ car 1430   ☐ harm, injure 250   xi

BF That *car* ran into you and *injured* you. You can't do anything yourself—the courts **have jurisdiction over** the matter.   [14 STROKES   RANK 1643]

1627 魏 魏 Wei dynasty

☐ listless, dejected 593   ☐ ghost, spirit 1591   w

Perhaps the **Wei** emperors chose this graph—composed of two *dejected* images—to show that they could rise above such matters.   [17 STROKES   RANK 1648]

1628 梯 梯 ladder

☐ tree 375   ☐ younger brother 1450   tī

BF **Ladders** are made from *trees*, and the sinuous nature of the '*younger brother*' part suggests its rungs.   [11 STROKES   RANK 1672]

1629 抛　抛　toss, fling, abandon

⬛ hand r 29　⬛⬛ man 311 (altered)　⬛ strength 1492　　pāo

The *hand* and coiled right arm of a *man* used great *strength* to **fling** the grenade as far away as possible.　　　　　　　　　　[7 STROKES　RANK 1692]

1630 身　身　human body

CMP Make way for the very pregnant lady as she travels to the left across the page. She's facing a heavy wind. It is her profile which suggests 'human body'.

　　　We see her in mid-stride. The vertical hooked stroke is the leg supporting the her weight. The curved stroke to its left shows the other leg in readiness to step forward. One arm is stretched in front to help with balance, while the fingers of her other hand are splayed across her stomach in a protective gesture. Remember, there's a strong wind blowing, and a bit of cloth—a protective kerchief?—blows up obscuring her face and head.

1631 身　身　body

BF

⬛ human body 1630　　shēn

[7 STROKES　RANK 164]

1632 躺　躺　lie down

⬛ body 1631　⬛ still, yet 1139　　tǎng

A tired worker takes her *body* and **lies down** on the company cot. We are looking at it head on from ground level. The square head is covered by the blanket. Her two feet stick out from the other end, and the vertical stick in the middle represents her hands lying together.　　　　[15 STROKES　RANK 1608]

1633 射　射　to shoot

⬛ body 1631　⬛ inch 210　　shè

Her *body* **shot** one-*inch* daggers with such a force they stopped the attackers in their tracks.　　　　　　　　　　　　　　　　[10 STROKES　RANK 703]

1634 谢　谢　thank

⬛ speech r 615　⬛ to shoot 1633　　xiè

Some people have a macabre sense of amusement. Here's a guy who *requested* the chance to be present at an execution, death by *firing* squad. Afterwards, he **thanked** his hosts profusely.　　　　　　　　　[12 STROKES　RANK 897]

1635 ナ　ナ　**moving hand**

CMP You see here a greatly altered hand (§27). The use of the action path (§1421) for the arm suggests motion.

1636 左　左　**left**   ■ moving hand 1635   ▣ labor, work 7   z

You might think you see a *hand moving* in *productive labor*, but the hand dominates the labor in relative size to emphasize that there's more movement than there is work—a typical inefficiency when most people use their **left** hand to try and do something.   [5 STROKES   RANK 782]

Unit 67

Masculine and Feminine

1637 佐　佐　assist　　　　　　　　　　■ man r 953　■ left 1636　　zuǒ

BF *Left*-handed people are so clumsy that they need a *man* to **assist** them when they try to do meaningful work. (The current author is a lefty.)

[7 STROKES　RANK 2081]

1638 右　右　right (-hand)　　　　■ moving hand 1635　■ mouth 41　　yòu

BF The **right hand** is so important because it's the *moving hand* we eat with—the hand we use to shove food into our *mouths*.　　[5 STROKES　RANK 783]

1639 若　若　seem, like, if　　　　□ grass r 94　■ right (-hand) 1638　　ruò

Using a thread made from *grass*, you use your dexterous *right hand* to repair the **seams** (sounds like **seems**!) of your clothes.　　[8 STROKES　RANK 651]

1640 惹　惹　to provoke, exasperate

　　　　　■ grass r 94　■ right (-hand) 1638　■ heart (fat) 906　　rě

Mowing the *grass* with the *right hand* only is one of those silly yet *emotional* things that teens do to **provoke** their parents.　　[12 STROKES　RANK 2272]

1641 布　布　cloth　　　　　　■ moving hand 1635　■ towel 130　　bù

Imagine a *moving hand* actively working with a *towel*. The implication is we're treating the *towel* as raw material, and working it into finished **cloth** for sale or use.　　[5 STROKES　RANK 380]

1642 无　无　un-, -less　■ moving hand 1635　☐ one 2　◪ mineshaft 135　v

I *move* my *hand*, and nastily grab the *one* thing that means the most to my beloved. Unfeelingly, I heart**less**ly throw it down the *mineshaft* **without** a backward glance.　[4 STROKES　RANK 105]

1643 抚　抚　comfort, console　◧ hand r 29　◪ un-, -less 1642　f

The touch of a human *hand* **consoles** a mourner by helping him feel *less* pain.　[7 STROKES　RANK 1720]

1644 尤　尤　blame, fault

◧ moving hand 1635　☐ dab 169　◪ mineshaft 135　y

BF It's dark and gloomy, so I can't see all the details, but somebody's *moving hand* carries a *small something* to the edge of the *mineshaft*, and drops it down. It's surely the smoking gun evidence that would solve the brutal crime. If I could see the person, I would know who's to **blame**.　[4 STROKES　RANK 1099]

1645 扰　扰　disturb, bother　◧ hand r 29　◪ blame, fault 1644　r

In the middle of my first decent sleep in over 36 hours, you tripped, and landed with your *hand* right in my face. It's your *fault* I woke up, and I'll never forgive you for **disturbing** me.　[7 STROKES　RANK 1483]

1646 忧　忧　worry, anxiety　◧ heart (skinny) 930　◪ blame, fault 1644　y

BF *Emotions* caused by *blame* are **worry** and **anxiety**.　[7 STROKES　RANK 1461]

1647 优　优　excellent, superior　◧ man r 953　◪ blame, fault 1644　y

BF This *man* I know always manages *not* to be overcome by feelings of *guilt*. What an **excellent** way to be!　[6 STROKES　RANK 774]

1648 就　就　then　◧ capital city 1077　◪ blame, fault 1644　ji

(This is an extremely common word with an abundance of meanings, of which 'then' is among the most common.) If a particularly dreadful crime is your *fault*, **then** you may suffer *capital* punishment!　[12 STROKES　RANK 27]

649 龙 龙 dragon   ■ blame, fault 1644 ▯ action path 1421   lóng

Look at this character as a pictograph. You see a man with an injured right leg; the *action path* is some massive bandage or cast. The patient or prisoner is trying to walk, but it's such an effort that a drop of sweat flies in the air. And he's not really walking, either—he's just **draggin'** (sounds like **dragon**!) himself along.   [5 STROKES   RANK 696]

650 庞 庞 very large   ▯ shelter r 681 ■ dragon 1649   páng

BF Look how the *dragon* sticks out from its *shelter* because it's so **very large**!   [8 STROKES   RANK 1849]

651 沈 沈 to sink

▯ water r 523 ■ moving hand 1635 (altered) ▯ mineshaft 135   chén

Someone has flooded the *mineshaft* with *water*. You're struggling to hold yourself up—those are your fingers at the ends of the *moving hand*, trying to grab onto the edge of the mine—but it's a losing battle. You're slowly **sinking**.   [7 STROKES   RANK 1681]

652 灰 灰 gray, ash   ■ moving hand 1635 ▤ fire 1101   huī

If you use your *hand* to put out the *fire*, it will get covered with **gray ash**.   [6 STROKES   RANK 1311]

653 恢 恢 extensive, vast   ▯ heart (skinny) 930 ▯ gray, ash 1652   huī

BF A giant *heart* is somehow being stretched vertically. The taller it gets, the more its color turns from healthy pinkish red to *ashen gray*. At the end of this procedure, the heart has become **extensive** and **vast**.   [9 STROKES   RANK 1364]

654 宏 宏 great, grand

▯ roof 247 ■ moving hand 1635 ▤ private 750   hóng

BF In the *privacy* of my **grand** and palatial home, under my own *roof*, I can *move my hand* as much as I want with no fear of breaking things (as sometimes happened in the past!).   [7 STROKES   RANK 1798]

1655 雄 雄 **male, mighty**

⬛ moving hand 1635   ⬛ private 750   ⬛ short-tailed bird 992   **x**

BF You can tell the **mighty** army is made up solely of **men**. They're all *moving their hands* in silly salutes, even the *privates*, and their fancy uniforms invites comparison with fancy *short-tailed birds*.   [12 STROKES   RANK 1054]

1656 犹 犹 **just as, just like**   ⬛ dog r 898   ⬛ dog 332 (altered)   **y**

We'll use this term to mean **similarity** or **the same as**.

If you look at wildly distinct breeds of *dogs* (Irish wolfhounds and Boston terriers), it's hard to believe they belong to the **same** species.

[7 STROKES   RANK 1230]

1657 获 获 **capture, catch**   ⬜ grass r 94   ⬛ just as, just like 1656 (altered)   **h**

BF I use *two dogs* to **capture** prey in the *grassy* fields and meadows.

[10 STROKES   RANK 688]

1658 诺 诺 **to promise**   ⬛ speech r 615   ⬛ seem, like, if 1639   **n**

BF His love *speech seemed like* eternal **promises** of undying love, but he was as deceitful as all the others. She felt her life was ruined.

[10 STROKES   RANK 969]

1659 袭 袭 **raid, make a surprise attack**

⬛ dragon 1649   ⬛ clothing 839   **x**

BF Who would suspect a herd of *dragons* wearing tutus, Speedo swim trunks, and other outrageous *clothing* would be preparing a **surprise attack** on the settlers?   [11 STROKES   RANK 1213]

1660 怖 怖 **fear, be afraid**   ⬛ heart (skinny) 930   ⬛ cloth 1641   **b**

BF When you are in the grip of extreme **fear**, it feels like someone has wrapped your *heart* in a *cloth* strip which they are pulling tight.

[8 STROKES   RANK 1776]

1661 笼　笼　**cage, coop, basket**   ☐ bamboo r 243   ■ dragon 1649   lóng

BF How do you build a **cage** for a *dragon*? Very carefully. It turns out *bamboo* is the best, for it flexes without breaking.   [11 STROKES   RANK 1928]

1662 羊　羊　**running sheep**

CMP Take the sheep (§1147) and replace its backbone by the action path (§1421) to suggest a moving or **running sheep**.

Unit 68

Widdershins

1663 差 差 **lack, short of** ■ running sheep 1662 ▪ labor, work 7 cƕ

Here's a pesky *running sheep* that has destroyed our *work*, a shelter for those inclement days herding sheep. The work has to be redone; we **lack** completion. [9 STROKES RANK 732]

1664 羞 羞 **shame, embarrass** ■ running sheep 1662 ▪ hideous 37 xi

We find ourselves in the middle of a fairy tale. The beautiful princess has been enchanted so as to appear *hideous* to one and all. To protect against the **shame** and **embarrassment** she feels when the handsome prince enters, she hides behind one of the *running sheep* in the king's herds. [10 STROKES RANK 2048]

1665 着 着 **indicates continuing progress**

■ running sheep 1662 ▪ eye 78 zƕ

Little *sheep never keep still.* The shepherd uses his *eye* to keep track of their **continuing progress.** [11 STROKES RANK 41]

1666 判 判 **judge, decide**

▯ running sheep 1662 (altered) ▯ knife r 166 (altered) pà

The trial is winding up. The jury sees all the evidence—a *mutilated sheep corpse* (two legs missing) and a bloody *knife*, and now it's up to them to **decide** the verdict. [7 STROKES RANK 719]

667 丬 廾 **action scaffolding**

☐ one 2   ■ action path 1421   ■ scepter 5

CMP The curved stroke represents a path on which something travels up. When it gets to the top, it rests on the horizontal stroke of the simple scaffolding structure which supports it.

668 升 升 **raise, hoist**   ☐ dab 169   ■ action scaffolding 1667   shēng

The *bit* at the top of the *scaffolding* represents something that moved up, so it's being **hoisted up**.   [4 STROKES   RANK 837]

669 弄 弄 **make, do, manage**   ☐ king 11   ■ action scaffolding 1667   nòng

The *king* on the *scaffolding* oversees his subjects, and **manages** their lives.

[7 STROKES   RANK 1053]

670 卉 卉 **kinds of grasses**   ■ ten 6   ■ action scaffolding 1667   huì

BF How do we fasten together the struts that make up the *scaffolding*? From a short distance, this glyph looks like a sheaf of tall, uncut **grass of many varieties**, waving in the breeze. And that's what we'll use, several varieties—metaphorically, *ten*—as cords to bind the rods together.

[5 STROKES   RANK 3341]

671 奔 奔 **head for**   ■ big 330   ■ kinds of grasses 1670   bēn

That pile of *grass clippings* on my neighbor's lawn is so *big* that all the circus elephants are **heading for** it.   [8 STROKES   RANK 1285]

1672 井　井　well　　　■ action scaffolding 1667　▢ one 2　　j

1　The *single* bar near the top of the *scaffolding* represents *one* aqueduct for water pumped from a nearby **well**.

2　The horizontals and (near) verticals represent the division of land into neighboring fields. The only reason they can flourish despite their proximity to each other is the central **well**, which provides plenty of water for every *one* of the farmers.

3　The criss-cross pattern of lines represents a protective grid across the top of the **well**. You can drop your bucket down to get water, but kids and other large things can't fall through.　　　[4 STROKES　RANK 1431]

1673 开　开　operate　　　■ action scaffolding 1667　▢ one 2　　k

There's *one* person on top of the *scaffolding*, and it's she who gets to **operate** all the machinery.　　　[4 STROKES　RANK 94]

1674 刑　刑　punishment, sentence　　　▮ operate 1673　▮ knife r 166　　x

BF The prisoner has received the most severe **punishment** and **sentencing** possible—decapitation, and we are a little too late to witness the grisly act. On the left is the headless body, and we see the shoulders and arms, and the two legs; one is dangling out to the left in a final gallows twitch. The huge *knife* which can so easily lop off a human head is also present.

[6 STROKES　RANK 1087]

1675 型　型　mold, model, pattern

　　　　▬ punishment, sentence 1674　▬ earth, soil 9　　x

BF Each society sets up a **pattern** of proper behavior for its citizens. Violate this code? Following *punishment*, you'll rest in the *earth*, either permanently (capital offense) or not (early prisons were dug into the *earth*).

[9 STROKES　RANK 556]

1676 研　研　to grind　　　▯ stone, rock 1386　▯ operate 1673　　y

Oops—the giant *rock* slipped off the *scaffolding*, and **ground** the unlucky pedestrian to a bloody pulp. (You can see the 'mouth' on the bottom, as someone screams briefly in agony.)　　　[9 STROKES　RANK 447]

1677 并　并　**an intensifier**　　　◻ eight (v) 1047　　◼ operate 1673　　bìng

(An *intensifier* is a word like *really* or *truly*. In modern Mandarin, 并 may only be used in front of a negative: This book is *really* uninteresting.)

　　Operating a machine is an example of an activity, and affixing a sign of '*abundance*' to it **intensifies** this sense of activity. Activity is work, and no one likes work, so in this way, 并 acquires a negative association.

[6 STROKES　RANK 141]

1678 拼　拼　**spell**　　　◼ hand r 29　　◻ an intensifier 1677　　pīn

In the United States, we have spelling bees, while in China, where '**spelling**' refers to the proper composition of a character, appreciation of **spelling** goes *hand* in *hand* with appreciation of fine calligraphy. In either case, **spelling** evokes *intense* feelings.　　　[9 STROKES　RANK 1820]

1679 屏　屏　**hold one's breath**　　　◻ corpse 703　　◼ an intensifier 1677　　bǐng

BF The unburied *corpse* has begun to smell, and its stench is *intensely* bad. Mourners have to **hold their breath** or else they'll pass out.

[9 STROKES　RANK 1891]

1680 耕　耕　**plow, till**　　　◼ tree 375　　◻ two 3 (altered)　　◼ well 1672　　gēng

In ancient times, they made **plows** out of *two trees*, one for the handle and one for the 'blade'. The lengths of the strokes in '*two*' are altered to emphasize that the handle was longer than the part that digs into the soil. The four strokes of the '*well*' map out the pattern of furrows in the soil.　　[10 STROKES　RANK 1850]

1681 形　形　**form, shape**　　　◼ operate 1673　　◻ feathers 1285　　xíng

BF Eeks—a serious accident at the farm. The old man was *operating* the tractor, and ran someone over! It's pretty bad—we can see the *feathery* tracks on the ground where the body was dragged, but the actual **shape** of the body is still hidden under the machine itself.　　　[7 STROKES　RANK 269]

1682 讲　讲　**talk, speak, speaking of**　　　◼ speech r 615　　◼ well 1672　　jiǎng

The genie's *speech* rose mysteriously from the *well* and asked us to **speak** our wishes to him more clearly.　　　[6 STROKES　RANK 555]

1683 异 异 different, strange, unusual

■ self* 852 (altered)   ■ action scaffolding 1667   y

BF Our manager, fat and bald, is quite a character. Here he is, the great man him*self*, climbing up the *scaffolding* to hang a 'Happy New Year' sign in Chinese. Everyone thought it was **strange** and **unusual**.

[6 STROKES   RANK 709]

1684 舛 舛 error, incongruous

■ evening, dusk 655   □ action scaffolding 1667 (altered)   c

BF Working at *evening* time under improper conditions (such as poor lighting) leads to outrageous **errors**. Just look at what a poor job they made of the *scaffolding*!   [6 STROKES   RANK 4694]

1685 舞 舞 dance

□ man 311 (altered)   ■ ten (times 4) 6   ■ bar 1   ■ error, incongruous 1684   w

Forty people, mostly *men*, on the **dance** *floor*, all newbies. It's bound to lead to *errors* and *incongruities*—just look at the tall woman dancing with the male midget, and listen to the cries from people whose toes have been stepped on!   [14 STROKES   RANK 1144]

1686 戒 戒 guard against, warn

■ halberd 359   ■ action scaffolding 1667   ji

BF The *scaffolding* serves as a perfect setting to stand, *sword* poised, to **guard against** evildoers trying to kidnap the princess.   [7 STROKES   RANK 1566]

1687 械 械 machinery, mechanical

□ tree 375   □ guard against, warn 1686   xi

BF In order to make the *tree* suitable to *guard us against danger*, we need to work it with some **machinery**.   [11 STROKES   RANK 1657]

1688 刂 刂 steadfast soul

CMP A person engaged in many activities nevertheless always returns to a fixed point, symbolized by a scepter, to do their duty.

Unit 69

Arms Akimbo

1689 归 归 **go back, return** ▐ steadfast soul 1688 ▐ boar's head 34 guī

The new servant appears completely reliable. This *steadfast soul* has to sweep up every morning using the special *boar bristle* broom, and so always **returns** in time to do this every morning. [5 STROKES RANK 933]

1690 帅 帅 **handsome** ▐ steadfast soul 1688 ▐ towel 130 shuài

This guy, known as a *steadfast soul* somehow decided to appear dressed only in a *towel* 'round his middle. How sexy and **handsome** he looks!

[5 STROKES RANK 1888]

1691 师 师 **teacher, master** ▐ steadfast soul 1688 ▐ money, currency 230 shī

BF A **teacher** must set an example of *steadfastness* and that's what they pay him for. See the *money* he gets?

The little 'dab' on top of 'towel' also makes me think '**teacher**'. The dab is a small piece of chalk for the blackboard, and the towel serves as blackboard eraser. [6 STROKES RANK 333]

The characters 帅 'handsome' and 师 'teacher' (§§1690, 1691) differ by a single, small stroke. Teachers can, I suppose, be handsome, but they carry around that little piece of chalk all the time.

1692 班 班 **team, class**

▐ king 11 ▐▐ steadfast soul 1688 (altered) ▐ king 11 bān

The two grids on either side represent organized groups of people, perhaps sitting in rows as in a **team** or **class**. They are are all *steadfast people* acting together, the kind you can rely on, and the best kind to have on a **team** or in a **class**. [10 STROKES RANK 884]

1693 卯 卯 listening ear

■ basket, box 152   ⊔ action path 1421   ▮ single ear 157

CMP Symbolically, we see sound traveling via the *action path* into the sound *box*, where it's amplified magically so the *ear* can **listen** to it.

1694 聊 聊 to chat   ▮ ear 82   ▮ listening ear 1693   liá

What activity do *ears* play a large part in? When your best friend gets ready to share some juicy gossip during a **chat**, that's when you're *all ears*!

[11 STROKES   RANK 1932]

1695 柳 柳 willow   ▮ tree 375   ▮ listening ear 1693   liǔ

BF The famous **willow** *trees* of China participate in an impressive event. During storms, the wind through the branches produces a clearly audible rustling to the *listening ear*.   [9 STROKES   RANK 1557]

1696 丿 丿| dancing girl

CMP As in other components focusing on moving people, we just see the young woman's legs, at the moment she's in a graceful pirouette.

1697 介 介 introduce   ▭ man 311   ▬ dancing girl 1696   jiè

BF We are present at the **introduction** of a *man* to his future bride, a graceful young woman. The *man* just stands there, too nervous to budge, while the *girl* is so poised she has no trouble displaying her skill at *dancing*.

[4 STROKES   RANK 831]

1698 价 价 price   ▮ man r 953   ⊔ introduce 1697   jià

We saw in §1697 that the moment two young people meet serves to explain the character 介 'introduce'. But in those long-ago days, this *introduction* would not have taken place without the intervention of a professional matchmaker. There *he* is on the left, come to collect the **price** for his services.

[6 STROKES   RANK 409]

1699 界 界 **boundary, scope**   ▢ field 57   ▆ introduce 1697   jiè
BF Buying a new property, a new *field*, requires *getting to know* all about it—its peculiarities, its pretty spots, stony areas, and so on. Then you will know the full **scope** and extent of this new acquisition.   [9 STROKES   RANK 288]

1700 乔 乔 **tall**   ▬ heaven 333   ▆ dancing girl 1696   qiáo
BF The *dancing girl* gets closer to *heaven* because she's so **tall**. Of course, this is an exaggeration, which is why we use a slightly exaggerated form of 天, 'heaven'.
　　To me, this graph looks like a tall fashion model dressed in a fall jacket standing in a typical fashion pose.   [6 STROKES   RANK 1488]

1701 娇 娇 **fragile, frail**   ▮ woman 581   ▯ tall 1700   jiāo
The odd-looking *woman* is not only very *tall*, but has an emaciated, anorexic-looking body. She looks so **fragile** she might just shatter.
          [9 STROKES   RANK 2158]

1702 桥 桥 **bridge**   ▮ tree 375   ▯ tall 1700   qiáo
Tall trees made primordial engineers devise ways to build **bridges**. They used them as natural supports over which they could loop strong vines or they chopped the trees down and lay them over narrow valleys.
          [10 STROKES   RANK 1292]

1703 养 养 **support, provide for**
          ▯ eight (v) 1047   ▬ mighty tree 1358   ▣ dancing girl 1696   yǎng
With the *abundance* of *mighty trees* on his property, the farmer has enough extra money to devote to his *dancing girl*friend and to **support** her in the style in which she'd like to become accustomed.   [9 STROKES   RANK 760]

1704 鼻 鼻 **nose**

■ self 202   ■ field 57   ■ one 2   ■ dancing girl 1696   b

BF The top component alerts us to the depiction of a person's *self*, but it's easy to interpret everything else pictographically. The middle '*field*' is this person's snub **nose**, bordered below by a thin mustache. Underneath is either the fold of skin directly below all our **noses**, or (if you prefer) two lines of exhaled breath.

[14 STROKES   RANK 1335]

1705 毫 毫 **long, fine hair**

■ tall 1700 (altered)   ■ hair 231   h

A *tall* strand of *hair* is a metaphor for one that is **long** and **fine**.

[11 STROKES   RANK 879]

1706 弗 弗 **not (literary)**

■ bow (weapon) 859   ■ dancing girl 1696   f

The *dancing girl* played with the *bow*. What a mistake—in short order, she had tangled everything into a big **knot** (sounds like '**not**').

[5 STROKES   RANK 1257]

1707 佛 佛 **Buddha**

■ man r 953   ■ not (literary) 1706   f

Who is *not* a *man*? The great **Buddha**, who is like a god.

[7 STROKES   RANK 771]

1708 费 費 **cost, spend, expend**

■ not (literary) 1706   ■ cowrie 430   f

Spent too much money? Result: *not* any *money* left in your wallet.

[9 STROKES   RANK 486]

1709 阶 階 **stairs, rank or step**

■ hills 735   ■ introduce 1697   ji

BF *He'll* (sounds like '*hill*') *introduce* me to the boss, so I can ride in the executive elevator, and don't have to take the **stairs** to my office all the time.

[6 STROKES   RANK 745]

1710 尹 尹 **pinned bug**   ▯ action path 1421   ▭ boar's head 34 (altered)

CMP The upper trident savagely, even brutally, (think of the teeth of a *wild boar*) **pins** the flying insect (that's whose *action path* we see) to the wall. It is a metaphor for being trapped—in a job, existence, or other situation.

From a different angle, it looks like something flew into a secure cage. You can only check in—you can't check out!

1711 伊 伊 **he, she**   ▮ man r 953   ▯ pinned bug 1710   yī

A *person* may feel *trapped* forever in their **gender role**.

[6 STROKES   RANK 761]

1712 君 君 **monarch, lord**   ▮ pinned bug 1710   ▭ mouth 41   jūn

It's hard to believe, but interviews with **monarchs** reveal that they regard themselves as being imprisoned in their jobs, forced to serve as figureheads for the duration of their reigns. Does that not make them the metaphorical equal of a *talking head pinned to a board*?   [7 STROKES   RANK 985]

1713 群 群 **herd, crowd, flock**   ▮ monarch, lord 1712   ▯ sheep 1147   qún

Sheep are metaphors for creatures that blindly follow their *leader*, whatever he does. These concepts together illustrate a **herd** or **flock**.

[13 STROKES   RANK 570]

1714 肅 肅 **respectful, solemn**

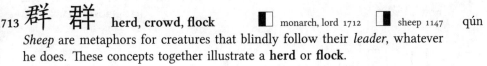 ▮ dancing girl 1696   ▪ eight 1048   ▭ pinned bug 1710 (altered)   sù

BF Watch the finale of a Broadway extravaganza (at least part of it). See *how many dancing showgirls*! Courtesy of their stylized choreography, their performance onstage makes them resemble gaudy *butterflies pinned to a board*. Nevertheless, their choreography is so well-done, that you cannot help sitting in **respectful** attention.

The path of the pinned bug has been straightened out so it fits inside the character square.   [8 STROKES   RANK 1518]

Unit 70
The Thing Speaks for Itself

1715 嘯 嘯 **to whistle**   ■ mouth 41   ▢ respectful, solemn 1714   X
Finally, you catch your breath from the beauty of this presentation (§1714).
You use your *mouth* to make a *respectful* sound of appreciation—you **whistle**!
                           [11 STROKES   RANK 2301]

1716 蕭 蕭 **desolate, bleak**   ▢ grass r 94   ■ respectful, solemn 1714   X
BF Ever see a truly well-tended lawn? Each blade of *grass* seems to stand
respectfully at attention. Impressive, but in the end, you notice there's no
sign of homeyness—no games, no chairs to sit in, no nothin'. How **desolate**,
how **bleak**.   [11 STROKES   RANK 1898]

1717 刀 刀 **safe place**   ▢ action path 1421   ■ place of refuge 111
CMP This character combines an *active path* (§1421) with the *place of refuge*
(§111). It's very similar to 'borders' (§127), but Chinese scribes seem to make
a point of emphasizing the dynamic left side in some characters and leaving
it straight in others.

    This component often suggests a **safe place**, environment, or period in
which to work.

1718 丹 丹 **red, cinnabar**   ■ safe place 1717   ▦ cover 268   dā
Cover the heavy jar which is the only *safe place* to store the lab's supply of
mercury, whose ore (by the way) is **cinnabar**.   [4 STROKES   RANK 1280]

1719 月 月   **moon, month**   ■ safe place 1717   ⊟ two 3 (altered)   yuè

Nighttime. Observe the reflection of the full **moon** in a lake, with the left and right boundaries displaying the edges of its silver path. The lake's surface isn't completely still, and the two horizontals represent a few small wavelets.

This glyph often represents an altered form of 'meat' (normally 肉), and commonly will represent a body part in this variation.   [4 STROKES   RANK 169]

1720 肩 肩   **shoulder**   ▯ door of house 724   ▮ moon, month 1719   jiān

Your **shoulder** is the *part of the body* most suitable for bursting through *doors*.   [8 STROKES   RANK 1415]

1721 脏 脏   **filthy**   ▮ moon, month 1719   ▮ village 687   zāng

By light of the *moon*, the *village* takes a bath to rid itself of the **filth** tourists bring in. What a sight—all the quaint old buildings daintily stepping into the river and washing all over!   [10 STROKES   RANK 1634]

1722 青 青   **nature's color, unripe**   ▮ plentiful 12 (altered)   ▬ moon, month 1719   qīng

Nature's colors are the ones that predominate in natural growth—blue and green. It was thought that harsh sun was inimical to such growth, but *plentiful moonlight* was responsible for lush harvests. Interestingly, the Chinese associate 'green' with 'unripe', as do we English speakers.   [8 STROKES   RANK 497]

1723 忄青 忄青   **sentiment, sensibility**   ▮ heart (skinny) 930   ▮ nature's color, unripe 1722   qíng

BF **Sentiment** is an *emotion* often associated with *nature* and her *colors*.

[11 STROKES   RANK 120]

1724 明 明   **bright, clear**   ▮ day, sun 63   ▮ moon, month 1719   míng

BF Having the *sun* and *moon* act together is a charming metaphor for **brightness**.   [8 STROKES   RANK 121]

1725 有 有 **have**　　　🔲 moving hand 1635　🔲 moon, month 1719　　yǒ

The *moon*, in an inferior position because it is in the background, shines over the earth's bounty. You *move your hand* over it all to indicate that you **have** it all—it's all yours.　　　　　　　　　　　　[6 STROKES   RANK 8]

1726 前 前 **before, in front of**

　　　　🔲 stop! 181 (altered)　🔲 moon, month 1719　🔲 knife r 166　qi

As a child, I once tried following a rainbow to find the legendary pot of gold. It was a clear night, so I followed the radiance of the *moon*, lighting a clear path whose edges were *knife*-edge sharp. Eventually, I had to *stop* when the walls of the town were **in front of** me, keeping me inside and the gold outside.　　　　　　　　　　　　[9 STROKES   RANK 93]

1727 那 那 **which? what? how?**

　　　　🔲 moon, month 1719 (altered)　🔲 town 745　nǎ

What an odd dream! It was nighttime, and the *moon* raced through the streets of the *town* on little lunar feet, which was why the stripes lag behind its enclosing part. **How** is this possible? **What** is going on?

　　　　　　　　　　　　[6 STROKES   RANK 38]

1728 周 周 **week**　　🔲 safe place 1717　🔲 earth, soil 9　🔲 mouth 41　zh

In ancient days, people sweated the *earth* to survive, either through farming or by hunting. In those days, recreation involved using your *mouth*—talking, singing, joking, screaming, and so on. The **week** is an *environment* during which people carried out these two types of actions.　　[8 STROKES   RANK 490]

1729 雕 雕 **carve, engrave**　　🔲 week 1728　🔲 short-tailed bird 992　di

The eagle, a famous *short-tailed bird*, is attacking the sheep! But it's so *weak* (sounds like '*week*') that it can't tear the sheep to pieces, but can only **carve** some bloody gashes in the sheep's body.　　　　[16 STROKES   RANK 1829]

1730 用 用   to use   ■ safe place 1717   ▌▌ middle 45 (altered)   yòng

Within a *safe place*, everyone has chores to keep the enclosure safe and strong. Of *central* importance are tools whose **use** lightens everyone's work. '*Middle*' is slightly abbreviated, as a reminder that tools alter the material they work on.   [5 STROKES   RANK 51]

1731 拥 拥   to embrace, hold   ▌ hand r 29   ▌▌ to use 1730   yōng

I'm no Casanova, but even I know that *hands* have a central *use* in a passionate **embrace**.   [8 STROKES   RANK 1059]

1732 甫 甫   just now, only

       ■ to use 1730 (altered)   ▭ one 2   ▢ dab 169   fǔ

The people have been striving for months to set up a new monument, a symbol of their victorious struggle against oppression. They've **just now** finished! The tall central rod is held up by several *useful* tools. A *single* crosspiece shelters all citizens, and a *dab* of cloth flutters defiantly as it catches the breeze.

     When this character appears as a component in other characters, we may attach to it the meaning of '**monument**' or '**statue**'.   [7 STROKES   RANK 2152]

1733 捕 捕   catch, seize   ▌ hand r 29   ▌▌ just now, only 1732   bǔ

I **caught** the murderer *just now* using only my *hands*, and we strung him up on the new *monument* as a warning. Watch his *hands* flutter in the breeze.   [10 STROKES   RANK 1312]

1734 浦 浦   water's edge   ▌ water r 523   ▌▌ just now, only 1732   pǔ

BF The *water* in the huge tsunami pounded the new war *memorial* causing it to topple. It was so heavy that all the land around it started sinking, and now it's at the **water's edge**.   [10 STROKES   RANK 2161]

1735 蒲 蒲   cattail   ▭ grass r 94   ■ water's edge 1734   pú

The fuzzy **cattail** is a beloved and decorative *grass* you can find at the *water's edge*.   [13 STROKES   RANK 2344]

1736 博 博 **win, gain**   ▮ ten 6   ▯ just now, only 1732   ▮ inch 210   b

BF In a horse race, the *inch* by which the winner *just now* nosed out the second-place horse leads to an incredible and unexpected **win**; that's what the '*ten*' means.   [12 STROKES   RANK 965]

1737 傅 傅 **teacher, instructor**

▮ man r 953   ▯ just now, only 1732   ▮ inch 210   f

BF That *man* is a terrific **teacher**! He *just now* taught me what an *inch* is.   [12 STROKES   RANK 1887]

1738 溥 溥 **broad, extensive**

▮ water r 523   ▮ just now, only 1732   ▮ inch 210   p

BF The *water* in the pool near the *memorial* is a popular gathering place, and is full of the *inch*-long bits of stale bread that kids throw in for the ducks. The bread floats, and instantly spreads over a **broad** and **extensive** area.   [STROKES   RANK 3882]

1739 薄 薄 **thin, flimsy**   ▯ grass r 94   ▮ broad, extensive 1738   b

Our cheapskate neighbor planted a small amount of *grass* seed over a very *broad* area—a stupid way to save money. The lawn grew in **thin** and sparse and cheapened the entire neighborhood.   [16 STROKES   RANK 1433]

1740 能 能 **can, able**

▮ private 750   ▮ moon, month 1719   ▮ compared with 146 (altered)   n

We see *privacy* piled upon a *month* juxtaposed with an upended *comparison*. How does that suggest '**can**'? Better to interpret this character as a suggestive picture. '*Month*' itself looks like a **can**, and a thirsty teenager's *nose* appears above it as she is about to take a swig. The *ladle*-like shapes on the right (§142) show her shiny curls falling forward in delicate ringlets.

[10 STROKES   RANK 35]

Curiouser and Curiouser, Too

1741 朋 朋 friend   ▊ meat 317 (altered)   ▊ meat 317 (altered)   péng

BF Yes, each of these components does look like 'month', but the scribes also associated this shape with '*meat*'. Here, imagine *two meaty* creatures—people or dogs or whatever—strolling along companionably, because they're **friends**.

[8 STROKES RANK 882]

1742 鵬 鵬 roc   ▊ friend 1741   ▊ bird 885   péng

Despite the ferocity of this large fabulous *bird*, sailors considered the **roc** to be a *friendly bird*. How so? If they do manage to subdue it, they can feast off its flesh for a long, long time.   [13 STROKES RANK 1926]

1743 郁 郁 lush   ▊ have 1725   ▊ town 745   yù

BF You *have towns* only in locations which are sufficiently **lush** to support their growth.   [8 STROKES RANK 1915]

1744 霸 霸 overlord

     ▊ rain 85   ▊ animal hide 101   ▊ moon, month 1719   bà

It's no fun being a peasant in ancient China! Each town is under the iron thumb of their **overlord**, compelled to offer *monthly* tribute. Tonight it's *raining* barrels, but we still have to deliver our quota of *leather hides* to the castle.   [21 STROKES RANK 1838]

1745 甬 甬 corridor, path   ▊ private 750   ▊ to use 1730   yǒng

BF The **corridors** leading to the interior of the house are for *private use* only!

[7 STROKES RANK 4038]

1746 痛 痛 **painful**   ☐ sick 697   ☐ corridor, path 1745   tò
Comparing the interior of a house to the body, the patient's *sickness* was spreading throughout the *corridors*. This was very **painful** to the patient.

[12 STROKES   RANK 730]

1747 涌 涌 **gush, well up**   ☐ water r 523   ☐ corridor, path 1745   y
The terrorists have blown up the dam! *Water* is flowing through the innermost *corridors* of all the houses, **gushing up** everywhere.   [10 STROKES   RANK 1642]

1748 勇 勇 **brave, valiant**   ☐ corridor, path 1745   ☐ strength 1492   y
BF The soldiers charging down the dark, gloomy *corridor* were quite *strong*, but even so it was such a scary place that we knew they were also quite **brave**.   [9 STROKES   RANK 1206]

1749 角 角 **horn, corner, angle**   ☐ knife 1489 (altered)   ☐ to use 1730   ji
Craftsmen *use a knife* to carve various objects out of animal bones and **horns**.

[7 STROKES   RANK 736]

1750 解 解 **untie, undo, take off**
☐ horn, corner, angle 1749   ☐ knife 1489   ☐ ox 186   ji
The not-too-bright farmer is doing something with the *ox*. It looks like he's got the *knife* on the animal's *horn*, and is trying to **take it off**. The *ox* looks ready to kill him, and can you blame it?   [13 STROKES   RANK 201]

1751 期 期 **period of time**   ☐ his, her, its, theirs 1093   ☐ moon, month 1719   q
BF All the family, the distant cousins and recluses got together for a fabulous vacation. Now *their* **time** together is over, as the *moon* comes forward to cover them.   [12 STROKES   RANK 253]

1752 望   望   **observe, gaze into distance**

■ perish 269   ⊔ moon, month 1719   ■ king 11   wàng

Perhaps this character refers to an old but persistent myth. If you **gaze** at the *king* by the light of the *moon*, you will surely *perish*.   [11 STROKES   RANK 326]

1753 清   清   **clear, clear up**   ▯ water r 523   ▮ nature's color, unripe 1722   qīng

The effect of *natural colors* in the *waters* of a pristine tropical lagoon is one of perfect **clarity**.   [11 STROKES   RANK 335]

1754 确   确   **true, authentic**   ▮ stone, rock 1386   ▮ horn, corner, angle 1749   què

BF The carved image of the *horn* on the *stone* seal **authenticates** the oath.   [12 STROKES   RANK 331]

1755 睛   睛   **eyeball**   ▮ eye 78   ▮ nature's color, unripe 1722   jīng

BF Nowadays, people wear ornate glasses and contact lenses to camouflage and disguise the *eyes* that nature originally gave us. Look for an *eye* that's a *natural color* to see a genuine **eyeball**.   [13 STROKES   RANK 934]

1756 请   请   **ask, invite, polite request**

▮ speech r 615   ▮ nature's color, unripe 1722   qǐng

Somebody *speaks* most *naturally* when they're making a **request**.   [10 STROKES   RANK 421]

1757 猜   猜   **guess**   ▮ dog r 898   ▮ nature's color, unripe 1722   cāi

Those *natural colored dogs* that run in packs—it's hard to **guess** their breed.   [11 STROKES   RANK 1598]

1758 精   精   **perfect, excellent**   ▮ rice 1127   ▮ nature's color, unripe 1722   jīng

Nowadays, people think that *natural-colored* brown *rice* is the **perfect** way to consume rice, as opposed to the white, refined variety.   [14 STROKES   RANK 435]

1759 调 调   tune, air   ▯ speech r 615   ▮ week 1728   dí
He whistled the same **tune** all *week* long to keep from going crazy at the
job. He didn't care for the other guys on his shift, so he rarely *spoke* to
them.   [10 STROKES   RANK 400]

1760 静 静   still, quiet, calm   ▯ nature's color, unripe 1722   ▮ struggle 463   jìng
When *nature* overcomes the *struggling* of its inhabitants, then **calm** and **still**
conditions prevail, even if all too temporarily.   [14 STROKES   RANK 722]

1761 朝 朝   dynasty   ▯ ten 6   ▮ morning 70   ▮ moon, month 1719   cháo
BF Chinese scholars often associate **dynastic** reigns with heavenly phenomena.
Here, they compare the period of a **dynasty** with the pearly light you see
early in the day (10 o'clock) with a more extended period of time, written as
'*month*'.   [12 STROKES   RANK 593]

1762 潮 潮   trendy, chic   ▯ water r 523   ▮ dynasty 1761   cháo
BF **Trendiness** is an elusive quality. It personifies what's *current* (hence, the
'*water*' component) in the world of high fashion and also what is supposed
to be superior, symbolized by the '*dynasty*' component.
                                                          [15 STROKES   RANK 1302]

1763 脸 脸   face, countenance
                                ▮ moon, month 1719   ▮ together, unanimous 1351   liǎn
A beautiful June night. Under the light of the full *moon*, the crowd looks up
together to see the fireworks, which illuminate their collective **faces**.
                                                          [11 STROKES   RANK 615]

1764 哪 哪   which?* what?* how?*
                                ▮ mouth 41   ▮ which? what? how? 1727   nǎ
The '*mouth*' emphasizes the vocal aspect to '**which, what, and how**'.
                                                          [9 STROKES   RANK 652]

1765 胜　胜　win victory, succeed, excel

▮ moon, month 1719　▮ give birth to 191　shèng

By the light of the full *moon*, the ancient princess *gave birth to* a mighty prince, who **won** great **victories** for the Chinese people.　[9 STROKES　RANK 743]

1766 脚　脚　foot, leg, base　▮ moon, month 1719　▮ now (storytelling) 760　jiǎo

By the light of the *moon*, his *tale* sounded completely true, but thinking on it overnight, I realized he didn't have a **leg** to stand on.　[11 STROKES　RANK 790]

Unit 72

August Moon

1767 胡 胡 **beard, mustache** 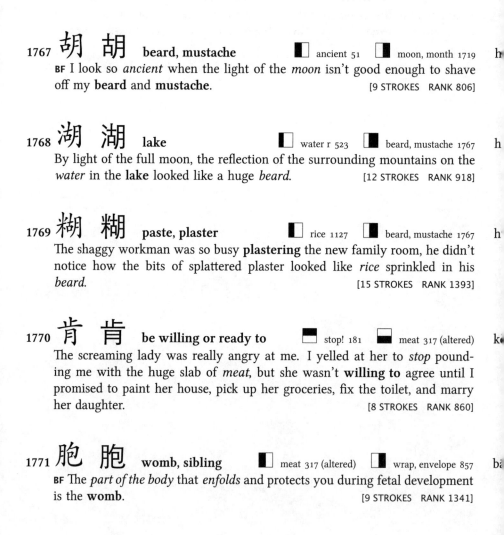 ancient 51 ☐ moon, month 1719 h
BF I look so *ancient* when the light of the *moon* isn't good enough to shave off my **beard** and **mustache**. [9 STROKES RANK 806]

1768 湖 湖 **lake** ☐ water r 523 ☐ beard, mustache 1767 h
By light of the full moon, the reflection of the surrounding mountains on the *water* in the **lake** looked like a huge *beard*. [12 STROKES RANK 918]

1769 糊 糊 **paste, plaster** ☐ rice 1127 ☐ beard, mustache 1767 h
The shaggy workman was so busy **plastering** the new family room, he didn't notice how the bits of splattered plaster looked like *rice* sprinkled in his *beard*. [15 STROKES RANK 1393]

1770 肯 肯 **be willing or ready to** ☐ stop! 181 ☐ meat 317 (altered) k
The screaming lady was really angry at me. I yelled at her to *stop* pounding me with the huge slab of *meat*, but she wasn't **willing to** agree until I promised to paint her house, pick up her groceries, fix the toilet, and marry her daughter. [8 STROKES RANK 860]

1771 胞 胞 **womb, sibling** ☐ meat 317 (altered) ☐ wrap, envelope 857 b
BF The *part of the body* that *enfolds* and protects you during fetal development is the **womb**. [9 STROKES RANK 1341]

1772 阴 阴　feminine principle in nature

■ hills 735　　□ moon, month 1719　　yīn

The light of the *moon* shining gently on the rounded *hills* in the distance reminds any viewer of a woman's breasts, putting them in mind of the **feminine side of nature**.　　　　[6 STROKES　RANK 987]

1773 臂 臂　arm, upper arm

□ law 1256　　■ moon, month 1719　　bì

BF The crescent *moon* is shaped like the upraised **arm** of a policeman getting ready to seize the crook and uphold the *law*.　　　[17 STROKES　RANK 1688]

1774 嘴 嘴　mouth, snout, bill

□ mouth 41　　□ this 233　　■ horn, corner, angle 1749　　zuǐ

How does this character differ in meaning from '*mouth*' (§41)? Well, *this* kind of '**mouth**' has more structure—it includes the *bony and angular* structures that belong to it.　　　　　[16 STROKES　RANK 1010]

1775 盟 盟　alliance, pact, league

■ bright, clear 1724　　■ blood 209 (altered)　　méng

BF Opposing parties get together and use *blood* to *clarify* under *bright light* of day their relationships with each other. Thus is born an **alliance** between neighboring countries.　　　　[13 STROKES　RANK 1163]

1776 触 触　touch, contact, strike

■ horn, corner, angle 1749　　■ insect 890　　chù

The angry hive of *bees* chased me into a *corner*. I was deeply fearful of **contact** with them, as I am very allergic to their stings.　　[13 STROKES　RANK 1207]

1777 衡 衡　weigh, measure

■ firm, business 1035　　■ horn, corner, angle 1749 (altered)　　■ big 330　　héng

BF The two halves of '*firm, business*' are mirror images, more or less, of each other. They show equal weighing pans balanced at the ends of a *big* piece of *horn*. Scales used by *businesses* to **weigh** their goods look like this.　　　　　[16 STROKES　RANK 1340]

1778 胆　胆　bravery, audacity　　　■ moon, month 1719　⬗ dawn 65　dǎ

Prince Charming demonstrates his **bravery** yet again. He'll be in the Enchanted Forest from late night until *dawn*, his only companion the light of the full *moon*.　　　　　[9 STROKES　RANK 1352]

1779 腰　腰　waist

■ meat 317 (altered)　⬓ west 291 (altered)　⬕ woman 581　yā

Western standards for *feminine* beauty focus on a few *body parts*, including a slender **waist**.　　　　[13 STROKES　RANK 1458]

1780 箭　箭　arrow*　　　⬒ bamboo r 243　■ before, in front of 1726　jià

In the hands of a master archer, the *bamboo* **arrows** swiftly fly *in front of* the advancing army.　　　　[15 STROKES　RANK 1496]

1781 娜　娜　lithe, graceful　　⬕ woman 581　⬗ which? what? how? 1727　nu

BF This *particular woman* is distinguished by her **graceful** athletic abilities.

[9 STROKES　RANK 1584]

1782 脉　脉　arteries and veins

■ meat 317 (altered)　⬓ forever, always 560　m

The right part looks like '*water*' (§545), but altered a bit. After all, the **arteries and veins** are the *parts of the body* which channel the main fluid of the body, blood.　　　　[9 STROKES　RANK 1594]

1783 铺　铺　spread, extend　　⬕ gold r 1327　⬗ just now, only 1732　pū

The *monument* (§1732) is hard to see. They *just* covered it in *gold leaf,* and that **extends** the area of visibility many times over.　　[12 STROKES　RANK 1613]

1784 朕 朕 **royal 'we'**   ▮ moon, month 1719   ▮ shut, close 1113   **zhèn**
Heavenly bodies such as the *moon* form part a pronoun involving the Emperor.
The *'close'* part refers to the exclusivity of the Emperor; normally, access to
his person was *closed* to the common citizen. The left *'moon'* looks like an
eye, and so this graph represents **I** when used by the Emperor, the **royal**
'we'.   [10 STROKES   RANK 3054]

1785 腾 騰 **gallop, prance**   ▮ royal 'we' 1784 (altered)   ▮ horse 878   **téng**
BF You're a *horse* honored to be able to carry the *royal* '*we*'. Would you do
anything but **prance** and **gallop** in the expected manner?
                                                               [13 STROKES   RANK 1635]

1786 熊 熊 **bear (animal)**   ▮ can, able 1740   ▮ fire r 796   **xióng**
Ever throw a *can* into a *bonfire*? Nothing happens for a few minutes, and
then there's a sudden explosion as the inside pressure of the boiled stuff
overcomes the strength of the *can*. **Bears** are like that. They look so big
and cute, but internal passions seethe, and suddenly you've got a vicious,
man-eating monster on your hands.   [14 STROKES   RANK 1741]

1787 肝 肝 **liver**   ▮ meat 317 (altered)   ▮ dry 10   **gān**
The **liver** is the *body part* that drunks need to keep '*dry*' if they don't want
to succumb to cirrhosis.   [7 STROKES   RANK 1760]

1788 肤 膚 **skin**   ▮ meat 317 (altered)   ▮ man (spiffy) 337   **fū**
BF The *body part* the handsome *man* likes best is his **skin**.
                                                               [8 STROKES   RANK 1790]

1789 肿 腫 **to swell**   ▮ moon, month 1719   ▮ middle 45   **zhǒng**
In the *middle* of the *month*, when the *moon* aligns with the earth in a certain
way, extra high tides make the seas **swell** up.   [8 STROKES   RANK 1792]

1790 肚　肚　belly*, abdomen*　　　■ meat 317 (altered)　　■ earth, soil 9　　d

BF That fat man's **belly** is the *part of the body* closest to the *earth*.

[7 STROKES   RANK 1800]

1791 膜　膜　membrane, film, thin coating

■ meat 317 (altered)　　■ do not, not 349　　n

BF A **membrane** is the *body part* that covers choice cuts of *meat* (steaks, chops) when an animal is freshly butchered. *Do not* eat this!

[14 STROKES   RANK 1945]

1792 晴　晴　clear, fine (of weather)

■ day, sun 63　　■ nature's color, unripe 1722　　q

By light of *day*, the *green* forest looks especially **fine**.

[12 STROKES   RANK 1968]

Unit 73

Righteous Anger

1793 丷 丷 **harmonious crossing**

CMP There's something especially peaceful and graceful about this arrangement when these curves are well drawn.

1794 义 义 **justice, righteousness**

■ harmonious crossing 1793 ⊔ dab 169   yì

BF In three well-placed strokes, you see someone rejoicing—hands raised in thanksgiving to heaven—as **justice** triumphs over corruption and intolerance.

[3 STROKES   RANK 208]

1795 仪 仪 **rites**

■ man r 953   ■ justice, righteousness 1794   yí

BF There is an ancient trend among *men* and women: after achieving a *just* victory, they display the urge to commemorate this occasion with special religious **rites**.

[5 STROKES   RANK 1283]

1796 又 又 **hand, also**

□ one 2   ■ harmonious crossing 1793   yòu

This pictograph of a right **hand** (see the thumb and index finger pinch together on the left?) represents the **hand** which, for most people, is the most, uh, dexterous. The symbol for *harmony*, which resembles *one* closed fist, reinforces the concept of dexterity.

What's the connection with **also**? Your right hand is so accomplished that you can easily perform a sequence of actions with barely a break in between. Not only can you do *one* thing, but **also** the second, and **also** the third, and so on.

[2 STROKES   RANK 126]

1797 对 对 **correct, right**   ☐ hand, also 1796   ☐ inch 210   duì

The *hand* we see belongs to a skilled draftsman, measuring each wall opening and fixture on the blueprint to the last fraction of an *inch*. If he does his job job **correctly** the house will stand forever.   [5 STROKES   RANK 33]

1798 友 友 **friend, associate**   ☐ moving hand 1635   ☐ hand, also 1796   yǒ

BF *Hands*, one supporting the other, is a charming visualization of the nature of **friend**ship.   [4 STROKES   RANK 594]

1799 发 发 **send out, deliver**   ■ friend, associate 1798   ☐ eight 1048   fā

You need to **deliver** your message to the world. *Eight friends* volunteer to be your emissaries.   [5 STROKES   RANK 47]

1800 取 取 **take, get, obtain**   ☐ ear 82   ☐ hand, also 1796   qǔ

I **take** your *ear* with my *hand* and pull hard to **get** you to do what I want.   [8 STROKES   RANK 323]

1801 最 最 **most, -est**   ☐ day, sun 63   ■ take, get, obtain 1800   zu

You're a greedy son of a gun. You always want the **most** of anything. Wherever the *sun* shines, you seem to feel that anything there is yours for the *taking*.   [12 STROKES   RANK 139]

1802 娶 娶 **take a wife**   ☐ take, get, obtain 1800   ■ woman 581   qǔ

In the very unlamented old days, a man **takes a wife** by, uh, *taking* a *woman*.   [11 STROKES   RANK 2494]

1803 议 议 **confer, discuss**   ☐ speech r 615   ☐ justice, righteousness 1794   yì

How do you determine a *just* system of government? Many *speeches* on the subject of *justice* contribute to **conferences** and **discussions** on that subject.   [5 STROKES   RANK 368]

1804 文 文 **language, culture**

■ justice, righteousness 1794 (altered)   ▢ one 2   wén

BF *One* system of *justice* prevails over a society united by *one* **language** and **culture**.   [4 STROKES   RANK 148]

1805 刘 刘 **kill, massacre**   ▌ language, culture 1804   ▐ knife r 166   liú

Using a *knife* or other serious weapon on many members of a *culture* sounds like a genocidal **massacre** to me.   [6 STROKES   RANK 751]

1806 齐 齐 **to make even**   ▢ language, culture 1804   ▬ dancing girl 1696   qí

Let's watch the *dancing girl* for a bit. Hands *crossed in front* of her, the horizontal stroke represents her shoulders, which must be **kept even** as she dances.   [6 STROKES   RANK 1063]

1807 挤 挤 **crowd, jostle**   ▐ hand r 29   ▐ to make even 1806   jǐ

A malicious *hand* approaches the poor waiter carrying the tray of snacks *on an even keel* so they don't fall. Why does he **jostle** the waiter so?
                                    [9 STROKES   RANK 1661]

1808 济 济 **cross a river**   ▐ water r 523   ▐ to make even 1806   jì

BF Imagine having to carry stuff on your head and shoulders carefully to get it **across the river** safe, sound, and dry. In the *water*, the main thing is *to keep* everything *even*, so nothing falls.   [9 STROKES   RANK 360]

1809 纹 纹 **vein, grain**   ▐ silk r 807   ▐ language, culture 1804   wén

Two of the great hallmarks of civilization are clothes and *language*. The *silken* embroidery threads which decorate fine clothing and the patterns of written *language* suggest the patterns formed by **veins** of minerals in stone or the swirls in wood **grain**.   [7 STROKES   RANK 1768]

1810 艮 艮   tough, hard to chew

◻ eye 78 (altered)   ◼ harmonious crossing 1793 (altered)   gè

You've just bitten something that's *very* **hard to chew**. It's so **tough** that you scrunch up your *eye* with the effort of biting down (explaining the altered '*eye*'). There's no *harmony* here, which further explains the chopped up *harmonious crossing*.   [6 STROKES   RANK 4564]

1811 很 很   very

◻ left step 1034   ◻ tough, hard to chew 1810   hě

That guy over there is the one they make jokes about—it's **very** *hard* for him to *chew* gum and *walk* at the same time!   [9 STROKES   RANK 138]

1812 父 父   father

◻ eight 1048   ◼ harmonious crossing 1793   fù

In theory, when a **father** does his job properly, the family experiences an *abundance* of *harmony*. But all too often, children and spouses ignore or flout his sage advice, resulting in plenty of tears for the besieged **father**. Here the dual dabs of '*eight*' resemble the tears of bitterness that **fathers** can experience bringing their children to adulthood.   [4 STROKES   RANK 589]

1813 爷 爷   grandpa

◻ father 1812   ◼ guard, protect 113 (altered)   yé

BF A **grandfather** is like a *father* with additional emphasis on *protection*. If you compare this '*protection*' with §113, you'll notice that it's missing its base. **Grandfathers** have to *protect* and defend more than one household, and they have no single home base.   [6 STROKES   RANK 1007]

1814 交 交   meet, intersect

◻ six 1062   ◼ harmonious crossing 1793   jiā

A **meeting place** is where *roads cross*. Let's meet for drinks after work, at *six*.   [6 STROKES   RANK 320]

1815 咬 咬   bite, nip

◻ mouth 41   ◻ meet, intersect 1814   yǎ

When the horizontal parts of your *mouth intersect* with something in between, that's a **bite**.   [9 STROKES   RANK 1658]

1816 较 较 **comparatively** ◧ car 1430 ◨ meet, intersect 1814 jiào

Classic *cars* and their owners gather at *meets* to rate each other **comparatively**. [10 STROKES RANK 491]

1817 校 校 **school** ◧ tree 375 ◨ meet, intersect 1814 xiào

BF **Schools** must have been one of the most important structures in the ancient Chinese world. In those days, a large interior space was created by leaning tall *trees* together across each side of the schoolhouse. These trees *intersected* and supported each other. [10 STROKES RANK 633]

1818 艾 艾 **to end, stop** ⬒ grass r 94 ⬓ harmonious crossing 1793 ài

You can **stop** the flow of water, *harmoniously* gurgling through the *crossed* pipes, by damming the drain with a wad of *grass*. [5 STROKES RANK 1291]

Unit 74

Quaint Histories

1819 哎 哎 hey!   ▮ mouth 41   ▮ to end, stop 1818   āi

Hey, look at that guy! By plugging his lips into the hole in the dike, he used his *mouth* to *stop* the leak.   [8 STROKES   RANK 2294]

1820 杀 杀 kill   ▬ harmonious crossing 1793   ▬ few, little 1475   ▬ one 2   s

To me, this character represents a view of *one* dead person's face, the face of someone who's been **killed**. The *harmonious cross* represents the closed eyes of the victim, the hooked vertical is the nose, and the other dabs look like creases in his face.   [6 STROKES   RANK 587]

1821 刹 刹 to brake a car   ▮ kill 1820   ▮ knife r 166   s

Metaphorically speaking, *killing* the motion of a *car* is the application of the *knife* edges of the **brake** mechanism.   [8 STROKES   RANK 2249]

1822 赵 赵 kingdom of Zhao   ▬ to walk 421   ▮ harmonious crossing 1793   z

The ancient **kingdom of Zhao** was one of the so-called Warring States that flourished 2200 years ago. As a result of its military prowess, it was possible for people *to walk* around in *harmony* with no fear of personal danger.   [9 STROKES   RANK 1169]

1823 希 希 hope

▭ harmonious crossing 1793   ▬ moving hand 1635   ▬ towel 130   x

Moving hands harmoniously crossed in supplication, covered by a special, embroidered *towel*—thus begins the ceremony of **hope**.   [7 STROKES   RANK 508]

1824 稀 稀 **sparse**   ▣ rice or grain 409   ▢ hope 1823   xī

Too much *hope* at the conclusion of the *grain* harvest means the harvest was too **sparse** for everyone's well-being.   [12 STROKES   RANK 1788]

1825 冈 冈 **mountain ridge**   ▰ borders 127   ▣ harmonious crossing 1793   gāng

BF We're looking down at a topographical map. Within the *borders* of the region are *crossed* strokes representing the spines of intersecting **mountain ridges**.   [4 STROKES   RANK 2047]

1826 刚 刚 **hard, firm, strong**   ▣ mountain ridge 1825   ▢ knife r 166   gāng

The minerals and the topsoil of the *mountain ridge* are so **firm** and **hard** that we need a *knife* of some sort to dig through it.   [6 STROKES   RANK 621]

1827 纲 纲 **guiding principle**   ▣ silk r 807   ▢ mountain ridge 1825   gāng

Guiding principles were so important in traditional Chinese culture, that here we see two visual references to it. First of all is the *silken* thread which guides us and pulls us in the proper direction. Next are the *mountain ridges* which serve as paths for our intrepid traveler. One false step, and it's curtains!   [7 STROKES   RANK 1934]

1828 网 网 **net**   ▰ borders 127   ▣ harmonious crossing (times 2) 1793   wǎng

BF Within *borders* there are plenty of *crisscrossing* strands. That's the design of an old-fashioned fishing **net**.

It's possible to confuse the meanings of 冈 'mountain ridge' and 网 'net'. Even though the ridge is bigger, the net is a more complicated structure, and that's why 网 is visually more complex than 冈.   [6 STROKES   RANK 605]

1829 区 区 **administrative division**

                           ▣ basket, box 152   ▣ harmonious crossing 1793   qū

BF The purpose of dividing a large country like China into a variety of **administrative districts** is to establish and maintain *harmony* within the *box*-like borders of the region.   [4 STROKES   RANK 265]

1830 驱 驱 drive (carriage, horse)

■ horse 878   ▣ administrative division 1829   q'

BF To get to the *division* headquarters, I must **drive** my *horse*.

[7 STROKES   RANK 1511]

1831 凶 凶 fiendish, ferocious

■ receptacle 155   ▣ harmonious crossing 1793   x

Like Pandora's box, this *receptacle* is open to the sky, and we see the how all the buoyant forces of *harmony* seems to be rising and escaping. What's left? In the absence of harmony, **fiendishness** and **ferocity** thrive.

[4 STROKES   RANK 1378]

Here are three characters whose meanings may blend together in a student's mind. How can we distinguish between 冈, 区, and 凶 ('mountain ridge', 'administrative division', and 'fiendish')? All three contain a cross within an open square.

The open part of the square suggests a means of escape for the character meaning. Mountain ridges are so heavy, they fall out the bottom. Ferocity is a boiling hot emotion, and the steam rises out the top. To flee a fiendish administrator, you flee to another district, alongside the old one.

1832 恼 恼 get mad

■ heart (skinny) 930   ▣ cover 268   ■ fiendish, ferocious 1831   n.

Sometimes things don't go your way. Here's one poor soul, whose *heart* is swollen in agitation. He's trying to keep a *cover* on the feelings of *ferocity* that threaten to overcome him. In short, he's **getting mad**.

[9 STROKES   RANK 1704]

1833 丈 丈 male elder relative

▢ ten 6 (altered)   ■ harmonious crossing 1793 (altered)   z

BF '*Ten*' is an allusion to a high number or quantity. Here, it is a polite way to refer significant age. So, a *harmony* plus *ten* suggests the respect due to an **older male relative**.

[3 STROKES   RANK 1242]

1834 仗 仗 **battle** ⬛ man r 953 ⬜ male elder relative 1833 zhàng

BF You see *two men,* but that's all that would fit in the character. They symbolize a larger group of men that stand together, egging each other on, anticipating victory, as they prepare for **battle.** [5 STROKES RANK 1712]

1835 史 史 **history** ⬛ harmonious crossing 1793 (altered) ⬜ middle 45 (altered) shǐ

BF The *Middle* Kingdom (China) brought and maintained *harmony* in the Far East. That's the region's **history** in a nutshell. [5 STROKES RANK 456]

1836 吏 吏 **minor official** ⬛ history 1835 ⬜ one 2 lì

BF **Minor officials** are the ones adding to the *historical* record, using their pens (which look like *'ones'*) to write stuff for future historians.

[6 STROKES RANK 2311]

1837 使 使 **have sb do sth** ⬛ man r 953 ⬜ minor official 1836 shǐ

Minor officials are minor because almost any other *person* can come in to their office and **have them do something for them.** [8 STROKES RANK 119]

1838 更 更 **even more** ⬛ history 1835 ⬜ two 3 gèng

History has *twice* as many surprises as I expected. It's **even more** interesting than I thought! [7 STROKES RANK 221]

1839 便 便 **cheap** ⬛ man r 953 ⬜ even more 1838 pián

BF If stuff is **cheap,** then a *man* can buy *even more* of it! [9 STROKES RANK 271]

1840 硬 硬 **hard, stiff** ⬛ stone, rock 1386 ⬜ even more 1838 yìng

Consider a medium-sized *rock.* It's hard to imagine anything *even more* **stiff** or **hard,** but if you could, this character would describe it.

[12 STROKES RANK 1170]

1841 鞭 鞭 a whip ▮ animal hide 101 ▯ cheap 1839 b▸

A **whip** only uses a thin strip of *animal hide*, so it's *cheap*.

[18 STROKES   RANK 2250]

1842 皮 皮 leather, skin ▮ cliff r 671 ▯ scepter 5 ▪ hand, also 1796 p▸

Here's how to prepare the hide of an animal as **leather**. Carefully hang it over a *cliff* and use one *hand* to anchor it. Beat it with a *big stick* in your other *hand* to make it soft and supple.   [5 STROKES   RANK 741]

1843 皱 皱 wrinkle ▮ hay for fodder 462 ▮ leather, skin 1842 z▸

The older you get, the more **wrinkles** you display, and the more you are apt to attempt crackpot diets. My 'favorite' is the *hay* diet for smoother *skin*.

[10 STROKES   RANK 1954]

1844 被 被 quilt, passive marker ▮ clothing r 838 ▮ leather, skin 1842 b▸

BF You use bits of old *clothing* and scraps of *leather* to create a **quilt**.

This character is most commonly encountered with the passive meaning 'by' (as in, the dog was bitten *by* the boy).   [10 STROKES   RANK 154]

Unit 75

Dance of Death

845 贤 贤 **worthy, virtuous**

◧ subject of a ruler 17 (altered)　◧ hand, also 1796　▬ cowrie 430　xián

BF Only the truly **worthy** *subjects of the king* could *handle* the king's *money*. ('*Subject*' 臣 is greatly altered so it will fit into the small space allotted to it.)　[8 STROKES　RANK 1943]

846 痕 痕 **mark, trace**　◧ sick 697　◧ tough, hard to chew 1810　hén

BF Recently, I was dreadfully *sick* and in the hospital. I recuperated—I guess—but the hospital food didn't help. It was *tough* and *hard to chew*. I still bear the **marks** of my illness.　[11 STROKES　RANK 1938]

847 函 函 **case, casket**　◧ le 1399　▬ fiendish, ferocious 1831 (altered)　hán

BF The *ferocious* bandit and his gang terrified the locals for decades. What a *change*, now that he's in his **casket** and planted safely in the ground.

[8 STROKES　RANK 1950]

848 爵 爵 **nobility**

◧ hands raised high 1345　◧ net r 107　◧ tough, hard to chew 1810 (altered)　◧ inch 210　jué

BF These banquets of **nobility** are no fun. The meat is *tough* and they measure their weak wine by the *inch*. *Hands* are constantly *raised high* in toast to the king, but the protocol is so fixed that guests feel like they are trapped in *nets*.　[17 STROKES　RANK 1925]

1849 辰 辰 time, day, occasion

◰ cliff r 671   ◼ tough, hard to chew 1810 (altered)   C

An old-**time** procedure to improve the taste of food was to take *tough* meat and toss it over a *cliff* to tenderize it. It was always a memorable **occasion** when the tribal elders decided to employ this method.

[7 STROKES   RANK 2317]

1850 晨 晨 **morning, daybreak**   ▢ day, sun 63   ◼ time, day, occasion 1849   C

BF The *time of day* when you can see the *sun* peaking over the horizon marks the onset of **daybreak**.

[11 STROKES   RANK 1388]

1851 辱 辱 **disgrace, insult**   ◰ time, day, occasion 1849   ◼ inch 210   r

BF In ancient China, you could measure prestige by the amount of seating room allotted to you at special *occasions*. A minister given only an *inch* could mark this as a special sign of **insult** and **disgrace**, and he knew for sure his days in power were numbered.

[10 STROKES   RANK 1907]

1852 唇 唇 lip   ◼ time, day, occasion 1849 (altered)   ▣ mouth 41   C

BF Her **lips** were trembling on that special *occasion* when I proposed marriage. Her *mouth* opened in surprised pleasure—or was it amused contempt? (It was hard to tell!).

[10 STROKES   RANK 1880]

1853 坚 坚 **hard, solid**

◼ subject of a ruler 17 (altered)   ▢ hand, also 1796   ◼ earth, soil 9   j

BF Bowing down, the loyal *subject* supports himself with his *hands* on the *earth* knowing that the surface will be **hard** and **solid**.   [7 STROKES   RANK 748]

1854 紧 紧 tight, taut

◼ subject of a ruler 17 (altered)   ▢ hand, also 1796   ◼ silk 206 (altered)   j

The *king's* loyal *subject* is helping out today in the *silk* factories. Using his *hands*, he's helping spin the *silk* thread by holding the strands **taut** and **tight**.

[10 STROKES   RANK 560]

1855 及　及　**and, in, on**　　■ man 311　◩ hand, also 1796　◪ extra stuff　jí

The '*extra stuff*' in the character is like a link binding a *hand* to *someone else*, combining two *people*, that is, one *person* **and** another. We use this component to represent multiple positions.　　[3 STROKES　RANK 198]

1856 度　度　**degree, other small unit**

□ shelter r 681　◪ horned animal 100　◪ hand, also 1796　dù

The new *bull* needs some serious taming before we can bring him inside the *shelter*. By **degrees**, under my *hand*, he starts behaving like a member of the family!　　[9 STROKES　RANK 184]

1857 渡　渡　**cross water, ferry across**

□ water r 523　◪ degree, other small unit 1856　dù

The river—creek, actually—is pretty narrow. I could **cross it** by swimming if the *water* wasn't so cold (not many *degrees*).　　[12 STROKES　RANK 1406]

1858 拨　拨　**poke, stir, turn**　　◪ hand r 29　□ send out, deliver 1799　bō

Actions like **stirring, poking, turning**, and so forth are *hand* motions that have been *sent out* for a purpose.　　[8 STROKES　RANK 1807]

1859 吸　吸　**absorb, suck up**　　□ mouth 41　◪ and, in, on 1855　xī

To use your *mouth* to **suck up** the coffee that spilled, you'll need to place your lips in *many different positions*.　　[6 STROKES　RANK 924]

1860 级　级　**level, rank, grade**　　◪ silk r 807　◪ and, in, on 1855　jí

Customers demand quality when they buy *silk*—after all, they're paying a lot of money for it. Early on, it became important to sort *silks* by means of a standard **grading** system. Merchants show off the sorted *silks* in *many different places* in the store so they don't get mixed up.　　[6 STROKES　RANK 415]

1861 极 极 **extremely, extremity**   ∎ tree 375   ⊔ and, in, on 1855   jí

BF That tall *tree* is perfect for the municipal Christmas *tree—*it's **extremely** tall. We intensify its festive nature by placing ornaments *in many different positions.*   [7 STROKES   RANK 363]

1862 报 报 newspaper

∎ hand r 29   ⊔⊓ single ear 157   ∎ hand, also 1796   b

Disregard the meaning of the *'single ear'*. What you see are *two hands* doing their best to support the unruly sheets of paper that comprise a full-sized **newspaper**. See how the paper towers above the *hands* and threatens to fall over the right *hand.*   [7 STROKES   RANK 234]

1863 反 反 **oppose, anti-**   ⌐ cliff r 671   ∎ hand, also 1796   fǎ

Your punishment for **opposing** the rebel army: you hang over the *cliff* by your *hands* until you either fall or manage to pull yourself up.

[4 STROKES   RANK 237]

1864 版 版 edition, newspaper page

∎ slice, flake 1485   ⊔ oppose, anti- 1863   b

Stories on a **newspaper page** provide *slices* of life in *opposition* to our own. But since bad news sells better than good news, most stories emphasize tragedy and stories of *opposition.*   [8 STROKES   RANK 810]

1865 变 变 transform, change into

∎ trade, industry 1117 (altered)   ∎ hand, also 1796   b

The *hand* of a strong executive or CEO can totally **transform** an *industry*. The *industry* here has been turned upside-down.   [8 STROKES   RANK 225]

1866 受 受   **receive**

☐ hands raised high 1345   ▤ smooth cover 280   ▬ hand, also 1796   **shòu**

The bottom-most *hand* belongs to the university president bestowing diplomas on graduation day. The body of students with *hands raised high* can't wait to **receive** their diplomas, each in a protective *smooth cover.*

[8 STROKES   RANK 238]

1867 授 授   **instruct, teach**   ▮ hand r 29   ▯ receive 1866   **shòu**

BF Effective **teachers** use *hand* motions and gestures to ensure the students *receive* their **instruction.**   [11 STROKES   RANK 968]

1868 服 服   **clothes, garment**

▮ moon, month 1719   ▯ single ear 157   ▯ hand, also 1796   **fú**

Think of a macabre Halloween costume as the **garment** we see here. The Demon Barber has slabs of *meat* and body parts like *ears* and *hands* dangling from his torso.   [8 STROKES   RANK 365]

1869 权 权   **right, power, authority**   ▮ tree 375   ▯ hand, also 1796   **quán**

I know this *tree* is on your land, but I can approach it and put my *hand* on it because I have special **authority.**   [6 STROKES   RANK 297]

1870 难 难   **difficult, hard**   ▮ hand, also 1796   ▯ short-tailed bird 992   **nán**

Ever try to use your *hand* to catch a *bird?* Don't bother—it's very **hard** to do.   [10 STROKES   RANK 295]

Unit 76

Sharper than a Serpent's Tooth

1871 眼　眼　**eye, aperture**　　　🔲 eye 78　🔲 tough, hard to chew 1810　y

When we get a cinder in our **eye**, it's pretty painful, but think how things are for giants. Instead of cinders, they get *eye*-shaped almonds, *tough* as nails, that float on their **eye**balls, making life temporarily unbearable for them.　　　[11 STROKES　RANK 281]

1872 卽　即　**approach, be near**

🔲 tough, hard to chew 1810 (altered)　🔲 single ear 157　jí

I was tired of the *tough, hard to chew* food that my evil stepmother kept feeding me. One day, I **approached** her as I could and spit a mouthful at her. I hit her in the *ear*. I thought she would kill me.　　　[7 STROKES　RANK 293]

1873 艮　良　**good, fine**　　　🔲 dab 169　🔲 tough, hard to chew 1810　li

BF Imagine you're a prisoner in some third-world dictatorship. Everything they feed you is *tough* and *hard to chew*. But on the ruler's birthday, the meat is a *little bit* better quality. By comparison with the normal fare, how **fine** it seems!　　　[7 STROKES　RANK 835]

1874 郎　郎　**young man**　　　🔲 good, fine 1873 (altered)　🔲 town 745　lá

Bustling *towns* and big cities attract **young men** because they are *fine* places to live with lots to do and many other young people to meet.

[8 STROKES　RANK 1457]

875 狼　狼　wolf　　　■ dog r 898　■ good, fine 1873　　láng

Dogs and **wolves** are clearly close relatives. Somehow, although wild *dogs* always seem somewhat mangy, **wolves** always seem to retain their natural grace, majesty, and *fineness*.　　　　　　　[10 STROKES　RANK 1708]

876 限　限　set a limit, restrict　　■ hills 735　■ tough, hard to chew 1810　　xiàn

Well-trained soldiers can do anything, but there are **restrictions**. For example, the rocky *hills* limit the distance they can march, and the *toughness* of their rations limits their energy and stamina.　　　　[8 STROKES　RANK 613]

877 狠　狠　ruthless, relentless　　■ dog r 898　■ tough, hard to chew 1810　　hěn

I've never seen a *dog* too full to go after food. No matter how *tough* the piece of meat might be, the *dog* is **relentless**, and never lets go.

[9 STROKES　RANK 1654]

878 恨　恨　hate　　　■ heart (skinny) 930　■ tough, hard to chew 1810　　hèn

Hatred is a *tough* and all-consuming *emotion*.　[9 STROKES　RANK 1295]

879 根　根　plant roots　　■ tree 375　■ tough, hard to chew 1810　　gēn

No part of an ornamental tree makes good eating, but in times of famine you do the best you can. Moreover, no part of a *tree* is chewable, but the **plant roots** of the *tree* are *tough*, but chewable.　　[10 STROKES　RANK 352]

880 跟　跟　with, follow　　■ foot r 946　■ tough, hard to chew 1810　　gēn

Somehow the soldier got a *tough* nut in his boot, lodged against a sensitive part of his *foot*, but the pace of marching is too swift for him to stop and remove it. The painful nut travels **with** him for the duration of the maneuvers.

[13 STROKES　RANK 541]

881 银　银　silver　　　■ gold r 1327　■ tough, hard to chew 1810　　yín

Gold has the reputation for being a soft, malleable metal. If you want a *tougher* precious metal, you'll need to invest in **silver**.

[11 STROKES　RANK 757]

1882 既 既 already, then

■ tough, hard to chew 1810 (altered)   ■ un-, -less 1642 (altered)   j

Un-less I get help soon, that *tough* piece of food I recklessly ate has **already** made me deathly ill.   [9 STROKES   RANK 724]

1883 观 观 look at, watch, observe

■ hand, also 1796   ■ see 301   ₤

BF If you hold that exquisitely carved statuette in your *hand*, you can *also see* it close up, and better **observe** all its superior qualities.   [6 STROKES   RANK 334]

1884 支 支 prop up, support

■ ten 6   ■ hand, also 1796   ₂

Someone's *hand* is balancing the *ten*-pound weight, trying to **support** it.   [4 STROKES   RANK 437]

1885 技 技 skill, ability

■ hand r 29   ■ prop up, support 1884   j

BF The juggler uses his *hand* to *support* several balls in the air at once. What **skill**!   [7 STROKES   RANK 422]

1886 枝 枝 branch of tree

■ tree 375   ■ prop up, support 1884   ₂

Trees support their **branches**.   [8 STROKES   RANK 1491]

1887 鼓 鼓 drum, rouse

■ ten 6   ■ bean 1168   ■ prop up, support 1884   ₤

I just managed to *prop up ten beans* on the window sill. Suddenly, a mighty clap of sound rent the air, scattering the beans to kingdom come. Someone had just beat their **drum** as loud as they could.   [13 STROKES   RANK 1123]

1888 仅 仅 barely, merely

■ man r 953   ■ hand, also 1796   j

Think back to ancient days. Without the use of machines, relying only on the power provided by *hands* and feet, *men* and women could **barely** survive.   [4 STROKES   RANK 494]

889 双   双   **pair, both, dual**   ▌▌ hand, also (times 2) 1796   **shuāng**

To do most things well, use **both** *hands*.   [4 STROKES   RANK 581]

890 祭   祭   **offer sacrifice**

         ▄ meat 317 (altered)   ▄ hand, also 1796 (altered)   ▄ show, indicate 1064   **jì**

Priests **offer sacrifice** to their gods in a ritualized ceremony. They place a slab of *meat* on the altar using their *hands*, hoping that patterns in the burns will *show* them hidden knowledge.   [11 STROKES   RANK 1782]

891 察   察   **inspect, scrutinize**   ▢ roof 247   ▄ offer sacrifice 1890   **chá**

BF Better bring the *sacrificial offering* in from the sun, under the *roof* of the temple so the priest can carefully **scrutinize** it away from prying eyes.

         [14 STROKES   RANK 564]

892 擦   擦   **rub, scrape**   ▌ hand r 29   ▄ inspect, scrutinize 1891   **cā**

The priest uses his *hand* on the burnt offering to *scrutinize* it and **scrape** or **rub** away some of the soot to see what messages have been sent to him from heaven.   [17 STROKES   RANK 1761]

893 坡   坡   **slope, plain**   ▌ earth, soil 9   ▄ leather, skin 1842   **pō**

The *ground* is covered by a large sheet of *leather*. Because of natural imperfections in the *leather* and in the *soil*, it's not exactly straight and level—it's **sloped**.   [8 STROKES   RANK 1550]

894 玻   玻   **glass**   ▌ king 11   ▄ leather, skin 1842   **bō**

BF In olden days, windows and containers of the peasantry were made of *animal skins*. Finally, they invented **glass**, quite expensively at first, which performed the same services for the *king*.   [9 STROKES   RANK 1769]

895 波   波   **wave, ripple of water**   ▌ water r 523   ▄ leather, skin 1842   **bō**

BF They wash the old *leather* cape by beating it in the *water*. They beat it with such energy as to create huge **waves** and **ripples**.   [8 STROKES   RANK 664]

1896 婆　婆　old woman, matron, mother-in-law

▢ wave, ripple of water 1895　▮ woman 581　p

BF Who's the *woman* so good at *making waves* in my house? Why, it's my mother-in-law, who else!?　　　　　　[11 STROKES   RANK 1347]

Unit 77

Categorical Imperatives

897 疲 疲 **tired, weary** ☐ sick 697 ☐ leather, skin 1842   pí
BF The old doctor has had it with patients! He is so **weary** of treating *sick* and *leathery* people who never stop complaining and are slow to pay their bills.   [10 STROKES RANK 1778]

898 彼 彼 **other party, that, those**
            ☐ left step 1034 ☐ leather, skin 1842   bǐ
I hate dancing at parties. My *left foot* somehow always lands on the *leather* shoe of my partner's foot. After awhile, no **other party** will dance with me. As a result, I need to leave and find some **other party** to have fun at.   [8 STROKES RANK 1256]

899 颇 颇 **slanting, tilting** ☐ leather, skin 1842 ☐ page, leaf 444   pō
BF Look at the old boxer. The *back of his head* is tough and *leathery*, so stiff that he can't raise his head fully. The back of his neck is always **slanting**.
       [11 STROKES RANK 1560]

900 破 破 **broken, damaged** ☐ stone, rock 1386 ☐ leather, skin 1842   pò
The giant alligator swallowed a giant *stone* at some point. When trappers caught him, killed him, and skinned him, the dried *skin* could no longer support the *rock*, which burst through and **damaged** the *skin*.
       [10 STROKES RANK 604]

1901 夜 夜 night, evening

◻ cover 268 ◼ man r 953 ◰ evening 479 ◼ harmonious crossing 1793

What can a *man* do under *cover* of *night*? *Harmonious*, peaceful things actually, **night**time and sleepy time things.   [8 STROKES   RANK 665]

1902 脑 脑 brain

◼ meat 317 (altered) ◻ cover 268 ◼ fiendish, ferocious 1831

The **brain** is the *body part* where, according to shrinks everywhere, lie everybody's most *fiendish* and *ferocious* thoughts. We learn to *cover* all this ugliness or else no one could ever live with anyone else.   [10 STROKES   RANK 646]

1903 假 假 fake, phony, false

◼ man r 953 ◼ two 3 ◼ leather, skin 1842 (altered)

A *man* wearing a *second skin* is a powerful metaphor for **falseness**.   [11 STROKES   RANK 636]

1904 急 急 impatient, anxious

◻ and, in, on 1855 (altered) ◼ heart (fat) 906

BF *Too much stuff going on* engenders *emotions* in sensitive people, typically those of **impatience** and **anxiety**.   [9 STROKES   RANK 657]

1905 食 食 eat*

◼ man 311 ◼ good, fine 1873

Putting something *good* and *fine* within a *person* is the same as giving them something to **eat**.   [9 STROKES   RANK 671]

1906 汉 汉 ethnic Chinese

◼ water r 523 ◼ hand, also 1796

BF Historians are now confident that extensive systems of *water* connections and *manual* dexterity are key to the development of any civilization, especially the **ethnic Chinese**.   [5 STROKES   RANK 711]

1907 树 树 tree*

◻ tree 375 ◼ correct, right 1797

It's *correct* to think of a *tree* as a **tree**.   [9 STROKES   RANK 697]

1908 欢 欢　**happy, pleased**　▣ hand, also 1796　▢ owe, lack 465　huān
BF I use my *hand* to finally pay off the loan I *owe*. I don't know who's **happier**—me, for getting the monkey off my back, or my pal, who gets his money back.　[6 STROKES　RANK 685]

1909 怪 怪　**surprising, strange**
　　　　　　　▢ heart (skinny) 930　▣ hand, also 1796　▣ earth, soil 9　guài
Hearts and *hands* are raining down on the *earth*. Whoa, how **strange!**
　　　　　　　　　　　　　　　　　[8 STROKES　RANK 775]

1910 概 概　**approximate, general**　▢ tree 375　▣ already, then 1882　gài
BF The *tree already* fell on the forest ranger when I got there. I was **approximately** two minutes too late!　[13 STROKES　RANK 791]

1911 释 释　**set free, explain**
　　　　　　　▣ distinguish, differentiate 1322　▢ hand, also 1796　▢ earth, soil 9 (altered)　shì
BF The police have rounded up a crowd of troublemakers. Who of them should we **set free**? We *distinguish* the innocent from the guilty in an odd way, which seems to work somehow. The ones with their *hands* on the *earth* are so bewildered that they must be innocent.　[12 STROKES　RANK 813]

1912 曼 曼　**handsome, graceful**　▭ brave 79 (altered)　▬ hand, also 1796　màn
BF The *brave* soldier, demonstrating perfect fighting skills with his *hands*, impressed us as being very **handsome** and **graceful**.　[11 STROKES　RANK 1224]

1913 漫 漫　**brim over, overflow**
　　　　　　　▣ water r 523　▢ handsome, graceful 1912　màn
He *gracefully* lowered his hand into the tub of *water*, but no matter how *graceful*, it still made the tub **overflow**.　[14 STROKES　RANK 1455]

1914 慢 慢 slow   ■ heart (skinny) 930   ■ handsome, graceful 1912   n
Handsome men usually made her *heart* beat fast, but this guy was so rude, selfish, and ignorant, that he actually made her *heart* **slow** down.

[14 STROKES   RANK 822]

1915 欧 欧 Europe   ■ administrative division 1829   ■ owe, lack 465   ō
Europe, a bunch of *administrative divisions* formerly called countries, *lack* so many skills and resources that each can't make it on its own.

[8 STROKES   RANK 823]

1916 娘 娘 mum, mother   ■ woman 581   ■ good, fine 1873   n
My **mother** was the *best woman* that ever lived.   [10 STROKES   RANK 881]

1917 板 板 board, plank   ■ tree 375   ■ oppose, anti- 1863   b
You cut **planks** from a *tree*. You use the *planks* of a political platform to *oppose* the money-grubbing incumbent.   [8 STROKES   RANK 930]

1918 叔 叔 uncle   ■ on 175   ■ small 1063   ■ hand, also 1796   sh
When I was *small*, I used to climb *on* top of my **uncle**. What fun—and he *also* enjoyed it.   [8 STROKES   RANK 1422]

1919 督 督 supervise   ■ uncle 1918   ■ eye 78   d
BF My *uncle* entered the family business many years ago, and did well despite family ties. He stood eagle-*eyed* in the factory, **supervising** all aspects of the operation.   [13 STROKES   RANK 946]

1920 择 择 choose*, select*
    ■ hand r 29   ■ hand, also 1796   ■ earth, soil 9 (altered)   zé
BF All kinds of good stuff gets scattered on the *soil.* **Selectively**, I use *both hands* to pick up the best garbage from the *earth*.   [8 STROKES   RANK 961]

921 译 译 translate, interpret

■ speech r 615   ◩ hand, also 1796   ◪ earth, soil 9 (altered)   yì

I opened my mouth to *speak*, and the hostile strangers used their *hands* to
throw *soil* at me. You don't need an **interpreter** to figure their intentions.

[7 STROKES   RANK 1198]

922 泽 泽 marsh

☐ water r 523   ◩ hand, also 1796   ◪ earth, soil 9 (altered)   zé

BF This godforsaken **marsh** is a slimy mixture of *water* and *soil*. It's not made
for humans—my limbs are not very *handy*.   [8 STROKES   RANK 951]

Unit 78

Shadowy Realms

1923 圣 圣 **sage, saint**   ▢ hand, also 1796   ■ earth, soil 9

BF The **sage** man, *arms* crossed in front, rises above the *earth* towards heaven, as reward for his **saint**liness.   [5 STROKES   RANK 960]

1924 戏 戏 **drama, play, show**   ▯ hand, also 1796   ▯ halberd 359

The renegade samurai warrior is stealing the **show**. That's because he's the one with the *sword* in his *hand*, and no one wants to make him angry.   [6 STROKES   RANK 1033]

1925 隐 隐 **conceal, hide, latent**   ▯ hills 735   ■ impatient, anxious 1904

BF Blackbeard the Pirate is *anxious* to get back to the *hills*, for that's where his buried treasure lies **hidden**.   [11 STROKES   RANK 1034]

1926 稳 稳 **settled, steady, stable**

   ■ rice or grain 409   ■ impatient, anxious 1904

Careful—the cup of *rice* is filled to the top. If you are *anxious* or *impatient* while carrying, you won't hold it **steady**, and the *rice* will get all over the floor.   [14 STROKES   RANK 1055]

1927 趣 趣 **interesting, to interest**

   ■ to walk 421   ■ take, get, obtain 1800

BF That new item in the store window **interests** me quite a lot. I'll do whatever *walking* I have to do to *get* it.   [15 STROKES   RANK 1065]

928 奴　奴　**slave, enslave**　　◼ woman 581　◻ hand, also 1796　nú
BF Men put their *hands* onto *women* to make them **slaves** in traditional and ancient societies.　　　　　　　　[5 STROKES   RANK 1402]

929 努　努　**exert, strive**　　◻ slave, enslave 1928　◼ strength 1492　nǔ
BF Masters exhorted their *slaves* to use their utmost *strength*—to **exert** themselves.　　　　　　　　[7 STROKES   RANK 1081]

930 震　震　**shake, quake**　　◻ rain 85　◼ time, day, occasion 1849　zhèn
It's a memorable *occasion* whenever the *rain* pours down in sheets. Even though it's only *rain*, the earth seems to **shake** from the torrential onslaught.
　　　　　　　　[15 STROKES   RANK 1104]

931 振　振　**rouse, shake, vibrate**
　　　　　◼ hand r 29　◻ time, day, occasion 1849　zhèn
Normally, I was never allowed to disturb my father during his naps. But on this *occasion*, when my mother fell down drunk in front of the neighbors, I used my *hand* to **rouse** him from his sleep.　　[10 STROKES   RANK 1140]

932 缓　缓　**unhurried, delay, postpone**
　　　　◼ silk r 807　◻ receive 1866 (altered)　◼ moving hand 1635　huǎn
With my fancy *silk* duds on, I *receive* every one's honor and praise. Through it all, my *hand moves* slowly and **unhurriedly**, as befits someone as elegant as I.　　　　　　[12 STROKES   RANK 1111]

933 援　援　**help, aid, assist**
　　　　◼ hand r 29　◻ receive 1866 (altered)　◼ moving hand 1635　yuán
BF *Two hands* working together, so the poor victim will *receive* the best possible **aid** and **assistance**.　　　　[12 STROKES   RANK 1197]

1934 暖 暖 **warm, genial**

■ day, sun 63   █ receive 1866 (altered)   ▐ moving hand 1635   I

As I *wave my hand* in the air, it *receives* the beneficial rays of the *sun*. It feels so **warm** and pleasant.   [13 STROKES   RANK 1745]

1935 怒 怒 **become angry, indignant**

▢ slave, enslave 1928   ▬ heart (fat) 906   ▶

The *slave* is **indignant** at having to live as a *slave*.   [9 STROKES   RANK 1143]

1936 浪 浪 **wave, breaker**   ▐ water r 523   █ good, fine 1873   l

Nothing is *finer* than the raw energy of *watery* **breakers** pounding the beach. The structure of **waves** is impossibly complex, in line with the way this character is drawn.   [10 STROKES   RANK 1186]

1937 轰 轰 **bang, boom**   ▢ car 1430   ▬▬ hand, also (times 2) 1796   ▐

The backfire of a *car*. *Two hands* clapping. That's the kind of **booming** or **banging** this character represents.   [8 STROKES   RANK 1264]

1938 朗 朗 **clear*, bright***

█ good, fine 1873   ▐ moon, month 1719 (altered)   l

BF A *perfect moon* makes the evening **clear** and **bright** as day.

[10 STROKES   RANK 1276]

1939 叹 叹 **sigh, exclaim**   █ mouth 41   ▐ hand, also 1796   t

BF I rest my chin—along with my *mouth*—on my *hand* and breathe a great **sigh** of grief.   [5 STROKES   RANK 1299]

1940 粮 粮 **grain, food, provisions**   ▐ rice 1127   ▐ good, fine 1873   l

Rice makes mighty *fine* **provisions**.   [13 STROKES   RANK 1303]

1941 聚 聚 assemble, gather, get together

◻ take, get, obtain 1800 ◼ water 545 (altered) jù

We're all **getting together** on that pretty island in the bay. The friendly boatman *takes* everybody across the *water* to get there.

[14 STROKES   RANK 1306]

1942 叙 叙 talk, chat, narrate

◼ surplus, remainder 1073 ◻ hand, also 1796 xù

Now that work is finished, and we have *surplus* time on our *hands*, we can relax, **chat** a bit, and bring ourselves up to date.   [9 STROKES   RANK 1607]

1943 泛 泛 float, suffused with, non-specific

◻ water r 523 ◼ tired, weary 1897 fàn

BF I exercise in the *water* every day, but today I am just so *tired* that I'll just **float** calmly along instead.   [7 STROKES   RANK 1327]

1944 胸 胸 chest, bosom, thorax

◼ meat 317 (altered) ◪ wrap 636 ◪ fiendish, ferocious 1831 xiōng

Imagine *wrapping* all your *fiendish* inclinations in a piece of *meat*. Put it away in a **chest** and forget about it.   [10 STROKES   RANK 1356]

1945 废 废 useless, superfluous ◻ shelter r 681 ◼ send out, deliver 1799 fèi

BF Siege of Leningrad, winter 1943. We had to *send* him *out* of the *shelter*. He was **superfluous**, not pulling his own weight, threatening death to the rest of us.   [8 STROKES   RANK 1376]

1946 鸡 鸡 chicken ◼ hand, also 1796 ◻ bird 885 jī

Chicken is a *hand*-raised *bird*.   [7 STROKES   RANK 1391]

1947 聂 聂 whisper ◻ ear 82 ◼◼ hand, also (times 2) 1796 niè

I cup my *hands* to my *ears* to better hear what he said—for some reason, he insisted on **whispering**.   [10 STROKES   RANK 2797]

1948 摄 摂 **absorb, assimilate** ▯ hand r 29 ▮ whisper 1947 sł

BF If I *whisper* instead of yelling, the student is more apt to **absorb** what I'm saying. But a whack with my *hand* is the best way of all to keep their attention. [13 STROKES RANK 1403]

Unit 79
Two Up, Three Down

949 液 液 liquid, fluid ▮ water r 523 ▮ night, evening 1901 yè
BF Somehow, during the *night, watery* **liquid**—dew—appears on plants, flowers, and grass. [11 STROKES RANK 1451]

950 餐 餐 eat, meal ▮ eat* 1905 ▯ evil, vicious 657 (altered) ▯ hand, also 1796 cān
BF *Evil things* and wild beasts are subdued by the *hands* of hunters to provide **meals** for city folk. [16 STROKES RANK 1465]

951 拔 拔 uproot, pull out ▮ hand r 29 ▯ send out, deliver 1799 bá
There's a *hand* on the left and *also a hand* (see §1796) on the right. They're both tugging on the *tree- or plant-like thing* between them, trying to **uproot** it. [8 STROKES RANK 1502]

952 驶 驶 sail, (vehicle) moves quickly ▮ horse 878 ▮ history 1835 shǐ
Look at that *horse* go! Wow, it **moves so fast**, it's *history*! [8 STROKES RANK 1520]

953 桑 桑 mulberry tree ▯ hand, also (times 3) 1796 ▬ tree 375 sāng
BF The **mulberry** is a messy *tree*. It's prolific with its berries, many of which drop off and need picking up before they stain walkways. Many *hands* are needed for the harvesting and cleaning. [10 STROKES RANK 1528]

1954 剂 剂 **dose (medical)**   ⬛ to make even 1806   ⬛ knife r 166   j

BF Time to take your **pills**. Unfortunately, each **pill** contains several **doses**. Use a sharp *knife* to carefully cut each **pill** into pieces, and be extra careful to make each piece *even*, or else the **dosage** will vary unacceptably.

[8 STROKES   RANK 1546]

1955 劝 劝 **exhort, urge, persuade**   ⬛ hand, also 1796   ⬛ strength 1492   c

Urgent *hand* movements, coupled with great *strength* of character, endeavor to **persuade** you to buy the new product.   [4 STROKES   RANK 1562]

1956 钢 钢 **steel**   ⬛ gold r 1327   ⬛ mountain ridge 1825   ₈

The early view of **steel** was as a *precious metal* discovered mysteriously near the *ridges of mountains*.   [9 STROKES   RANK 1609]

1957 岗 岗 **mound**   ⬜ mountain 21   ⬛ mountain ridge 1825   ₈

The squished '*mountain*' on top together with '*ridge*' emphasizes the **mound**ness of the resulting character.   [7 STROKES   RANK 1795]

1958 邓 邓 **surname of Deng Xiaoping**

⬛ hand, also 1796   ⬛ town 745   c

Deng Xiaoping is a famous 20-century Chinese leader, through whose influence and abilities *town* economies thrived. The entire country became more active in economic activities, which is what '*hand*' symbolizes.

[4 STROKES   RANK 1614]

1959 艰 艰 **difficult, arduous**

⬛ hand, also 1796   ⬛ tough, hard to chew 1810   j

BF Something *tough* for your *hands* is an **arduous** task.

[8 STROKES   RANK 1647]

1960 寂 寂 **lonely, quiet**   ☐ roof 247 ◼ uncle 1918   jì

BF My **lonely** *uncle* spent his entire life under a single *roof*, never ever moving to a new house. Something about him was not quite right...

[11 STROKES   RANK 1739]

1961 叛 叛 **betray, rebel, revolt**   ◼ running sheep 1662 (altered) ☐ oppose, anti- 1863   pàn

BF The slaughterers have a trained *running sheep* to cause the herd to march quietly to slaughter. I *oppose* such tactics, which use a sheep to **betray** her comrades.

[9 STROKES   RANK 1779]

1962 夂 夂 **step forward**   ☐ action path 1421 ◼ hand, also 1796

CMP A young man walks steadily and with purpose. As he takes each **step forward**, his *hands* swing back and forth. The arc of the swing is the *action path*.

Sometimes, this component appears in a slightly altered form: 夂.

1963 傻 傻 **muddleheaded**

◼ man r 953 ☐ elder brother* 298 ☐ fiendish, ferocious 1831 ◼ step forward 1962   shǎ

A **muddleheaded** *man* just stands there while his *fiendish older brother steps* towards him with a knife (see that little 'dab' at the top?). Here's a dysfunctional family at work...

[13 STROKES   RANK 1989]

1964 陵 陵 **mausoleum, mound**

◼ hills 735 ☐ earth, soil 9 ◼ eight 1048 ◼ step forward 1962   líng

BF An *abundant* pile of *earth* is a poetic description of a **mound**. Located in the scenic *hills* outside of town, we *step forward* there solemnly to pay our respects to the leaders of the country.

[10 STROKES   RANK 1965]

1965 俊 俊 handsome*

■ man r 953   ⬜ permit, allow 771   ◼ step forward 1962   j

The **handsome** young *man* gets ready to *step forward* along the boulevard. His full length portrait appears on the left of this character. The right zooms on his noble, Grecian nose, and the stylish mustache below. Here, of course, we make a visual correspondence between his nose and mustache and '*permit, allow*'. (Refer again to §771 for the connection between '*permit*' and 'nose').

[9 STROKES   RANK 1847]

1966 蜂 蜂 bee, wasp   ■ insect 890   ⬜ step forward 1962   ◼ plentiful 12   f

Bees and **wasps** are known for their swarming behavior, in which a *plentiful* supply of the *insects* act together as they *move forward*.

[13 STROKES   RANK 1912]

1967 锋 锋 sword's cutting edge

■ gold r 1327   ⬜ step forward 1962   ◼ plentiful 12   f

BF With a **sword's cutting edge** made of *precious metal*, the samurai *steps forward* and skewers *three* of the attackers with a single thrust ('*plentiful*' is equivalent to three at one blow).   [12 STROKES   RANK 1671]

1968 复 复 turn around, repeat

⬜ size range 163 (altered)   ◼ step forward 1962   f

BF After you *step forward* through a *series of different* dance steps, you **repeat** everything all over again until the music stops.   [9 STROKES   RANK 426]

1969 腹 腹 belly, abdomen

■ meat 317 (altered)   ■ turn around, repeat 1968   f

BF In cows and other ruminants, the **stomach** is the *part of the body* where grass is digested *over and over again*.   [13 STROKES   RANK 1589]

1970 覆 覆 **overturn, cover**

■ west 291 (altered)   ▮ left step 1034   ▯ turn around, repeat 1968   fù

The sun was about to set in the *west*, so it was almost dark. I took a *step to the left*, for some reason *turned around*, and so managed to **overturn** some jars of new wine which were fermenting.   [18 STROKES   RANK 1823]

1971 履 履 **shoe***

□ corpse 703   ▮ left step 1034   ▯ turn around, repeat 1968   lǚ

BF Until the day we become a *corpse*, we are condemned to walk forever, taking *step* after *step*, *repeatedly*, in one pair of **shoes** or another.

[15 STROKES   RANK 1802]

1972 处 处 **get along with sb**   ▮ step forward 1962   ▯ foretell 170   chǔ

There's one reason why this guy always seems to *move forward* in life. It's as if he can *foretell* personalities which enable him to **get along with everybody**.

[5 STROKES   RANK 206]

1973 冬 冬 **winter**   ▭ step forward 1962   ▬ two 3 (altered)   dōng

Here's a person *moving forward*, but at *twice* their normal speed. Why? It's **winter**, and they want to keep warm.   [5 STROKES   RANK 1384]

1974 图 图 **picture, chart, map**   ■ enclosure 40   ▣ winter 1973   tú

Winter time, and the ground is frozen and covered with a permanent layer of snow. We can use this surface to scratch out **pictures** and **maps**. It's probably best to imagine that the *enclosing square* is really a *picture frame*.

[8 STROKES   RANK 476]

Unit 80

Step by Step

1975 疼 疼 **it hurts!** ☐ sick 697 ■ winter 1973 té
Whatever it is that makes you *sick, winter* makes it worse. Oh, how **it hurts!** [10 STROKES   RANK 1710]

1976 终 终 **end, finish** ▮ silk r 807 ☐ winter 1973 zh
The weavers spin the *silk* thread during *winter*time. They **finish** this task in time for the start of spring. [8 STROKES   RANK 558]

1977 窗 窗 **window**
☐ cave, den, hole 1098 ☐ dab 169 ■ enclosure 40 ■ step forward 1962 ch
There's a *hole* in the room's wall. It's *little*. It forms a rectangular *enclosure*, and through it you can see *people walking*. It's a **window**! [12 STROKES   RANK 1074]

1978 夏 夏 **summer** ■ page, leaf 444 (altered) ■ step forward 1962 xi
BF Every thing slows down in the **summer**. Even the hot breezes blowing the *leaves forward*, do it slowly. The abbreviated form of *'leaf'* accentuates this slowness. [10 STROKES   RANK 1126]

1979 麦 麦 **wheat** ☐ plentiful 12 (altered) ■ step forward 1962 m
The scholar sees **wheat** as one of the primary reasons that civilization makes progress (isn't that what *'stepping forward'* is all about?), especially when this resource is *plentiful*. But a more casual interpretation hinges on **wheat**'s use to make flour, and hence bread. The top of this character shows layers of bread, skewered with a cocktail toothpick, and resting on an artsy cocktail table. [7 STROKES   RANK 1171]

1980 酸 酸 sour, tart

■ new wine 303   ◩ permit, allow 771   ■ step forward 1962   suān

I *allowed* myself to sample some of that *new wine* I bought, but it was awful! It made my stomach rumble and feel like it was taking several *steps forward*. Worst of all, it tasted very **sour**.   [14 STROKES   RANK 1456]

1981 峰 峰 peak, summit

■ mountain 21   ◩ step forward 1962   ■ plentiful 12   fēng

When you've *stepped forward* as *many times* as you could while climbing the *mountain*, you find you can't go up anymore. You've reached the **peak**.   [10 STROKES   RANK 1473]

1982 凌 凌 thick ice

■ ice r 569   ◩ earth, soil 9   ■ walking man 287   ■ step forward 1962   líng

The **ice** is so **thick** that a *man walks* on the *ice* as confidently as if he were *stepping forward* on real *soil*.   [10 STROKES   RANK 1731]

1983 攴 攴 tap, rap

CMP Look carefully—there's the hammer coming down to **tap, tap, tap** on the small table.

1984 敲 敲 to strike, beat

■ high 275   ◩ tap, rap 1983   qiāo

This how you **knock** on a door—select a *high* spot, and then *tap* until someone opens up.   [14 STROKES   RANK 1732]

1985 叟 叟 old gentleman

■ tap, rap 1983 (altered)   ◩ speak 64 (altered)   sǒu

BF This sketch of a man emphasizes the boniness typical of an **old gentleman**.   [9 STROKES   RANK 3804]

1986 搜 搜 search, collect

■ hand r 29   ◩ old gentleman 1985   sōu

The *old gentlemen* uses his *hand* to **search** for things since his eyesight has pretty much gone now.   [12 STROKES   RANK 1564]

1987 瘦 瘦 **thin, lean** ☐ sick 697 ■ old gentleman 1985 S

The *old gentlemen* became *ill* from working too hard. We could all tell, because he steadily lost weight to become **thin** and **lean**.

[14 STROKES RANK 1841]

1988 艘 艘 **m for ships and vessels**

■ boat, ship 597 (altered) ☐ old gentleman 1985 S

The *old gentleman* on the *boat* is a scary sight. He **counts** his steps on the **boat** since his vision has become so poor. [15 STROKES RANK 1470]

1989 攵 攵 **wallop**

CMP Most of the time, the 'tap' component of §1983 appears in a simpler form like this, where you see the head of the hammer protruding below as part of the strike. This component confers an interpretation of action, or attack, or strike.

1990 攻 攻 **to assault, attack** ■ labor, work 7 ☐ wallop 1989 g

An **attack** is a *wallop* of such intensity that it involves *work* on the part of the invader. [7 STROKES RANK 588]

1991 玫 玫 **rose** ■ king 11 ☐ wallop 1989 n

BF How childish—the *king* is *walloping* his courtiers with a bunch of blood-red, long stem **roses**. It seems silly, but those thorns do hurt.

[8 STROKES RANK 2303]

1992 政 政 **government, political** ■ correct 183 ☐ wallop 1989 z

BF **Government** regulations can come down hard. **Government** ideas of *correct* behavior often *wallop* the heads and wallets of its citizens.

[9 STROKES RANK 150]

1993 故 故 reason, cause   ▮ ancient 51 ▮ wallop 1989   gù

BF Oops—is it my fault that my hammer caught the *ancient,* irreplaceable, and priceless vase with a mighty *wallop?* I guess that's the **reason** I've never been invited back.   [9 STROKES   RANK 572]

1994 做 做 do, make   ▮ man r 953 ▮ reason, cause 1993   zuò

Men with a passionate *cause* find inspiration to **make** great efforts to achieve their goals.   [11 STROKES   RANK 246]

1995 敌 敌 enemy, foe   ▮ tongue 225 ▮ wallop 1989   dí

BF Irresponsible rumor-mongering with your *tongue* packs as mighty a *wallop* as any weapon. It's easy for gossips and slanderers to make **enemies**.   [10 STROKES   RANK 523]

1996 牧 牧 herd   ▮ ox 186 ▮ wallop 1989   mù

BF Normally, *oxen* are placid and content. But crowded conditions in a **herd** can cause *oxen* to *wallop* and even gore each other.   [8 STROKES   RANK 1580]

1997 收 收 receive, accept   ▮ speak up! 92 ▮ wallop 1989   shōu

The homeowner is hard of hearing. *"Speak up!"* he yells to the mailman furiously *walloping* the door so the deaf guy can **accept** the package.   [6 STROKES   RANK 351]

1998 败 败 lose, be defeated   ▮ cowrie 430 ▮ wallop 1989   bài

Who would think! With *shells* as weapons, the enemy *pounded* our troops mercilessly, and we **were defeated**.   [8 STROKES   RANK 862]

1999 敢 敢 to dare   ▮ unexpected stroke ▮ ear 82 ▮ wallop 1989   gǎn

To listen with your *ear* to the call of an *unexpected challenge,* to *strike* while the iron is hot—such behavior is to accept a **dare**.   [11 STROKES   RANK 795]

2000 效 效 **imitate**   ▮ meet, intersect 1814   ▯ wallop 1989   ⊠

BF The beginning Chinese student tried on the right to **imitate** the form on the left. His intentions and goals failed to *intersect*, and he got a *wallop* on his ear as punishment.   [10 STROKES   RANK 551]

Unit 81

Poise

2001 教 教 **teach** ■ filial 1465 ■ wallop 1989 jiāo

In the old days, teachers were brutal. Students sat in the classroom out of a sense of *filial* duty, even though the **teacher** did nothing but *wallop* them for any and no reason. That was old-fashioned **teaching**. [11 STROKES RANK 191]

2002 敦 敦 **sincere**

■ cover 268 ■ mouth 41 ■ son, child 1402 ■ wallop 1989 dūn

Sincere feelings are those free from pretense or deceit. Perhaps the ancient scribes associated these feelings with *children* who simply un*cover* their *mouths* and say what they think. Sincere comments are so unusual in polite society that they *hit* the listener with great force. [12 STROKES RANK 1722]

2003 攸 攸 **distant, far**

■ man r 953 ■ unexpected vertical ■ wallop 1989 yōu

An ancient Chinese game of golf (or the equivalent). One *player* gives his golf ball, here shown in the form of a *small vertical stroke*, a mighty *wallop*. How **far** it travels! [7 STROKES RANK 3416]

2004 敕 敕 **imperial edict** ■ bundle, bunch 394 ■ wallop 1989 chì

BF For many people, even the best laws are *wallops* against individual liberty. In this viewpoint, an **imperial edict** is a *bunch* of liberty-constraining *blows*...

[11 STROKES RANK 3435]

2005 整 整 neat, tidy　　　　▭ imperial edict 2004 ▪ correct 183　z▮

BF …But if you follow those *imperial edicts* to the letter, and if you follow them *correctly*, then your life proceeds in a **neat** and **tidy** manner.

[16 STROKES   RANK 416]

2006 数 数 number, figure　　　▮ trouble, blunder 1137 ▯ wallop 1989　s▮

To overcome your *troubles*, imagine *walloping* them hard, so hard they shatter into a huge **number** of harmless fragments.　　　[13 STROKES   RANK 231]

2007 放 放 put, place　　　　▮ square, direction 1491 ▯ wallop 1989　f▮

Think of a board game like shuffleboard. When you *wallop* the puck, it travels in a certain *direction*. With a little luck and a modicum of skill, you **place** it in the proper *square*.　　　[8 STROKES   RANK 291]

2008 敖 敖 ramble　　　　　▯ exit 22 (altered) ▪ put, place 2007　á▮

BF On a nice spring morning, I prepare for a nice **rambling** walk by *exiting* my house without any thoughts of where I'm going to *put* my feet.

[10 STROKES   RANK 3573]

2009 傲 傲 proud, haughty　　　▯ man r 953 ▯ ramble 2008　à▮

No one tells this **haughty** *man* what to do! For example, when he takes a walk, he *rambles* wherever he wants.　　　[12 STROKES   RANK 1960]

2010 枚 枚 m for coins, small objects　▮ tree 375 ▯ wallop 1989　m▮

As you *wallop* the *tree* hard, lots of **small objects** (acorns?) tumble down.

[8 STROKES   RANK 1884]

2011 敏 敏 sharp, keen　　　　▮ every 600 ▯ wallop 1989　m▮

BF **Keenness** of mind is like **sharpness** in a blade. You maintain and enhance the **sharpness** with *every blow* of the smith's hammer.

[11 STROKES   RANK 1436]

2012 繁 繁 **complicated** ▢ sharp, keen 2011 ▮ silk r 807 (altered)   fán

BF High quality embroidery earns its reputation on the basis of the stitches of the **complicated** pattern it shows. These patterns remain *sharp* and the fabric must be *silk*.   [17 STROKES   RANK 1296]

2013 激 激 **surge, dash**

▮ water r 523   ▢ white 201   ▮ put, place 2007 (altered)   jī

The mighty waves of *water* **surging** against the rocky coast of Maine personify nature's power. *White* with foam, they pound the same *place* over and over.

[16 STROKES   RANK 710]

2014 缴 缴 **pay, hand over**

▮ silk r 807   ▢ white 201   ▮ put, place 2007 (altered)   jiǎo

Squares of *white silk*, so we may imagine, served as currency in the very old days, because they were valuable items and yet convenient to carry. We *place* one of these cloths on the counter in order to **pay** for something.

[16 STROKES   RANK 1834]

2015 各 各 **each, every** ▮ wallop 1989 (altered) ▮ mouth 41   gè

The bully *walloped* that guy in the head so hard that **each** and **every** tooth in his *mouth* rattled.   [6 STROKES   RANK 209]

2016 客 客 **visitor, guest** ▢ roof 247 ▮ each, every 2015   kè

Each and *every* person who stays under our *roof* as a **guest** merits the full range of our hospitality.   [9 STROKES   RANK 583]

2017 洛 洛 **a certain river** ▮ water r 523   ▮ each, every 2015   luò

BF *Each* and *every* drop of *water* that nature recycles finds itself in a **certain river** at some point.   [9 STROKES   RANK 978]

2018 落 落 **fall, drop behind**　　　☐ grass r 94　　■ a certain river 2017　　lˑ

The villagers regularly dump their *grass* clippings in the nearby *river* after they mow their lawns. The swiftness of the current grabs hold and whisks it out of sight, **leaving** the villagers **behind**.　　　[12 STROKES   RANK 496]

2019 络 络 **enmesh, wind**　　　■ silk r 807　　☐ each, every 2015　　lˑ

We're touring the *silk* factory. Be careful! For all their thinness and fineness, *each* and *every silk* thread can **enmesh** you in a trap from which you can't escape without damaging hundreds of dollars of merchandise.

[9 STROKES   RANK 1118]

2020 格 格 **lattice, grid**　　　☐ tree 375　　☐ each, every 2015　　g

In a **lattice**, *each* and *every* component square is identical to every other, and they are all made of *wood*.　　　[10 STROKES   RANK 325]

2021 路 路 **road, path, way**　　　☐ foot r 946　　☐ each, every 2015　　lˑ

To get somewhere, you put *each* and *every foot*step on the right **path**.

[13 STROKES   RANK 305]

2022 条 条 **strip, sth long and narrow**

■ wallop 1989 (altered)　　■ tree 375 (altered)　　tˑ

BF Go ahead—really *wallop* that *tree*! Lots of branches—**long and narrow** pieces of the *tree*—will fall all around you.　　　[7 STROKES   RANK 214]

2023 务 务 **affair, business matter**

☐ wallop 1989 (altered)　　■ strength 1492　　W

BF It's trite—but true, nevertheless—to compare **business matters** with athletic competitions. To succeed, you need to *wallop* your competitors with great *strength*.　　　[5 STROKES   RANK 245]

2024 额 额 forehead   ▮ each, every 2015   ▯ page, leaf 444   é

Walking home, the cold autumn wind tirelessly hammered me down. It felt like *each* and *every* blown *leaf* battered my **forehead**.

[15 STROKES   RANK 936]

2025 雾 雾 fog, mist   ▭ rain 85   ▰ affair, business matter 2023   wù

A real hot *business deal* is in the works—so hot that when it *rains*, it sizzles. The steaming vapor forms clouds of **fog** and **mist**.   [13 STROKES   RANK 1670]

2026 救 救 rescue, save, salvage   ▮ request, entreat 557   ▯ wallop 1989   jiù

We've captured one of the terrorists from the group who kidnapped my wife. We desperately want to **rescue** her, but the terrorist has resisted our *entreaties*. We're going to apply a few *wallops* to him to see if it will loosen his tongue.

[11 STROKES   RANK 872]

Unit 82

Prickly Personifications

2027 备 备 **prepare, get ready** ▭ wallop 1989 ▰ field 57 b

Everyone loves the spring, except perhaps the farmer. Farmers work furiously to **prepare** their *fields* for planting. Weeding, hoeing, aerating the soil, and so on are necessary steps which do great violence to the soil, symbolically a '*walloping*' to the *field*. [8 STROKES   RANK 397]

2028 改 改 **transform, change** ▮ self* 852 ▯ wallop 1989 g

You can always tell a professional boxer. Over the years, he *himself* will have received so many *wallops* that his appearance will be greatly **changed**.

[7 STROKES   RANK 350]

2029 致 致 **send, deliver** ▮ to, until 755 ▯ wallop 1989 z

I *wallop* that stubborn little donkey *until* he's ready to obey me, and then I **send** it with an important message to **deliver**. [10 STROKES   RANK 524]

2030 微 微 **micro, tiny, minute**

▮ left step 1034 ▯ mountain 21 ▰ dollar 293 ▯ wallop 1989 v

BF The American *dollar* just isn't what it used to be. Foreign economies are *walloping* it. Moreover, the American economy is *left stepping* into a *mountain* of debt. Result—the purchasing power of the *dollar* is a **tiny** fraction of what it used to be. [13 STROKES   RANK 653]

2031 攸 攸   thus, that which   ▮ man 311   ▯ scepter 5   ▮ wallop 1989   yōu

BF Phrases like 'thus' or 'that which' often introduce factors that **cause results to happen**.

The *man* takes a *stick* and *wallops* a few heads to make sure these people **do what he wants**.   [7 STROKES   RANK 3416]

2032 修 修   embellish, decorate

▮ thus, that which 2031 (altered)   ▮ feathers 1285   xiū

The colorful *feathers* on the club I used to *get my own way* serve as useful **decoration**, for they hide my aggressive nature.   [9 STROKES   RANK 740]

2033 敬 敬   respect, offer politely

▮ thoughtless, careless 653   ▮ wallop 1989   jìng

He felt great shame at the way he *thoughtlessly walloped* his teacher in the face, even though it was an accident. Thereafter, he never failed to **respect** this great master to try compensate for this *careless* insult.

[12 STROKES   RANK 1209]

2034 警 警   warn, alert   ▮ respect, offer politely 2033   ▮ speech 270   jǐng

BF The thug *spoke politely* to the shopkeeper, but no one was fooled. It was really a **warning**. Pay up, or the store gets torched.   [19 STROKES   RANK 687]

2035 降 降   surrender, capitulate

▮ hills 735   ▮ wallop 1989 (altered)   ▮ fort   xiáng

We swarmed down from the *hills*, giving their *forts* a real *walloping*. They had no choice but to **surrender**.   [8 STROKES   RANK 744]

2036 隆 隆   prosperous, booming

▮ surrender, capitulate 2035 (altered)   ▮ give birth to 191   lóng

BF After the Japanese *surrender* in 1945, the United States embarked on a program to cause the *rebirth* of the Japanese economy. This successful program led to wildly **prosperous** times for this country.   [11 STROKES   RANK 1400]

2037 略 略 **summary, outline** ▪ field 57 ▫ each, every 2015 (altered) l

BF Here's a **summary**, a **brief outline** of the farmer's business strategy. See that *field*? Well, he aims to plant as much as he can in that one and in *each* and *every* other one he owns. [11 STROKES RANK 704]

2038 露 露 **dew** ▪ rain 85 ▪ road, path, way 2021 l

BF Was it *raining* overnight? The *road* is moist. But no—it's just a heavy **dew**. [21 STROKES RANK 841]

2039 散 散 **break up, distribute** ▪ contented cows 1297 ▫ wallop 1989 ▪ meat 317 (altered) S

The *contented cow* is not going to be contented for much longer. With a mighty *wallop* from a cleaver, the slaughterer will soon be able to take various cuts of *meat* and **distribute** them to customers near and far.

[12 STROKES RANK 866]

2040 撒 撒 **scatter, sprinkle** ▪ hand r 29 ▪ break up, distribute 2039 S

You've *broken up* the stale bread you brought with you to the park, and you use your *hand* to **scatter** it to the ducks who wait impatiently for this tasty snack. [15 STROKES RANK 1445]

2041 阁 阁 **pavilion, chamber** ▪ door 196 ▪ each, every 2015 g

BF *Each* and *every door* to the emperor's palace deliberately looked the same as *every* other one. Thieves and saboteurs would have a more difficult time determining the whereabouts of the emperor's private **chambers**.

[9 STROKES RANK 1682]

2042 乙 乙 **whole arm**

CMP The curve on the right strongly resembles an **entire arm**, the 'corner' of the curve representing the elbow. (In fact, this character did stand for 'elbow' in former times.) The horizontal top shows a bit of shoulder, to emphasize the bodily resemblance.

2043 飞 飞 **to fly** ⬛ whole arm 2042 ⬛ wings fēi
飞 shows an early attempt at **flying**. Some enterprising inventor attached
wings to his *arms*, and flapped away! [3 STROKES RANK 347]

2044 艺 艺 **skill, art** ⬛ grass r 94 ⬛ whole arm 2042 yì
BF An intricately woven tapestry of strands of *grass*, draped over some one's
whole arm, shows off their great **skill**. [4 STROKES RANK 786]

2045 忆 忆 **recall, remember** ⬛ heart (skinny) 930 ⬛ whole arm 2042 yì
BF Here's a display of cooperation between the *emotional* side of a person and
their physical side, represented by their *whole arm*. **Remembering** shows this
cooperation. [4 STROKES RANK 1333]

2046 九 九 **nine** ⬛ action path 1421 ⬛ whole arm 2042 jiǔ
How many common body parts comprise the mechanism of the *whole arm*?
Let's see, there's the shoulder, the upper arm, the forearm, wrist, palm, and
five fingers. That's ten. But the *action path* through the shoulder is like the
'forbid' symbol—it crosses out the shoulder. As a result, this is a schematic
of **nine** parts of the arm system. [2 STROKES RANK 445]

2047 瓦 瓦 **tile** ⬜ one 2 ⬛ ancient ladle 142 (altered) ⬛ whole arm 2042 wǎ
An eccentric mason places a **tile** in the ceiling. Holding it in place with
his *whole arm*, he forces grout between adjacent tiles with an odd-looking
spoon. [4 STROKES RANK 1195]

2048 仇 仇 **hatred** ⬛ man r 953 ⬛ nine 2046 chóu
The *man* on the right is using all *nine* parts of his arm to pound and beat the
man on the left. Great **hatred** accounts for this aggression.
[4 STROKES RANK 1536]

2049 杂 杂 **mixed, composite** ▢ nine 2046 ▤ one 2 ▆ small 1063   zá
A complicated recipe calls for *nine* ingredients, each of which appears in a
small amount. They come together to make *one* dish. This delicious dish is
an inspired **mixture**.   [6 STROKES   RANK 853]

2050 执 执 **grasp** ▮ hand r 29 ▮ nine 2046 ⬛ thing   zh
Here's a *hand* holding *nine things* tightly. It's **grasping** these *things*.
                                                           [6 STROKES   RANK 763]

2051 几 几 **several, how many?** ▮ action path 1421 ▮ whole arm 2042   jǐ
BF Lunch is over—time to get back to work. This big bruiser is ready to carry
several heavy machine components at a time, cradled in his massive *arms*.
That's *action* on the factory floor.   [2 STROKES   RANK 211]

2052 机 机 **machine** ▮ tree 375 ▮ several, how many? 2051   jī
BF Wood from *trees* was an early—the earliest?—high-tech building material.
How many **machines** and other tools could we construct from this material?
The answer is limited only by your imagination.   [6 STROKES   RANK 111]

Unit 83

A Musical Comedy Administration

2053 殳 殳 **ancient bamboo spear**

⬛ several, how many? 2051　◼ hand, also 1796　shū

BF Tools extend the capability of a naked and unarmed mortal. An **ancient bamboo spear** must have seemed the epitome of technological wonder, extending the power of one skilled warrior to be like that of *several hands* acting all at once.　　　　　[4 STROKES　RANK 6005]

2054 没 没 **have not**　⬜ water r 523　◼ ancient bamboo spear 2053　méi

Water on a wooden *spear* **has no** benefit. It dulls its edge and warps the fibers. What we thought was smooth wood is **not**—it **has** a knot!

[7 STROKES　RANK 72]

2055 染 染 **to dye**　◻ water r 523　◻ nine 2046　◼ tree 375　rǎn

In old times, **dying and dye craft** was a secret art. Figuratively speaking, *nine* chemicals derived from *trees* and plants were poured into *water* to create the finished **dye**.　　　　　[9 STROKES　RANK 1141]

2056 凡 凡 **commonplace**　⬛ several, how many? 2051　◼ dab 169　fán

BF A working definition of '**commonplace**' might focus on the middle ground between extremes, extremes like '*several*' and very '*few*'.

[3 STROKES　RANK 1013]

2057 讯 讯 **message, dispatch**　◼ speech r 615　◼ commonplace 2056　xùn

BF They hid the importance of the military **dispatch** from the enemy by using only *commonplace speech* in the text.　　　　[5 STROKES　RANK 1238]

2058 壳 壳 shell, housing, case

■ scholar 8   ▤ smooth cover 280   ▪ several, how many? 2051   k

The *scholar* needs some special *coverings* for a new piece of lab equipment. *How many?* With this new tool, she can make the **housings** herself for any of her future research needs.   [7 STROKES   RANK 1937]

2059 毅 毅 perseverance

■ erect, stand 1179   ◗ pig, boar 1425   ◧ ancient bamboo spear 2053   y

BF A young man *stands erect* for hours practicing the art of *ancient bamboo spearing*. He **perseveres** until such time as he can bring down a *boar* for the tribe.   [15 STROKES   RANK 1946]

2060 肌 肌 flesh, muscle   ◧ meat 317 (altered)   ◧ several, how many? 2051   jì

BF **Muscle** is the kind of *meaty tissue* that enables us to perform the *several* physical tasks we do each day.   [6 STROKES   RANK 1935]

2061 虎 虎 tiger

■ action path 1421   ◗ on 175   ◨ ancient ladle 142   ▪ several, how many? 2051   h

The **tiger** was special to the ancients. Capable of limitless *action*, it always leapt *onto* its prey. Magically, it replenished its *several* powers nightly using a special enchanted *ladle*.   [8 STROKES   RANK 1083]

2062 虑 虑 anxiety   ■ tiger 2061 (altered)   ◳ heart (fat) 906   lì

BF In the presence of a charging *tiger* our *heart* will be beating wildly. In the brief time you have left, you will be subject to severe **anxiety**.   [10 STROKES   RANK 901]

2063 挖 挖 dig, excavate

■ hand r 29   ◳ cave, den, hole 1098   ▪ whole arm 2042   w

Here you are, master archaeologist, on the verge of making the discovery of the century. You are so excited you use not only your *hand* in the *cave* but your *whole arm* to do the **excavation**.   [9 STROKES   RANK 1860]

064 乳   乳   **breast, milk**

☐ hands raised high 1345   ◼ son, child 1402   ◼ whole arm 2042 (altered)   rǔ

BF Here's the charming scene: a young mother nestles her infant *son* inside her *whole arm* which is *raised high* as she prepares to let him nurse at her **breast**.   [8 STROKES   RANK 1831]

065 贏   贏   **gain, win**

☐ perish 269   ◼ meat 317 (altered)   ◼ employee 440   ☐ several, how many? 2051 (altered)   yíng

Here's a kooky contest for some reality television show. Start with a pile of *meat* on the stage, and *several employees*, whose mouths have been *altered* with piercings, try to eat more than their opponents. They *perish* if they don't **win**.   [17 STROKES   RANK 1836]

066 气   气   **air, spirit, vital energy**

☐ man 311 (altered)   ▬ one 2   ◼ whole arm 2042   qì

(This character is famously difficult to translate into English!)

1   Originally, this character was drawn to mimic the curling boundaries of heavenly clouds.

2   The *man*, altered by the accident, lies like a corpse on the pavement. Suddenly, he moved *one* of his *whole arms* to show that **spirit** and **vital energy** remained in his body.   [4 STROKES   RANK 217]

067 汽   汽   **steam, vapor**   ◼ water r 523   ◼ air, spirit, vital energy 2066   qì

BF Vapor is precisely that kind of '*air*' originating from heated *water*.   [7 STROKES   RANK 1200]

068 设   设   **set up, found, establish**

◼ speech r 615   ◼ ancient bamboo spear 2053   shè

The warrior with the gift of *speech* and with the talents and abilities to use *ancient bamboo spears* was able to **establish** and **found** many cities and colonies.   [6 STROKES   RANK 302]

2069 风　凤　wind　■ commonplace 2056 (altered)　■ harmonious crossing 1793

For sailors and mariners, nothing is better than a *commonplace* **wind** which blows the ship quickly from port to port in a *harmonious crossing.*

[4 STROKES   RANK 348]

2070 疯　疯　mad, insane　■ sick 697　■ wind 2069

A person in the grip of **insanity** is a frightening sight. While *sick*, they appear to be buffeted backwards and forwards by the *winds* of their inner demons.

[9 STROKES   RANK 1549]

2071 究　究　study carefully, look into

■ cave, den, hole 1098　■ nine 2046

BF The entrance to the *cave*, actually an abandoned gold mine, looked spooky and dangerous. I forced myself to go in about *nine* feet to **look into** it.

[7 STROKES   RANK 429]

2072 凤　凤　phoenix　■ wind 2069 (altered)

In mythology, the **phoenix** bird soared like the *wind*, so it makes sense to alter the '*wind*' glyph to represent it. The 'harmonious crossing' innards become the '*hand, also*' component, which provides a horizontal perch for it when it needs a rest.　[4 STROKES   RANK 1504]

2073 势　势　power, force, influence　■ grasp 2050　■ strength 1492

BF Mao Zedong showed great *strength* in *grasping* the reins of power, and as a result his **power** during his lifetime and **influence** after his death were and remain noteworthy.

[8 STROKES   RANK 506]

2074 投　投　throw, fling　■ hand r 29　■ ancient bamboo spear 2053

I use my *hand* to take my *ancient bamboo spear* and **fling** at my super-annoying, 97-year-old mother-in-law. (Don't worry—she grabs it and **throws** it right back!)

[7 STROKES   RANK 516]

2075 段 段   section, part

▮ ear 82 (altered)   ▮ ancient bamboo spear 2053 (altered)   duàn

What a fight! The guy with the *ancient bamboo spear* has ripped away a **part** of the other guy's *ear*!   [9 STROKES   RANK 567]

2076 热 热   hot, fervent   ▬ grasp 2050   ▬ fire r 796   rè

The baby *grasped* the spoon that had been lying in the *fire*. She'll never do that again—it's **hot**.   [10 STROKES   RANK 606]

2077 沿 沿   alongside, edge, border

▮ water r 523   ▣ several, how many? 2051   ▣ mouth 41   yán

Those *several* marking stones each of which looks like a big open *mouth* marks the **edge** of the *water*.   [8 STROKES   RANK 1182]

2078 铅 铅   lead (metal)

▮ gold r 1327   ▣ several, how many? 2051   ▣ mouth 41   qiān

Lead is known as a *metal* with a low melting point. That's why you get those *several mouth*-shaped lumps when you dropped the **lead** solder on the hot stove.   [10 STROKES   RANK 2641]

Unit 84

Foolish Consistencies

2079 船 船 ship, vessel

⬛ boat, ship 597   ⬛ several, how many? 2051   ⬛ mouth 41   c▌

A large *boat*, one large enough to hold *several mouths*, is called a **ship**.

[11 STROKES   RANK 614]

2080 般 般 sort, kind   ⬛ boat, ship 597   ⬛ ancient bamboo spear 2053   b▌

When somebody thinks of Chinese *boats* they are usually thinking of the ones made with spars and masts that look like *ancient bamboo spears* lashed together. These are the **sort** called *Chinese junks*.   [10 STROKES   RANK 629]

2081 搬 搬 take away, remove, move (house)

⬛ hand r 29   ⬛ sort, kind 2080   b▌

That *sort* of thing just won't do. We use our *hands* to **remove** and get rid of it.   [13 STROKES   RANK 1766]

2082 股 股 thigh   ⬛ meat 317 (altered)   ⬛ ancient bamboo spear 2053   g▌

BF One *meaty* body part that is as long as an *ancient bamboo spear* is the **thigh**.   [8 STROKES   RANK 644]

2083 冗 冗 superfluous, redundant

⬛ smooth cover 280   ⬛ walking man 287 (altered)   r▮

BF That *man* should be helping the other workers, but he's *walking* around under the shade of the *roof*. If he doesn't watch out, they'll make him **redundant**!   [4 STROKES   RANK 3642]

2084 沉 沉 submerge, lower

◨ water r 523 ◧ superfluous, redundant 2083 chén

When organized crime makes you *redundant*, they throw your body in the *water* where it **submerges** to become shark food.   [7 STROKES   RANK 747]

2085 亢 亢 overbearing, haughty

▢ cover 268 ▮ several, how many? 2051 kàng

BF The emphasis is on a long neck, surmounted by a flat chin and snooty nose—the essence of **being overbearing**.   [4 STROKES   RANK 3268]

2086 抗 抗 resist, fight, defy ◧ hand r 29 ◧ overbearing, haughty 2085 kàng

BF That guy is so *overbearing* as to be obnoxious. Several people are ready to use their *hands* to **fight** him.   [7 STROKES   RANK 766]

2087 航 航 ship, craft ◧ boat, ship 597 ◧ overbearing, haughty 2085 háng

BF The kind of '**ship**' we have in mind is the kind that flies through the air, or a major sea vessel. Compared to ordinary *boats*, these **ships** seem *overbearing* and *haughty*.   [10 STROKES   RANK 773]

2088 亮 亮 light, bright ▭ tall 1700 (altered) ▬ several, how many? 2051 liàng

It's so dark by the evening campfire. *Several tall* campers take the hint, and shine flashlights all around, to make the occasion **bright** and **light**.

[9 STROKES   RANK 840]

2089 巩 巩 secure, solid ◧ labor, work 7 ◧ commonplace 2056 gǒng

BF It's hard *work* building a road. First, you gather together all kinds of *commonplace* rocks and stones and lay them on the roadbed. This will create a **secure** foundation.   [6 STROKES   RANK 2384]

2090 恐 恐 afraid, be frightened

▀ secure, solid 2089   ▀ heart (fat) 906 (altered)   k

During the earthquake, some masonry fell from the building which had formerly seemed so *secure*. Was anyplace safe? My *heart* beat wildly, and I became very **frightened**.   [10 STROKES   RANK 891]

2091 筑 筑 build, construct   ▀ bamboo r 243   ▀ secure, solid 2089   z

In olden times, you would **build** a house by taking *bamboo* stems and anchoring and attaching them in a particularly *secure* and *solid* manner.   [12 STROKES   RANK 1130]

2092 殿 殿 hall, palace, temple

▊ dead body 702   ▊ together 1302   ▊ ancient bamboo spear 2053   d

Only the king knows where the *dead bodies* are buried. The rebels who were *speared* to death are buried *together* deep in the bowels of the **palace**.   [13 STROKES   RANK 1555]

2093 孰 孰 who? what? which? (lit)

▊ enjoy 1403   ▊ nine 2046   ▪ things   s

The *nine* of us in our large family *enjoy* different *things*. It's hard keeping straight **which** of us enjoys **what**.   [11 STROKES   RANK 3568]

2094 熟 熟 ripe, cooked, familiar

▀ who? what? which? (lit) 2093   ▀ fire r 796   s

Who gets to sit in front of the *fire*? Family and friends—anyone who is **familiar**, that's who.   [15 STROKES   RANK 1035]

2095 亿 亿 hundred million   ▊ man r 953   ▊ whole arm 2042   y

The lenses in a pair of glasses are like a pair of zeroes. Since there are eight zeroes in the number '**hundred million**' (100,000,000), we would need four pair of glasses to represent this vast number. It's not easy to carry more than one pair in each hand, so one *man* will have to borrow his best friend's *whole arm* to carry all of them!   [3 STROKES   RANK 1057]

096 虚 虚 **empty, unoccupied**

▪ tiger 2061 (altered)   ▪ trade, industry 1117   xū

Somehow a *tiger* escaped from the zoo and ran into the *trade* office building. Needless to say, those offices quickly became **unoccupied**.

[11 STROKES   RANK 1071]

097 役 役 **military service, labor**

▪ left step 1034   ▪ ancient bamboo spear 2053   yì

BF Soldiers *march* (suggested by the '*left step*') with their *ancient bamboo spears*. This was the heart of **required military service**.

[7 STROKES   RANK 1245]

098 凭 凭 **lean on, rely on**

▪ assume a post 956   ▪ several, how many? 2051   píng

You *assume* a new *post* with *many* responsibilities. Why? Management knows they can **rely on** you.

[8 STROKES   RANK 1410]

099 凯 凯 **triumphant, victorious**

▪ how could it be? 854   ▪ several, how many? 2051   kǎi

BF The small-town team beat all odds and emerged **victorious**. *How could it be* that these *several* hicks and amateurs defeated our well-trained players?

[8 STROKES   RANK 1447]

100 佩 佩 **to girdle**   ▪ man r 953   ▪ commonplace 2056   ▪ towel 130   pèi

It's *commonplace* to see *men* wearing *towels* around their waists. They are called belts or **girdles**. The two outer curves of '*commonplace*' remind us of legs narrowing to the waist, where belts and **girdles** are normally worn.

[8 STROKES   RANK 1507]

101 飘 飘 **blow, drift about**   ▪ ticket 1068   ▪ wind 2069   piāo

When the *wind* rises, used, ripped *tickets* and other light-weight fragments **drift about** in the air.

[15 STROKES   RANK 1527]

2102 朵　朵　m for flowers　　　■ several, how many? 2051　■ tree 375　•

There are no components for flowers; '*tree*' is the closest. So, if you need to know *how many flowers* are in a bouquet, put these components together.

[6 STROKES   RANK 1571]

2103 躲　躲　hide, dodge, avoid　　■ body 1631　□ m for flowers 2102　•

Look at all these *flowers—so many I can't even count them*. It's easy to place my *body* behind them to try to **hide** from the hotel manager.

[13 STROKES   RANK 1644]

2104 瓶　瓶　bottle, vase, pitcher　　■ an intensifier 1677　□ tile 2047　|

BF Imagine cementing a couple of *tiles* together in a waterproof way to act as a **vase**. That's a pretty *intense* use of the *tiles*.　　　[10 STROKES   RANK 1703]

Unit 85

Silhouettes and Shadows

2105 疫 疫　**epidemic, plague**　▢ sick 697　▧ ancient bamboo spear 2053　yì
BF Epidemics are *sicknesses* that move rapidly through a town as if the *sick*ness traveled on swift but *ancient bamboo spears*.　[9 STROKES　RANK 1791]

2106 氧 氧　**oxygen**　▧ air, spirit, vital energy 2066　▧ sheep 1147　yǎng
Be careful when you buy *woolen* carpet. Burn a bit in the presence of **oxygen**. If it's real *wool*, the '*vital spirit*' of *sheep* it gives off will stink. Otherwise, if the fiber is synthetic, you've been cheated.　[10 STROKES　RANK 1863]

2107 乙 乙　**second in a series**　▧ whole arm 2042 (altered)　yǐ
Upside-down, this graph shows the number **two**!　[1 STROKES　RANK 1872]

2108 轨 轨　**course, path**　▧ car 1430　▢ nine 2046　guǐ
BF What are *nine cars* doing, being driven together? It must be a race, and their **path** defines the race **course**.　[6 STROKES　RANK 1883]

2109 乞 乞　**beg***　▢ man 311 (altered)　▧ whole arm 2042 (altered)　qǐ
This *man's whole arm* is overdeveloped. This comes from years of **begging**.　[3 STROKES　RANK 2429]

2110 吃 吃　**eat**　▢ mouth 41　▢ chopsticks　▧ whole arm 2042　chī
Someone's *whole arm* is using *chopsticks* to shovel food into their *mouths* as fast as they can. This is how they **eat**.　[6 STROKES　RANK 475]

2111 乾 乾 male principle, heaven

◼ ten 6   ◼ morning 70   ☐ man 311 (altered)   ◼ whole arm 2042   q

BF Every *morning*, for the last *ten* days in a row, *the man* has gotten up early to work out, and look how big his *whole arm* is compared with the rest of him! This is the **male principle** in action.   [11 STROKES   RANK 1999]

2112 ⺍ ⺍ great idea!

CMP You can always tell when characters in an animated cartoon have a brilliant idea, because a simulated light bulb flashes, showing rays emanating from the top of their head. The short strokes on top are the light rays, and the smooth cover is the top of a cartoon skull.

2113 学 学 study

☐ great idea! 2112   ◼ son, child 1402   X

The *child*'s head is a like an open tap. *Great ideas* flow from him non-stop. That's the fruit of hard **study**.   [8 STROKES   RANK 66]

2114 觉 觉 think

☐ great idea! 2112   ◼ see 301   j

The result of hard **thinking** is a *great idea*, so we can *see* our way to a clear solution.   [9 STROKES   RANK 327]

2115 晃 晃 to dazzle

☐ day, sun 63   ◼ great idea! 2112 (altered)   ◼ son 288   h

Great idea—'sun' and '*son*' sound the same but have different meanings! What a **dazzling** observation!   [10 STROKES   RANK 1796]

2116 兆 兆 omen

◼ north 145 (altered)   z

BF It's possible to decompose this character in terms of curves and dabs, but it's probably simpler to remember that this pictograph represents an unfortunate turtle whose shell has been borrowed, then baked. I interpret the upright curves as representing the pattern on the shell, and the oblique strokes are the cracks induced by the heat of baking. Ancient Chinese priests used these shells as **omens** to read the future.   [6 STROKES   RANK 2246]

2117 挑 挑 **select, pick**   ▌ hand r 29 ▐ omen 2116   tiāo
On the basis of the *omens*, I reach out with my *hand* and **pick** the lottery
ticket that will bring me untold riches for sure!   [9 STROKES   RANK 1309]

2118 跳 跳 **jump**   ▌ foot r 946 ▐ omen 2116   tiào
The evil child **jumps** on the turtle with his *feet*, smashing the *shell* to bits and
pieces and smithereens.   [13 STROKES   RANK 999]

2119 乘 乘 **multiply**   ▌ rice or grain 409 (altered) ▐▐ omen 2116 (altered)   chéng
When the harvest is good, the size of the crop is a **multiple** of last year's—a
good *omen*. Note that '*omen*' has been altered until it looks like 'north'
(§145).   [10 STROKES   RANK 1231]

2120 剩 剩 **remain, be left over**   ▌ multiply 2119 ▐ knife r 166   shèng
When stuff *multiplies*, we sometimes get more than we need. Use a *knife* to
cut off this surplus, and here's the bit that's **left over**.

          [12 STROKES   RANK 1446]

2121 愛 爱 **love**   ▢ dab 169 ▬ great idea! 2112 ▬ friend, associate 1798   ài
After years of enjoying each other's company, a *little* acquaintanceship blos-
somed into a truly *great idea*. My *friend* and I realized we were deeply in
love.   [10 STROKES   RANK 394]

2122 桃 桃 **peach**   ▌ tree 375 ▐ omen 2116   táo
Besides being used for eating, **peaches**—or more properly, their *tree*-like
pits—played a role in ancient religion. Priests read the wrinkles on the pits
as *omens*.   [10 STROKES   RANK 1839]

2123 辶 辶 **move forward**   ▢ dab 169 ▬ whole arm 2042 (altered) ▖ dab 169
CMP It's difficult to **walk forward** without moving your *arms*. The two dabs
here suggest this movement in the style of comic book-art.

2124 这 这 **this, these**   ☐ move forward 2123   ☐ language, culture 1804   z
'This' is used for a specific thing you have in mind. In your speech you *move forward* to this object, an important *cultural* artifact.   [7 STROKES   RANK 11]

2125 过 过 **cross, go over**   ☐ move forward 2123   ☐ inch 210   g
Crossing a street or **going over** a bridge is *moving forward* by a *fixed amount*.   [6 STROKES   RANK 46]

2126 道 道 **direction, way**   ☐ move forward 2123   ☐ head, leader 1167   d
If you *move forward* by following the proven *leader*, you'll surely be following the right **way**.   [12 STROKES   RANK 52]

2127 还 还 **still or yet**   ☐ move forward 2123   ☐ no! 1452   h
You try to *move forward*, but the powers that be do *not* allow it. Therefore, you **have yet** to reach your goal.   [7 STROKES   RANK 80]

2128 进 进 **enter**   ☐ move forward 2123   ☐ well 1672   ji
The enemy **moves forward** into the cave, but we've laid a trap! We've covered the *well* with a grid of sticks, which they don't notice. As they *move forward* in the gloom, we rejoice as they tumble down, screaming for mercy.   [7 STROKES   RANK 81]

2129 逆 逆 **go against, disobey**
☐ move forward 2123   ☐ running sheep 1662 (altered)   ☐ receptacle 155   n
The shepherd *moves forward* to catch the *running sheep* who escaped from the *pen*. The sheep is guilty of **disobeying** orders!   [9 STROKES   RANK 1975]

2130 迅 迅 **rapid**   ☐ move forward 2123   ☐ commonplace 2056 (altered)   x
BF Ambitious young people try their best to **rapidly** *move forward* away from their *commonplace* past, toward their bold and exciting future.   [6 STROKES   RANK 1090]

Unit 86

The Wretched of the Earth

131 途 途 road, journey

⬜ move forward 2123　■ surplus, remainder 1073　　tú

BF Roads and trade routes came to be established as merchants *moved forward* along the same paths to sell their *surpluses* for other products.

[10 STROKES　RANK 1085]

132 逢 逢 each time

⬜ move forward 2123　⬜ step forward 1962　◼ plentiful 12　　féng

Imagine a list of things *moving forward* into the future. As you *step forward*, you have have *plenty of resources* **each time** you deal with item.

[10 STROKES　RANK 2181]

133 缝 缝 sew, stitch　　⬛ silk r 807　⬜ each time 2132　　féng

Expert seamstresses and seamsters gain their reputations because *each time* they make a **stitch** in the *silk* clothes it's identical to every other.

[13 STROKES　RANK 1852]

134 连 连 join, link　　⬜ move forward 2123　⬜ car 1430　　lián

The circus has come to town! We stayed up late to watch the procession of *cars*, each *moving forward* in sync with every other car, as if they were all **linked** together. [7 STROKES　RANK 399]

135 莲 莲 water lily　　⬜ grass r 94　◼ join, link 2134　　lián

Those beautiful **water lilies** that grace a pond are not, as they appear, bunches of distinct plants. Rather, these *grasses* are all *linked* one to the other.

[10 STROKES　RANK 1837]

2136 邀 邀 **invite, request**

□ move forward 2123   ⬛ white 201   ⬛ put, place 2007 (altered)

It's the first time I've been **invited** over to meet my girlfriend's parents. For the occasion, I *put* on a *white* shirt, and I'm confidently *moving forward* towards her house.   [16 STROKES   RANK 1854]

2137 通 通 **lead to, go to**   ⬛ move forward 2123   ⬛ corridor, path 1745

Where do the *corridors* **lead to**? If you don't *move forward*, you'll never find out.   [10 STROKES   RANK 190]

2138 返 返 **return to**   ⬛ move forward 2123   ⬛ oppose, anti- 1863

After the *opposition* was quashed, the soldiers can *move forward* and **return** home.   [7 STROKES   RANK 1430]

2139 达 达 **attain, reach**   ⬛ move forward 2123   ⬛ big 330

It's your *big* day. Years of nose to the grindstone and slow but steady *movement forward* through the company are finally paying off. Today you **attain** your goal—vice-president in charge of advertising!   [6 STROKES   RANK 289]

2140 退 退 **retreat, retire**

⬛ move forward 2123   ⬛ tough, hard to chew 1810

The wacky soldiers found it *hard* to *chew* and *move forward* at the same time, so they had to **retreat**.   [9 STROKES   RANK 723]

2141 腿 腿 **leg**   ◻ moon, month 1719   ⬛ retreat, retire 2140

The army *retreated* by light of full *moon*. So as to remain quiet and not alert the enemy, they used their **legs** exclusively, forgoing the convenience of noisy cars or horses.   [13 STROKES   RANK 1351]

2142 运 运 **move, transport**   ⬛ move forward 2123   ⬛ cloud 751

I hate **moving**! **Transporting** stuff is so tiring and makes it seem far. A better attitude is to turn off your mind, and *move forward* in the direction of the distant *clouds* until it all gets done.   [7 STROKES   RANK 345]

2143 边   边   **side, margin, edge**   ⬜ move forward 2123   ⬛ strength 1492   biān
Stranded in the desert, we have no choice but to *move forward.* Using the last reserves of our *strength,* we hope to get to the **edge** of the sands before we give out.   [5 STROKES   RANK 316]

2144 近   近   **near, close to**   ⬜ move forward 2123   ⬛ catty 118   jìn
The rare Chinese table (Tang dynasty) is in danger of toppling and collapsing because it is *unbalanced.* We can *move forward* quickly enough to catch it because we happen to be **close to** it.   [7 STROKES   RANK 374]

2145 造   造   **build, fabricate**   ⬜ move forward 2123   ⬛ tell 189   zào
The clever inventor is so persuasive when he *tells* his backers what his plans are that he is able to *move forward* in the **fabrication** of his next invention.   [10 STROKES   RANK 354]

2146 远   远   **far, distant**   ⬜ move forward 2123   ⬛ dollar 293   yuǎn
The more **distant** are the places that you want to *move forward to* via train, the more *money* the ticket costs.   [7 STROKES   RANK 386]

2147 选   选   **choose, select**   ⬜ move forward 2123   ⬛ first 300   xuǎn
As he *moves forward* in life, he always seems to do better than anyone else, seems always to be *first.* He claims it's because he always **chooses** the best alternatives.   [9 STROKES   RANK 499]

2148 随   随   **follow, comply with, as soon as**   ⬛ hills 735   ⬜ move forward 2123   ⬛ have 1725   suí
The *hills* have come alive, as in some 50's sci-fi flick. They are *moving forward* toward the town, to take over the people's *possessions.* They are **complying with** the orders of the largest mountains (their chiefs), who have also come to life.   [11 STROKES   RANK 498]

2149 速 速 **fast, speed**   ■ move forward 2123   ■ bundle, bunch 394   S

BF As I *moved forward*, the *bundle* of reeds started to come apart. I've got to move **fast** if I want to get to the table before the reeds are all over the place.   [10 STROKES   RANK 617]

2150 适 适 **appropriate, suitable**   ■ move forward 2123   ■ tongue 225   S

BF Imagine Hansel and Gretel in the gingerbread house, but this time they're blindfolded with their hands tied behind them. They *move forward* carefully, using their *tongues* to make sure their route is still **suitable**.   [9 STROKES   RANK 663]

2151 述 述 **state, narrate, relate**   ■ move forward 2123   ■ art, skill 405   S

BF The *art* of **narrating** a story is just that—an *art*. Your narrative has to be interesting, but keep the action *moving forward*, or else you lose your audience.   [8 STROKES   RANK 674]

2152 送 送 **give a present**   ■ move forward 2123   ■ shut, close 1113   S

Oh, no! I forgot to **get** an anniversary **present** for my wife. As I *moved towards* the store, it *shut* its doors at closing time. What will I do now?   [9 STROKES   RANK 656]

2153 遍 遍 **all over, everywhere**   ■ move forward 2123   ■ flat, crushed 729   b

BF A giant, purple people-eater from outer space is chasing me. I'm *everywhere*, constantly *moving forward* so it doesn't catch me and *crush* me *flat*.   [12 STROKES   RANK 1012]

2154 遗 遗 **lose, leave behind**   ■ move forward 2123   ■ expensive 437   y

BF The train ticket was too *expensive* for me. The rest of the class got on the train which *moved forward* and **left me behind**.   [12 STROKES   RANK 892]

155 逐 逐 **pursue, chase** ⬛ move forward 2123 ⬛ pig, boar 1425 zhú

A little known fact: there are hundreds of thousands of feral *boars and pigs* running wild in this country, mostly down south. They make fine eating, but *moving forward* to **chase** and **pursue** them takes some skill.

[10 STROKES RANK 954]

156 迫 迫 **compel, force, coerce** ⬛ move forward 2123 ⬛ white 201 pò

BF I was *moving forward* in my car, when there suddenly must have been an accident, a serious one. For I woke up surrounded by people dressed in *white* **forcing** me to stay in bed, eat certain foods at certain times, and so on. [8 STROKES RANK 1006]

Unit 87

Autumnal Thoughts

2157 逃 逃 escape, flee ☐ move forward 2123 ■ omen 2116

BF It's time to leave home, and so **escape** the constraints of youth. It's a time of *moving forward* under the sure knowledge that the *omens* all predict good things for you. [9 STROKES   RANK 996]

2158 避 避 avoid, evade ☐ move forward 2123 ☐ law 1256

I *move forward* always under the protection of the *law*. That way, I never feel worried, anxious, or that I have to **avoid** and **evade** bill collectors, landlords, and police officers. [16 STROKES   RANK 991]

2159 遭 遭 encounter, by chance

☐ move forward 2123 ■ plaintiff and defendant 105

Both the *plaintiff and defendant* met each other **by chance** at the local supermarket. In this social setting, they resolved their differences, and so could *move forward* with their lives. [14 STROKES   RANK 1048]

2160 迎 迎 to welcome ☐ move forward 2123 ■ head held high 160

BF Our friends *move forward* to us. We haven't seen them since college! We *hold our heads high* as we prepare to **welcome** them. [7 STROKES   RANK 1069]

2161 透 透 penetrate, seep through

☐ move forward 2123 ■ to flower, put forth ears of grain 1593

We can *move forward* after an exceptional *harvest*. The reason was the new irrigation method we used, which allowed the water **seep through** to the plants effectively and efficiently. [10 STROKES   RANK 1077]

162 迹 迹 **mark, trace, remains** ⬛ move forward 2123 ⬛ also, too 1503   jì

BF Several things happen when you *move forward* on a trip. First, you get closer to your goal. But you *also* leave **traces** of yourself—footprints, tire tracks, credit card receipts, and so on—behind.   [9 STROKES RANK 1098]

163 迷 迷 **confused, be fascinated by**

⬛ move forward 2123 ⬛ rice 1127   mí

You're supposed to *move forward*, but the handful of *rice* you see scattered about in all directions summarizes your state of mind. You don't know which way to turn; you're all **confused**.   [9 STROKES RANK 1153]

164 违 违 **disobey, violate** ⬛ move forward 2123 ⬛ leather 115   wéi

BF I told my teen-age daughter she could not *go out* Saturday night. I threatened her with my *leather* belt if she **disobeyed** me.   [7 STROKES RANK 1184]

165 迟 迟 **late, tardy** ⬛ move forward 2123 ⬛ ruler 704   chí

I broke my walking stick, so I *went* to my friends' using a *ruler* instead. It was too short, I walked slower than normal, and I got there very **late**.

[7 STROKES RANK 1374]

166 迪 迪 **enlighten, guide** ⬛ move forward 2123 ⬛ let sb do sth 48   dí

BF I will let my students *move forward* and *do what they want*, but only up to a point. They are under my **guidance**.   [8 STROKES RANK 1440]

167 递 递 **hand over, transmit**

⬛ move forward 2123 ⬛ younger brother 1450   dì

Since the estate was **handed over** to the oldest son, *younger brothers* had to learn to *move forward* with their lives and not depend on family money.

[10 STROKES RANK 1538]

2168 巡 巡 patrol, make the rounds

⬛ move forward 2123   ⬛ river 1495 (altered)   ﾈ

BF Olden times, and **patrolling** the city's perimeter involved *moving along* the nearby *river*. [6 STROKES RANK 1544]

2169 逼 逼 force, press on towards

⬛ move forward 2123   ⬛ size range 163   ﾄ

Consider the explorers we all learned about in school. As they *moved forward* on their journey, they encountered *ranges* of all kinds—in climates, peoples, languages, food, and creature comforts. Still, they **pressed on towards** their goal. [12 STROKES RANK 1559]

2170 逻 逻 patrol   ⬛ move forward 2123   ⬛ catch birds with a net 663   ﾉ

BF The '*birds*' *you catch* while *moving forward* on **patrol** are a lot like the winged creatures in the air, just a bigger and more dangerous. [11 STROKES RANK 1591]

2171 遵 遵 abide by, obey   ⬛ move forward 2123   ⬛ honor, venerate 1214   ﾌ

BF You **abide by** your professor's rules when you *move forward* with *honor*. [15 STROKES RANK 1593]

2172 迁 迁 move*   ⬛ move forward 2123   ⬛ thousand 224   ﾄ

Moving house is *moving forward* a *large distance* from the old place. [6 STROKES RANK 1630]

2173 逊 逊 modest, inferior   ⬛ move forward 2123   ⬛ grandson 1410   ﾈ

BF My *grandson moves forward* with such confidence, that we all shrink back with a sense of **inferiority**. [9 STROKES RANK 1697]

2174 迈 迈 step, stride   ⬛ move forward 2123   ⬛ ten thousand 472   ﾄ

BF "A journey of *ten thousand forward movements* starts with a single **step**." [6 STROKES RANK 1698]

75 遥 遥   **distant, far, remote**

   ■ move forward 2123   ⬜ hands raised high 1345   ◨ dry mountainous bits 520   yáo

BF The passengers from the downed jet are stranded on the *dry mountain top*, frantically *waving their hands* in the air. We're *moving forward* to rescue them, but they are **far** away; see how small their hands appear.

[13 STROKES   RANK 1715]

76 夂 夂   **move on**

CMP Don't confuse this component with the component ⻌ 'move forward'! Here, the sinuous top-to-bottom curve suggests a relaxed person out for a stroll, and he's about to take a giant step, which is that curve extending towards the right. He's worn out his welcome with this bunch of relatives, and he's about to **move on**.

77 延 延   **prolong, postpone**

   ■ move on 2176   ⬜ action path 1421   ◨ stop! 181   yán

BF While someone is trying to *move on*, someone else is trying to *stop* him. Lot of attempted *action* here! That could easily **postpone** his departure and **prolong** his stay.   [6 STROKES   RANK 1103]

78 诞 诞   **birth, birthday**   ■ speech r 615   ■ prolong, postpone 2177   dàn

BF I hate celebrating someone's **birthday**. Because of all the boring *speeches*, I have to *postpone* my midday nap.   [8 STROKES   RANK 1997]

79 之 之   **relationship marker**   ■ move forward 2123 (altered)   zhī

This character participates in several constructs which show a relationship between the things surrounding it. It's a type of grammatical marker. Readers of a certain age will agree that the central swash-like form closely resembles the **mark** of Zorro! The little *dab* on top reminds us that this is a small, particle-like word.

     Also: note how the character looks like a subtly distorted version of the '*move forward*' radical (§2123). Good **relationships** in life make it easy for us to *move forward* from one achievement to the next.   [3 STROKES   RANK 44]

2180 建　建　establish, set up

▢ move on 2176　◼ pen, writing instrument 39

A hallmark of civilization: with the stroke of a *pen*, you can *move on* to **establish** new things—companies, cities, treaties, and so on.

[8 STROKES   RANK 244]

2181 健　健　healthy, strong

◧ man r 953　◼ establish, set up 2180

BF A *man* (any person, actually) who lives in a secure and well-*set-up* house helps insure his continued **health** and **strength**.   [10 STROKES   RANK 979]

2182 键　键　key (lock, computer)

▢ gold r 1327　◼ establish, set up 2180

You get to the *gold* that's in the banking *establishment* by using a **key** to open the door.   [13 STROKES   RANK 1471]

Unit 88

Pacific Overtures

183 廷 廷 **imperial court**

⬛ move on 2176　▢ dab 169　⬛ earth, soil 9　tíng

BF A person *moves on* to the *infinitesimal* piece of *earth* where he must stand to address the emperor in his **court**. [6 STROKES RANK 1626]

184 庭 庭 **hall, front courtyard**　▢ shelter r 681　⬛ imperial court 2183　tíng

BF You can only take *shelter* at the *imperial court* in the **front courtyard**. [9 STROKES RANK 931]

185 蜓 蜓 **dragonfly**　⬛ insect 890　⬛ imperial court 2183　tíng

BF The only *insect* good enough for the *imperial court* is the graceful, beautiful, eye catching **dragonfly**. [12 STROKES RANK 4083]

186 挺 挺 **straighten up (physically)**　⬛ hand r 29　⬛ imperial court 2183　tǐng

No time for slouching today! We're visiting the *imperial court*. Use your *hand* to **straighten yourself up**. [9 STROKES RANK 1467]

187 艇 艇 **small boat**　⬛ boat, ship 597　⬛ imperial court 2183　tǐng

BF Only **small boats** are allowed at the *imperial court*, *boats* which are smaller than those of the emperor. [12 STROKES RANK 1372]

2188 乏 乏 tired*, weary*

☐ action path 1421 (altered) ◼ relationship marker 2179

This character *connects* me with a seriously stunted *action path*. I guess I don't feel like much action today. I am just too **tired**. [4 STROKES RANK 1399]

2189 巴 巴 dancing snake

CMP This component displays a hooded cobra **snake** doing its **dance**. Rising up on its tail, marked hood fully extended, it exerts a hypnotic effect on its viewers.

2190 巴 巴 cling to, be near

◼ dancing snake 2189

It's impossible to take your eyes away from the *dancing snake*, especially if you **are near** it. Audience eyes **cling** to its movements as if there were a physical connection between it and them. [4 STROKES RANK 546]

2191 把 把 hold or grasp

◼ hand r 29   ☐ dancing snake 2189

It looks like the *dancing snake* is going to attack. As a gesture of defense, you use your *hand* to **grasp** the snake securely, before any harm is done.

[7 STROKES RANK 110]

2192 色 色 color, look

☐ man 311 (altered)   ◼ dancing snake 2189

The *tourist* was hypnotized by the fakir and his *dancing snake*. It wasn't so much the dancing as it was the brilliant **colors** and patterns on the skin of the tropical reptile, so different from anything back home. [6 STROKES RANK 304]

2193 绝 绝 cut off, sever, unique

◼ silk r 807   ☐ color, look 2192 (altered)

BF Somehow, during the manufacturing process, the *silk*'s *color* changed abruptly from brilliant red to muddy green. Immediately, we **cut off** power to the machines. [9 STROKES RANK 562]

2194 吧 吧 **let's do this (particle)** ⬛ mouth 41 ⬜ dancing snake 2189 ba

Don't just stand there—move! That's what emerges from my *mouth* when I want you to move sharply away from the *dancing snake* I just saw under your chair. It's impolite in Chinese just to make a command; we use 吧 to soften it. [7 STROKES   RANK 470]

2195 爸 爸 **dad** ⬛ father 1812 ⬛ cling to, be near 2190 bà

When the child is still young enough to climb over her *father* and *cling* to him, then the *father* is still more of a **dad** than a *father*. [8 STROKES   RANK 1050]

2196 肥 肥 **fat, fertile, rich** ⬛ meat 317 (altered) ⬜ dancing snake 2189 féi

The *dancing snake* used to be **fat**, but all that dancing made his *body* thin. [8 STROKES   RANK 1620]

2197 饣 饣 **eat r** ⬜ man r 953 (altered) ⬛ scepter 5 (altered)

CMP Our Chinese scribes are emphasizing the 'eat till you drop' aspect of **eating**, the kind of eating you see at festivals, receptions, and all-you-can-eat buffets. The *scepter* acts like a piston or press, forcing ever more food into the *guest's* mouth.

2198 饱 饱 **full, satiated** ⬛ eat r 2197 ⬜ wrap, envelope 857 bǎo

I don't *wrap* up my *eating* sessions until I am totally **full**. [8 STROKES   RANK 1998]

2199 饲 饲 **feed (animals)** ⬛ eat r 2197 ⬜ company 112 sì

BF Following the long-standing *company* policy of keeping key employees content, they give us humongous amounts of food at lunch. We *eat* so much, that outside observers compare us to **animal feeding** frenzies. [8 STROKES   RANK 1971]

2200 饿 饿 **hungry** ⬛ eat r 2197 ⬛ I 361 è

I *eat* when I'm **hungry**—how about you? [10 STROKES   RANK 1911]

2201 饭 饭 cooked rice   ▮ eat r 2197   ▮ oppose, anti- 1863   f

Teenagers are *rebels* you're stuck with. For instance, they cram nothing but junk food into themselves, and don't *eat* the nutritious **rice cooked** for them.   [7 STROKES   RANK 935]

2202 饮 饮 swallow liquid or insults   ▮ eat r 2197   ▮ owe, lack 465   y

Insults are all about emphasizing the miserable stuff you *eat* as well as the qualities you *lack*.   [7 STROKES   RANK 1569]

2203 饰 饰 decoration, ornament   ▮ eat r 2197   ▮ market 273 (altered)   s

BF In olden times, when did people dress up and **decorate** themselves? To go to the *market*, originally a place where people gathered to buy and sell things to *eat*.   [8 STROKES   RANK 1604]

2204 爪 爪 clawed foot

CMP If you've ever owned a cat, this sketch of a cat with extended **claws** about to pounce on a tender knee or bared midriff will ring true.

2205 爪 爪 claw   ▮ clawed foot 2204   z

[4 STROKES   RANK 2363]

2206 畏 畏 fear   ▮ field 57   ▮ claw 2205 (altered)   v

BF **Fear** of the unknown is particularly terrifying. Imagine a farmer out in his *field*, and there in front of his panic-stricken eyes are the giant *claw*-marks of an animal he's never seen before.   [9 STROKES   RANK 2039]

2207 喂 喂 feed   ▮ mouth 41   ▮ fear 2206   v

If you **feed** that wild animal, go ahead. Just toss the raw steak into its *mouth*, and you won't need to *fear* it.   [12 STROKES   RANK 1988]

208 抓 抓 **grab, seize, arrest**   ■ hand r 29   ■ claw 2205   zhuā

You **grab** the crook by **seizing** him with your *hand*, like a *claw*.

[7 STROKES   RANK 992]

Unit 89

Urban Trendsetters

2209 爬　爬　**crawl, creep, scramble**

　　　　　　　　　　　　■ claw 2205　　■ cling to, be near 2190

Animals who have evolved to **crawl** generally have *claws* that make it easy to *cling* to a surface.　　　　　　　　　　　　[8 STROKES　RANK 1426]

2210 内　内　**animal track**

CMP Learn to recognize the stylized pattern of some **animal**'s paw print as it leaves a **track**. This component, also a radical, appears here drawn with four strokes; there is also a 5-stroke variant which appears at the bottoms of characters like 偶 and 遇 among others.

2211 愚　愚　**stupid, foolish**

　　　　　　　　　■ field 57　　■ animal track 2210　　■ heart (fat) 906

BF Apparently some coyote was so **stupid** as to trap himself inside one of the farmer's *fields*. Although the farmer can't see it, the *animal* left plenty of *tracks*. Trapped animals are always dangerous, so the farmer's *heart* is beating in anxiety.　　　　　　　　　　　　[13 STROKES　RANK 1895]

2212 偶　偶　**by chance**　　■ man r 953　　■ field 57　　■ animal track 2210

People and animals generally avoid each other. But sometimes, **by chance**, their *tracks* cross. This *farmer* encountered some wildlife in one of his *fields*.

　　　　　　　　　　　　[11 STROKES　RANK 1361]

213 离 离 **leave, depart**

☐ cover 268   ◧ fiendish, ferocious 1831   ◧ animal track 2210   lí

The *animal tracks* in the forest led us to the *ferocious* aardvark. We were able to get in a *covered* box which we then threw in the river. A job well done, we felt free to **leave** and go home for dinner.   [10 STROKES   RANK 418]

214 璃 璃 **glazed tile**   ◧ jade 221   ◧ leave, depart 2213   lí

BF Because of the economic downturn, the *jade* business has fallen to nothing. As the taste for *jade left* the buying public, they turned to decorative **glazed tile** as a cheaper alternative.   [14 STROKES   RANK 1894]

215 遇 遇 **meet, encounter**

☐ move forward 2123   ◧ field 57   ◧ animal track 2210   yù

BF *Moving toward* his home, the farmer followed some *animal tracks* in his *fields* which led to an unexpected **meeting** with the coyote preying on his flocks.   [12 STROKES   RANK 899]

216 属 属 **category**   ◧ corpse 703   ◧ various animal parts   shǔ

Picture a naturalist trying to **categorize** a new specimen. She's got the *body*, and various other body parts, including some *little bits* (§169), the *mouth* (§41), and *various other parts* (§2210).   [12 STROKES   RANK 610]

217 云 云 **child r**

CMP The strokes of this component are stylized, but it's easy to imagine this form as 子 'son' drawn upside-down. To the original scribes, this represented the head-first position of birth, so this form represents a **child**.

218 育 育 **rear, raise, educate**   ◧ child r 2217   ◧ meat 317 (altered)   yù

BF If you feed a *child meat*, you nourish and **raise** her properly.

[8 STROKES   RANK 609]

2219 流　流　flow, drift　■ water r 523　■ child r 2217　■ river 1495

Like Moses in the bulrushes, picture a small *child* in a basker surrounded by flowing *river water*. Of course, the baby's basket is going to go with the **flow** as well.　[10 STROKES　RANK 396]

2220 疏　疏　sparse, scattered

■ foot r 946 (altered)　■ child r 2217　■ river 1495

BF As the *baby* in the basket was flowing in the *river*, I used my *foot* to try and stop it. But see the sharp point at the top of the altered '*foot*' component? I was wearing pointy shoes that day, and the point struck the basket and destroyed it. The strands became **scattered** all over the place. Don't even ask what happened to the baby!　[12 STROKES　RANK 1897]

2221 亥　亥　near midnight　■ child r 2217　■ man 311

Children are something, especially when they're little. **Near midnight**, a *parent* must check on them.　[6 STROKES　RANK 3179]

2222 刻　刻　engrave, carve　■ near midnight 2221　■ knife r 166

A nighttime serial killer is terrorizing the city. *Near midnight*, this depraved person uses a *knife* to **carve** a mysterious message on the skin of his victims.　[8 STROKES　RANK 618]

2223 该　该　ought to, should　■ speech r 615　■ near midnight 2221

It's *near midnight*! Who's *speaking* outside? They **ought to** be asleep!　[8 STROKES　RANK 319]

2224 核　核　nut, kernel, fruit pit　■ tree 375　■ near midnight 2221

BF The crispest **nuts** come from the top of the *tree*. If I use a clock dial to represent the location on the *tree*, the prime harvest area is the part of the tree '*nearest midnight*'.　[10 STROKES　RANK 828]

2225 孩 孩 child*   ▮ child 1186 ▮ near midnight 2221   hái

BF The *small boy* gets restive *near midnight*. But that's life when you bring up a **child**.   [9 STROKES   RANK 533]

2226 弃 弃 discard, abandon, give up

                              ▯ child r 2217 ▮ action scaffolding 1667   qì

BF Oh, no! The drug-addled mother on top of the *scaffolding* is about to toss her *child* off if she doesn't get drug money. How could anyone **abandon** their children in such a depraved way?   [7 STROKES   RANK 1105]

2227 撤 撤 remove, take away, withdraw

                 ▮ hand r 29 ▮ rear, raise, educate 2218 ▮ wallop 1989   chè

The ancient Confucian system of *education*: plenty of *corporal punishment*. Such a system guaranteed the **removal** of any love of learning.

                                                              [15 STROKES   RANK 1270]

2228 礻 礻 show r   ▮ show, indicate 1064 (altered)

CMP Look closely to see how the strokes of §1064, 示, have been scrunched and slightly deformed to fit in half a character.

2229 祖 祖 ancestor   ▮ show r 2228 ▮ moreover 15   zǔ

BF The Duke of Bla-Bla's **ancestral** records will *show* you all you want to know about his family. They (the records, not the **ancestors**) are stored in that *bookshelf* over there.   [9 STROKES   RANK 1025]

2230 礼 礼 ceremony, rite   ▮ show r 2228 ▮ mineshaft 135   lǐ

BF In ancient times, recruits to an army were ceremonially led to the edge of a deep *mineshaft* where they **ritually** threw their civilian clothes away to *show* their allegiance to king and country! This was a **ceremony**, a rite of passage, to mark the transformation from civilian to soldier.   [5 STROKES   RANK 926]

2231 福　福　**good fortune**　　　⬛ show r 2228　⬜ size range 163　f

Good fortune means a large, happy family, all in good health. You can easily tell such a family—clean clothes in *a range of* sizes often hang outside to dry to *show* their good fortune.　　　[13 STROKES   RANK 683]

2232 祝　祝　**express good wishes**

⬛ show r 2228　⬜ mouth 41　⬛ walking man 287　z

In this instance, we interpret the '*show*' component as flowing lines of words issuing from a *man*'s *mouth* as he *walks* to and fro, carried away by the emotion of the occasion. These **express good wishes** for the coming holiday!

[9 STROKES   RANK 1651]

2233 祥　祥　**propitious**　　　⬛ show r 2228　⬜ sheep 1147　x

BF The high priest *shows* the fine *sheep* to the congregation. It is a **propitious** offering to the gods.　　　[10 STROKES   RANK 1674]

2234 祸　祸　**misfortune, disaster**

⬛ show r 2228　⬜ mouth 41　⬛ inside* 318　h

The tall stranger looks just like a regular guy. But as you get to know him, he (symbolized by the *mouth*) *shows* you his *inner*, darker self, which has been plagued by **misfortune**.　　　[11 STROKES   RANK 1870]

Unit 90

Dastardly Effects

235 神　神　**god, divinity**　　■ show r 2228　■ express 47　　shén
Gods are created by mankind as a way to *show* how the world works and *express* eternal truths.　　[9 STROKES　RANK 227]

236 社　社　**society, group**　　■ show r 2228　■ earth, soil 9　　shè
In a mature **society** of people, things are so congested in the towns that the *earth* barely *shows* between all the buildings and structures.

[7 STROKES　RANK 270]

237 视　视　**regard, look at**　　■ show r 2228　■ see 301　　shì
BF You **look at** or *see* something that someone *shows* you.

[8 STROKES　RANK 438]

238 𠂤　𠂤　**stair steps**
CMP This component displays two **stair steps** with a hand rail on the left. Grand staircases have many more steps than this, but this is all we can fit in.

239 官　官　**government official**　　□ roof 247　■ stair steps 2238　　guān
Watch this foolish and self-important **government official** as he swaggers down the grand *staircase* of the government *building* to his puny cubicle in the umpteenth sub-basement.　　[8 STROKES　RANK 432]

2240 管 管 **run, manage, have charge of**

⬒ bamboo r 243 ⬓ government official 2239

BF The *government official* **in charge of** the *bamboo* grove is doing a lousy job. Look how the plants tower above the building, like giant weeds.

[14 STROKES RANK 252]

2241 追 追 **chase, pursue**

▙ move forward 2123 ▜ stair steps 2238 ◳ dab 169

The toughest part of the **chase** scenes in the latest action flick are the tireless *moves* up and down *small flights of stairs.* [9 STROKES RANK 768]

2242 馆 馆 **guest accommodation**

◧ eat r 2197 ◨ government official 2239

BF The most obnoxious types of guests used to be freeloading *government officials.* They forced citizens to provide them with **guest accommodations**, and they *ate* food greedily, because they weren't paying.

[11 STROKES RANK 1011]

2243 遣 遣 **send, dispatch**

▙ move forward 2123 ⬒ middle 45 ⬒ one 2 ◼ stair steps 2238

BF Get out of my way! I *move forward* up the *stair steps* of the *central* post office to **send** *one* letter before it closes. [13 STROKES RANK 1780]

2244 丂 丂 **breath against mirror**

CMP Observe how the horizontal mirror stops and disturbs the smooth flow of the line of breath.

2245 巧 巧 **clever, ingenious**

◧ labor, work 7 ◨ breath against mirror 2244

He gets so involved in his own **ingenuity** that he forgets how tired he gets. He *works* so hard, you can see is *breath fogging the mirror.*

[5 STROKES RANK 1219]

2246 号 号 **number in a series** ☐ mouth 41 ▮ breath against mirror 2244   hào

The car accident was **one of a number** for the young driver. We hold the mirror up to his *mouth* without seeing any *breath* at all.

[5 STROKES   RANK 487]

2247 专 专 **concentrated, focused**

▮ breath against mirror 2244 (altered) ☐ one 2 ⌐▪ dab 169   zhuān

He pursed his lips so they made a *small* area while *breathing* so his *breath* would be **concentrated** into a *small* area on the mirror.

[4 STROKES   RANK 485]

2248 传 传 **pass on, impart** ▐ man r 953 ▐ concentrated, focused 2247   chuán

During his life, the *man* was so *focused* on the traditions of his craft, that he made sure to **impart** them to his children and disciples.

[6 STROKES   RANK 332]

2249 转 转 **turn, shift, change** ▐ car 1430 ▐ concentrated, focused 2247   zhuǎn

One good way to *concentrate* the motion of a *car* is to make a sharp **turn**.

[8 STROKES   RANK 376]

2250 考 考 **give or take a test**

☐ old 1506 (altered) ▮ breath against mirror 2244   kǎo

Omigod! The *old* guy sitting on the chair just slumped to the floor unconscious. Is he dead? We'll **give** him the *breath-against-a-mirror* **test** to see.   [6 STROKES   RANK 495]

2251 亏 亏 **loss, unfair treatment**

☐ one 2 ▮ breath against mirror 2244   kuī

I **lost** everything in a business gone bad. The only thing left to me was *one* mirror. I practiced *breathing against it* to keep reminding myself I wasn't yet dead.   [3 STROKES   RANK 1738]

2252 夸 夸 **boast, exaggerate**

■ big 330 ⊟ one 2 ▤ breath against mirror 2244

A **boast** is like *one big breath*.   [6 STROKES   RANK 1955]

2253 跨 跨 **step, stride, straddle**   ▮ foot r 946 ▮ boast, exaggerate 2252

With an *exaggerated* movement of your *foot*, you **step** over and **straddle** the fallen enemy combatant and capture him.   [13 STROKES   RANK 1774]

2254 丬 丬 **plank**

CMP this is the left half of a *tree* (§375). You make **planks** from pieces of *trees*.

2255 壮 壮 **strong, robust**   ▮ plank 2254 ▮ scholar 8

Use a *plank* to attack a puny *scholar* (and so force him to exercise) to make him **robust and strong**.   [6 STROKES   RANK 1432]

2256 装 裝 **adorn, dress up**   ▬ strong, robust 2255 ▬ clothing 839

You could tell the injured man was getting better and more *robust*—he was taking more interest in his *clothing* and even **dressing up**.

[12 STROKES   RANK 467]

2257 状 狀 **form, shape, state of things**   ▮ plank 2254 ▮ dog 332

BF An amazing *dog*—he stays sober no matter how much liquor his owner gives him. He still walks straight along a *plank*, and his **state** is perfect.

[7 STROKES   RANK 624]

2258 奖 奖 **award, prize, reward**

▯ plank 2254 ▮ evening, dusk 655 ▬ big 330

Our club gives a Golden *Plank* **Award** to the member who builds the *biggest* project out of *planks* in the *evening*, using no artificial light.

[9 STROKES   RANK 1233]

2259   氏   氏   **plant root ball**

CMP The horizontals suggest the top layer of fertile soil. Through it, several roots snake down, seeking moisture and nutrition.

2260   氏   氏   **surname**   ■ plant root ball 2259   shì

The *roots of a plant* are like the **family ancestors** that define a family. The *plant root ball* bears the **surname** of its predecessors.   [4 STROKES   RANK 1500]

Unit 91

Finale Ultimo

2261 昏 昏 dusk   □ plant root ball 2259   ▰ day, sun 63   h

BF The stray roots of a mysterious, giant *plant root ball* grow over the face of the *sun*, reducing its light. It looks like **dusk**.   [8 STROKES   RANK 1561]

2262 婚 婚 wed, marry   ▯ woman 581   ▯ dusk 2261   h

BF This man feels bound by China's family traditions, and is not happy. The arranged **marriage** with his parents' choice of a *woman* means he will never see his true love again. The world darkens—to him all is perpetual *dusk*.

[11 STROKES   RANK 942]

2263 氐 氐 basic, thoroughgoing   ▰ plant root ball 2259   ⌐ dab 169   d

BF *Plants root balls* are vigorous. You can cut away a huge amount of the root system, for example, and as long as you leave the *small* nucleus you have the **basic** material from which the plant can flourish.   [5 STROKES   RANK 4355]

2264 抵 抵 support, sustain   ▮ hand r 29   ▯ basic, thoroughgoing 2263   d

The giant, but *basic* tree stump looks like it could fall over at any time. The *little* stone underneath helps balance it, but it still threatens passersby. I guess I'll have to stand here and use my *hand* to **support** it.   [8 STROKES   RANK 1119]

2265 底 底 bottom, base   ▯ shelter r 681   ▰ basic, thoroughgoing 2263   d

Here the *basic* part of a *shelter* is the **base** of the roof.   [8 STROKES   RANK 543]

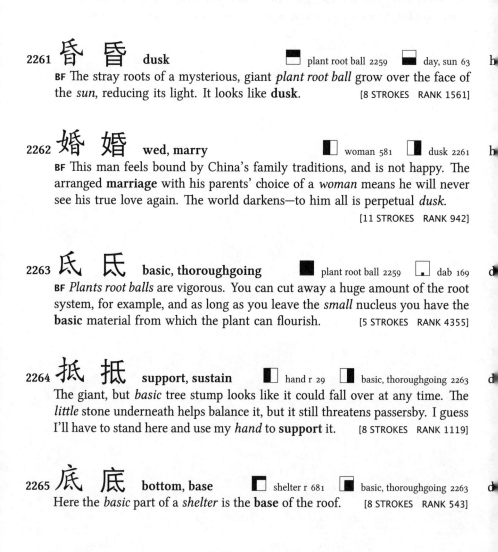

2266 低 低 **let droop, hang down**

☐ man r 953   ☐ basic, thoroughgoing 2263   dī

The *basic* price for the new car was so great that the *man* **hung his head** in despair.   [7 STROKES RANK 592]

2267 纸 纸 **paper**   ☐ silk r 807   ☐ plant root ball 2259   zhǐ

Here's some weird **paper**. The pulp is made from *plant root balls*, and *silk threads* line the edge. The overall effect is one of luxurious craftsmanship.

[7 STROKES RANK 1020]

2268 方 方 **banner, follow me!**

☐ square, direction 1491   ☐ man 311 (altered)

CMP *Men* follow each other in the same *direction* under the influence of a **charismatic leader** ("**follow me!**") or under the representation of such leadership—a **banner**.

2269 族 族 **clan, race, tribe, group**

☐ banner, follow me! 2268   ☐ arrow 334   zú

The dark side of **tribal** membership: under the misguided direction of the wrong kind of *leader*, people use their *arrows* against other groups.

[11 STROKES RANK 549]

2270 旋 旋 **revolve, circle, spin**

☐ banner, follow me! 2268   ☐ foot 419 (altered)   xuán

BF The world **revolves** about the great leader. I will *follow* on *foot* wherever he flies his *banner*.   [11 STROKES RANK 1383]

2271 旗 旗 **banner, flag, emblem**

☐ banner, follow me! 2268   ☐ his, her, its, theirs 1093   qí

BF *It's* (sounds like '*its*') time! The campaign to regain the mother land has begun. *Follow* the **banner** on the road to glory.   [14 STROKES RANK 1407]

2272 游　游　swim, float

　　　■ water r 523　　■ banner, follow me! 2268　　■ son, child 1402

BF Hey, you in the *water*! *Follow me* to help save the dolphin *children* which are in danger of becoming stranded in the shallows. Don't try to walk through the water, it takes too long. You'll have to **swim**.　　[12 STROKES　RANK 695]

2273 施　施　execute, carry out

　　　　　　■ banner, follow me! 2268　　■ also*, too* 140

BF I need help. *Follow me*, and you *too* can share in the glory as we assist in the **execution** of our leader's master plan.　　[9 STROKES　RANK 553]

2274 旅　旅　trip, travel　　■ banner, follow me! 2268　　■ clothing 839 (altered)

BF We'll have a grand time on our **trip**! *Follow me!*—but don't forget to pack your *clothing*.　　[10 STROKES　RANK 950]

2275 臼　臼　mortar and pestle

CMP This drawing is strictly suggestive. We'll also associate this component with a dangerous hole or cavity.

2276 臼　臼　mortar　　　　　　　　　■ mortar and pestle 2275

BF It looks like the *pestle* will crush you to bits in the jaw-like grip of the **mortar**.　　[6 STROKES　RANK 4066]

2277 陷　陷　fall into, get bogged down

　　　　　■ hills 735　　■ man 311 (altered)　　■ mortar 2276

The *man* comes down from the *hills*, **falls into** a weird *hole*. It has branches and rocks which impede his escape—he's **bogged down** and must wait for help.　　[10 STROKES　RANK 1262]

2278 毀 毀 **destroy, ruin**

        ■ mortar 2276   ■ labor, work 7   ■ ancient bamboo spear 2053   huǐ

The conquerors, well-equipped with their *ancient bamboo spears*, have laid waste to our lands. Bombs have created *ragged holes* in our fields, and all public *works* have been razed to the ground. The **ruin** and **destruction** is complete.   [13 STROKES   RANK 1160]

2279 插 插 **insert, stick in**

        ■ hand r 29   ■ dry 10   ■ mortar 2276   chā

The powder has to be completely *dry* before you **insert** it by *hand* in the *mortar* for further grinding. Otherwise, you get this dreadful, muddy gunk.

    [12 STROKES   RANK 1495]

2280 鼠 鼠 **mouse, rat**

        ■ mortar 2276   ■ toothy jaws   ■ long tail   shǔ

BF Here's a cute (?) little animal with *toothy jaws* and a *long tail*, but so small it could fit into the opening of a *mortar*. It's a **mouse**!   [13 STROKES   RANK 1693]

Appendix
On-line Resources

On-line resources come in two flavors: **(1)** review and reinforcement; and **(2)** everything else. You can find all these at our Website

www.EZChinesey.com

all (unless otherwise noted) freely available. This appendix describes the material that has been prepared at the time this book was completed. But we're always adding fresh material, so check back often to see what's new!

All these files use the so-called PDF format, and you may download, preview, and print these files using any program (such as Adobe Acrobat™, and there are many others for all computer platforms) that can handle this type of file.

Review and reinforcement
'Review files' include flash cards, end-of-unit review lists, and graded reading practice. Each comes with its personal collection of pros and cons.

Flashcards
No serious study of Chinese characters is complete without some kind of flashcard system.

There is a large file at the EZChinesey Website called easyflash.pdf you can use to print flashcards. The cards are printed according to the units in this book, so there's usually a few blank cards at the end of each unit. Let's first discuss the mundane physical details of flash card production, which turn out to be not so mundane at all.

First off, *our* flash cards break with tradition in size. Ours are relatively small—the size of business cards. Decks of these small cards are easy to carry, convenient for purse or shirt pocket, and a snap to shuffle. To print them, you'll need to load your printer with 'card stock' paper in the color of your choice (ordinary paper doesn't really have sufficient heft).

The cards themselves are printed with lines at all four edges. To print the cards, make sure you **only print** the odd-numbered pages in the file!! (For the teacher's pets among you, you *can* print the cards in two passes. On the first pass, choose 'odd numbered pages only' to print the tops. Take these sheets turn them over and/or rotate them by one hundred-eighty degrees, and print the even numbered pages to get the backs. Experiment with a few pages until you get it right. The backs of these cards contain character and pronunciation information.) The primary cards show the character, its definition, its pronunciation, panel number and page, rank, and unit number. That's the easy part. Now, how do you separate the cards? To be sure, if you load your printer with micro-perforated computer business card stock, each of our cards will be nicely centered on one of these cards. But there are problems. These forms often don't take well to printing (especially in two passes); they often come apart at the seams. Moreover, they are punishingly expensive. If you use top-of-the-line card stock, you'll be spending in excess of $220 just for these cards! Some large stationery companies provide their own brand cards, such as Quill Office Products at www.quill.com (item 7-20393Q), but these don't fold cleanly, and leave all your cards with fuzzy edges. Moreover, they aren't all exactly uniform in size. But the cost for this book's-worth of cards is less than $50, a much thriftier alternative.

But whether regular stock or computer forms, you are still faced with the problem of 'bursting' all those cards. With micro-perforated cards, sit yourself down in front of the television, lose yourself in your favorite action flick, and start folding and tearing.

In case you've opted for solid card stock, what are your options? Office paper cutters are fine but time consuming. Scissors will surely raise blisters on your hands before you're through, and the finished cards will look distressingly ragged regardless of the care you take. My solution has been to use a little-known office appliance specifically designed for the cutting of business cards. This gadget, costing less than $100, cleanly cuts a single sheet into ten cards in two passes, and it's fun to use. Maybe you'll find, as I have, that blank business cards are perfect for making notes to yourself, so the utility of this gadget persists long after you've become a Chinese character expert. Visit us at www.EZChinesey.com to order one.

You'll also find a separate file from which you can print 'dividers' for the finished cards. In addition to divider-sized cards labeled 'Unit 1' through 'Unit 91' there are also dividers with the alphabet, and a page of blank tabs. These last are in case you become so enamored of these cards that you adapt existing information systems to them.

But even after your cards are cut and collated, how do you manage the piles and piles of cards that this process inevitably generates? Surprisingly, there don't appear to be *any* commercial products for business cards which are comparable to index card boxes. By chance, I determined that boxes containing Pennsylvania Dutch sourdough pretzels (in the snack section of your local supermarket, in the pretzel section) will serve admirably, but watch out—these pretzels are quietly addictive! Once you've finished a box, cut off the bottom (or side) to use for your card trays. In my area, metropolitan New

York City, no brand is any more useful than any other (but I do have my taste favorites).

In summary: flashcards have several advantages. They are traditional, convenient, and comfortable—there's nothing like massaging a pack of flash cards. On the other hand, they require labor to prepare them, and some care to store them properly.

End of unit reviews

Review material for the end of each unit is an attempt to provide a convenient review technique without the drawbacks of flash cards (cutting problems, storage concerns). This material appears in the file GBSureview.pdf.

Originally, this kind of material consisted of three lists—a list of pinyin (from which you could quiz yourself on characters and meanings), characters (to review pronunciation and meaning), and definitions (characters and pronunciation). This material was in columns, and you can imagine running up and down each column, reading sometimes from left to right, or from right to left for the sake of variety. However, no matter how you staggered these patterns, you couldn't be sure that you were memorizing the order in which this material was listed rather than the actual content.

For this reason, for each unit, this tripartite grouping is now presented in each of several "shuffles." So, for example, the columns displaying the actual characters are presented once in the order of the text, and thereafter in three random shuffles. The format remains the same, but the re-shuffling provides variety and spice. You can practice this material up and down, left to right, and vice versa on a total of four layouts (the original plus three shuffles), lessening the chance that you are inadvertently memorizing the order rather than the content.

Moreover, it's easy to print this material, for it's formatted for letter-size output. While these sheets may not be as convenient as flashcards, you can easily trash and re-print them as necessary.

Graded practice

'Graded practice' refers to material that you can practice reading or translating, meticulously arranged in such a way that each of its entries uses *only* material that has been presented previously.

There are several Chinese-English dictionary files whose compilers have graciously made them available. The grand-daddy of them all is the CEDICT project started by Paul Denisowski in 1997 which aimed to provide a complete downloadable Chinese-to-English dictionary, accompanied by pronunciation in pinyin. It has recently returned to life under the name CC-CEDICT, and is currently available from

www.mdbg.net/chindict/chindict.php?page=cedict.

Please observe the conditions of its license, which more or less allows you to use this data for both non-commercial and commercial purposes provided that you: mention where you got the data from (attribution) and that in case you improve or add to the data you will share these changes under the same license (share alike). At this time (summer, 2009), there are more than 84,000 entries in this dictionary.

Anyway, since dictionary files are text files, it has proved possible to re-order their entries in such a way that entries depend only on words and syllables that came before. The resulting files have been formatted and typeset, and are quite lengthy (over 500 pages as of summer, 2008). As the compilers of the parent dictionary files augment their files, we will update these practice reading files. The reading practice file originating from the CEDICT project is ezreaderup.pdf.

Other Material
Other on-line references are less compelling. They consist mainly of helpful indices to the book, some useful study aids, and a dictionary look-up shortcut; you should feel free to consult them as time and your needs permit.

Indices of Components and Definitions

Greetings—we hope you've journeyed with us to the end! If you got here by dint of hard work, you will have learned a total of 2280 characters and components, which is how many panels there are in this volume. Of this number, 2178 are independent, legal characters, while 102 are components, with which independent characters are constructed.

These indices present the components and definitions found in this volume, separately, in alphabetical order.

The component index lists all components in alphabetical order. Each index entry contains the panel number, the component, its name, and its page. A total of 102 distinct components appear in this book.

The definition index immediately follows. Character information is alphabetized by the brief definitions that is part of the title line of the panel. Leading asterisks are ignored in the alphabetization process. (Remember, a leading asterisk indicates a grammatical function rather than a definition. A trailing asterisk indicates a meaning that has previously appeared with a different character.) We ignore any leading 'to', 'the', or other short word that is part of the definition. (For example, 'bat' would be ambiguous—is this a noun or a verb?—but 'to bat' helps resolve this ambiguity.) Because these leading 'to's are also ignored during alphabetization, 'to bat' would appear towards the beginning of the b's, and *not* under 'to bat'.

In addition to the definition, each entry contains contains the corresponding character, pinyin, panel number, and the page number in italics.

Component Index

Definition Index

Buddha, kind-hearted person 萨 sà §1260 *(253)*
Buddhist temple 寺 sì §213 *(54)*
build 搭 dā §513 *(111)*
build, construct 筑 zhù §2091 *(412)*
build, fabricate 造 zào §2145 *(421)*
building, house 宇 yǔ §259 *(63)*
bundle, bunch 束 shù §394 *(89)*
bureau, office 局 jú §705 *(147)*
burn, cook, run a fever 烧 shāo §1261 *(253)*
burn, ignite 燃 rán §1272 *(255)*
burnt, scorched 焦 jiāo §1001 *(203)*
burst, break through 溃 kuì §567 *(121)*
bury 埋 mái §72 *(25)*
busy 忙 máng §935 *(191)*
but 但 dàn §965 *(196)*
button 纽 niǔ §811 *(167)*
to button 扣 kòu §59 *(21)*
buy 买 mǎi §340 *(78)*
buy, purchase 购 gòu §791 *(163)*
by chance 偶 ǒu §2212 *(434)*
cage, coop, basket 笼 lóng §1661 *(329)*
calculate, compute 算 suàn §1228 *(247)*
call to, name 称 chēng §1238 *(249)*
call, call out to 唤 huàn §469 *(103)*
call, convene 召 zhào §1552 *(309)*
can, able 能 néng §1740 *(344)*
can, may 堪 kān §1095 *(221)*
can; may 可 kě §60 *(22)*
cancer 癌 ái §698 *(146)*
cannon, firecracker 炮 pào §1253 *(252)*
canon, dictionary 典 diǎn §1308 *(262)*
capital city 京 jīng §1077 *(218)*
capture, catch 获 huò §1657 *(328)*
capture, take prisoner 俘 fú §1408 *(282)*
car 车 chē §1430 *(286)*
card 卡 kǎ §179 *(47)*
careful, cautious 谨 jǐn §1307 *(262)*
carry a burden 荷 hè §964 *(196)*
carry on your head 顶 dǐng §446 *(99)*
carry, take along 携 xié §1515 *(302)*
carry, take, lift 提 tí §238 *(59)*
carve, engrave 雕 diāo §1729 *(342)*
case, casket 函 hán §1847 *(365)*
castrate, spay 奄 yān §455 *(101)*
cat 猫 māo §905 *(184)*
catch birds with a net 罗 luó §663 *(140)*
to catch, capture 捉 zhuō §420 *(94)*
catch, seize 捕 bǔ §1733 *(343)*
category 属 shǔ §2216 *(435)*
cattail 蒲 pú §1735 *(343)*
catty 斤 jīn §118 *(36)*
cauldron for meat or cereal 鬲 lì §279 *(66)*
cautious, careful 慎 shèn §1059 *(215)*
cave, den, hole 穴 xué §1098 *(222)*
celebrate 庆 qìng §685 *(143)*
cereal grain stalk 稿 gǎo §412 *(91)*
cereal, grain 谷 gǔ §1060 *(215)*
ceremony, rite 礼 lǐ §2230 *(437)*
a certain river 洛 luò §2017 *(397)*
certain, some 某 mǒu §397 *(89)*
chair 椅 yǐ §408 *(91)*
change, alter 移 yí §669 *(141)*
change, transform 化 huà §1016 *(206)*
chant softly 哦 é §362 *(82)*

chant, recite 吟 yín §1380 *(276)*
chapter, section 章 zhāng §1198 *(241)*
character, word 字 zì §1415 *(283)*
chase, pursue 追 zhuī §2241 *(440)*
to chat 聊 liáo §1694 *(336)*
cheap 便 pián §1839 *(363)*
cheat, hoodwink 蒙 mēng §1590 *(316)*
check, examine 检 jiǎn §1355 *(271)*
check, investigate 查 chá §390 *(88)*
cherish, value highly 惜 xī §1301 *(261)*
chest, bosom, thorax 胸 xiōng §1944 *(383)*
chicken 鸡 jī §1946 *(383)*
child 童 tóng §1186 *(239)*
child* 孩 hái §2225 *(437)*
chilly, sad 凄 qī §614 *(131)*
choose, select 选 xuǎn §2147 *(421)*
choose*, select* 择 zé §1920 *(378)*
cinnamon 桂 guì §387 *(87)*
clan, race, tribe, group 族 zú §2269 *(445)*
clan, sect, faction 宗 zōng §1247 *(251)*
clap 拍 pāi §204 *(52)*
clause in document 款 kuǎn §1225 *(247)*
claw 爪 zhuǎ §2205 *(432)*
clean 洁 jié §528 *(114)*
clean, net (price) 净 jìng §578 *(124)*
clear* 楚 chǔ §424 *(94)*
clear*, bright* 朗 lǎng §1938 *(382)*
clear, clear up 清 qīng §1753 *(347)*
clear, fine (of weather) 晴 qíng §1792 *(354)*
clear, obvious 昭 zhāo §1554 *(309)*
clever, ingenious 巧 qiǎo §2245 *(440)*
clever, sharp 灵 líng §1105 *(223)*
cliff, crag 岩 yán §1388 *(278)*
cling to, be near 巴 bā §2190 *(430)*
cloth 布 bù §1641 *(325)*
clothes, garment 服 fú §1868 *(369)*
clothing 衣 yī §839 *(172)*
cloud 云 yún §751 *(155)*
cluck 咕 gū §54 *(21)*
cluster 丛 cóng §315 *(74)*
coal 煤 méi §1269 *(254)*
coarse 粗 cū §1129 *(228)*
coerce, force 胁 xié §1572 *(313)*
cold 冷 lěng §1378 *(276)*
cold, glacial 寒 hán §1316 *(264)*
color 颜 yán §1296 *(260)*
color, look 色 sè §2192 *(430)*
colorful 彩 cǎi §1350 *(270)*
come close to 接 jiē §1185 *(239)*
come 来 lái §1128 *(228)*
comfort, console 抚 fǔ §1643 *(326)*
comment, criticize 评 píng §1162 *(234)*
commerce, trade 贸 mào §1525 *(304)*
commonplace 凡 fán §2056 *(405)*
companion, partner 伴 bàn §1165 *(234)*
company 司 sī §112 *(34)*
comparatively 较 jiào §1816 *(359)*
compared with 比 bǐ §146 *(41)*
compassionate, kind 慈 cí §927 *(189)*
compel, force, coerce 迫 pò §2156 *(423)*
compensate, pay for 赔 péi §1277 *(256)*
compensate, repay 偿 cháng §1265 *(254)*
compete, contend 竞 jìng §1192 *(240)*
compete, game, competition 赛 sài §1314 *(263)*
compile, edit 辑 jí §1440 *(288)*

fortress 堡 bǎo §988 *(201)*
foundation, site 址 zhǐ §242 *(59)*
four 四 sì §289 *(69)*
fourth 丁 dīng §25 *(15)*
fragile, brittle 脆 cuì §863 *(177)*
fragile, frail 娇 jiāo §1701 *(337)*
fragrant 香 xiāng §411 *(91)*
fragrant, virtuous (name) 芳 fāng §1624 *(322)*
frequently, repeatedly 频 pín §1620 *(321)*
fresh, new 鲜 xiān §1255 *(252)*
friend 朋 péng §1741 *(345)*
friend, associate 友 yǒu §1798 *(356)*
frighten 吓 xià §180 *(47)*
from 从 cóng §313 *(73)*
fruit 果 guǒ §388 *(87)*
full of trees 森 sēn §377 *(85)*
full, complete 满 mǎn §541 *(116)*
full, overflowing 弥 mí §1284 *(257)*
full, satiated 饱 bǎo §2198 *(431)*
gain, win 赢 yíng §2065 *(407)*
gallop, prance 腾 téng §1785 *(353)*
garden 园 yuán §294 *(69)*
gasp for breath 喘 chuǎn §90 *(29)*
gather together 汇 huì §532 *(115)*
gather, collect 集 jí §1003 *(203)*
gather, unite 统 tǒng §824 *(169)*
gathering place, field 场 chǎng §1546 *(308)*
general, universal 普 pǔ §1124 *(227)*
generation 世 shì §106 *(33)*
Germany 德 dé §1039 *(211)*
get along with sb 处 chǔ §1972 *(389)*
get mad 恼 nǎo §1832 *(362)*
ghost, spirit 鬼 guǐ §1591 *(316)*
giggle 嘻 xī §1170 *(236)*
to girdle 佩 pèi §2100 *(413)*
give a present 送 sòng §2152 *(422)*
give birth to 生 shēng §191 *(50)*
give birth to* 产 chǎn §1221 *(246)*
give or take a test 考 kǎo §2250 *(441)*
give up 舍 shě §328 *(76)*
give 给 gěi §819 *(168)*
give* 予 yǔ §763 *(157)*
give** 与 yǔ §645 *(136)*
give, present 奉 fèng §1363 *(273)*
glad to, enjoy 乐 lè §1240 *(249)*
glass 玻 bō §1894 *(373)*
glazed tile 璃 lí §2214 *(435)*
glory, splendor 华 huá §1018 *(207)*
go against, disobey 逆 nì §2129 *(418)*
go back, return 归 guī §1689 *(335)*
go on a journey 征 zhēng §1037 *(210)*
go to, attend 赴 fù §423 *(94)*
go 去 qù §754 *(156)*
goblin, demon 妖 yāo §588 *(125)*
god, divinity 神 shén §2235 *(439)*
gold 金 jīn §1157 *(233)*
good fortune 福 fú §2231 *(438)*
good, fine 良 liáng §1873 *(370)*
good, kind 善 shàn §1149 *(232)*
good, OK 好 hǎo §1405 *(281)*
goods 货 huò §1019 *(207)*
gorge, canyon 峡 xiá §1281 *(257)*
gourd 卢 lú §712 *(148)*
government office 署 shǔ §1463 *(292)*
government official 官 guān §2239 *(439)*

government, political 政 zhèng §1992 *(392)*
grab, seize, arrest 抓 zhuā §2208 *(433)*
gradually 渐 jiàn §1438 *(287)*
grain, food, provisions 粮 liáng §1940 *(382)*
grain, granule, pellet 粒 lì §1280 *(257)*
grandpa 爷 yé §1813 *(358)*
grandson 孙 sūn §1410 *(282)*
grasp 执 zhí §2050 *(404)*
grasp, hold 持 chí §214 *(54)*
grass 草 cǎo §95 *(30)*
gray, ash 灰 huī §1652 *(327)*
great, grand 宏 hóng §1654 *(327)*
great, imposing 伟 wěi §981 *(199)*
green jade 碧 bì §1387 *(277)*
green 绿 lù §825 *(169)*
to grind 研 yán §1676 *(332)*
guard against, warn 戒 jiè §1686 *(334)*
guard, defend against 防 fáng §1561 *(311)*
guard, defend 守 shǒu §254 *(61)*
guard, protect 卫 wèi §113 *(35)*
guess 猜 cāi §1757 *(347)*
guest accommodation 馆 guǎn §2242 *(440)*
guest, visitor 宾 bīn §1539 *(307)*
guide, lead 导 dǎo §871 *(178)*
guide, lead, induce 诱 yòu §1594 *(316)*
guiding principle 纲 gāng §1827 *(361)*
gulf, bay 湾 wān §1578 *(314)*
gush, well up 涌 yǒng §1747 *(346)*
hair 毛 máo §231 *(57)*
halberd 戈 gē §359 *(82)*
half, semi 半 bàn §1164 *(234)*
hall, front courtyard 庭 tíng §2184 *(429)*
hall, palace, temple 殿 diàn §2092 *(412)*
halt, stay 驻 zhù §882 *(180)*
hamlet 村 cūn §407 *(91)*
hand over, transmit 递 dì §2167 *(425)*
hand 手 shǒu §27 *(15)*
hand, also 又 yòu §1796 *(355)*
handkerchief 帕 pà §205 *(52)*
handle a matter 将 jiāng §1488 *(297)*
handsome 帅 shuài §1690 *(335)*
handsome* 俊 jùn §1965 *(388)*
handsome, graceful 曼 màn §1912 *(377)*
handsome, talented 隽 juàn §1514 *(302)*
hang 挂 guà §30 *(16)*
hang, suspend 吊 diào §131 *(38)*
happy 欣 xīn §497 *(108)*
happy, joyful 愉 yú §1510 *(301)*
happy, pleased 欢 huān §1908 *(377)*
harbor, port 港 gǎng §1311 *(263)*
hard pressed 困 kùn §395 *(89)*
hard, firm, strong 刚 gāng §1826 *(361)*
hard, solid 坚 jiān §1853 *(366)*
hard, stiff 硬 yìng §1840 *(363)*
hardworking 辛 xīn §1200 *(242)*
harm, injure 害 hài §250 *(61)*
harmonize, cooperate, assist 协 xié §1571 *(313)*
harness, draw a cart 驾 jià §1541 *(307)*
harsh, severe, serious 厉 lì §678 *(142)*
hasten 奔 bēn §433 *(96)*
hasten, hurry 趋 qū §495 *(108)*
hasty 匆 cōng §1508 *(301)*
hat 帽 mào §132 *(38)*
hat, cap 冠 guān §297 *(70)*
hate 恨 hèn §1878 *(371)*

hatred 仇 chóu §2048 *(403)*
have a rest 歇 xiē §652 *(138)*
have fun, amuse oneself 玩 wán §295 *(70)*
have jurisdiction over 辖 xiá §1626 *(322)*
have not yet 未 wèi §381 *(86)*
have not 没 méi §2054 *(405)*
have sb do sth 使 shǐ §1837 *(363)*
have 有 yǒu §1725 *(342)*
hay for fodder 刍 chú §462 *(102)*
he 他 tā §1015 *(206)*
he, she 伊 yī §1711 *(339)*
head for 奔 bēn §1671 *(331)*
head 头 tóu §339 *(78)*
head, leader 首 shǒu §1167 *(235)*
healthy, peaceful, abundant 康 kāng §692 *(145)*
healthy, strong 健 jiàn §2181 *(428)*
to heap up 堆 duī §993 *(202)*
hear, listen 听 tīng §119 *(36)*
hear, smell 闻 wén §200 *(51)*
heart 心 xīn §907 *(185)*
heaven 天 tiān §333 *(77)*
heavy 重 zhòng §228 *(57)*
to help 帮 bāng §747 *(154)*
help, aid, assist 援 yuán §1933 *(381)*
help, assist, aid 助 zhù §1564 *(312)*
hemp, pocked, pitted 麻 má §694 *(145)*
herd 牧 mù §1996 *(393)*
herd, crowd, flock 群 qún §1713 *(339)*
hero 英 yīng §354 *(81)*
heroic 侠 xiá §1178 *(237)*
hey! 哎 āi §1819 *(360)*
hide 潜 qián §542 *(117)*
hide, conceal 藏 cáng §945 *(193)*
hide, dodge, avoid 躲 duǒ §2103 *(414)*
hideous 丑 chǒu §37 *(18)*
high mountain peak 岳 yuè §122 *(36)*
high 高 gāo §275 *(65)*
hinder, block 阻 zǔ §738 *(152)*
hinder, impede 妨 fáng §1536 *(306)*
hinder, obstruct 碍 ài §1391 *(278)*
his, her, its, theirs 其 qí §1093 *(221)*
historical record 纪 jì §856 *(175)*
history 史 shǐ §1835 *(363)*
hit 打 dǎ §33 *(17)*
hog, pig 猪 zhū §1586 *(315)*
hold in the palm 托 tuō §236 *(58)*
hold one's breath 屏 bǐng §1679 *(333)*
hold or carry in arms 抱 bào §876 *(179)*
hold or grasp 把 bǎ §2191 *(430)*
hold your head high 昂 áng §161 *(44)*
hold, grasp, shake hands 握 wò §784 *(162)*
hole, aperture 孔 kǒng §1412 *(282)*
hole, cavity 洞 dòng §533 *(115)*
home 家 jiā §1426 *(285)*
honest and upright 廉 lián §691 *(144)*
honest, sincere 诚 chéng §630 *(134)*
honor, venerate 尊 zūn §1214 *(244)*
honorable 荣 róng §402 *(90)*
hope 希 xī §1823 *(360)*
horizontal stroke 横 héng §1306 *(262)*
horn, corner, angle 角 jiǎo §1749 *(346)*
horse 马 mǎ §878 *(179)*
hot, fervent 热 rè §2076 *(409)*
house 房 fáng §1560 *(311)*

house, room 屋 wū §783 *(161)*
how can one help? 奈 nài §1215 *(244)*
how come? why? 嗯 ńg §917 *(187)*
how could it be? 岂 qǐ §854 *(174)*
how, why 怎 zěn §1449 *(289)*
how, why, when 曷 hé §647 *(137)*
huge 巨 jù §18 *(12)*
huh? what? 么 me §1422 *(284)*
huh? 乎 hū §1158 *(233)*
hum, croon 哼 hēng §1401 *(280)*
human relationship 伦 lún §1020 *(207)*
Hunan province (abbrev) 湘 xiāng §548 *(118)*
hundred (fraudproof) 佰 bǎi §966 *(197)*
hundred million 亿 yì §2095 *(412)*
hundred 百 bǎi §203 *(52)*
hungry 饿 è §2200 *(431)*
hunt, chase 猎 liè §1321 *(265)*
I (woman's form) 妾 qiè §1184 *(238)*
I 我 wǒ §361 *(82)*
ice 冰 bīng §577 *(124)*
idea, meaning 意 yì §1191 *(240)*
idle 闲 xián §400 *(90)*
if, in case 倘 tǎng §1145 *(231)*
imitate 效 xiào §2000 *(394)*
imitate, copy, resemble 仿 fǎng §1601 *(318)*
immortal 仙 xiān §969 *(197)*
impatient, anxious 急 jí §1904 *(376)*
imperial court 廷 tíng §2183 *(429)*
imperial edict 敕 chì §2004 *(395)*
imperial robes 衮 gǔn §1270 *(254)*
impoverished, exhausted 穷 qióng §1607 *(319)*
in advance 预 yù §786 *(162)*
in an instant 顷 qǐng §458 *(101)*
in disorder 乱 luàn §232 *(57)*
in the direction of 顺 shùn §1496 *(298)*
in the direction of, toward 往 wǎng §1041 *(211)*
in the end 竟 jìng §1193 *(240)*
in; at; to 于 yú §26 *(15)*
inch 寸 cùn §210 *(53)*
incline, lean 倾 qīng §1021 *(207)*
inclined to one side 偏 piān §1027 *(208)*
inclined to 侧 cè §1011 *(205)*
incomplete, deficient 残 cán §666 *(140)*
increase 添 tiān §1080 *(218)*
increase, add 增 zēng §1173 *(236)*
incredible 玄 xuán §776 *(159)*
indicates continuing progress 着 zhe §1665 *(330)*
indicates sth just happened 才 cái §1467 *(293)*
indication of excitement, doubt 啦 la §1181 *(238)*
inferior 亚 yà §1119 *(226)*
inferior, low quality 劣 liè §1533 *(306)*
initiate, inaugurate 创 chuàng §869 *(178)*
injure, wound 伤 shāng §1568 *(312)*
ink, ink stick 墨 mò §805 *(166)*
inquire 询 xún §641 *(136)*
insect 虫 chóng §890 *(182)*
insert, stick in 插 chā §2279 *(447)*
inside 里 lǐ §71 *(24)*
inside* 内 nèi §318 *(74)*
inspect, scrutinize 察 chá §1891 *(373)*
inspect, supervise 监 jiān §237 *(59)*
to instruct, exhort 咐 fù §972 *(198)*
instruct, teach 授 shòu §1867 *(369)*

recall, remember 忆 yì §2045 *(403)*
receive 受 shòu §1866 *(369)*
receive, accept 收 shōu §1997 *(393)*
recognize, know 认 rèn §627 *(133)*
record, file, law case 案 àn §605 *(129)*
record, write down 录 lù §549 *(118)*
red 红 hóng §810 *(167)*
red, be flushed 赤 chì §1504 *(300)*
red, cinnabar 丹 dān §1718 *(340)*
refined 斯 sī §1096 *(222)*
reflect, mirror 鉴 jiàn §1224 *(246)*
reflect, shine 映 yìng §355 *(81)*
regard, look at 视 shì §2237 *(439)*
region, area 域 yù §364 *(83)*
regret, repent 悔 huǐ §941 *(192)*
relationship marker 之 zhī §2179 *(427)*
relatives 亲 qīn §1202 *(242)*
relax 舒 shū §765 *(158)*
rely, depend on 赖 lài §491 *(106)*
remain, be left over 剩 shèng §2120 *(417)*
remember 记 jì §855 *(175)*
remote, secluded 幽 yōu §795 *(163)*
remove, do away with 除 chú §1236 *(248)*
remove, take away, withdraw 撤 chè §2227
   (437)
rent 租 zū §414 *(92)*
reputation, fame 誉 yù §1278 *(257)*
request, entreat 求 qiú §557 *(120)*
rescue, save, salvage 救 jiù §2026 *(399)*
resemble 像 xiàng §1519 *(303)*
reside 居 jū §707 *(148)*
residence, house 宅 zhái §264 *(64)*
resist or repel 拒 jù §31 *(17)*
resist, fight, defy 抗 kàng §2086 *(411)*
respect, adulate 崇 chóng §1268 *(254)*
respect, offer politely 敬 jìng §2033 *(401)*
respectful 恭 gōng §1309 *(262)*
respectful, dignified 穆 mù §1289 *(258)*
respectful, solemn 肃 sù §1714 *(339)*
responsibility 责 zé §439 *(97)*
rest content 安 ān §604 *(129)*
to rest 休 xiū §986 *(200)*
restrain, restrict 抑 yì §162 *(44)*
retain, stay 留 liú §1523 *(303)*
retreat, retire 退 tuì §2140 *(420)*
return to 返 fǎn §2138 *(420)*
return 回 huí §42 *(19)*
revive, Suzhou 苏 sū §1563 *(311)*
revolve, circle, spin 旋 xuán §2270 *(445)*
rice or grain 禾 hé §409 *(91)*
rice 米 mǐ §1127 *(227)*
rich, wealthy 富 fù §251 *(61)*
ride or sit astride 骑 qí §883 *(181)*
rifle, gun 枪 qiāng §870 *(178)*
right (-hand) 右 yòu §1638 *(325)*
right, power, authority 权 quán §1869 *(369)*
ripe, cooked, familiar 熟 shú §2094 *(412)*
rise (water, prices) 涨 zhǎng §1544 *(307)*
rise 起 qǐ §860 *(176)*
rites 仪 yí §1795 *(355)*
river 川 chuān §1495 *(298)*
river* 河 hé §529 *(114)*
river, Yangtze 江 jiāng §524 *(114)*
road, journey 途 tú §2131 *(419)*
road, path, way 路 lù §2021 *(398)*

rob, plunder 劫 jié §1540 *(307)*
robe, gown 袍 páo §875 *(178)*
roc 鹏 péng §1742 *(345)*
rod, stick 棍 gùn §460 *(101)*
roll, turn, scram! 滚 gǔn §1271 *(255)*
room for a special purpose 堂 táng §1140
   (230)
room 间 jiān §198 *(51)*
room* 室 shì §757 *(157)*
root or stem of plant 本 běn §378 *(85)*
rope 绳 shéng §816 *(168)*
rose 玫 méi §1991 *(392)*
rot, fester 烂 làn §1156 *(233)*
rotten, putrid, stale 腐 fǔ §1033 *(209)*
round 圆 yuán §443 *(98)*
round, circular 团 tuán §1468 *(293)*
rouse, shake, vibrate 振 zhèn §1931 *(381)*
royal 'we' 朕 zhèn §1784 *(353)*
rub 摩 mó §695 *(145)*
rub, scrape 擦 cā §1892 *(373)*
rule, order 程 chéng §416 *(93)*
ruler 尺 chǐ §704 *(147)*
rules and regulations 规 guī §338 *(78)*
run into, collide 撞 zhuàng §1187 *(239)*
run 跑 pǎo §950 *(193)*
run, manage, have charge of 管 guǎn §2240
   (440)
rush 赶 gǎn §422 *(94)*
Russian 俄 é §985 *(200)*
rustling sound 瑟 sè §1444 *(288)*
ruthless, relentless 狠 hěn §1877 *(371)*
sacrificial animal 牺 xī §292 *(69)*
sad, sorrow 悲 bēi §909 *(186)*
sage, saint 圣 shèng §1923 *(380)*
sail, (vehicle) moves quickly 驶 shǐ §1952
   (385)
salt 盐 yán §506 *(110)*
salty 咸 xián §371 *(84)*
same, similar 同 tóng §129 *(38)*
sand 沙 shā §1479 *(295)*
sausage 腊 là §1319 *(264)*
say, be called 谓 wèi §631 *(134)*
scale, climb 登 dēng §1251 *(251)*
scatter, sprinkle 撒 sǎ §2040 *(402)*
scholar 士 shì §8 *(10)*
school 校 xiào §1817 *(359)*
scold, curse 骂 lì §272 *(65)*
scold, reprimand 斥 chì §177 *(46)*
scorching hot 炎 yán §1102 *(223)*
sea 海 hǎi §601 *(128)*
seal, stamp 印 yìn §158 *(43)*
search, collect 搜 sōu §1986 *(391)*
search, demand, exact 索 suǒ §833 *(171)*
search, seek 寻 xún §217 *(55)*
season 令 lìng §1373 *(274)*
season* 季 jì §1407 *(282)*
seat 座 zuò §688 *(144)*
second in a series 乙 yǐ §2107 *(415)*
2nd in seniority 仲 zhòng §959 *(195)*
secret 秘 mì §1443 *(288)*
section, group 组 zǔ §812 *(167)*
section, part 段 duàn §2075 *(409)*
secure, solid 巩 gǒng §2089 *(411)*
see 见 jiàn §301 *(71)*
seedling 苗 miáo §97 *(30)*
seek 找 zhǎo §360 *(82)*

seem, appear 似 sì §1024 *(208)*
seem, like, if 若 ruò §1639 *(325)*
seize 夺 duó §425 *(94)*
select, pick 挑 tiāo §2117 *(417)*
self 自 zì §202 *(52)*
self* 己 jǐ §852 *(174)*
selfish, personal, private 私 sī §790 *(162)*
sell 卖 mài §341 *(79)*
sell* 售 shòu §1028 *(208)*
send out, deliver 发 fā §1799 *(356)*
send, deliver 致 zhì §2029 *(400)*
send, dispatch 遣 qiǎn §2243 *(440)*
send, mail, consign 寄 jì §500 *(109)*
sentence 句 jù §639 *(135)*
sentiment, sensibility 情 qíng §1723 *(341)*
separate, impede 隔 gé §744 *(153)*
serious, earnest 郑 zhèng §1115 *(225)*
serve, wait upon 侍 shì §963 *(196)*
set a limit, restrict 限 xiàn §1876 *(371)*
set free, explain 释 shì §1911 *(377)*
set up, found, establish 设 shè §2068 *(407)*
settled, steady, stable 稳 wěn §1926 *(380)*
seven 七 qī §137 *(39)*
several, how many? 几 jǐ §2051 *(404)*
sew, stitch 缝 féng §2133 *(419)*
shadow, reflection 影 yǐng §1290 *(259)*
shake, quake 震 zhèn §1930 *(381)*
shake, wave 摇 yáo §1346 *(269)*
shallow, superficial 浅 qiǎn §547 *(118)*
shame, embarrass 羞 xiū §1664 *(330)*
share, portion 份 fèn §1576 *(313)*
sharp, acute 锐 ruì §1329 *(266)*
sharp, keen 敏 mǐn §2011 *(396)*
she 她 tā §595 *(126)*
sheath, cover 套 tào §1516 *(302)*
shed, take off 脱 tuō §1254 *(252)*
sheep 羊 yáng §1147 *(231)*
shell, housing, case 壳 ké §2058 *(406)*
shield 盾 dùn §733 *(152)*
shine, illuminate 照 zhào §1555 *(309)*
ship, craft 航 háng §2087 *(411)*
ship, vessel 船 chuán §2079 *(410)*
shipboard cabin or hold 舱 cāng §867 *(177)*
shoe 鞋 xié §102 *(32)*
shoe* 履 lǚ §1971 *(389)*
to shoot 射 shè §1633 *(323)*
shop 店 diàn §684 *(143)*
shore, coast 岸 àn §680 *(143)*
short of stature 矮 ǎi §594 *(126)*
short, brief 短 duǎn §1171 *(236)*
short-tailed bird 隹 zhuī §992 *(202)*
shoulder 肩 jiān §1720 *(341)*
show, indicate 示 shì §1064 *(215)*
shut, close 关 guān §1113 *(224)*
shut*, close* 闭 bì §1469 *(294)*
side 旁 páng §1520 *(303)*
side, margin, edge 边 biān §2143 *(421)*
sigh, exclaim 叹 tàn §1939 *(382)*
sign one's name 签 qiān §1357 *(272)*
silent, keep silent 默 mò §804 *(165)*
silk 帛 bó §206 *(52)*
silk* 丝 sī §809 *(166)*
silver 银 yín §1881 *(371)*
simple, simplified 简 jiǎn §245 *(60)*
sincere 敦 dūn §2002 *(395)*
sincere, honest 愿 yuàn §926 *(188)*

sing 唱 chàng §75 *(25)*
single, sole 单 dān §1166 *(234)*
to sink 沈 chén §1651 *(327)*
sit 坐 zuò §321 *(75)*
situation 况 kuàng §572 *(123)*
six 六 liù §1062 *(215)*
skill, ability 技 jì §1885 *(372)*
skill, art 艺 yì §2044 *(403)*
skin 肤 fū §1788 *(353)*
slanting, tilting 颇 pō §1899 *(375)*
slave, enslave 奴 nú §1928 *(381)*
sleep 睡 shuì §286 *(68)*
sleep, dormancy 眠 mián §715 *(149)*
sleeve 袖 xiù §840 *(172)*
slice, flake 片 piàn §1485 *(297)*
slide, glide, sneak off 溜 liū §1524 *(304)*
slightly, somewhat 稍 shāo §1235 *(248)*
slippery, smooth, cunning 滑 huá §564 *(121)*
slope, plain 坡 pō §1893 *(373)*
slow 慢 màn §1914 *(378)*
slowly, gently 徐 xú §1263 *(253)*
small boat 艇 tǐng §2187 *(429)*
small box 盒 hé §516 *(112)*
small 小 xiǎo §1063 *(215)*
smear, apply 涂 tú §1075 *(217)*
smelt, refine 炼 liàn §1584 *(314)*
smoke 烟 yān §1108 *(224)*
smooth 亨 hēng §1400 *(280)*
snake, serpent 蛇 shé §897 *(183)*
snow 雪 xuě §87 *(28)*
so, therefore 乃 nǎi §1513 *(302)*
society, group 社 shè §2236 *(439)*
soft, pliant 软 ruǎn §1592 *(316)*
soft, supple, gentle 柔 róu §1613 *(320)*
soldier 兵 bīng §1483 *(296)*
solid 固 gù §53 *(20)*
solid, substantial 实 shí §342 *(79)*
solitary, isolated 孤 gū §1413 *(283)*
some 些 xiē §234 *(58)*
son 儿 ér §288 *(68)*
son, child 子 zǐ §1402 *(280)*
Song dynasty 宋 sòng §487 *(106)*
song 歌 gē §489 *(106)*
sorrow, lament 哀 āi §849 *(174)*
sort, kind 般 bān §2080 *(410)*
soul, spirit, mood 魂 hún §1608 *(319)*
sound 音 yīn §1189 *(239)*
sound, voice 声 shēng §722 *(150)*
soup 汤 tāng §1527 *(304)*
sour, tart 酸 suān §1980 *(391)*
source of river, fountainhead 源 yuán §677
    (142)
South Korea 韩 hán §117 *(35)*
south 南 nán §1209 *(243)*
sow, broadcast 播 bō §1324 *(265)*
sparrow 雀 què §1081 *(218)*
sparse 稀 xī §1824 *(361)*
sparse, scattered 疏 shū §2220 *(436)*
speak 曰 yuē §64 *(22)*
speak, talk 说 shuō §1052 *(213)*
special, unusual 特 tè §215 *(54)*
speech 言 yán §270 *(64)*
spell 拼 pīn §1678 *(333)*
spike, sharp point 芒 máng §277 *(66)*
spit 吐 tǔ §55 *(21)*
split, divide up 裂 liè §847 *(173)*

Pin Yin Index

Here are all characters listed according to their pīnyīn pronunciation. The parenthesized number following the pīnyīn is the number of homonyms listed; we omit this information if there are no homonyms. Characters with the same pronunciation are arranged by frequency order. The numbers refer, though, to the panel in which they appear in this work, and its page number (in italics).

Let's summarize some interesting information. First, let's agree that a "pronunciation" refers to a single pīnyīn transcription, so that (for example) 'bā', 'bǎ', and 'ba' are three pronunciations. For any valid pronunciations, there will be one or more characters with that pronunciation.

In this index, there are 939 different pronunciations.
There are 426 pronunciations which map to 1 character.
There are 224 pronunciations which map to 2 characters.
There are 128 pronunciations which map to 3 characters.
There are 67 pronunciations which map to 4 characters.
There are 39 pronunciations which map to 5 characters.
There are 18 pronunciations which map to 6 characters.
There are 12 pronunciations which map to 7 characters.
There are 8 pronunciations which map to 8 characters.
There are 5 pronunciations which map to 9 characters.
There are 3 pronunciations which map to 10 characters.
There are 2 pronunciations which map to 11 characters.
There is 1 pronunciation which maps to 12 characters.
There are 3 pronunciations which map to 14 characters.
There is 1 pronunciation which maps to 16 characters.
There are 2 pronunciations which map to 17 characters.

The biggest winners in this syllable-to-character lottery are the syllables 'shì' and 'yì' which each map to 17 distinct characters. The syllable 'jì' maps to 16 characters, while 'fù', 'lì', and 'yù' each map to fourteen. 'Xī' maps to twelve, and 'jiàn' and 'wèi' map to eleven characters apiece. Finally, we'll mention that 'jí', 'jiān', and 'jù' each map to ten characters.

a	啊 §740	phrase suffix (153)	
ā	阿 §739	particle before names (153)	
āi (3)	埃 §793	dirt, dust (163)	
	哀 §849	sorrow, lament (174)	
	哎§1819	hey! (360)	
ái	癌 §698	cancer (146)	
ǎi	矮 §594	short of stature (126)	
ài (3)	爱§2121	love (417)	

	艾§1818	to end, stop (359)
	碍§1391	hinder, obstruct (278)
ān	安 §604	rest content (129)
àn (4)	案 §605	record, file, law case (129)
	按 §606	press, push down, according to (129)
	暗§1190	dark, dim (239)
	岸 §680	shore, coast (143)

áng	昂 §161	hold your head high *(44)*
áo	敖 §2008	ramble *(396)*
ào (3)	奥 §1135	profound, abstruse *(229)*
	澳 §1273	bay, cove *(256)*
	傲 §2009	proud, haughty *(396)*
ba	吧 §2194	let's do this (particle) *(431)*
bā (2)	八 §1048	eight *(213)*
	巴 §2190	cling to, be near *(430)*
bá	拔 §1951	uproot, pull out *(385)*
bǎ	把 §2191	hold or grasp *(430)*
bà (3)	爸 §2195	dad *(431)*
	罢 §758	stop, cease *(157)*
	霸 §1744	overlord *(345)*
bái	白 §201	white *(51)*
bǎi (4)	百 §203	hundred *(52)*
	摆 §759	place, put, arrange *(157)*
	柏 §401	cypress *(90)*
	佰 §966	hundred (fraudproof) *(197)*
bài (2)	败 §1998	lose, be defeated *(393)*
	拜 §28	do obeisance, salute *(15)*
bān (3)	般 §2080	sort, kind *(410)*
	班 §1692	team, class *(335)*
	搬 §2081	take away, remove, move (house) *(410)*
bǎn (2)	版 §1864	edition, newspaper page *(368)*
	板 §1917	board, plank *(378)*
bàn (4)	办 §1550	do, manage, set up *(308)*
	半 §1164	half, semi *(234)*
	伴 §1165	companion, partner *(234)*
	扮 §1512	dress up as, disguise as *(302)*
bāng (2)	帮 §747	to help *(154)*
	邦 §746	nation state *(154)*
bǎng	膀 §1521	upper arm, shoulder *(303)*
bāo (3)	包 §857	wrap, envelope *(176)*
	胞 §1771	womb, sibling *(350)*
	剥 §568	to peel, shell, skin *(121)*
báo	薄 §1739	thin, flimsy *(344)*
bǎo (4)	保 §987	protect, defend *(201)*
	宝 §255	treasure, precious jewel *(61)*
	堡 §988	fortress *(201)*
	饱 §2198	full, satiated *(431)*
bào (4)	报 §1862	newspaper *(368)*
	暴 §1312	sudden and violent, savage *(263)*
	抱 §876	hold or carry in arms *(179)*
	爆 §1313	explode, burst, quick-fry *(263)*
bēi (4)	背 §483	bear, shoulder *(105)*
	悲 §909	sad, sorrow *(186)*
	杯 §1453	cup *(290)*
	卑 §1486	low, inferior *(297)*
běi	北 §145	north *(41)*
bèi (5)	被 §1844	quilt, passive marker *(364)*
	备 §2027	prepare, get ready *(400)*
	贝 §430	cowrie *(95)*
	倍 §1197	-fold *(241)*
	辈 §1435	lifetime *(287)*
bēn (2)	奔 §1671	head for *(331)*
	贲 §433	hasten *(96)*
běn	本 §378	root or stem of plant *(85)*
bī	逼 §2169	force, press on towards *(426)*
bí	鼻 §1704	nose *(338)*
bǐ (4)	比 §146	compared with *(41)*
	笔 §246	pen *(60)*
	彼 §1898	other party, that, those *(375)*
	匕 §142	ancient ladle *(40)*
bì (8)	必 §1442	must *(288)*
	避 §2158	avoid, evade *(424)*
	毕 §148	finish, conclude *(41)*
	币 §230	money, currency *(57)*
	闭 §1469	shut*, close* *(294)*
	壁 §1257	wall, cliff, rampart *(252)*
	臂 §1773	arm, upper arm *(351)*
	碧 §1387	green jade *(277)*
biān (3)	边 §2143	side, margin, edge *(421)*
	编 §834	weave, plait *(171)*
	鞭 §1841	a whip *(364)*
biǎn	扁 §729	flat, crushed *(151)*
biàn (4)	变 §1865	transform, change into *(368)*
	遍 §2153	all over, everywhere *(422)*
	辩 §1267	argue, dispute, debate *(254)*
	辨 §1222	distinguish between *(246)*
biāo	标 §1066	to mark, label *(216)*
biǎo	表 §841	external, surface *(172)*
bié	别 §1548	do not, must not *(308)*
bīn	宾 §1539	guest, visitor *(307)*
bīng (2)	兵 §1483	soldier *(296)*
	冰 §577	ice *(124)*
bǐng (2)	屏 §1679	hold one's breath *(333)*
	丙 §474	third in series *(104)*
bìng (2)	并 §1677	an intensifier *(333)*
	病 §701	disease, fall sick *(147)*
bō (4)	波 §1895	wave, ripple of water *(373)*
	播 §1324	sow, broadcast *(265)*
	玻 §1894	glass *(373)*
	拨 §1858	poke, stir, turn *(367)*
bó (4)	伯 §970	father's elder brother *(197)*
	博 §1736	win, gain *(344)*
	勃 §1619	flourishing, thriving *(321)*
	帛 §206	silk *(52)*
bǔ (3)	补 §845	mend, patch *(173)*
	捕 §1733	catch, seize *(343)*
	卜 §170	foretell *(45)*
bù (5)	不 §1452	no! *(290)*
	部 §1182	part, section *(238)*
	步 §1501	step *(299)*
	布 §1641	cloth *(325)*
	怖 §1660	fear, be afraid *(328)*
cā	擦 §1892	rub, scrape *(373)*
cāi	猜 §1757	guess *(347)*
cái (3)	才 §1467	indicates sth just happened *(293)*
	材 §1471	timber *(294)*
	裁 §846	cut, cut cloth *(173)*
cǎi (2)	采 §1348	pick, gather *(270)*
	彩 §1350	colorful *(270)*
cài (2)	财 §1470	wealth, riches *(294)*
	菜 §1349	dish, course, veggies *(270)*
cān (2)	参 §1292	take part in, participate *(259)*
	餐 §1950	eat, meal *(385)*
cán	残 §666	incomplete, deficient *(140)*

	脆 §863	fragile, brittle (177)		递§2167	hand over, transmit (425)
cūn	村 §407	hamlet (91)	diǎn (2)	点 §797	dot (164)
cún	存§1459	store, preserve (292)		典§1308	canon, dictionary (262)
cùn	寸 §210	inch (53)	diàn (3)	电 §138	electricity (40)
cuò (2)	错§1332	bad, wrong, mistaken (267)		店 §684	shop (143)
	措§1299	arrange (261)		殿§2092	hall, palace, temple (412)
dā	搭 §513	build (111)	diāo	雕§1729	carve, engrave (342)
dá (2)	达§2139	attain, reach (420)	diào (3)	调§1759	tune, air (348)
	答 §512	answer (111)		掉 §185	to drop, fall (48)
dǎ	打 §33	hit (17)		吊 §131	hang, suspend (38)
dà	大 §330	big (76)	diē	跌 §949	fall, tumble (193)
dāi (2)	待§1042	stay (211)	dīng (2)	丁 §25	fourth (15)
	呆 §393	foolish, stupid (88)		盯 §80	stare (26)
dǎi	歹 §657	evil, vicious (139)	dǐng	顶 §446	carry on your head (99)
dài (5)	代 §983	take the place of (199)	dìng (2)	定 §248	decide* (60)
	带 §283	bring, band, belt (67)		订 §617	draw up, agree on (131)
	戴§1317	wear, put on (clothes) (264)	diū	丢 §761	lose, misplace (157)
	袋§1031	pouch, bag, pocket (209)	dōng (2)	东§1429	east (286)
	贷§1032	loan, borrow (209)		冬§1973	winter (389)
dān (3)	单§1166	single, sole (234)	dǒng (2)	懂 §937	understand, know (191)
	担 §67	undertake (24)		董 §229	director (57)
	丹§1718	red, cinnabar (340)	dòng (2)	动§1494	move (298)
dǎn	胆§1778	bravery, audacity (352)		洞 §533	hole, cavity (115)
dàn (5)	但 §965	but (196)	dōu	都§1461	all (292)
	淡§1103	bland, weak (223)	dǒu (2)	斗 §218	cup-shaped (55)
	旦 §65	dawn (22)		抖 §219	tremble (55)
	蛋 §896	egg (183)	dòu	豆§1168	bean (235)
	诞§2178	birth, birthday (427)	dū	督§1919	supervise (378)
dāng	当§1341	work as, become (268)	dú (3)	独 §900	alone, only (184)
dǎng (2)	党§1143	political party (231)		读 §633	read aloud, attend school (134)
	挡§1342	ward off, block (269)		毒 §609	poison (130)
dàng (2)	荡§1611	swing, shake, wash away (320)	dǔ	赌§1464	bet, gamble (292)
	档§1344	files, archives (269)	dù (4)	度§1856	degree, other small unit (367)
dāo	刀§1489	knife (297)		杜 §385	prevent (87)
dǎo (3)	导 §871	guide, lead (178)		渡§1803	cross water, ferry across (367)
	倒 §991	topple, fall over (201)		肚§1790	belly*, abdomen* (354)
	岛 §888	island (182)	duān	端§1196	end, extremity (241)
dào (3)	到 §756	arrive (156)	duǎn	短§1171	short, brief (236)
	道§2126	direction, way (418)	duàn (2)	断§1132	break, snap, cut (228)
	盗 §579	steal, rob (124)		段§2075	section, part (409)
de (2)	的 §643	of (136)	duī	堆 §993	to heap up (202)
	得§1036	verbal particle (210)	duì (3)	对§1797	correct, right (356)
dé	德§1039	Germany (211)		队 §737	team (152)
dēng (2)	登§1251	scale, climb (251)		兑§1049	exchange, convert (213)
	灯§1107	lamp, light (223)	dūn (2)	吨 §151	ton (42)
děng	等 §244	wait (60)		敦§2002	sincere (395)
dèng	邓§1958	surname of Deng Xiaoping (386)	dùn (2)	顿 §484	m for meals (105)
dī (2)	低§2266	let droop, hang down (445)		盾 §733	shield (152)
	滴§1207	drip (243)	duō	多 §656	many, much (139)
dí (2)	敌§1995	enemy, foe (393)	duó	夺§425	seize (94)
	迪§2166	enlighten, guide (425)	duǒ (2)	朵§2102	m for flowers (414)
dǐ (3)	底§2265	bottom, base (444)		躲§2103	hide, dodge, avoid (414)
	抵§2264	support, sustain (444)	é (3)	额§2024	forehead (399)
	氐§2263	basic, thoroughgoing (444)		俄 §985	Russian (200)
dì (6)	地 §141	earth, ground (40)		哦 §362	chant softly (82)
	第§1451	ordinal prefix (290)	è (3)	恶§1120	evil (226)
	帝§1204	emperor* (242)		饿§2200	hungry (431)
	弟§1450	younger brother (289)		厄 §873	trapped in difficult situation (178)
	蒂§1208	base of fruit (243)	ēn	恩 §916	kindness, favor (187)

ér (2)	而 §83	express add'l but contrasting info (26)	
	儿 §288	son (68)	
ěr (2)	尔 §1227	you, thou (247)	
	耳 §82	ear (26)	
èr	二 §3	two (9)	
fā	发 §1799	send out, deliver (356)	
fá (3)	罚 §278	punish, penalize (66)	
	乏 §2188	tired*, weary* (430)	
	伐 §984	cut down (199)	
fǎ	法 §762	method (157)	
fān (2)	翻 §1326	turn over, cross over (266)	
	番 §1323	kind (265)	
fán (3)	凡 §2056	commonplace (405)	
	烦 §1109	vexed, annoyed (224)	
	繁 §2012	complicated (397)	
fǎn (2)	反 §1863	oppose, anti- (368)	
	返 §2138	return to (420)	
fàn (4)	范 §559	pattern, model, example (120)	
	犯 §901	violate, offend, commit crime (184)	
	饭 §2201	cooked rice (432)	
	泛 §1943	float, suffused with, non-specific (383)	
fāng (2)	方 §1491	square, direction (298)	
	芳 §1624	fragrant, virtuous (name) (322)	
fáng (3)	房 §1560	house (311)	
	防 §1561	guard, defend against (311)	
	妨 §1536	hinder, impede (306)	
fǎng (2)	访 §1589	visit, call on, seek (315)	
	仿 §1601	imitate, copy, resemble (318)	
fàng	放 §2007	put, place (396)	
fēi (3)	非 §13	not (11)	
	飞 §2043	to fly (403)	
	菲 §99	luxuriant (31)	
féi	肥 §2196	fat, fertile, rich (431)	
fěi	匪 §153	bandit (42)	
fèi (2)	费 §1708	cost, spend, expend (338)	
	废 §1945	useless, superfluous (383)	
fēn (3)	分 §1490	divide, separate (297)	
	纷 §1535	numerous, confused (306)	
	芬 §1534	sweet smell, fragrance (306)	
fěn	粉 §1616	powder (321)	
fèn (3)	份 §1576	share, portion (313)	
	奋 §426	act vigorously (95)	
	愤 §939	anger (192)	
fēng (7)	风 §2069	wind (408)	
	封 §212	m for correspondence (54)	
	丰 §12	plentiful (11)	
	峰 §1981	peak, summit (391)	
	疯 §2070	mad, insane (408)	
	锋 §1967	sword's cutting edge (388)	
	蜂 §1966	bee, wasp (388)	
féng (2)	缝 §2133	sew, stitch (419)	
	逢 §2132	each time (419)	
fèng (2)	奉 §1363	give, present (273)	
	凤 §2072	phoenix (408)	
fó	佛 §1707	Buddha (338)	
fǒu (2)	否 §1456	negate (291)	
	缶 §521	archaeological vessel (113)	
fū (2)	夫 §337	man (spiffy) (78)	

	肤 §1788	skin (353)	
fú (9)	服 §1868	clothes, garment (369)	
	福 §2231	good fortune (438)	
	符 §1029	tally, symbol, sign (208)	
	弗 §1706	not (literary) (338)	
	伏 §1007	bend over (204)	
	幅 §164	width of cloth (44)	
	浮 §1409	float (282)	
	扶 §348	use a hand to support (80)	
	俘 §1408	capture, take prisoner (282)	
fǔ (4)	府 §973	mansion (198)	
	腐 §1033	rotten, putrid, stale (209)	
	抚 §1643	comfort, console (326)	
	甫 §1732	just now, only (343)	
fù (14)	复 §1968	turn around, repeat (388)	
	父 §1812	father (358)	
	负 §481	bear, carry on shoulders (105)	
	富 §251	rich, wealthy (61)	
	副 §168	vice- (45)	
	付 §971	pay (197)	
	附 §974	add, attach (198)	
	妇 §584	woman* (125)	
	腹 §1969	belly, abdomen (388)	
	赋 §503	endow, bestow (109)	
	覆 §1970	overturn, cover (389)	
	赴 §423	go to, attend (94)	
	傅 §1737	teacher, instructor (344)	
	咐 §972	to instruct, exhort (198)	
gāi	该 §2223	ought to, should (436)	
gǎi	改 §2028	transform, change (400)	
gài (3)	概 §1910	approximate, general (377)	
	盖 §1126	cover* (227)	
	丐 §644	beg (136)	
gān (3)	干 §10	dry (10)	
	甘 §103	sweet (33)	
	肝 §1787	liver (353)	
gǎn (3)	感 §925	feel, sense (188)	
	敢 §1999	to dare (393)	
	赶 §422	rush (94)	
gāng (4)	刚 §1826	hard, firm, strong (361)	
	钢 §1956	steel (386)	
	纲 §1827	guiding principle (361)	
	冈 §1825	mountain ridge (361)	
gǎng (2)	港 §1311	harbor, port (263)	
	岗 §1957	mound (386)	
gāo	高 §275	high (65)	
gǎo (2)	搞 §276	do, work, manage, etc (65)	
	稿 §412	cereal grain stalk (91)	
gào	告 §189	tell (49)	
gē (4)	哥 §62	elder brother (22)	
	歌 §489	song (106)	
	割 §262	cut apart, sever (63)	
	戈 §359	halberd (82)	
gé (5)	格 §2020	lattice, grid (398)	
	革 §101	animal hide (31)	
	隔 §744	separate, impede (153)	
	阁 §2041	pavilion, chamber (402)	
	葛 §650	kudzu vine (138)	
gè (2)	个 §312	non-specific measure word (73)	

烈	§799	strong, intense *(164)*
裂	§847	split, divide up *(173)*
猎	§1321	hunt, chase *(265)*
劣	§1533	inferior, low quality *(306)*
lín (3) 林	§376	forest *(85)*
临	§239	face, overlook *(59)*
邻	§1384	neighbor, neighborhood, neighboring *(277)*
líng (7) 灵	§1105	clever, sharp *(223)*
零	§1375	zero *(275)*
龄	§1376	age, years *(275)*
凌	§1982	thick ice *(391)*
玲	§1374	exquisitely made *(274)*
陵	§1964	mausoleum, mound *(387)*
铃	§1383	bell *(277)*
lǐng 领	§1377	neck *(276)*
lìng (2) 令	§1373	season *(274)*
另	§1547	other, another *(308)*
liū 溜	§1524	slide, glide, sneak off *(304)*
liú (3) 流	§2219	flow, drift *(436)*
留	§1523	retain, stay *(303)*
刘	§1805	kill, massacre *(357)*
liǔ 柳	§1695	willow *(336)*
liù 六	§1062	six *(215)*
lóng (3) 龙	§1649	dragon *(327)*
隆	§2036	prosperous, booming *(401)*
笼	§1661	cage, coop, basket *(329)*
lóu (2) 楼	§1138	multi-story building *(229)*
娄	§1137	trouble, blunder *(229)*
lú (2) 卢	§712	gourd *(148)*
炉	§1112	stove *(224)*
lǔ 鲁	§486	stupid, dull, vulgar *(106)*
lù (4) 路	§2021	road, path, way *(398)*
陆	§741	land, continent *(153)*
露	§2038	dew *(402)*
录	§549	record, write down *(118)*
luàn 乱	§232	in disorder *(57)*
luè (2) 略	§2037	summary, outline *(402)*
掠	§1085	plunder *(219)*
lún (3) 伦	§1020	human relationship *(207)*
轮	§1507	wheel, wheel-like *(301)*
仑	§457	order, coherence *(101)*
lùn 论	§632	discuss, talk *(134)*
luó (2) 罗	§663	catch birds with a net *(140)*
逻	§2170	patrol *(426)*
luò (3) 落	§2018	fall, drop behind *(398)*
洛	§2017	a certain river *(397)*
络	§2019	enmesh, wind *(398)*
lǚ (3) 旅	§2274	trip, travel *(446)*
吕	§43	bamboo pitch pipes *(19)*
履	§1971	shoe* *(389)*
lǜ (4) 律	§1040	law, rule *(211)*
率	§832	rate, proportion *(171)*
虑	§2062	anxiety *(406)*
绿	§825	green *(169)*
ma (2) 吗	§881	yes or no? *(179)*
嘛	§696	particle of persuasion *(145)*
mā 妈	§893	mom *(182)*
má 麻	§694	hemp, pocked, pitted *(145)*
mǎ (3) 马	§878	horse *(179)*
玛	§879	agate *(179)*
码	§1396	number *(279)*
mà 骂	§880	curse, abuse *(179)*
mái 埋	§72	bury *(25)*
mǎi 买	§340	buy *(78)*
mài (4) 卖	§341	sell *(79)*
麦	§1979	wheat *(390)*
脉	§1782	arteries and veins *(352)*
迈	§2174	step, stride *(426)*
mǎn 满	§541	full, complete *(116)*
màn (3) 慢	§1914	slow *(378)*
曼	§1912	handsome, graceful *(377)*
漫	§1913	brim over, overflow *(377)*
máng (3) 忙	§935	busy *(191)*
茫	§538	vast, without borders *(116)*
芒	§277	spike, sharp point *(66)*
māo 猫	§905	cat *(184)*
máo (2) 毛	§231	hair *(57)*
矛	§1612	lance, pike, spear *(320)*
mǎo 卯	§1522	early morning *(303)*
mào (4) 贸	§1525	commerce, trade *(304)*
冒	§79	brave *(26)*
貌	§904	appearance, aspect *(184)*
帽	§132	hat *(38)*
me 么	§1422	huh? what? *(284)*
méi (7) 没	§2054	have not *(405)*
梅	§602	plum flower or tree *(129)*
眉	§723	eyebrow *(150)*
媒	§611	matchmaker, go-between *(130)*
煤	§1269	coal *(254)*
枚	§2010	m for coins, small objects *(396)*
玫	§1991	rose *(392)*
měi (2) 美	§1148	beautiful *(232)*
每	§600	every *(128)*
mèi 妹	§592	younger sister *(126)*
men 们	§978	plural marker *(199)*
mēn 闷	§911	stuffy, muggy *(186)*
mén 门	§196	door *(51)*
mēng 蒙	§1590	cheat, hoodwink *(316)*
méng 盟	§1775	alliance, pact, league *(351)*
měng 猛	§1418	fierce, valiant *(283)*
mèng (2) 梦	§668	dream *(141)*
孟	§1411	eldest among brothers *(282)*
mí (2) 迷	§2163	confused, be fascinated by *(425)*
弥	§1284	full, overflowing *(257)*
mǐ 米	§1127	rice *(227)*
mì (2) 密	§1562	thick, dense, intimate *(311)*
秘	§1443	secret *(288)*
mián (2) 棉	§508	cotton *(110)*
眠	§715	sleep, dormancy *(149)*
miǎn (2) 免	§477	dismiss, fire, exempt *(104)*
勉	§1567	strive to, do with effort *(312)*
miàn 面	§84	face, aspect *(27)*
miáo (2) 描	§98	to trace *(31)*
苗	§97	seedling *(30)*
miào (2) 妙	§1477	wonderful *(295)*
庙	§683	temple *(143)*
miè 灭	§1104	extinguish *(223)*
mín 民	§714	people, masses *(149)*

mǐn (3)	敏 §2011	sharp, keen *(396)*	niè	聶 §1947	whisper *(383)*
	皿 §110	vessel, dish *(34)*	nín	您 §1243	you (formal) *(249)*
	黾 §136	tadpole *(39)*	níng	凝 §1420	congeal, curdle *(284)*
míng (3)	明 §1724	bright, clear *(341)*	nìng	宁 §257	rather, would rather *(62)*
	名 §661	personal name *(140)*	niú	牛 §186	ox *(49)*
	鸣 §887	bird or animal cry *(181)*	niǔ (2)	纽 §811	button *(167)*
mìng	命 §517	life, fate *(112)*		扭 §38	twist, wrench *(18)*
mō	摸 §350	touch, grope *(80)*	nóng (2)	农 §843	agriculture *(173)*
mó (5)	模 §404	model, imitation *(90)*		浓 §844	dense, thick *(173)*
	摩 §695	rub *(145)*	nòng	弄 §1669	make, do, manage *(331)*
	魔 §1595	devil, evil spirit, monster *(316)*	nú	奴 §1928	slave, enslave *(381)*
	磨 §1395	polish, wear down, pester *(279)*	nǔ	努 §1929	exert, strive *(381)*
			nù	怒 §1935	become angry, indignant *(382)*
	膜 §1791	membrane, film, thin coating *(354)*	nuǎn	暖 §1934	warm, genial *(382)*
			nuó	娜 §1781	lithe, graceful *(352)*
mǒ	抹 §384	put on, apply, smear *(87)*	nuò	诺 §1658	to promise *(328)*
mò (5)	莫 §349	do not, not *(80)*	nǚ	女 §581	woman *(124)*
	默 §804	silent, keep silent *(165)*	ō	噢 §1136	oh! (surprised understanding) *(229)*
	末 §383	end, tip *(86)*			
	墨 §805	ink, ink stick *(166)*	ōu	欧 §1915	Europe *(378)*
	漠 §543	desert *(117)*	ǒu	偶 §2212	by chance *(434)*
móu	谋 §634	work for, seek *(134)*	pá	爬 §2209	crawl, creep, scramble *(434)*
mǒu	某 §397	certain, some *(89)*	pà (2)	怕 §934	to fear, be afraid *(190)*
mǔ (2)	母 §596	mother *(127)*		帕 §205	handkerchief *(52)*
	姆 §599	mother, nursemaid *(128)*	pāi	拍 §204	clap *(52)*
mù (7)	目 §78	eye *(26)*	pái (2)	排 §32	put in order *(17)*
	木 §375	tree *(85)*		牌 §1487	plate, tablet *(297)*
	幕 §453	stage curtain *(100)*	pán	盘 §610	dish, current market price *(130)*
	牧 §1996	herd *(393)*			
	穆 §1289	respectful, dignified *(258)*	pàn (2)	判 §1666	judge, decide *(330)*
	墓 §454	tomb *(101)*		叛 §1961	betray, rebel, revolt *(387)*
	慕 §1216	admire* *(245)*	pāng	乒 §1482	ping-pong* *(296)*
ná	拿 §515	take *(111)*	páng (2)	旁 §1520	side *(303)*
nǎ (2)	那 §1727	which? what? how? *(342)*		庞 §1650	very large *(327)*
	哪 §1764	which?* what?* how?* *(348)*	pàng	胖 §1223	fat, stout, plump *(246)*
nà	纳 §818	accept, receive *(168)*	pāo	抛 §1618	toss, fling, abandon *(323)*
nǎi (2)	乃 §1513	so, therefore *(302)*	páo	袍 §875	robe, gown *(178)*
	奶 §1604	breast*, milk* *(318)*	pǎo	跑 §950	run *(193)*
nài (2)	耐 §216	bear, endure *(54)*	pào (2)	炮 §1253	cannon, firecracker *(252)*
	奈 §1215	how can one help? *(244)*		泡 §858	blister, bubble *(176)*
nán (4)	难 §1870	difficult, hard *(369)*	péi (3)	培 §1195	bank up with earth *(241)*
	南 §1209	south *(243)*		陪 §1276	accompany *(256)*
	男 §1565	male *(312)*		赔 §1277	compensate, pay for *(256)*
	喃 §1210	mumbling *(244)*	pèi (2)	配 §861	join together *(176)*
nǎo (2)	脑 §1902	brain *(376)*		佩 §2100	to girdle *(413)*
	恼 §1832	get mad *(362)*	pēn	喷 §434	spurt, spout, gush *(96)*
nào	闹 §274	make a noise *(65)*	péng (3)	朋 §1741	friend *(149)*
ne	呢 §718	particle with many uses *(149)*		彭 §1291	surname of Peng *(259)*
nèi	内 §318	inside* *(74)*		鹏 §1742	roc *(345)*
néng	能 §1740	can, able *(344)*	pèng	碰 §1389	touch, bump *(278)*
ňg	嗯 §917	how come? why? *(187)*	pī	批 §147	annotate *(41)*
ní (2)	尼 §717	nun *(149)*	pí (2)	皮 §1842	leather, skin *(364)*
	泥 §720	mud, clay *(150)*		疲 §1897	tired, weary *(375)*
nǐ (2)	你 §1072	you *(217)*	pǐ	匹 §290	be a match for *(69)*
	拟 §498	plan, intend *(109)*	pì	辟 §1256	law *(252)*
nì	逆 §2129	go against, disobey *(418)*	piān (2)	篇 §730	piece of writing *(151)*
nián	年 §192	year *(50)*		偏 §1027	inclined to one side *(208)*
niàn	念 §1372	read aloud *(274)*	pián	便 §1539	cheap *(363)*
niáng	娘 §1916	mum, mother *(378)*	piàn (2)	片 §1485	slice, flake *(297)*
niǎo	鸟 §885	bird *(181)*		骗 §894	deceive, swindle *(183)*

rǎo	扰§1645	disturb, bother (326)	shāo (2)	烧§1261	burn, cook, run a fever (253)
rào	绕 §822	wind, coil (168)		稍§1235	slightly, somewhat (248)
rě	惹§1640	to provoke, exasperate (325)	shaó	勺 §642	spoon (136)
rè	热§2076	hot, fervent (409)	shǎo	少§1475	few, little (295)
rén (2)	人 §311	man (73)	shào	绍§1556	connect, introduce (309)
	仁 §954	benevolence (194)	shé (3)	折 §120	broken (stick, rope) (36)
rěn	忍§1597	bear, endure, forbear (317)		蛇 §897	snake, serpent (183)
rèn (3)	任 §956	assume a post (194)		舌 §225	tongue (56)
	认 §627	recognize, know (133)	shě	舍 §328	give up (76)
	刃§1596	blade edge (317)	shè (5)	社§2236	society, group (439)
rēng	扔§1530	throw, toss (304)		设§2068	set up, found, establish (407)
réng	仍§1566	still, yet, again and again (312)		射§1633	to shoot (323)
rì	日 §63	day, sun (22)		涉§1502	wade, ford (299)
róng (3)	容§1229	allow, tolerate (247)		摄§1948	absorb, assimilate (384)
	荣 §402	honorable (90)	shēn (4)	身§1631	body (323)
	融 §895	melt, thaw (183)		深§1100	deep (222)
rǒng	冗§2083	superfluous, redundant (410)		申 §47	express (19)
róu	柔§1613	soft, supple, gentle (320)		伸 §960	stretch, extend (195)
ròu	肉 §317	meat (74)	shén (2)	什 §955	what (194)
rú	如 §585	be like (125)		神§2235	god, divinity (439)
rǔ (2)	乳§2064	breast, milk (407)	shěn	审 §252	examine, go over (61)
	辱§1851	disgrace, insult (366)	shèn (2)	甚§1094	very, extremely (221)
rù	入 §482	enter, receive, take in (105)		慎§1059	cautious, careful (215)
ruǎn	软§1592	soft, pliant (316)	shēng (4)	生 §191	give birth to (50)
ruì (2)	瑞 §89	auspicious (29)		声 §722	sound, voice (150)
	锐§1329	sharp, acute (266)		升§1668	raise, hoist (331)
rùn (2)	润 §544	moist, soft (117)		牲 §194	domestic animal (50)
	闰 §199	intercalary month (51)	shéng	绳 §816	rope (168)
ruò (2)	若§1639	seem, like, if (325)	shěng	省§1478	economize, be frugal (295)
	弱 §126	weak, feeble, inferior (37)	shèng (3)	胜§1765	win victory, succeed, excel (349)
sǎ	撒§2040	scatter, sprinkle (402)			
sà	萨§1260	Buddha, kind-hearted person (253)		圣§1923	sage, saint (380)
				剩§2120	remain, be left over (417)
sāi	塞§1315	fill, stuff in (264)	shī (6)	师§1691	teacher, master (335)
sài	赛§1314	compete, game, competition (263)		失 §427	lose (95)
				施§2273	execute, carry out (446)
sān	三 §4	three (9)		诗 §625	poem, poetry (133)
sàn	散§2039	break up, distribute (402)		尸 §703	corpse (147)
sāng (2)	丧 §493	mourning (108)		湿§1122	wet, damp (227)
	桑§1953	mulberry tree (385)	shí (7)	时 §211	time (54)
sǎo	扫 §35	sweep (17)		实 §342	solid, substantial (79)
sè (2)	色§2192	color, look (430)		十 §6	ten (10)
	瑟§1444	rustling sound (288)		识§1089	know, recognize (219)
sēn	森 §377	full of trees (85)		石§1386	stone, rock (277)
sēng	僧§1174	monk (237)		食§1905	eat* (376)
shā (4)	杀§1820	kill (360)		拾§1511	pick up (111)
	沙§1479	sand (295)	shǐ (6)	使§1837	have sb do sth (363)
	莎§1480	katydid (295)		始 §782	begin, start (161)
	刹§1821	to brake a car (360)		史§1835	history (363)
shá	啥 §329	what? (dialect) (76)		驶§1952	sail, (vehicle) moves quickly (385)
shǎ	傻§1963	muddleheaded (387)			
shān	山 §21	mountain (14)		矢 §334	arrow (77)
shǎn	闪 §322	lightning (75)		豕§1425	pig, boar (285)
shàn (2)	善§1149	good, kind (232)	shì (17)	是 §184	is (48)
	扇 §728	fan, leaf (151)		事 §165	matter, affair (44)
shāng (2)	商§1188	trade, business (239)		世 §106	generation (33)
	伤§1568	injure, wound (312)		市 §273	market (56)
shǎng	赏§1144	admire (231)		式 §357	model, standard (81)
shàng (2)	上§175	on (46)		士 §8	scholar (10)
	尚§1139	still, yet (230)		示§1064	show, indicate (215)

téng (2)	腾 §1785	gallop, prance (353)
	疼 §1975	it hurts! (390)
tī	梯 §1628	ladder (322)
tí (2)	提 §238	carry, take, lift (59)
	题 §471	topic, subject, title (103)
tǐ	体 §989	body* (201)
tì	替 §347	for, on behalf of (80)
tiān (2)	天 §333	heaven (77)
	添 §1080	increase (218)
tián (3)	田 §57	field (21)
	填 §1258	fill in, stuff (252)
	甜 §227	sweetness (56)
tiāo	挑 §2117	select, pick (417)
tiáo	条 §2022	strip, sth long and narrow (398)
tiào	跳 §2118	jump (417)
tiē	贴 §432	paste, stick to (96)
tiě	铁 §1333	iron (267)
tīng (2)	听 §119	hear, listen (36)
	厅 §673	public rooms, hall (141)
tíng (5)	停 §1008	stop, pause (204)
	庭 §2184	hall, front courtyard (429)
	廷 §2183	imperial court (429)
	亭 §281	pavilion, kiosk (66)
	蜓 §2185	dragonfly (429)
tǐng (2)	艇 §2187	small boat (429)
	挺 §2186	straighten up (physically) (429)
tōng	通 §2137	lead to, go to (420)
tóng (3)	同 §129	same, similar (38)
	童 §1186	child (239)
	铜 §1339	copper (268)
tǒng	统 §824	gather, unite (169)
tòng	痛 §1746	painful (346)
tōu	偷 §1605	steal, pilfer (318)
tóu (2)	头 §339	head (78)
	投 §2074	throw, fling (408)
tòu	透 §2161	penetrate, seep through (424)
tū	突 §1239	dash forward (249)
tú (4)	图 §1974	picture, chart, map (389)
	徒 §1043	disciple, pupil, follower (212)
	途 §2131	road, journey (419)
	涂 §1075	smear, apply (217)
tǔ (2)	土 §9	earth, soil (10)
	吐 §55	spit (21)
tù	兔 §476	rabbit (104)
tuán	团 §1468	round, circular (293)
tuàn	彖 §1602	determine, make a judgment (318)
tuī	推 §994	push (202)
tuǐ	腿 §2141	leg (420)
tuì	退 §2140	retreat, retire (420)
tūn	吞 §452	swallow, gulp down (100)
tún	屯 §150	stockpile, store up (42)
tuō (3)	托 §236	hold in the palm (58)
	脱 §1254	shed, take off (252)
	拖 §496	pull, drag, haul (108)
tuǒ	妥 §1347	appropriate, proper (269)
wā	挖 §2063	dig, excavate (406)
wá	娃 §582	baby (124)
wǎ	瓦 §2047	tile (403)

wài	外 §664	outside, external (140)
wān (2)	湾 §1578	gulf, bay (314)
	弯 §1577	bent, curved, crooked (313)
wán (3)	完 §296	finish, complete (70)
	玩 §295	have fun, amuse oneself (70)
	顽 §447	stupid, stubborn (99)
wǎn (4)	晚 §479	evening (104)
	碗 §1393	bowl (278)
	挽 §478	draw, pull (104)
	宛 §864	bent (177)
wàn	万 §472	ten thousand (103)
wāng	汪 §526	bow-wow (114)
wáng (2)	王 §11	king (11)
	亡 §269	perish (64)
wǎng (2)	往 §1041	in the direction of, toward (211)
	网 §1828	net (361)
wàng (2)	望 §1752	observe, gaze into distance (347)
	忘 §914	forget (187)
wēi (3)	威 §607	power, might (129)
	微 §2030	micro, tiny, minute (400)
	危 §862	danger, imperil (177)
wéi (7)	为 §1493	do, accomplish (298)
	维 §1026	fiber, hold together (208)
	围 §116	surround, enclose (35)
	唯 §995	only, alone (202)
	违 §2164	disobey, violate (425)
	韦 §115	leather (35)
	惟 §1000	way of thought, -ism (203)
wěi (4)	委 §593	listless, dejected (126)
	伟 §981	great, imposing (199)
	尾 §716	tail (149)
	伪 §1621	false, fake, bogus (321)
wèi (11)	位 §1183	m for persons (polite) (238)
	未 §381	have not yet (86)
	卫 §113	guard, protect (35)
	味 §382	taste, flavor (86)
	谓 §631	say, be called (134)
	慰 §1275	console, comfort (256)
	魏 §1627	Wei dynasty (322)
	胃 §461	stomach (102)
	喂 §2207	feed (432)
	畏 §2206	fear (432)
	尉 §1274	military official (256)
wēn	温 §536	lukewarm, to warm up (115)
wén (3)	文 §1804	language, culture (357)
	闻 §200	hear, smell (51)
	纹 §1809	vein, grain (357)
wěn (2)	稳 §1926	settled, steady, stable (380)
	吻 §1511	kiss (301)
wèn	问 §197	ask (51)
wō	窝 §1217	nest, lair (245)
wǒ	我 §361	I (82)
wò (3)	握 §784	hold, grasp, shake hands (162)
	沃 §566	fertile, rich (121)
	卧 §178	lie down, crouch (animals) (47)
wū (4)	屋 §783	house, room (161)
	乌 §886	crow (181)
	污 §562	dirty, filthy, foul (121)
	巫 §320	wizard (74)

译§1921　translate, interpret (379)
役§2097　military service, labor (413)
翼§1318　wing, flank (264)
忆§2045　recall, remember (403)
抑§162　restrain, restrict (44)
疫§2105　epidemic, plague (415)
毅§2059　perseverance (406)
弋§356　arrow type (81)

yīn (3)　因§345　because (79)
音§1189　sound (239)
阴§1772　feminine principle in nature (351)

yín (3)　银§1881　silver (371)
吟§1380　chant, recite (276)
寅§1244　3–5am (250)

yǐn (3)　引§872　lead, guide (178)
隐§1925　conceal, hide, latent (380)
饮§2202　swallow liquid or insults (432)

yìn　印§158　seal, stamp (43)

yīng (3)　应§1353　ought (271)
英§354　hero (81)
鹰§1006　eagle (204)

yíng (3)　营§282　battalion (67)
迎§2160　to welcome (424)
赢§2065　gain, win (407)

yǐng　影§1290　shadow, reflection (259)

yìng (2)　硬§1840　hard, stiff (363)
映§355　reflect, shine (81)

yōng　拥§1731　to embrace, hold (343)

yǒng (4)　永§560　forever, always (120)
勇§1748　brave, valiant (346)
涌§1747　gush, well up (346)
甬§1745　corridor, path (345)

yòng　用§1730　to use (343)

yōu (5)　优§1647　excellent, superior (326)
忧§1646　worry, anxiety (326)
幽§795　remote, secluded (163)
攸§2003　distant, far (395)
悠§2031　thus, that which (401)

yóu (6)　由§48　let sb do sth (19)
游§2272　swim, float (446)
油§527　oil (114)
尤§1644　blame, fault (326)
犹§1656　just as, just like (328)
邮§748　to post, mail (154)

yǒu (3)　有§1725　have (342)
友§1798　friend, associate (356)
酉§303　new wine (71)

yòu (4)　又§1796　hand, also (355)
右§1638　right (-hand) (325)
幼§1623　young (322)
诱§1594　guide, lead, induce (316)

yú (7)　于§26　in; at; to (15)
余§1073　surplus, remainder (217)
鱼§485　fish (105)
渔§561　fisherman (120)
愚§2211　stupid, foolish (434)
愉§1510　happy, joyful (301)
俞§1509　consent (301)

yǔ (6)　与§645　give** (136)

语§618　language (131)
予§763　give* (157)
雨§85　rain (28)
宇§259　building, house (63)
羽§123　feather, wing (37)

yù (14)　育§2218　rear, raise, educate (435)
预§786　in advance (162)
域§364　region, area (83)
遇§2215　meet, encounter (435)
玉§221　jade (55)
欲§1259　wish, desire, want (253)
愈§1606　the more—the more (318)
御§1045　control, manage (212)
狱§899　prison, jail (183)
誉§1278　reputation, fame (257)
郁§1743　lush (345)
豫§1518　pleased, content (303)
裕§1230　abundant (247)
聿§39　pen, writing instrument (18)

yuán (9)　原§676　original, unprocessed (142)
员§440　employee (97)
元§293　dollar (69)
源§677　source of river, fountainhead (142)
园§294　garden (69)
圆§443　round (98)
援§1933　help, aid, assist (381)
缘§1603　reason*, cause* (318)
袁§850　Yuan Shikai (174)

yuǎn　远§2146　far, distant (421)

yuàn (3)　院§742　courtyard (153)
愿§926　sincere, honest (188)
怨§929　blame, reproach, reprove (189)

yuē (2)　约§820　ask, invite (168)
曰§64　speak (22)

yuè (6)　月§1719　moon, month (341)
越§475　exceed (104)
阅§1051　read, review (213)
跃§947　leap, jump (193)
岳§122　high mountain peak (36)
悦§1050　pleased (213)

yún (2)　云§751　cloud (155)
匀§637　evenly divided (135)

yǔn　允§771　permit, allow (159)

yùn　运§2142　move, transport (420)

zá　杂§2049　mixed, composite (404)

zāi　灾§1266　disaster, calamity (254)

zài　载§1582　write down, year (314)

zài (2)　在§1458　located at (291)
再§128　again (37)

zán　咱§208　you and me (53)

zàn (2)　赞§435　support, assist (96)
暂§1439　temporarily (288)

zāng (2)　脏§1721　filthy (341)
臧§944　lucky, good (192)

zāo (2)　遭§2159　encounter, by chance (424)
糟§1131　spoiled (228)

zǎo　早§70　morning (24)

zào　造§2145　build, fabricate (421)

zé (4)　则§431　standard, norm (95)
责§439　responsibility (97)

	泽§1922	marsh (379)			织§1090	weave (220)
	择§1920	choose*, select* (378)			枝§1886	branch of tree (372)
zěn	怎§1449	how, why (289)	zhí (6)	直 §16	straight, vertical (12)
zēng	增§1173	increase, add (236)		值§1010	to be worth (205)
zhā	扎 §139	pierce, prick (40)		职§1088	duty, job (219)
zhà (2)	炸§1448	explode, burst (289)		执§2050	grasp (404)
	乍§1445	suddenly (289)		植 §392	plant, grow (88)
zhái	宅 §264	residence, house (64)		殖 §658	propagate (139)
zhài	债§1030	debt (209)	zhǐ (6)	只§1086	only (219)
zhān	占 §172	practice divination (46)		指 §144	finger (41)
zhǎn (2)	展 §842	expand, develop (172)		止 §181	stop! (48)
	斩§1437	behead (287)		纸§2267	paper (445)
zhàn (2)	战 §366	war (83)		旨 §143	intention, meaning (41)
	站§1199	stop, station (242)		址 §242	foundation, site (59)
zhāng (2)	张§1543	stretch, expand (307)	zhì (9)	制 §187	make, manufacture (49)
	章§1198	chapter, section (241)		至 §755	to, until (156)
zhǎng (2)	掌§1141	palm of the hand (230)		治 §769	manage, administer (158)
	涨§1544	rise (water, prices) (307)		质 §436	quality (96)
zhàng (4)	障§1262	obstruct, hinder (253)		致§2029	send, deliver (400)
	丈§1833	male elder relative (362)		志 §908	aspiration (185)
	帐§1625	curtain, canopy (322)		置 §109	to place, put (34)
	仗§1834	battle (363)		智 §429	wit (95)
zhāo (2)	招§1553	beckon, enlist (309)		秩 §504	order*, sequence* (109)
	昭§1554	clear, obvious (309)	zhōng (4)	中 §45	middle (19)
zhǎo	找 §360	seek (82)		终§1976	end, finish (390)
zhào (5)	照§1555	shine, illuminate (309)		钟§1334	bell, clock, time (267)
	赵§1822	kingdom of Zhao (360)		忠 §910	loyal (186)
	召§1552	call, convene (309)	zhǒng (2)	种 §415	m for kinds (93)
	罩 §174	bamboo fish trap (46)		肿§1789	to swell (353)
	兆§2116	omen (416)	zhòng (3)	重 §228	heavy (57)
zhe	着§1665	indicates continuing progress (330)		众 §314	multitude (73)
				仲 §959	2nd in seniority (195)
zhé	哲 §121	wise, sagacious (36)	zhōu (4)	周§1728	week (342)
zhě	者§1460	-er (292)		洲§1500	continent (299)
zhè	这§2124	this, these (418)		州§1499	state, province (299)
zhēn (4)	真§1058	real (214)		舟 §128	boat, ship (128)
	针§1336	needle, pin, injection (267)	zhǒu	帚 §133	broom* (39)
	珍§1286	precious thing (258)	zhòu (2)	宙 §261	all time, past, present, and future (63)
	侦§1012	to spy (205)			
zhěn	诊§1293	diagnose (259)		皱§1843	wrinkle (364)
zhèn (5)	阵§1573	battle array (313)	zhū (4)	诸§1585	all, various (315)
	镇§1335	trading center, garrison post (267)		朱 §379	vermilion (86)
				珠 §380	pearl (86)
	震§1930	shake, quake (381)		猪§1586	hog, pig (315)
	振§1931	rouse, shake, vibrate (381)	zhú (2)	逐§2155	pursue, chase (423)
	朕§1784	royal 'we' (353)		竹 §195	bamboo (50)
zhēng (4)	争 §463	struggle (102)	zhǔ	主 §220	master (55)
	征§1037	go on a journey (210)	zhù (8)	住 §980	to live (199)
	睁 §464	open (eyes) (102)		注 §539	pour (116)
	怔 §932	panic-stricken (189)		助§1564	help, assist, aid (312)
zhěng	整§2005	neat, tidy (396)		著§1462	write, compose (292)
zhèng (6)	正 §183	correct (48)		筑§2091	build, construct (412)
	政§1992	government, political (392)		驻 §882	halt, stay (180)
	证 §622	evidence, proof (132)		祝§2232	express good wishes (438)
	郑§1115	serious, earnest (225)		柱 §403	pillar, column (90)
	症 §699	disease (146)	zhuā	抓§2208	grab, seize, arrest (433)
	挣 §467	struggle, strive (103)	zhuǎ	爪§2205	claw (432)
zhī (5)	之§2179	relationship marker (427)	zhuān	专§2247	concentrated, focused (441)
	知 §428	know (95)	zhuǎn	转§2249	turn, shift, change (441)
	支§1884	prop up, support (372)	zhuāng (2)	装§2256	adorn, dress up (442)

www.**EZC**hinesey.com

Quick Order Form

Quick Order Form

Telephone orders: Call 1-631-866-6146 and please have your credit card ready.

Email orders: info@EZChinesey.com

Postal orders: EZChinesey.com, Dr. Alan Hoenig, P.O Box 2346, Huntington, NY 11743, USA. Telephone: 631-866-6146.

Please send copies of the following books. I understand that I may return any of them (in new, salable condition) within 30 days for **any** reason, no questions asked.

QUANTITY   NAME _____

_____

_____

Please send more FREE information on: (circle)

Other Books   Speaking/Seminars   Mailing Lists

Consulting

Name: _____

Address: _____

City, State, Zip: _____

Telephone: _____

Email Address: _____

Sales Tax: please 8.25% for anything shipped to New York addresses.

Postage & Handling: Within the US, add $6.00 for first book, and $3.00 for each additional copy. **International:** please inquire.

www.**EZC**hinesey.com

Quick Order Form

Quick Order Form

Telephone orders: Call 1-631-866–6146 and please have your credit card ready.
Email orders: info@EZChinesey.com
Postal orders: EZChinesey.com, Dr. Alan Hoenig, P.O Box 2346, Huntington, NY 11743, USA. Telephone: 631-866–6146.

Please send copies of the following books. I understand that I may return any of them (in new, salable condition) within 30 days for **any** reason, no questions asked.

QUANTITY   NAME _____

_____

_____

Please send more FREE information on: (circle)

Other Books   Speaking/Seminars   Mailing Lists

Consulting

Name: _____

Address: _____

City, State, Zip: _____

Telephone: _____

Email Address: _____

Sales Tax: please 8.25% for anything shipped to New York addresses.
Postage & Handling: Within the **US**, add $6.00 for first book, and $3.00 for each additional copy. **International:** please inquire.